THE CLASH OF POLITICAL IDEALS

THE CLASH OF POLITICAL IDEALS

A Source Book on Democracy, Communism
and the Totalitarian State

SELECTED AND ANNOTATED
BY
ALBERT R. CHANDLER
PROFESSOR OF PHILOSOPHY
OHIO STATE UNIVERSITY

SECOND EDITION

NEW YORK

APPLETON-CENTURY-CROFTS, INC.

PREFACE

This book is for all those who wish to learn something at first hand of the rival ideals of Democracy, Communism, Fascism, Nazism, and the Japanese nation.

Such a book could appear only in a country where the ideal of free discussion prevails. Totalitarian states do not wish their subjects to hear the case of their opponents. But democracy permits the public to hear all sides of every issue, and has faith that the public will in the long run choose the good and reject the evil.

Some say that "Ideas are the warriors of the world." Mazzini, for instance, while exhorting the Italians to achieve national unity, declared, "Ideas rule the world and its events. A revolution is the passage of an Idea from theory to practice. Whatever men say, material interests never have caused, and never will cause, a revolution. . . . Revolutions have their origin in the mind, in the very root of life, not in the material organism. A religion or a philosophy lies at the base of every revolution." (Quoted by Mario Palmieri at the beginning of his *Philosophy of Fascism*.)

On the other hand one of the founders of Communism declared that "the final causes of all social changes and political revolutions are to be sought, not in men's brains, not in man's better insight into eternal truth and justice, but in changes in the modes of production and exchange. They are to be sought, not in the *philosophy* but in the *economics* of each particular epoch." (Cited from Engels, *Anti-Dühring,* in the *Encyclopaedia of the Social Sciences,* article "Socialism.") In the *Communist Manifesto* we read, "The charges against Communism made from a religious, a philosophical, and, generally, from an ideological standpoint are not deserving of serious examination. Does it require deep intuition to comprehend that man's ideas, views, and conceptions, in one word, man's consciousness changes with every change in the conditions of his material existence, in his social relations and in his social life? What else does the history of ideas prove, than that intellectual production changes its character in proportion as material production has been changed? The ruling ideas of each age have ever been the ideas of its ruling class. When people speak of ideas that revolutionize society they do but express the fact that within the old society the elements of a new one have been created, and that the dissolution of the old ideas keeps even pace with the dissolution of the old conditions of existence. . . . When Christian ideas succumbed in the eighteenth century to rationalist ideas, feudal society fought its death battle with the then revolutionary bourgeoisie. The ideas of religious liberty and freedom of conscience merely gave expression to the sway of free competition within the domain of knowledge."

A third view regards ideas as tools or weapons. Powerful groups or leaders are guided, not by ideals but by interests and ambitions; they use ideas and ideals as propaganda to control the masses. In this case, be it noted, ideas and ideals are still effective causes, though operating only on the masses.

A fourth view employs the psychological theory of "rationalization," according to which many of our thoughts are interpretations of our own conduct which make it seem more rational or more noble than it really is. Business men scrambling for profits easily convince themselves that they are serving the public welfare. Persons hostile to Jews easily convince themselves that Jews are a danger to state and church, so that it is a patriotic and Christian duty to persecute them. Leaders who deceive themselves in this way can more readily deceive the masses, since their propaganda has the fervor of sincerity.

A fifth view combines the positive aspects of the first and second. This is represented by Mussolini when he writes, "Like all sound political conceptions, Fascism is action and it is thought; action in which doctrine is immanent, and doctrine arising from a given system of historical forces in which it is inserted, and working on them from within." (B. Mussolini, *Fascism, Doctrine and Institutions,* Rome, "Ardita" Publishers.) In simpler language, sound political ideas emerge from a social situation and react upon it to modify it; they are both effects and causes.

Whichever of these views we accept, the importance of studying the ideas connected with social movements remains. On the first view they are the basic causes of the movements. On the second, they are symptoms or reflections of the processes at work. On the third, since they are capable of moving the masses of men, they are symptomatic of the needs and passions of the masses; and since they are used by leaders for ulterior purposes, they may throw some light on the latter. On the fourth view, rationalizations at least indicate the standards, such as public welfare or Christianity, by which men are willing to be judged. On the fifth view, ideas are significant as both symptoms and partial causes of social movements.

In judging the ideas connected with a social movement it is unsafe to trust the descriptions given by its opponents. Even the most just and intelligent men can rarely give an adequate account of an opponent's view, and in the bitter and ardent struggles of our time, many of the debaters and propagandists are far from just or intelligent. It is better to hear a doctrine expounded by its friends, still better, by the leaders who shaped it and gave it currency. In this book great leaders and interpreters of conflicting social movements are allowed to speak for themselves. Let the reader listen and judge.

ALBERT R. CHANDLER.

PREFACE TO THE SECOND EDITION

In this edition the source material in the first nineteen chapters remains as before. Changes have been made in some of the introductions to bring them up to date, and some references to other books have been added. Copyright restrictions have again prevented extensive quotations from *Mein Kampf;* the summary of Hitler's views is therefore allowed to stand. Miss Thompson's expression of American aspirations in 1940 is the only item omitted.

The original compilation was made in 1940, when the clash of political ideals was manifested in armed conflict in Europe, and when many persons recognized the possibility that America and Japan would become involved in the struggle.

Now, in 1949, the material of the first nineteen chapters has been retained, because it still seems significant for the understanding of the war years and post war developments. Nine new chapters have been added in the hope of throwing further light on present and prospective issues. Selections from Roosevelt, Smith, and a declaration of the British Labor Party are included because of their bearing on current issues in democratic countries. The section on Communist strategy and tactics has a bearing on the communization of the border states between Russia and the Western powers, and on Communist activities throughout the world. The Tanaka Memorial throws light on Japanese war policies and possible future attitudes of the Japanese people. Selections from Chinese and Indian sources are concerned with revolutionary processes that have been going on for several decades and are increasingly significant for the rest of the world. The fears evoked by developments in atomic and bacteriological warfare, and disappointment regarding the United Nations, have given rise to renewed and widespread aspirations toward "a more perfect union" among the peoples of the world. These aspirations are given a definite form in the draft of a world constitution prepared by Robert M. Hutchins and his associates.

The editor hopes that this volume will help to widen and deepen the reader's insight into the problems of our time.

ALBERT R. CHANDLER

ACKNOWLEDGMENTS

Thanks are due to the following copyright-owners for permission to quote from the works indicated:

The Clarendon Press, Oxford, and the Jowett Trustees, *Thucydides,* translated by B. Jowett.
Doubleday, Doran and Company, Inc., New York, *American Individualism,* by Herbert Hoover.
International Publishers Co., New York, *What Is Leninism?* and *Stalin on the New Soviet Constitution.*
G. P. Putnam's Sons, New York, *Freedom and Culture,* by John Dewey.
The Vanguard Press, New York, *The State and Revolution,* by N. Lenin.

The University of Chicago Press, *Preliminary Draft of a World Constitution,* by Robert M. Hutchins and others.
George Allen & Unwin Ltd., *Mahatma Gandhi's Ideas,* by C. F. Andrews.

Especial thanks are due to the following copyright-owners for permission to quote without payment from the works indicated:

The America Press, New York, *On the Reconstruction of the Social Order,* by Pope Pius XI.
The University of Chicago Press, Chicago, *The New Testament, An American Translation,* by E. J. Goodspeed.
Henry Holt and Company, New York, *Government and Politics Abroad,* by H. R. Spencer, and *The New Soviet Constitution,* by Anna Louise Strong.
Houghton Mifflin Company, Boston, *Mein Kampf,* by Adolf Hitler.
G. P. Putnam's Sons, *Bushido,* by Inazo Nitobe.
Harper & Brothers, New York, *The Tanaka Memorial,* edited by Carl Crow.
The Atlantic Monthly, "Catholic and Patriot: Governor Smith Replies," 1927.

Harcourt, Brace and Company, Inc., *Progressive Democracy: Addresses and State Papers of Alfred E. Smith,* edited by Henry Moskowitz.

Oxford University Press, Inc., New York, *What Does Gandhi Want?* by T. A. Raman.

Lindsay Drummond Limited and Mr. V. Krishna Menon, *The Unity of India,* by Jahawarlal Nehru.

Acknowledgment is also due to Mr. Saul Padover for his courtesy in permitting the use of his *Democracy* by Thomas Jefferson (D. Appleton-Century Company, Inc.) as a source of Jefferson quotations.

CONTENTS

PAGE

1. THUCYDIDES ON ATHENIAN DEMOCRACY 1

*We alone regard a man who takes no part in public affairs, not as
a harmless, but as a useless character; and if few of us are
originators, we are all sound judges of a policy.**

2. CHRISTIAN LOVE IN THE NEW TESTAMENT . . . 7

*Love your enemies and pray for your persecutors.
Do not store up your riches on earth. . . .
. . . we have all—Jews or Greeks, slaves or free men—been baptized in one Spirit to form one body. . . .*

3. MILTON ON FREEDOM OF THOUGHT AND PUBLI-
CATION 15

*Let her [Truth] and Falsehood grapple; who ever knew Truth
put to the worse, in a free and open encounter?*

4. LOCKE ON CIVIL GOVERNMENT 21

*As much land as a man tills, plants, improves, cultivates, and can
use the product of, so much is his property.
The reason why men enter into society is the preservation of their
property; and the end while they choose and authorize a
legislative is that there may be laws made, and rules set, as
guards and fences to the properties of all the society. . . .
Wherever law ends, tyranny begins, if the law be transgressed to
another's harm. . . .*

5. JEFFERSON ON DEMOCRACY 40

*We hold these truths to be self-evident, that all men are created
equal; that they are endowed by their Creator with certain
unalienable Rights, that among these are Life, Liberty, and
the pursuit of Happiness. That to secure these rights, Governments are instituted among Men, deriving their just powers from the consent of the governed. . . .*

* All quotations here given will be found in the body of the book, where their
context will aid in their proper interpretation.

Where the press is free, and every man able to read, all is safe.

*A little rebellion, now and then, is a good thing, and as necessary
in the political world as storms in the physical.*

*To consider the judges alone as the ultimate arbiters of all con-
stitutional questions is a very dangerous doctrine indeed,
and one which would place us under the despotism of an oligarchy. . . .*

*If there is one principle more deeply rooted than any other in the
mind of every American, it is that we should have nothing
to do with conquest.*

6. THE FRENCH DECLARATION OF RIGHTS 56

*The law is an expression of the will of the community. All citi-
zens have a right to concur, either personally or by their representatives, in its formation.*

7. "THE FEDERALIST" ON THE AMERICAN CONSTITU-
TION 59

*. . . you must first enable the government to control the gov-
erned; and in the next place oblige it to control itself.*

*The interpretation of the laws is the proper and peculiar province
of the courts. . . . If, then, the courts are to be considered the
bulwarks of a limited Constitution against legislative encroachments, the consideration will afford a strong argument
for the permanent tenure of judicial offices. . . .*

8. GEORGE WASHINGTON ON FREEDOM, UNITY, AND
PEACE 73

*Of all the dispositions and habits, which lead to political pros-
perity, Religion, and Morality are indispensable supports.*

*The alternate domination of one faction over another, sharpened
by the spirit of revenge, natural to party dissension, which in
different ages has perpetrated the most horrid enormities, is
itself a frightful despotism.*

*'Tis our true policy to steer clear of permanent alliances, with any
portion of the foreign world. Taking care to keep ourselves,
by suitable establishments, on a respectable defensive posture,
we may safely trust to temporary alliances for extraordinary
emergencies.*

9. JOHN STUART MILL ON LIBERTY 88

*If all mankind minus one were of one opinion, and only one
person were of the contrary opinion, mankind would be no*

*more justified in silencing that one person, than he, if he had
the power, would be justified in silencing mankind.*

*Human nature is not a machine to be built after a model, and set
to do exactly the work prescribed for it, but a tree, which requires to grow and develop itself on all sides, according to
the tendency of the inward forces which make it a living
thing.*

*Precisely because the tyranny of opinion is such as to make ec-
centricity a reproach, it is desirable, in order to break through
that tyranny, that people should be eccentric.*

10. LINCOLN'S AMERICANISM 107

*It is rather for us to be here dedicated to the great task . . . that
this nation, under God, shall have a new birth of freedom;
and that government of the people, by the people, and for the
people, shall not perish from the earth.*

*With malice toward none; with charity for all; with firmness in
the right, as God gives us to see the right, let us strive . . .
to do all which may achieve and cherish a just and lasting
peace among ourselves and with all nations.*

11. WHITMAN ON THE PROSPECTS OF DEMOCRACY . . 110

*Political democracy, as it exists and practically works in America,
with all its threatening evils, supplies a training school for
making first class men.*

*Vive, the unpopular cause—the spirit that audaciously aims—the
never abandoned efforts, pursued the same amid opposing
proofs and precedents.*

*I say that democracy can never prove itself beyond cavil, until it
founds and luxuriantly grows its own forms of art, poems,
schools, theology, displacing all that exists, or that has been
produced anywhere in the past, under opposite influences.*

12. HOOVER ON AMERICAN INDIVIDUALISM 131

*. . . individuals with imaginative and administrative intelligence
. . . these rare individuals . . . can arise solely through the
selection that comes from the free-running mills of competition. They must be free to rise from the mass; they must be
given the attraction of premiums to effort.*

*We have learned that the impulse to production can only be
maintained at a high pitch if there is a fair division of the
product. We have also learned that fair division can only be*

PAGE

*obtained by certain restrictions on the strong and the domi-
nant.*

*Our mass of regulation of public utilities and our legislation
against restraint of trade is the monument to our intent to
preserve an equality of opportunity. This regulation is itself
proof that we have gone a long way toward the abandonment
of the "capitalism" of Adam Smith.*

13. DEWEY ON PROGRESSIVE DEMOCRACY 138

*. . . literary persons have been chiefly the ones in this country
who have fallen for Marxist theory, since they are the ones
who, having the least amount of scientific attitude, swallow
most readily the notion that "science" is a new kind of infallibility. . . . Scientific method is not forced to have an Inner
Council to declare just what is Truth. . . . It welcomes a
clash of "incompatible opinions" as long as they can produce
observed facts in their support.*

*There is no physical acid which has the corrosive power possessed
by intolerance directed against persons because they belong
to a group that bears a certain name.*

*Just because the cause of democratic freedom is the cause of the
fullest possible realization of human potentialities, the latter
when they are suppressed and oppressed will in time rebel
and demand an opportunity for manifestation.*

14. THE COMMUNIST MANIFESTO 158

*The history of all hitherto existing society is a history of class
struggles.*

*You are horrified at our intending to do away with private prop-
erty. But in your existing society private property is already
done away with for nine-tenths of the population; its existence for the few is solely due to its non-existence in the hands
of the nine-tenths.*

*In proportion as the exploitation of one individual by another is
put an end to, the exploitation of one nation by another will
be put an end to. In proportion as the antagonism between
classes within the nation vanishes, the hostility of one nation
to another will come to an end.*

*The Communists disdain to conceal their views and aims. They
openly declare that their ends can be attained only by the
forcible overthrow of all existing social conditions. Let the
ruling classes tremble at a Communist Revolution. The pro-*

*letarians have nothing to lose but their chains. They have a
world to win.*

15. LENIN AND STALIN: MARXISM IN THE TWENTIETH
     CENTURY 181

   *Lenin: . . . the expropriation of the capitalists will result inevi-
     tably in a gigantic development of the productive forces of
     human society. The State will be able to wither away com-
     pletely when society has realized the formula: "From each ac-
     cording to his ability; to each according to his need."*
   *Constitution of the U.S.S.R., Article 124: In order to insure to citi-
     zens freedom of conscience, the church in the U.S.S.R. is sep-
     arated from the State, and the school from the church. Free-
     dom of religious worship and freedom of anti-religious
     propaganda is recognized for all citizens.*
   *Ibid., Article 123: . . . any advocacy of racial or national exclu-
     siveness or hatred or contempt is punishable by law.*
   *Stalin: . . . I think that the Constitution of the U.S.S.R. is the
     only thoroughly democratic constitution in the world.*

16. MUSSOLINI ON FASCISM 206

   *Fascism denies that the majority, by the simple fact that it is a
     majority, can direct human society; it denies that numbers
     alone can govern by means of a periodical consultation, and
     it affirms the immutable, beneficial, and fruitful inequality
     of mankind . . .*
   *Fascism, now and always, believes in holiness and heroism; that
     is to say, in actions influenced by no economic motive, direct
     or indirect . . . Fascism denies that the class-war can be the
     preponderant force in the transformation of society.*
   *The Fascist State professes no theology, but a morality, and in the
     Fascist State religion is considered as one of the deepest mani-
     festations of the spirit of man, thus it is not only respected
     but defended and protected.*
   *Fascism . . . believes neither in the possibility nor the utility of
     perpetual peace. . . . War alone brings up to the highest
     tension all human energy and puts the stamp of nobility on
     the peoples who have the courage to meet it.*
   *Peoples which are rising, or rising again after a period of de-
     cadence, are always imperialist; any renunciation is a sign of
     decay and of death.*

PAGE

17. HITLER ON NAZI METHODS AND ASPIRATIONS . . 215

The very nature of organization *implies that it can exist only
if the broad masses, motivated by sentiment, serve a highest
intellectual leadership. A company of two hundred men, all
mentally equally able, could in the long run be disciplined
only with greater difficulty than a company of one hundred
and ninety mentally less able and ten who are more highly
educated.*

*. . . the great masses . . . will more easily fall victims to a great
lie than to a small one, since they themselves perhaps also lie
sometimes in little things, but would certainly still be too
much ashamed of too great lies. . . .*

*. . . the world approaches a great change. And there can only be
the sole question whether it turns out for the benefit of Aryan
mankind or for the profit of the eternal Jew.*

*That foreign policy will be acknowledged as correct only if, a
bare century from now, two hundred and fifty million Germans are living on this continent . . . as peasants and workers mutually guaranteeing each other's life by their productivity.*

18. THE SPIRIT OF JAPAN 225

Perceiving what is right, and doing it not, argues lack of courage.

*Imagine boys—and girls too—brought up not to resort to the
shedding of a tear or the uttering of a groan for the relief of
their feelings,—and there is a physiological problem whether
such effort steels their nerves or makes them more sensitive.*

*We admire him as truly great, who, in the menacing presence
of death, retains his self-possession; who, for instance, can
compose a poem under impending peril, or hum a strain in
the face of death.*

19. PIUS XI ON RECONSTRUCTING THE SOCIAL ORDER 239

*. . . the right to own private property has been given to man by
nature or rather by the Creator Himself, not only in order
that individuals may be able to provide for their own needs
and those of their families, but also that by means of it, the
goods which God destined for the human race may truly
serve this purpose.*

*Just as the unity of human society cannot be built upon class war-
fare, so the proper ordering of economic affairs cannot be left
to free competition alone.*

*. . . it is patent that in our days not alone is wealth accumulated,
but immense power and despotic domination is concentrated
in the hands of a few. . . . This accumulation of power . . .
is a natural result of limitless free competition which permits
the survival of those only who are strongest, which often
means those who fight most relentlessly, who pay least heed
to the dictates of conscience.*

*. . . certain forms of property must be reserved to the State, since
they carry with them an opportunity of domination too great
to be left to private individuals without injury to the community at large.*

*. . . bodily labor, which was decreed by Providence for the good
of man's body and soul even after original sin, has everywhere been changed into an instrument of strange perversion:
for dead matter leaves the factory ennobled and transformed,
where men are corrupted and degraded.*

*For this pitiable ruin of souls, which if continued will frustrate
all efforts to reform society, there can be no other remedy
than a frank and sincere return to the teaching of the Gospel.*

20. FRANKLIN D. ROOSEVELT ON THE DEMOCRATIC
WELFARE STATE 270

*We of the Republic sensed the truth that democratic government
has innate capacity to protect its people against disasters once
considered inevitable, to solve problems once considered unsolvable.*

*I see one-third of a nation ill-housed, ill-clad, ill-nourished. It is
not in despair that I paint you this picture . . . because the
Nation, seeing and understanding the injustice in it, proposes
to paint it out.*

21. ALFRED E. SMITH ON CATHOLICISM AND AMER-
ICAN POLITICS 275

*The American prelates of our Church stoutly defend our consti-
tutional declaration of equality of all religions before the law.*

22. THE BRITISH LABOR PARTY: DEMOCRATIC SOCIAL-
ISM 279

*Those key industries and services, upon which the well-being of
the nation depends, must be transferred to public ownership.*

*The provision by the community, for its members, of security
against the economic deprivations of unemployment, ill health,*

*and old age, and of services which develop bodily and mental
health and generous living, is in the forefront of Labor's program.*

*Ill-health is a loss to the nation, against which the nation owes its
citizens the best possible safeguards.*

23. COMMUNIST STRATEGY AND TACTICS 287

*It is particularly important for this purpose of winning over the
majority of the proletariat, to capture the trade unions. . . .*

*When a revolutionary situation is developing, the Party advances
certain transitional slogans and partial demands corresponding to the concrete situation; but these demands and slogans
must be bent to the revolutionary aim of capturing power
and of overthrowing bourgeois capitalist society.*

*When the revolutionary tide is not rising, the Communist Parties
must advance partial slogans and demands that correspond
to the everyday needs of the toilers, and combine them with
the fundamental tasks of the Communist International.*

*. . . the Sections of the Communist International submit to only
one discipline, viz., international proletarian discipline. . . .*

24. JAPANESE IMPERIALISM: THE TANAKA MEMORIAL 296

*In the future if we want to control China, we must first crush the
United States just as in the past we had to fight in the Russo-
Japanese War. . . . In order to conquer the world, we must
first conquer China. If we succeed in conquering China the
rest of the Asiatic countries and the South Sea countries will
fear us and surrender to us. . . . This is the plan left to us by
Emperor Meiji, the success of which is essential to our national existence.*

25. CONFLICTING IDEALS IN CHINA 302

*Sun Yat-Sen: . . . if we want to restore our race's standing, besides uniting all into a great national body, we must first recover our ancient morality—then, and only then, can we plan
how to attain again to the national position we once held.*

*Mao Tse-Tung: We can never let the few capitalists and landlords
"manipulate the life of the people," nor can we construct a
capitalist society of the European or American style. . . . we
cannot separate ourselves from the assistance of the Soviet
Union. . . . The world now depends on Communism as its
star of salvation, and so does China.*

PAGE

26. POLITICAL AIMS AND METHODS IN INDIA 313

*The Karachi Resolution, 1931. . . . No disability attaches to any
citizen by reason of his or her religion, caste, creed or sex, in
regard to public employment, office of power or honor, and
in the exercise of any trade or calling.*

*Gandhi: Passive Resistance is an all-sided sword . . . it blesses
him who uses it, and also him against whom it is used. . . .
The sword of Passive Resistance does not require a scabbard,
and one cannot be forcibly dispossessed of it. . . . It is easy
to see that Soul-Force is infinitely superior to body-force.*

*Gandhi in 1942: Both Britain and America lack the moral basis
for engaging in this war unless they put their own houses in
order by making it their fixed determination to withdraw
their influence and power from Africa and Asia and remove
the color bar.*

*Nehru in 1939: Liberty and democracy have no meaning without
equality, and equality cannot be established so long as the
principal instruments of production are privately owned.*

27. TOWARD ONE WORLD 325

*. . . iniquity and war inseparably spring from the competitive
anarchy of the national states. . . . therefore the age of nations must end, and the era of humanity begin.*

28. EPILOGUE 334

*. . . there is hope that if men of each tradition will live up to the
best in their tradition, the spirit of brotherhood implied in
each tradition will prevail.*

GENERAL REFERENCES 335

THE CLASH OF POLITICAL IDEALS

1

THUCYDIDES ON ATHENIAN DEMOCRACY

[Thucydides (about 460 to about 399 B. C.) wrote the history of the Peloponnesian War, in which democratic Athens and oligarchic Sparta fought intermittently for nearly thirty years. In the first winter of the war (431 B. C.) the Athenians held a public funeral for those who had fallen in battle. Pericles, the leading statesman of Athens, gave the oration, which Thucydides reports. As to the fidelity of the report, we have no evidence except Thucydides' general comment on the speeches incorporated in his history: "As to the speeches which were made either before or during the war, it was hard for me and for others who reported them to me, to recollect the exact words. I have therefore put into the mouth of each speaker the sentiments proper to the occasion, expressed as I thought he would be likely to express them, while at the same time I endeavored, as nearly as I could, to give the general purport of what was actually said." (Book I, Chapter 22, Jowett's translation, Oxford University Press.) Whatever the relative contributions of Pericles and Thucydides to this oration, it stands as an authentic expression of the ideals of Athenian democracy.

Benjamin Jowett, the translator, is best known for his unrivaled translation of Plato's dialogues, and as the subject of the doggerel stanza,

> My name is Benjamin Jowett,
> I am Master of Balliol College;
> Whatever is knowledge, I know it,
> And what I don't know is not knowledge.

After commenting on the custom of giving an oration on such occasions, Pericles continues (Book II, Chapters 36-43, Jowett's translation):]

'I will speak first of our ancestors, for it is right and seemly that now, when we are lamenting the dead, a tribute should be paid to their memory. There has never been a time when they did not inhabit this land, which by their valor they have handed down from generation to generation, and we

1

have received from them a free state. But if they were worthy of praise, still more were our fathers, who added to their inheritance, and after many a struggle transmitted to us their sons this great empire. And we ourselves assembled here to-day, who are still most of us in the vigor of life, have carried the work of improvement further, and have richly endowed our city with all things, so that she is sufficient for herself both in peace and war. Of the military exploits by which our various possessions were acquired, or of the energy with which we or our fathers drove back the tide of war, Hellenic or Barbarian, I will not speak; for the tale would be long and is familiar to you. But before I praise the dead, I should like to point out by what principles of action we rose to power, and under what institutions and through what manner of life our empire became great. For I conceive that such thoughts are not unsuited to the occasion, and that this numerous assembly of citizens and strangers may profitably listen to them.

'Our form of government does not enter into rivalry with the institutions of others. We do not copy our neighbors, but are an example to them. It is true that we are called a democracy, for the administration is in the hands of the many and not of the few. But while the law secures equal justice to all alike in their private disputes, the claim of excellence is also recognized; and when a citizen is in any way distinguished, he is preferred to the public service, not as a matter of privilege, but as the reward of merit. Neither is poverty a bar, but a man may benefit his country whatever be the obscurity of his condition. There is no exclusiveness in our public life, and in our private intercourse we are not suspicious of one another, nor angry with our neighbor if he does what he likes; we do not put on sour looks at him which, though harmless, are not pleasant. While we are thus unconstrained in our private intercourse, a spirit of reverence pervades our public acts; we are prevented from doing wrong by respect for the authorities and for the laws, having an especial regard to those which are ordained for the protection of the injured as well as to those unwritten laws which bring upon the transgressor of them the reprobation of the general sentiment.

'And we have not forgotten to provide for our weary spirits many relaxations from toil; we have regular games and sacrifices throughout the year; our homes are beautiful and elegant; and the delight which we daily feel in all these things helps to banish melancholy. Because of the greatness of our city the fruits of the whole earth flow in upon us; so that we enjoy the goods of other countries as freely as of our own.

'Then, again, our military training is in many respects superior to that of our adversaries. Our city is thrown open to the world, and we never expel a foreigner or prevent him from seeing or learning anything of which the secret if revealed to an enemy might profit him. We rely not upon management or trickery, but upon our own hearts and hands. And in the matter of education, whereas they from early youth are always undergoing laborious exercises which are to make them brave, we live at ease, and yet are equally ready to face the perils which they face. And here is the proof. The Lacedaemonians come into Attica not by themselves, but with their whole confederacy following; we go alone into a neighbor's country; and although our opponents are fighting for their homes and we on a foreign soil, we have seldom any difficulty in overcoming them. Our enemies have never yet felt our united strength; the care of a navy divides our attention, and on land we are obliged to send our own citizens everywhere. But they, if they meet and defeat a part of our army, are as proud as if they had routed us all, and when defeated they pretend to have been vanquished by us all.

'If then we prefer to meet danger with a light heart but without laborious training, and with a courage which is gained by habit and not enforced by law, are we not greatly the gainers? Since we do not anticipate the pain, although, when the hour comes, we can be as brave as those who never allow themselves to rest; and thus too our city is equally admirable in peace and in war. For we are lovers of the beautiful, yet simple in our tastes, and we cultivate the mind without loss of manliness. Wealth we employ, not for talk and ostentation, but when there is a real use for it. To avow poverty with us is no disgrace; the true disgrace is in doing nothing to avoid it. An Athenian citizen does not neglect the state because he takes care of his own household; and even those of us who are engaged in business have a very fair idea of politics. We alone regard a man who takes no interest in public affairs, not as a harmless, but as a useless character; and if few of us are originators, we are all sound judges of a policy. The great impediment to action is, in our opinion, not discussion, but the want of that knowledge which is gained by discussion preparatory to action. For we have a peculiar power of thinking before we act and of acting too, whereas other men are courageous from ignorance but hesitate upon reflection. And they are surely to be esteemed the bravest spirits who, having the clearest sense both of the pains and pleasures of life, do not on that account shrink from danger. In doing good, again, we are unlike others;

we make our friends by conferring, not by receiving favors. Now he who confers a favor is the firmer friend, because he would fain by kindness keep alive the memory of an obligation; but the recipient is colder in his feelings, because he knows that in requiting another's generosity he will not be winning gratitude but only paying a debt. We alone do good to our neighbors not upon a calculation of interest, but in the confidence of freedom and in a frank and fearless spirit. To sum up: I say that Athens is the school of Hellas, and that the individual Athenian in his own person seems to have the power of adapting himself to the most varied forms of action with the utmost versatility and grace. This is no passing and idle word, but truth and fact; and the assertion is verified by the position to which these qualities have raised the state. For in the hour of trial Athens alone among her contemporaries is superior to the report of her. No enemy who comes against her is indignant at the reverses which he sustains at the hands of such a city; no subject complains that his masters are unworthy of him. And we shall assuredly not be without witnesses; there are mighty monuments of our power which will make us the wonder of this and of succeeding ages; we shall not need the praises of Homer or of any other panegyrist whose poetry may please for the moment, although his representation of the facts will not bear the light of day. For we have compelled every land and every sea to open a path for our valor, and have everywhere planted eternal memorials of our friendship and of our enmity. Such is the city for whose sake these men nobly fought and died; they could not bear the thought that she might be taken from them; and every one of us who survive should gladly toil on her behalf.

'I have dwelt upon the greatness of Athens because I want to show you that we are contending for a higher prize than those who enjoy none of these privileges, and to establish by manifest proof the merit of these men whom I am now commemorating. Their loftiest praise has been already spoken. For in magnifying the city I have magnified them, and men like them whose virtues made her glorious. And of how few Hellenes can it be said as of them, that their deeds when weighed in the balance have been found equal to their fame! Methinks that a death such as theirs has been gives the true measure of a man's worth; it may be the first revelation of his virtues, but is at any rate their final seal. For even those who come short in other ways may justly plead the valor with which they have fought for their country; they have blotted out the evil with the good, and have benefited the state more by their public services than they have injured her by their private actions. None of these men were enervated by wealth or hesitated to resign the pleasures of life; none of them put off the evil day in the hope, natural to poverty, that a man, though poor, may one day become rich. But, deeming that the punishment of their enemies was sweeter than any of these things, and that they could fall in no nobler cause, they determined at the hazard of their lives to be honorably avenged, and to leave the rest. They resigned to hope their unknown chance of happiness; but in the face of death they resolved to rely upon themselves alone. And when the moment came they were minded to resist and suffer, rather than to fly and save their lives; they ran away from the word of dishonor, but on the battlefield their feet stood fast, and in an instant, at the height of their fortune, they passed away from the scene, not of their fear, but of their glory.

'Such was the end of these men; they were worthy of Athens, and the living need not desire to have a more heroic spirit, although they may pray for a less fatal issue. The value of such a spirit is not to be expressed in words. Any one can discourse to you for ever about the advantages of a brave defense, which you know already. But instead of listening to him I would have you day by day fix your eyes upon the greatness of Athens, until you become filled with the love of her; and when you are impressed by the spectacle of her glory, reflect that this empire has been acquired by men who knew their duty and had the courage to do it, who in the hour of conflict had the fear of dishonor always present to them, and who, if ever they failed in an enterprise, would not allow their virtues to be lost to their country, but freely gave their lives to her as the fairest offering which they could present at her feast. The sacrifice which they collectively made was individually repaid to them; for they received again each one for himself a praise which grows not old, and the noblest of all sepulchers—I speak not of that in which their remains are laid, but of that in which their glory survives, and is proclaimed always and on every fitting occasion both in word and deed. For the whole earth is the sepulcher of famous men; not only are they commemorated by columns and inscriptions in their own country, but in foreign lands there dwells also an unwritten memorial of them, graven not on stone but in the hearts of men. Make them your examples, and, esteeming courage to be freedom and freedom to be happiness, do not weigh too nicely the perils of war. The unfortunate who has no hope of a change for the better has less reason to throw away his life than the prosperous who, if he survive, is always liable to a change for the worse, and to whom any accidental fall makes the most serious difference. To a man of spirit, cowardice and disaster coming together are far more bitter than death striking him unperceived at a time when he is full of courage and animated by the general hope.'

[Pericles concludes with some further exhortations, especially to the relatives of the dead.

For the interpretation of Athenian democracy the reader may consult G. H. Sabine, *A History of Political Theory*, pages 11–19, W. S. Ferguson, *Greek Imperialism*, Chapter II, and A. Zimmern, *The Greek Commonwealth*.]

2

CHRISTIAN LOVE IN THE NEW TESTAMENT

[The Christian ideal of brotherly love has been invoked in support of various forms of social organization. The following passages from the New Testament are basic expressions of this ideal. Too often the sonorous phrases of the King James version evoke merely a mood of vague exaltation. For that reason I have chosen to present Goodspeed's version, whose plain, everyday, twentieth century language challenges us to ask what practical meaning these ideas may have to-day.

Professor Goodspeed, the translator, is the author of many books in the field of New Testament studies, and a special student of the papyri which record the colloquial speech of the period. After long service at the University of Chicago, he became emeritus in 1937.]

The Sermon on the Mount *

When he [Jesus] saw the crowds of people he went up on the mountain. There he seated himself, and when his disciples had come up to him, he opened his lips to teach them. And he said,

"Blessed are those who feel their spiritual need, for the Kingdom of Heaven belongs to them!

"Blessed are the mourners, for they will be consoled!

"Blessed are the humble-minded, for they will possess the land!

"Blessed are those who are hungry and thirsty for uprightness, for they will be satisfied!

"Blessed are the merciful, for they will be shown mercy!

"Blessed are the pure in heart, for they will see God!

"Blessed are the peacemakers, for they will be called God's sons!

"Blessed are those who have endured persecution for their uprightness, for the Kingdom of Heaven belongs to them!

* From *The Gospel according to Matthew*, chapters 5, 6, and 7, in *The New Testament, An American Translation*, by E. J. Goodspeed, University of Chicago Press, 1923.

"Blessed are you when people abuse you, and persecute you, and falsely say everything bad of you, on my account. Be glad and exult over it, for you will be richly rewarded in heaven, for that is the way they persecuted the prophets who went before you!

"You are the salt of the earth! But if salt loses its strength, how can it be made salt again? It is good for nothing but to be thrown away and trodden underfoot. You are the light of the world! A city that is built upon a hill cannot be hidden. People do not light a lamp and put it under a peck-measure; they put it on its stand and it gives light to everyone in the house. Your light must burn in that way among men so that they will see the good you do, and praise your Father in heaven.

"Do not suppose that I have come to do away with the Law or the Proph-ets. I have not come to do away with them but to enforce them. For I tell you, as long as heaven and earth endure, not one dotting of an *i* or crossing of a *t* will be dropped from the Law until it is all observed. Anyone, there-fore, who weakens one of the slightest of these commands, and teaches others to do so, will be ranked lowest in the Kingdom of Heaven; but any-one who observes them and teaches others to do so will be ranked high in the Kingdom of Heaven. For I tell you that unless your uprightness is far superior to that of the scribes and Pharisees, you will never even enter the Kingdom of Heaven!

"You have heard that the men of old were told 'You shall not murder,' and 'Whoever murders will have to answer to the court.' But I tell you that anyone who gets angry with his brother will have to answer to the court, and anyone who speaks contemptuously to his brother will have to answer to the great council, and anyone who says to his brother 'You cursed fool!' will have to answer for it in the fiery pit! So when you are presenting your gift at the altar, if you remember that your brother has any grievance against you, leave your gift right there before the altar and go and make up with your brother; then come back and present your gift. Be quick and come to terms with your opponent while you are on the way to court with him, or he may hand you over to the judge, and the judge may hand you over to the officer, and you will be thrown into prison. I tell you, you will never get out again until you have paid the last penny!

"You have heard that men were told 'You shall not commit adultery.' But I tell you that anyone who looks at a woman with desire has already committed adultery with her in his heart. But if your right eye makes you fall, tear it out and throw it away, for you might better lose one part of your body than have it all thrown into the pit! If your right hand makes you fall, cut it off and throw it away! For you might better lose one part of your body than have it all go down to the pit!

"They were told, 'Anyone who divorces his wife must give her a certificate of divorce.' But I tell you that anyone who divorces his wife on any ground, except unfaithfulness, makes her commit adultery, and anyone who marries her after she is divorced commits adultery.

"Again, you have heard that the men of old were told, 'You shall not swear falsely, but you must fulfil your oaths to the Lord.' But I tell you not to swear at all, either by heaven, for it is God's throne, or by the earth, for it is his footstool, or by Jerusalem, for it is the city of the great king. You must not swear by your own head, for you cannot make one single hair white or black. But your way of speaking must be 'Yes' or 'No.' Anything that goes beyond that comes from the evil one.

"You have heard that they were told, 'An eye for an eye and a tooth for a tooth.' But I tell you not to resist injury, but if anyone strikes you on your right cheek, turn the other to him too; and if anyone wants to sue you for your shirt, let him have your coat too. And if anyone forces you to go one mile, go two miles with him. If anyone begs from you, give to him, and when anyone wants to borrow from you, do not turn away.

"You have heard that they were told, 'You must love your neighbor and hate your enemy.' But I tell you, love your enemies and pray for your persecutors, so that you may show yourselves true sons of your Father in heaven, for he makes his sun rise on bad and good alike, and makes the rain fall on the upright and the wrongdoers. For if you love only those who love you, what reward can you expect? Do not the very tax-collectors do that? And if you are polite to your brothers and no one else, what is there remarkable in that? Do not the very heathen do that? So you are to be perfect, as your heavenly Father is.

"But take care not to do your good deeds in public for people to see, for, if you do, you will get no reward from your Father in heaven. So when you are going to give to charity, do not blow a trumpet before yourself, as the hypocrites do, in the synagogues and the streets, to make people praise them. I tell you, that is all the reward they will get! But when you give to charity, your own left hand must not know what your right hand is doing, so that your charity may be secret, and your Father who sees what is secret will reward you.

"When you pray, you must not be like the hypocrites, for they like to pray standing in the synagogues and in the corners of the squares, to let people see them. I tell you, that is the only reward they will get! But when you pray, go into your own room, and shut the door, and pray to your Father who is unseen, and your Father who sees what is secret will reward you. And when you pray, do not repeat empty phrases as the heathen do, for they imagine that their prayers will be heard if they use words enough. You must not be like them. For God, who is your Father, knows what you need before you ask him. This, therefore, is the way you are to pray:

'Our Father in heaven,

Your name be revered!

Your kingdom come!

Your will be done on earth as it is done in heaven!

Give us today bread for the day,

And forgive us our debts, as we have forgiven our debtors.

And do not subject us to temptation,

But save us from the evil one.'

For if you forgive others when they offend you, your heavenly Father will forgive you too. But if you do not forgive others when they offend you, your heavenly Father will not forgive you for your offenses.

"When you fast, do not put on a gloomy look, like the hypocrites, for they neglect their personal appearance to let people see that they are fasting. I tell you, that is all the reward they will get. But when you fast, perfume your hair and wash your face, so that no one may see that you are fasting, except your Father who is unseen, and your Father who sees what is secret will reward you.

"Do not store up your riches on earth, where moths and rust destroy them, and where thieves break in and steal them, but store up your riches in heaven, where moths and rust cannot destroy them, and where thieves cannot break in and steal them. For wherever your treasure is, your heart will be also. The eye is the lamp of the body. If then your eye is sound, your whole body will be light, but if your eye is unsound, your whole body will be dark. If, therefore, your very light is darkness, how deep the darkness will be! No slave can belong to two masters, for he will either hate one and love the other, or stand by one and make light of the other. You cannot serve God and money. Therefore, I tell you, do not worry about life, wondering what you will have to eat or drink, or about your body, wondering what you will have to wear. Is not life more important than food, and the body than clothes? Look at the wild birds. They do not sow or reap, or store their food in barns, and yet your heavenly Father feeds them. Are you not of more account than they? But which of you with all his worry can add a single hour to his life? Why should you worry about clothing? See how the wild flowers grow. They do not toil or spin, and yet I tell you, even Solomon in all his splendor was never dressed like one of them. But if God so beautifully dresses the wild grass, which is alive today and is thrown into the furnace tomorrow, will he not much more surely clothe you, you who have so little faith? So do not worry and say, 'What shall we have to eat?' or 'What shall we have to drink?' or 'What shall we have to wear?' For these are all things the heathen are in pursuit of, and your heavenly Father knows well that you need all this. But you must make his kingdom, and uprightness before him, your greatest care, and you will have all these other things besides. So do not worry about tomorrow, for tomorrow will have worries of its own. Let each day be content with its own ills.

"Pass no more judgments upon other people, so that you may not have judgment passed upon you. For you will be judged by the standard you judge by, and men will pay you back with the same measure you have used with them. Why do you keep looking at the speck in your brother's eye, and pay no attention to the beam that is in your own? How can you say to your brother, 'Just let me get that speck out of your eye,' when all the time there is a beam in your own? You hypocrite! First get the beam out of your own eye, and then you can see to get the speck out of your brother's eye.

"Do not give what is sacred to dogs, and do not throw your pearls before pigs, or they will trample them under their feet and turn and tear you in pieces. Ask, and what you ask will be given you. Search, and you will find what you search for. Knock, and the door will open to you. For it is always the one who asks who receives, and the one who searches who finds, and the one who knocks to whom the door opens. Which of you men when his son asks him for some bread will give him a stone? Or if he asks for a fish, will he give him a snake? So if you, bad as you are, know enough to give your children what is good, how much more surely will your Father in heaven give what is good to those who ask him for it! Therefore, you must always treat other people as you would like to have them treat you, for this sums up the Law and the Prophets.

"Go in at the narrow gate. For the road that leads to destruction is broad and spacious, and there are many who go in by it. But the gate is narrow and the road is hard that leads to life, and there are few that find it.

"Beware of false prophets, who come to you disguised as sheep but are ravenous wolves underneath. You can tell them by their fruit. Do people pick grapes off thorns, or figs off thistles? Just so any sound tree bears good fruit, but a poor tree bears bad fruit. No sound tree can bear bad fruit, and no poor tree can bear good fruit. Any tree that does not bear good fruit is cut down and burned. So you can tell them by their fruit. It is not everyone who says to me 'Lord! Lord!' who will get into the Kingdom of Heaven, but only those who do the will of my Father in heaven. Many will say to me on that Day, 'Lord! Lord! Was it not in your name that we prophesied, and by your name that we drove out demons, and by your name that we did many mighty acts?' Then I will say to them plainly, 'I never knew you! Go away from me, you who do wrong!'

"Everyone, therefore, who listens to this teaching of mine and acts upon it, will be like a sensible man who built his house on rock. And the rain fell, and the rivers rose, and the winds blew, and beat about that house, and it did not go down, for its foundations were on rock. And anyone who listens to this teaching of mine and does not act upon it, will be like a foolish man who built his house on sand. And the rain fell and the rivers rose, and the winds blew and beat about that house, and it went down, and its downfall was complete."

When Jesus had finished this discourse, the crowds were astounded at his teaching, for he taught them like one who had authority and not like their scribes.

Paul on Spiritual Gifts and Love *

About spiritual gifts, brothers, I do not want you to be misinformed. You know that when you were heathen you would stray off, as impulse directed, to idols that could not speak. Therefore, I must tell you that no one who is speaking under the influence of the Spirit of God ever says, "Curse Jesus!" and no one can say, "Jesus is Lord!" without being under the influence of the holy Spirit.

Endowments vary, but the Spirit is the same, and forms of service vary, but it is the same Lord who is served, and activities vary, but God who produces them all in us all is the same. Each one is given his spiritual illumination for the common good. One man receives through the Spirit the power to speak wisely, another, by the same Spirit, receives the power to

* From *The First Letter to the Corinthians*, Goodspeed's translation, chapters 12 and 13.

express knowledge, another, from his union with the same Spirit receives faith, another, by one and the same Spirit, the ability to cure the sick, another, the working of wonders, another, inspiration in preaching, another, the power of distinguishing the true Spirit from false ones, another various ecstatic utterances, and another, the ability to explain them. These are all produced by one and the same Spirit, and apportioned to each of us just as the Spirit chooses.

For just as the body is one and yet has many parts, and all the parts of the body, many as they are, form one body, so it is with Christ. For we have all—Jews or Greeks, slaves or free men—been baptized in one Spirit to form one body, and we have all been saturated with one Spirit. For the body does not consist of one part but of many. If the foot says, "As I am not a hand, I am not a part of the body," that does not make it any less a part of the body. And if the ear says, "As I am not an eye, I am not a part of the body," that does not make it any less a part of the body. If all the body were eye, how would we hear? If it were all ear, how could we have a sense of smell? As it is, God has arranged the parts, every one of them in the body as he wished them to be. If they were all one part, where would the body be? As it is, there are many parts, but one body. The eye cannot say to the hand, "I do not need you," or the head to the feet, "I do not need you." On the contrary, the parts of the body that are considered most delicate are indispensable, and the parts of it that we think common, we dress with especial care, and our unpresentable parts receive especial attention which our presentable parts do not need. God has so adjusted the body and given such especial distinction to its inferior parts that there is no clash in the body, but its parts all alike care for one another. If one part suffers, all the parts share its sufferings. If a part has honor done it, all the parts enjoy it too. Now you are Christ's body, and individually parts of it. And God has placed people in the church, first as apostles, second as inspired preachers, third as teachers, then wonder-workers; then come ability to cure the sick, helpfulness, administration, ecstatic speaking. Is everyone an apostle? Is everyone an inspired preacher? Is everyone a teacher? Is everyone a wonder-worker? Is everyone able to cure the sick? Can everyone speak ecstatically? Can everyone explain what it means? But you must cultivate the higher endowments.

I will show you a far better way. If I can speak the languages of men and even of angels, but have no love, I am only a noisy gong or a clashing cymbal. If I am inspired to preach and know all the secret truths and possess all knowledge, and if I have such perfect faith that I can move mountains, but have no love, I am nothing. Even if I give away everything I own, and give myself up, but do it in pride, not love, it does me no good. Love is patient and kind. Love is not envious and boastful. It does not put on airs. It is not rude. It does not insist on its rights. It does not become angry. It is not resentful. It is not happy over injustice, it is only happy with truth. It will bear anything, believe anything, hope for anything, endure anything. Love will never die out. If there is inspired preaching, it will pass away. If there is ecstatic speaking, it will cease. If there is knowledge, it will pass away. For our knowledge is imperfect and our preaching is imperfect. But when perfection comes, what is imperfect will pass away. When I was a child, I talked like a child, I thought like a child, I reasoned like a child. When I became a man, I put aside my childish ways. For now we are looking at a dim reflection in a mirror, but then we shall see face to face. Now my knowledge is imperfect, but then I shall know as fully as God knows me. So faith, hope, and love endure. These are the great three, and the greatest of them is love.

3

MILTON ON FREEDOM OF THOUGHT
AND PUBLICATION

[John Milton (1608–1674) published his *Areopagitica* November 25, 1644. The circumstances were as follows. On June 14, 1643, Parliament passed a law requiring all publications to be licensed by one of the official censors and to be registered with the Stationers' Company. Many publications appeared without conforming to this law, among them Milton's treatise on *The Doctrine and Discipline of Divorce*. The Stationers complained to Parliament against Milton and others. Milton's *Areopagitica* is his plea to Parliament for repeal of the law. The law was not repealed, but it was so discredited by Milton's polemic and the opposition of Cromwell and the Army Independents that it ceased to be enforced.

After the restoration of the Stuarts the licensing system was revived in 1662. Parliament let it lapse in 1695 and since then the British press has been free.

Already in the preface to his treatise on divorce above mentioned he had commented in picturesque terms upon the hostility encountered by advocates of new truth: ". . . for truth is as impossible to be soiled by any outward touch as the sunbeam; though this ill hap wait on her nativity, that she never comes into the world, but like a bastard, to the ignominy of him that brought her forth; till time, the midwife rather than the mother of truth, have washed and salted the infant, declared her legitimate, and churched the father of his young Minerva, from the needless causes of his purgation."

These words so impressed Thomas Hardy that in his poem "Lausanne" he makes the spirit of Gibbon inquire

> How fares the truth now?—Ill?
> .   .   .   .
> Still rule those minds on earth
> At whom sage Milton's wormwood words were hurled:
>   "Truth like a bastard comes into the world
> Never without ill-fame to him who gives her birth"?]

15

Areopagitica *

* * *

I deny not, but that it is of greatest concernment in the Church and Commonwealth, to have a vigilant eye how books demean themselves as well as men; and thereafter to confine, imprison, and do sharpest justice on them as malefactors. For books are not absolutely dead things, but do contain a potency of life in them to be as active as that soul was whose progeny they are; nay, they do preserve as in a vial the purest efficacy and extraction of that living intellect that bred them. I know they are as lively, and as vigorously productive, as those fabulous dragon's teeth; and being sown up and down, may chance to spring up armed men. And yet, on the other hand, unless wariness be used, as good almost kill a man as kill a good book. Who kills a man kills a reasonable creature, God's image; but he who destroys a good book, kills reason itself, kills the image of God, as it were in the eye. Many a man lives a burden to the earth; but a good book is the precious life-blood of a master spirit, embalmed and treasured up on purpose to a life beyond life. 'Tis true, no age can restore a life, whereof perhaps there is no great loss; and revolutions of ages do not oft recover the loss of a rejected truth, for the want of which whole nations fare the worse.

* * *

For books are as meats and viands are; some of good, some of evil substance; and yet God, in that unapocryphal vision, said without exception, Rise, Peter, kill and eat, leaving the choice to each man's discretion. Wholesome meats to a vitiated stomach differ little or nothing from unwholesome; and best books to a naughty mind are not unappliable to occasions of evil. Bad meats will scarce breed good nourishment in the healthiest concoction; but herein the difference is of bad books, that they to a discreet and judicious reader serve in many respects to discover, to confute, to forewarn, and to illustrate. Whereof what better witness can ye expect I should produce, than one of your own now sitting in Parliament, the chief of learned men reputed in this land, Mr. Selden; whose volume of natural and national laws proves, not only by great authorities brought together, but by exquisite reasons and theorems almost mathematically demonstra-

* From *Milton's Areopagitica*, Everyman edition, E. P. Dutton and Company, Inc.

tive, that all opinions, yea errors, known, read, and collated, are of main service and assistance toward the speedy attainment of what is truest. I conceive, therefore, that when God did enlarge the universal diet of man's body, saving ever the rules of temperance, He then also, as before, left arbitrary the dieting and repasting of our minds; as wherein every mature man might have to exercise his own leading capacity.

*　　*　　*

Good and evil we know in the field of this world grow up together almost inseparably; and the knowledge of good is so involved and interwoven with the knowledge of evil, and in so many cunning resemblances hardly to be discerned, that those confused seeds which were imposed upon Psyche as an incessant labor to cull out, and sort asunder, were not more intermixed. It was from out the rind of one apple tasted, that the knowledge of good and evil, as two twins cleaving together, leaped forth into the world. And perhaps this is that doom which Adam fell into of knowing good and evil, that is to say of knowing good by evil. As therefore the state of man now is; what wisdom can there be to choose, what continence to forbear without the knowledge of evil? He that can apprehend and consider vice with all her baits and seeming pleasures, and yet abstain, and yet distinguish, and yet prefer that which is truly better, he is the true wayfaring Christian.

I cannot praise a fugitive and cloistered virtue, unexercised and unbreathed, that never sallies out and sees her adversary, but slinks out of the race, where that immortal garland is to be run for, not without dust and heat. Assuredly we bring not innocence into the world, we bring impurity much rather; that which purifies us is trial, and trial is by what is contrary. That virtue therefore which is but a youngling in the contemplation of evil, and knows not the utmost that vice promises to her followers, and rejects it, is but a blank virtue, not a pure; her whiteness is but an excremental * whiteness. Which was the reason why our sage and serious poet Spenser, whom I dare be known to think a better teacher than Scotus or Aquinas, describing true temperance under the person of Guion, brings him in with his palmer through the cave of Mammon, and the bower of earthly bliss, that he might see and know, and yet abstain. Since therefore the knowledge and survey of vice is in this world so necessary to the con-

---

* "Of the nature of an outgrowth or excrescence" (Murray, *New English Dictionary*), i. e. superficial.—Editor.

stituting of human virtue, and the scanning of error to the confirmation of truth, how can we more safely, and with less danger, scout into the regions of sin and falsity than by reading all manner of tractates and hearing all manner of reason? And this is the benefit which may be had of books promiscuously read.

* * *

. . . When a man writes to the world, he summons up all his reason and deliberation to assist him; he searches, meditates, is industrious, and likely consults and confers with his judicious friends; after all which done he takes himself to be informed in what he writes, as well as any that writ before him. If, in this the most consummate act of his fidelity and ripeness, no years, no industry, no former proof of his abilities can bring him to that state of maturity, as not to be still mistrusted and suspected, unless he carry all his considerate diligence, all his midnight watchings and expense of Palladian * oil, to the hasty view of an unleisured licenser, perhaps much his younger, perhaps far his inferior in judgment, perhaps one who never knew the labor of book-writing, and if he be not repulsed or slighted, must appear in print like a puny with his guardian, and his censor's hand on the back of his title to be his bail and surety that he is no idiot or seducer, it cannot be but a dishonor and derogation to the author, to the book, to the privilege and dignity of Learning.

* * *

And lest some should persuade ye, Lords and Commons, that these arguments of learned men's discouragement at this your Order are mere flourishes, and not real, I could recount what I have seen and heard in other countries, where this kind of inquisition tyrannizes; when I have sat among their learned men, for that honor I had, and been counted happy to be born in such a place of philosophic freedom, as they supposed England was, while themselves did nothing but bemoan the servile condition into which learning amongst them was brought; that this was it which had damped the glory of Italian wits; that nothing had been there written now these many years but flattery and fustian. There it was that I found and visited the famous Galileo, grown old a prisoner to the Inquisition, for

[* "Of or pertaining to Pallas [Athene], the goddess of wisdom; hence pertaining to wisdom, knowledge or study" (Murray, *New English Dictionary*).]

thinking in astronomy otherwise than the Franciscan and Dominican licensers thought.

*   *   *

Truth indeed came once into the world with her Divine Master, and was a perfect shape most glorious to look on: but when He ascended, and His Apostles after Him were laid asleep, then straight arose a wicked race of deceivers, who, as that story goes of the Egyptian Typhon with his conspirators, how they dealt with the good Osiris, took the virgin Truth, hewed her lovely form into a thousand pieces, and scattered them to the four winds. From that time ever since, the sad friends of Truth, such as durst appear, imitating the careful search that Isis made for the mangled body of Osiris, went up and down gathering up limb by limb, still as they could find them. We have not yet found them all, Lords and Commons, nor ever shall do, till her Master's second coming; He shall bring together every joint and member, and shall mould them into an immortal feature of loveliness and perfection. Suffer not these licensing prohibitions to stand at every place of opportunity, forbidding and disturbing them that continue seeking, that continue to do our obsequies to the torn body of our martyred saint.

*   *   *

And now the time in special is, by privilege to write and speak what may help to the further discussing of matters in agitation. The temple of Janus with his two controversial faces might now not unsignificantly be set open. And though all the winds of doctrine were let loose to play upon the earth, so Truth be in the field, we do injuriously, by licensing and prohibiting, to misdoubt her strength. Let her and Falsehood grapple; who ever knew Truth put to the worse, in a free and open encounter? Her confuting is the best and surest suppressing. He who hears what praying there is for light and clearer knowledge to be sent down among us, would think of other matters to be constituted beyond the discipline of Geneva, framed and fabricked already to our hands. Yet when the new light which we beg for shines in upon us, there be who envy and oppose, if it come not first in at their casements. What a collusion * is this, whenas we are exhorted by the wise man to use diligence, to seek for wisdom as for hidden treasures

[* A trick or ambiguity in words or reasoning" (Murray, *New English Dictionary*).]

early and late, that another order shall enjoin us to know nothing but by statute? When a man hath been laboring the hardest labor in the deep mines of knowledge; hath furnished out his findings in all their equipage; drawn forth his reasons as it were a battle ranged; scattered and defeated all objections in his way; calls out his adversary into the plain, offers him the advantage of wind and sun, if he please, only that he may try the matter by dint of argument: for his opponents then to skulk, to lay ambushments, to keep a narrow bridge of licensing where the challenger should pass, though it be valor enough in soldiership, is but weakness and cowardice in the wars of Truth.

For who knows not that Truth is strong, next to the Almighty? She needs no policies, nor stratagems, nor licensings to make her victorious; those are the shifts and the defenses that error uses against her power. Give her but room, and do not bind her when she sleeps, for then she speaks not true, as the old Proteus did, who spake oracles only when he was caught and bound, but then rather she turns herself into all shapes, except her own, and perhaps tunes her voice according to the time, as Micaiah * did before Ahab, until she be adjured into her own likeness. Yet is it not impossible that she may have more shapes than one. What else is all that rank of things indifferent, wherein Truth may be on this side or on the other, without being unlike herself? What but a vain shadow else is the abolition of those ordinances, that hand-writing nailed to the cross? What great purchase is this Christian liberty which Paul † so often boasts of? His doctrine is, that he who eats or eats not, regards a day or regards it not, may do either to the Lord. How many other things might be tolerated in peace, and left to conscience, had we but charity, and were it not the chief stronghold of our hypocrisy to be ever judging one another?

* I Kings xxii. 4–28, especially 13–15.—EDITOR.
† See Galatians iii, iv, v.—EDITOR.

4

LOCKE ON CIVIL GOVERNMENT

[John Locke (1632–1704) published his *Two Treatises of Government* early in 1690 not long after the fall of the Stuarts and the establishment of the new Protestant and constitutional monarchy in 1688. "Locke's theories, as expressed in these treatises and in the letters upon 'Toleration,' supplied the whigs with their political philosophy for the next century; and although he and his followers were content with a partial application, they in fact laid the foundation of the more thoroughgoing doctrines of Bentham and the later radicals" (*Dictionary of National Biography,* article on John Locke).]

An Essay Concerning the True Original, Extent and End of Civil Government *

CHAPTER II

Of the State of Nature

4. To understand political power aright, and derive it from its original, we must consider what estate all men are naturally in, and that is, a state of perfect freedom to order their actions, and dispose of their possessions and persons as they think fit, within the bounds of the law of Nature, without asking leave or depending upon the will of any other man.

A state also of equality, wherein all the power and jurisdiction is reciprocal, no one having more than another, there being nothing more evident than that creatures of the same species and rank, promiscuously born to all the same advantages of Nature, and the use of the same faculties, should also be equal one amongst another, without subordination or subjection, unless the lord and master of them all should, by any manifest declaration

* From *Two Treatises of Civil Government,* Everyman edition, E. P. Dutton and Company, Inc., with a few corrections from *Two Treatises of Government,* London, 1764.

of his will, set one above another, and confer on him, by an evident and clear appointment, an undoubted right to dominion and sovereignty.

* * *

6. But though this be a state of liberty, yet it is not a state of license; though man in that state have an uncontrollable liberty to dispose of his person or possessions, yet he has not liberty to destroy himself, or so much as any creature in his possession, but where some nobler use than its bare preservation calls for it. The state of Nature has a law of Nature to govern it, which obliges every one, and reason, which is that law, teaches all mankind who will but consult it, that being all equal and independent, no one ought to harm another in his life, health, liberty or possessions; for men being all the workmanship of one omnipotent and infinitely wise Maker; all the servants of one sovereign Master, sent into the world by His order and about His business; they are His property, whose workmanship they are made to last during His, not one another's pleasure. And, being furnished with like faculties, sharing all in one community of Nature, there cannot be supposed any such subordination among us that may authorize us to destroy one another, as if we were made for one another's uses, as the inferior ranks of creatures are for ours. Every one as he is bound to preserve himself, and not to quit his station wilfully, so by the like reason, when his own preservation comes not in competition, ought he as much as he can to preserve the rest of mankind, and not unless it be to do justice on an offender, take away or impair the life, or what tends to the preservation of the life, the liberty, health, limb, or goods of another.

7. And that all men may be restrained from invading others' rights, and from doing hurt to one another, and the law of Nature be observed, which willeth the peace and preservation of all mankind, the execution of the law of Nature is in that state put into every man's hands, whereby every one has a right to punish the transgressors of that law to such a degree as may hinder its violation. For the law of Nature would, as all other laws that concern men in this world, be in vain if there were nobody that in the state of Nature had a power to execute that law, and thereby preserve the innocent and restrain offenders; and if any one in the state of Nature may punish another for any evil he has done, every one may do so. For in that state of perfect equality, where naturally there is no superiority or jurisdiction of one over another, what any may do in prosecution of that law, every one must needs have a right to do.

8. And thus, in the state of Nature, one man comes by a power over another, but yet no absolute or arbitrary power to use a criminal, when he has got him in his hands, according to the passionate heats or boundless extravagancy of his own will, but only to retribute to him so far as calm reason and conscience dictate, what is proportionate to his transgression, which is so much as may serve for reparation and restraint. For these two are the only reasons why one man may lawfully do harm to another, which is that we call punishment. In transgressing the law of Nature, the offender declares himself to live by another rule than that of reason and common equity, which is that measure God has set to the actions of men for their mutual security, and so he becomes dangerous to mankind; the tie which is to secure them from injury and violence being slighted and broken by him, which being a trespass against the whole species, and the peace and safety of it, provided for by the law of Nature, every man upon this score, by the right he hath to preserve mankind in general, may restrain, or where it is necessary, destroy things noxious to them, and so may bring such evil on any one who hath transgressed that law, as may make him repent the doing of it, and thereby deter him, and, by his example, others from doing the like mischief. And in this case, and upon this ground, every man hath a right to punish the offender, and be executioner of the law of Nature.

* * *

10. Besides the crime which consists in violating the laws, and varying from the right rule of reason, whereby a man so far becomes degenerate, and declares himself to quit the principles of human nature and to be a noxious creature, there is commonly injury done, and some person or other, some other man, receives damage by his transgression; in which case, he who hath received any damage has (besides the right of punishment common to him, with other men) a particular right to seek reparation from him that hath done it. And any other person who finds it just may also join with him that is injured, and assist him in recovering from the offender so much as may make satisfaction for the harm he hath suffered.

* * *

12. By the same reason may a man in the state of Nature punish the lesser breaches of that law, it will, perhaps, be demanded, with death? I answer: Each transgression may be punished to that degree, and with so

much severity, as will suffice to make it an ill bargain to the offender, give him cause to repent, and terrify others from doing the like.

*   *   *

14. It is often asked as a mighty objection, where are, or ever were, there any men in such a state of Nature? To which it may suffice as an answer at present, that since all princes and rulers of "independent" governments all through the world are in a state of Nature, it is plain the world never was, nor never will be, without numbers of men in that state. I have named all governors of "independent" communities, whether they are, or are not, in league with others; for it is not every compact that puts an end to the state of Nature between men, but only this one of agreeing together mutually to enter into one community, and make one body politic; other promises and compacts men may make one with another, and yet still be in the state of Nature. The promises and bargains for truck, etc., between the two men in the desert island, mentioned by Garcilasso de la Vega, in his history of Peru; or between a Swiss and an Indian, in the woods of America, are binding to them, though they are perfectly in a state of Nature in reference to one another for truth, and keeping of faith belongs to men as men, and not as members of society.*

*   *   *

CHAPTER V

Of Property

24. Whether we consider natural reason, which tells us that men, being once born, have a right to their preservation, and consequently to meat and drink and such other things as Nature affords for their subsistence, or "revelation," which gives us an account of those grants God made of the world to Adam, and to Noah and his sons, it is very clear that God, as King David says (Psalm cxv. 16), "has given the earth to the children of men," given it to mankind in common. But, this being supposed, it seems to some a very great difficulty how any one should ever come to have a property in anything, I will not content myself to answer, that, if it be difficult to make out "property" upon a supposition that God gave the world to Adam and his posterity in common, it is impossible that any man but one

[* This sentence corrected according to the edition of 1764.]

universal monarch should have any "property" upon a supposition that God gave the world to Adam and his heirs in succession, exclusive of all the rest of his posterity; but I shall endeavor to show how men might come to have a property in several parts of that which God gave to mankind in common, and that without any express compact of all the commoners.

25. God, who hath given the world to men in common, hath also given them reason to make use of it to the best advantage of life and convenience. The earth and all that is therein is given to men for the support and comfort of their being. And though all the fruits it naturally produces, and beasts it feeds, belong to mankind in common, as they are produced by the spontaneous hand of Nature, and nobody has originally a private dominion exclusive of the rest of mankind in any of them, as they are thus in their natural state, yet being given for the use of men, there must of necessity be a means to appropriate them some way or other before they can be of any use, or at all beneficial, to any particular men. The fruit or venison which nourishes the wild Indian, who knows no enclosure, and is still a tenant in common, must be his, and so his—*i.e.,* a part of him, that another can no longer have any right to it before it can do him any good for the support of his life.

26. Though the earth and all inferior creatures be common to all men, yet every man has a "property" in his own "person." This nobody has any right to but himself. The "labor" of his body and the "work" of his hands, we may say, are properly his. Whatsoever, then, he removes out of the state that Nature hath provided and left it in, he hath mixed his labor with it, and joined to it something that is his own, and thereby makes it his property. It being by him removed from the common state Nature placed it in, it hath by this labor something annexed to it that excludes the common right of other men. For this "labor" being the unquestionable property of the laborer, no man but he can have a right to what that is once joined to, at least where there is enough, and as good left in common for others.

27. He that is nourished by the acorns he picked up under an oak, or the apples he gathered from the trees in the wood, has certainly appropriated them to himself. Nobody can deny but the nourishment is his. I ask, then, when did they begin to be his? when he digested? or when he ate? or when he boiled? or when he brought them home? or when he picked them up? And it is plain, if the first gathering made them not his, nothing else could. That labor put a distinction between them and common. That added something to them more than Nature, the common

mother of all, had done, and so they became his private right. And will any one say he had no right to those acorns or apples he thus appropriated because he had not the consent of all mankind to make them his? Was it a robbery thus to assume to himself what belonged to all in common? If such a consent as that was necessary, man had starved, notwithstanding the plenty God had given him. We see in commons, which remain so by compact, that it is the taking any part of what is common, and removing it out of the state Nature leaves it in, which begins the property, without which the common is of no use. And the taking of this or that part does not depend on the express consent of all the commoners. Thus, the grass my horse has bit, the turfs my servant has cut, and the ore I have digged in any place, where I have a right to them in common with others, become my property without the assignation or consent of anybody. The labor that was mine, removing them out of that common state they were in, hath fixed my property in them.

*   *   *

31. But the chief matter of property being now not the fruits of the earth and the beasts that subsist on it, but the earth itself, as that which takes in and carries with it all the rest, I think it is plain that property in that too is acquired as the former. As much land as a man tills, plants, improves, cultivates, and can use the product of, so much is his property. He by his labor does, as it were, enclose it from the common. Nor will it invalidate his right to say everybody else has an equal title to it, and therefore he cannot appropriate, he cannot enclose, without the consent of all his fellow-commoners, all mankind. God, when He gave the world in common to all mankind, commanded man also to labor, and the penury of his condition required it of him. God and his reason commanded him to subdue the earth—*i.e.,* improve it for the benefit of life and therein lay out something upon it that was his own, his labor. He that, in obedience to this command of God, subdued, tilled, and sowed any part of it, thereby annexed to it something that was his property, which another had no title to, nor could without injury take from him.

32. Nor was this appropriation of any parcel of land, by improving it, any prejudice to any other man, since there was still enough and as good left, and more than the yet unprovided could use. So that, in effect, there was never the less left for others because of his enclosure for himself. For

he that leaves as much as another can make use of does as good as take nothing at all. Nobody could think himself injured by the drinking of another man, though he took a good draught, who had a whole river of the same water left him to quench his thirst. And the case of land and water, where there is enough of both, is perfectly the same.

* * *

40. Nor is it so strange as, perhaps, before consideration, it may appear, that the property of labor should be able to overbalance the community of land, for it is labor indeed that puts the difference of value on everything; and let any one consider what the difference is between an acre of land planted with tobacco or sugar, sown with wheat or barley, and an acre of the same land lying in common without any husbandry upon it, and he will find that the improvement of labor makes the far greater part of the value. I think it will be but a very modest computation to say, that of the products of the earth useful to the life of man, nine-tenths are the effects of labor. Nay, if we will rightly estimate things as they come to our use, and cast up the several expenses about them—what in them is purely owing to Nature and what to labor—we shall find that in most of them ninety-nine hundredths are wholly to be put on the account of labor.

* * *

42. To make this a little clearer, let us but trace some of the ordinary provisions of life, through their several progresses, before they come to our use, and see how much they receive of their value from human industry. Bread, wine, and cloth are things of daily use and great plenty; yet notwithstanding acorns, water, and leaves, or skins must be our bread, drink and clothing, did not labor furnish us with these more useful commodities. For whatever bread is more worth than acorns, wine than water, and cloth or silk than leaves, skins or moss, that is wholly owing to labor and industry. The one of these being the food and raiment which unassisted Nature furnishes us with; the other provisions which our industry and pains prepare for us, which how much they exceed the other in value, when any one hath computed, he will then see how much labor makes the far greatest part of the value of things we enjoy in this world; and the ground which produces the materials is scarce to be reckoned in as any, or at most, but a very small part of it; so little, that even amongst us,

land that is left wholly to nature, that hath no improvement of pasturage, tillage, or planting, is called, as indeed it is, waste; and we shall find the benefit of it amount to little more than nothing.

*   *   *

87. Man being born, as has been proved, with a title to perfect freedom and an uncontrolled enjoyment of all the rights and privileges of the law of Nature, equally with any other man, or number of men in the world, hath by nature a power not only to preserve his property—that is, his life, liberty, and estate, against the injuries and attempts of other men, but to judge of and punish the breaches of that law in others, as he is persuaded the offense deserves, even with death itself, in crimes where the heinousness of the fact, in his opinion, requires it. But because no political society can be, nor subsist, without having in itself the power to preserve the property, and in order thereunto punish the offenses of all those of that society, there, and there only, is political society where every one of the members hath quitted this natural power, resigned it up into the hands of the community in all cases that exclude him not from appealing for protection to the law established by it. And thus all private judgment of every particular member being excluded, the community comes to be umpire, and by settled standing rules, indifferent and the same to all parties; and by men having authority from the community for their execution, decides all the differences that may happen between any members of that society concerning any matter of right, and punishes those offenses which any member hath committed against the society with such penalties as the law has established; whereby it is easy to discern who are, and are not, in political society together.* Those who are united into one body, and have a common established law and judicature to appeal to, with authority to decide controversies between them and punish offenders, are in civil society one with another; but those who have no such common appeal, I mean on earth, are still in the state of Nature, each being, where there is no other, judge for himself and executioner; which is, as I have before showed it, the perfect state of Nature.

*   *   *

90. And hence it is evident that absolute monarchy, which by some men is counted for the only government in the world, is indeed inconsistent

[* This sentence corrected according to the edition of 1764.]

with civil society, and so can be no form of civil government at all. For the end of civil society being to avoid and remedy those inconveniences of the state of Nature which necessarily follow from every man's being judge in his own case, by setting up a known authority to which every one of that society may appeal upon any injury received, or controversy that may arise, and which every one of the society ought to obey. Wherever any persons are who have not such an authority to appeal to, and decide any difference between them there, those persons are still in the state of Nature. And so is every absolute prince in respect of those who are under his dominion.

91. For he being supposed to have all, both legislative and executive, power in himself alone, there is no judge to be found, no appeal lies open to any one, who may fairly and indifferently, and with authority decide, and from whence relief and redress may be expected of any injury or inconveniency that may be suffered from him, or by his order. So that such a man, however entitled, Czar, or Grand Signior,* or how you please, is as much in the state of Nature, with all under his dominion, as he is with the rest of mankind. For wherever any two men are, who have no standing rule and common judge to appeal to on earth, for the determination of controversies of right betwixt them, there they are still in the state of Nature, and under all the inconveniencies of it, with only this woeful difference to the subject, or rather slave of an absolute prince. That whereas, in the ordinary state of Nature, he has a liberty to judge of his right, according to the best of his power to maintain it; but whenever his property is invaded by the will and order of his monarch, he has not only no appeal, as those in society ought to have, but, as if he were degraded from the common state of rational creatures, is denied a liberty to judge of, or defend his right, and so is exposed to all the misery and inconveniences that a man can fear from one, who being in the unrestrained state of Nature, is yet corrupted with flattery and armed with power.

* * *

CHAPTER VIII

OF THE BEGINNING OF POLITICAL SOCIETIES

95. Men being, as has been said, by nature all free, equal, and independent, no one can be put out of this estate and subjected to the political

* The Sultan of Turkey.—EDITOR.

power of another without his own consent, which is done by agreeing with other men, to join and unite into a community for their comfortable, safe, and peaceable living, one amongst another, in a secure enjoyment of their properties, and a greater security against any that are not of it. This any number of men may do, because it injures not the freedom of the rest; they are left, as they were, in the liberty of the state of Nature. When any number of men have so consented to make one community or government, they are thereby presently incorporated, and make one body politic, wherein the majority have a right to act and conclude the rest.

96. For, when any number of men have, by the consent of every individual, made a community, they have thereby made that community one body, with a power to act as one body, which is only by the will and determination of the majority. For that which acts * any community, being only the consent of the individuals of it, and it being one body, must move one way, it is necessary the body should move that way whither the greater force carries it, which is the consent of the majority, or else it is impossible it should act or continue one body, one community, which the consent of every individual that united into it agreed that it should; and so every one is bound by that consent to be concluded by the majority. And therefore we see that in assemblies empowered to act by positive laws where no number is set by that positive law which empowers them, the act of the majority passes for the act of the whole, and of course determines as having, by the law of Nature and reason, the power of the whole.

* * *

98. For if the consent of the majority shall not in reason be received as the act of the whole, and conclude every individual, nothing but the consent of every individual can make anything to be the act of the whole, which, considering the infirmities of health and avocations of business, which in a number though much less than that of a commonwealth, will necessarily keep many away from the public assembly; and the variety of opinions and contrariety of interests which unavoidably happen in all collections of men, it is next impossible ever to be had. And, therefore, if coming into society be upon such terms, it will be only like Cato's coming into the theatre, *tantum ut exiret*.† Such a constitution as this would make the mighty leviathan of a shorter duration than the feeblest creatures, and not let it outlast the day it was born in, which cannot be supposed till we

* Sets in motion.—EDITOR.
† Merely to go out again.—EDITOR.

can think that rational creatures should desire and constitute societies only
to be dissolved. For where the majority cannot conclude the rest, there they
cannot act as one body, and consequently will be immediately dissolved
again.

99. Whosoever, therefore, out of a state of Nature unite into a community, must be understood to give up all the power necessary to the ends
for which they unite into society to the majority of the community, unless
they expressly agreed in any number greater than the majority. And this
is done by barely agreeing to unite into one political society, which is all
the compact that is, or needs be, between the individuals that enter into or
make up a commonwealth. And thus, that which begins and actually constitutes any political society is nothing but the consent of any number of
freemen capable of majority, to unite and incorporate into such a society.
And this is that, and that only, which did or could give beginning to any
lawful government in the world.

*   *   *

119. Every man being, as has been showed, naturally free, and nothing
being able to put him into subjection to any earthly power, but only his
own consent, it is to be considered what shall be understood to be a sufficient declaration of a man's consent to make him subject to the laws of
any government. There is a common distinction of an express and a tacit
consent, which will concern our present case. Nobody doubts but an express consent of any man, entering into any society, makes him a perfect
member of that society, a subject of that government. The difficulty is,
what ought to be looked upon as a tacit consent, and how far it binds—
i.e., how far any one shall be looked on to have consented, and thereby
submitted to any government, where he has made no expressions of it at
all. And to this I say, that every man that hath any possession or enjoyment
of any part of the dominions of any government doth hereby give his tacit
consent, and is as far forth obliged to obedience to the laws of that government, during such enjoyment, as any one under it, whether this his possession be of land to him and his heirs for ever, or a lodging only for a
week; or whether it be barely traveling freely on the highway; and, in
effect, it reaches as far as the very being of any one within the territories
of that government.

120. To understand this the better, it is fit to consider that every man
when he at first incorporates himself into any commonwealth, he, by his

uniting himself thereunto, annexes also, and submits to the community those possessions which he has, or shall acquire, that do not already belong to any other government. For it would be a direct contradiction for any one to enter into society with others for the securing and regulating of property, and yet to suppose his land, whose property is to be regulated by the laws of the society, should be exempt from the jurisdiction of that government to which he himself, and the property of the land, is a subject. By the same act, therefore, whereby any one unites his person, which was before free, to any commonwealth, by the same he unites his possessions, which were before free, to it also; and they become, both of them, person and possession, subject to the government and dominion of that commonwealth as long as it hath a being. Whoever therefore, from thenceforth, by inheritance, purchases, permission, or otherwise enjoys any part of the land so annexed to, and under the government of that commonweal, must take it with the condition it is under—that is, of submitting to the government of the commonwealth, under whose jurisdiction it is, as far forth as any subject of it.

* * *

CHAPTER XVIII

OF TYRANNY

199. As usurpation is the exercise of power which another hath a right to, so tyranny is the exercise of power beyond right, which nobody can have a right to; and this is making use of the power any one has in his hands, not for the good of those who are under it, but for his own private, separate advantage. When the governor, however entitled, makes not the law, but his will, the rule, and his commands and actions are not directed to the preservation of the properties of his people, but the satisfaction of his own ambition, revenge, covetousness, or any other irregular passion.

* * *

202. Wherever law ends, tyranny begins, if the law be transgressed to another's harm; and whosoever in authority exceeds the power given him by the law, and makes use of the force he has under his command to compass that upon the subject which the law allows not, ceases in that to be a magistrate, and acting without authority may be opposed, as any other

man who by force invades the right of another. This is acknowledged in subordinate magistrates. He that hath authority to seize my person in the street may be opposed as a thief and a robber if he endeavors to break into my house to execute a writ, notwithstanding that I know he has such a warrant and such a legal authority as will empower him to arrest me abroad. And why this should not hold in the highest, as well as in the most inferior magistrate, I would gladly be informed. Is it reasonable that the eldest brother, because he has the greatest part of his father's estate, should thereby have a right to take away any of his younger brothers' portions? Or that a rich man, who possessed a whole country, should from thence have a right to seize, when he pleased, the cottage and garden of his poor neighbor? The being rightfully possessed of great power and riches, exceedingly beyond the greatest part of the sons of Adam, is so far from being an excuse, much less a reason for rapine and oppression, which the endamaging another without authority is, that it is a great aggravation of it. For exceeding the bounds of authority is no more a right in a great than a petty officer, no more justifiable in a king than a constable. But so much the worse in him as that he has more trust put in him, is supposed, from the advantage of education and counselors, to have better knowledge and less reason to do it, having already a greater share than the rest of his brethren.

* * *

CHAPTER XIX

Of the Dissolution of Government

211. He that will, with any clearness, speak of the dissolution of government, ought in the first place to distinguish between the dissolution of the society and the dissolution of the government. That which makes the community, and brings men out of the loose state of Nature into one politic society, is the agreement which every one has with the rest to incorporate and act as one body, and so be one distinct commonwealth. The usual, and almost only way whereby this union is dissolved, is the inroad of foreign force making a conquest upon them. For in that case (not being able to maintain and support themselves as one entire and independent body) the union belonging to that body, which consisted therein, must necessarily cease, and so every one return to the state he was in before, with a liberty

to shift for himself and provide for his own safety, as he thinks fit, in some other society. Whenever the society is dissolved, it is certain the government of that society cannot remain.

* * *

219. There is one way more whereby such a government may be dissolved, and that is: When he who has the supreme executive power neglects and abandons that charge, so that the laws already made can no longer be put in execution; this is demonstratively to reduce all to anarchy, and so effectively to dissolve the government. For laws not being made for themselves, but to be, by their execution, the bonds of the society to keep every part of the body politic in its due place and function; when that totally ceases, the government visibly ceases, and the people become a confused multitude without order or connection. Where there is no longer the administration of justice for the securing of men's rights, nor any remaining power within the community to direct the force, or provide for the necessities of the public, there certainly is no government left. Where the laws cannot be executed it is all one as if there were no laws, and a government without laws is, I suppose, a mystery in politics inconceivable to human capacity, and inconsistent with human society.

220. In these, and the like cases, when the government is dissolved, the people are at liberty to provide for themselves by erecting a new legislative differing from the other by the change of persons, or form, or both, as they shall find it most for their safety and good. For the society can never, by the fault of another, lose the native and original right it has to preserve itself, which can only be done by a settled legislative and a fair and impartial execution of the laws made by it. But the state of mankind is not so miserable that they are not capable of using this remedy till it be too late to look for any. To tell people they may provide for themselves by erecting a new legislative, when, by oppression, artifice, or being delivered over to a foreign power, their old one is gone, is only to tell them they may expect relief when it is too late, and the evil is past cure. This is, in effect, no more than to bid them first be slaves, and then to take care of their liberty, and, when their chains are on, tell them they may act like free men. This, if barely so, is rather mockery than relief, and men can never be secure from tyranny if there be no means to escape it till they are perfectly under it; and therefore it is that they have not only a right to get out of it, but to prevent it.

221. There is, therefore, secondly, another way whereby governments are dissolved, and that is, when the legislative, or the prince, either of them act contrary to their trust.

For the legislative acts against the trust reposed in them when they endeavor to invade the property of the subject, and to make themselves, or any part of the community, masters or arbitrary disposers of the lives, liberties, or fortunes of the people.

222. The reason why men enter into society is the preservation of their property; and the end while they choose and authorize a legislative is that there may be laws made, and rules set, as guards and fences to the properties of all the society, to limit the power and moderate the dominion of every part and member of the society. For since it can never be supposed to be the will of the society that the legislative should have a power to destroy that which every one designs to secure by entering into society, and for which the people submitted themselves to legislators of their own making: whenever the legislators endeavor to take away and destroy the property of the people, or to reduce them to slavery under arbitrary power, they put themselves into a state of war with the people, who are thereupon absolved from any farther obedience, and are left to the common refuge which God hath provided for all men against force and violence. Whensoever, therefore, the legislative shall transgress this fundamental rule of society, and either by ambition, fear, folly, or corruption, endeavor to grasp themselves, or put into the hands of any other, an absolute power over the lives, liberties, and estates of the people, by this breach of trust they forfeit the power the people had put into their hands for quite contrary ends, and it devolves to the people, who have a right to resume their original liberty, and by the establishment of a new legislative (such as they shall think fit), provide for their own safety and security, which is the end for which they are in society. What I have said here concerning the legislative in general holds true also concerning the supreme executor, who having a double trust put in him, both to have a part in the legislative and the supreme execution of the law, acts against both, when he goes about to set up his own arbitrary will as the law of the society. He acts also contrary to his trust when he employs the force, treasure, and offices of the society to corrupt the representatives and gain them to his purposes, when he openly pre-engages the electors, and prescribes, to their choice, such whom he has, by solicitation, threats, promises, or otherwise, won to his designs, and employs them to bring in such who have promised beforehand what to

vote and what to enact. Thus to regulate candidates and electors, and new-model * the ways of election, what is it but to cut up the government by the roots, and poison the very fountain of public security? For the people having reserved to themselves the choice of their representatives as the fence to their properties, could do it for no other end but that they might always be freely chosen, and so chosen, freely act and advise as the necessity of the commonwealth and the public good should, upon examination and mature debate, be judged to require. This, those who give their votes before they hear the debate, and have weighed the reasons on all sides, are not capable of doing. To prepare such an assembly as this, and endeavor to set up the declared abettors of his own will, for the true representatives of the people, and the law-makers of the society, is certainly as great a breach of trust, and as perfect a declaration of a design to subvert the government, as is possible to be met with. To which, if one shall add rewards and punishments visibly employed to the same end, and all the arts of perverted law made use of to take off and destroy all that stand in the way of such a design, and will not comply and consent to betray the liberties of their country, it will be past doubt what is doing. What power they ought to have in the society who thus employ it contrary to the trust [which] went along with it in its first institution, is easy to determine; and one cannot but see that he who has once attempted any such thing as this cannot any longer be trusted.

223. To this, perhaps, it will be said that the people being ignorant and always discontented, to lay the foundation of government in the unsteady opinion and uncertain humor of the people, is to expose it to certain ruin; and no government will be able long to subsist if the people may set up a new legislative whenever they take offense at the old one. To this I answer, quite the contrary. People are not so easily got out of their old forms as some are apt to suggest. They are hardly to be prevailed with to amend the acknowledged faults in the frame they have been accustomed to. And if there be any original defects, or adventitious ones introduced by time or corruption, it is not an easy thing to get them changed, even when all the world sees there is an opportunity for it. This slowness and aversion in the people to quit their old constitutions has in the many revolutions which have been seen in this kingdom, in this and former ages, still kept us to, or after some interval of fruitless attempts, still brought us back again to our old legislative of king, lords and commons; and whatever provoca-

* Remodel.—EDITOR.

tions have made the crown be taken from some of our princes' heads, they never carried the people so far as to place it in another line.

224. But it will be said this hypothesis lays a ferment for frequent rebellion. To which I answer:

First: no more than any other hypothesis. For when the people are made miserable, and find themselves exposed to the ill usage of arbitrary power, cry up their governors as much as you will for sons of Jupiter, let them be sacred and divine, descended or authorized from Heaven; give them out for whom or what you please, the same will happen. The people generally ill treated, and contrary to right, will be ready upon any occasion to ease themselves of a burden that sits heavy upon them. They will wish and seek for the opportunity, which in the change, weakness, and accidents of human affairs, seldom delays long to offer itself. He must have lived but a little while in the world, who has not seen examples of this in his time; and he must have read very little who cannot produce examples of it in all sorts of governments in the world.

225. Secondly: I answer, such revolutions happen not upon every little mismanagement in public affairs. Great mistakes in the ruling part, many wrong and inconvenient laws, and all the slips of human frailty will be borne by the people without mutiny or murmur. But if a long train of abuses, prevarications, and artifices, all tending the same way, make the design visible to the people, and they cannot but feel what they lie under, and see whither they are going, it is not to be wondered that they should then rouse themselves, and endeavor to put the rule into such hands which may secure to them the ends for which government was at first erected, and without which, ancient names and specious forms are so far from being better, that they are much worse than the state of Nature or pure anarchy; the inconveniencies being all as great and as near, but the remedy farther off and more difficult.

*　*　*

228. But if they who say it lays a foundation for rebellion mean that it may occasion civil wars or intestine broils to tell the people they are absolved from obedience when illegal attempts are made upon their liberties or properties, and may oppose the unlawful violence of those who were their magistrates when they invade their properties, contrary to the trust put in them, and that, therefore, this doctrine is not to be allowed, being so destructive to the peace of the world; they may as well say, upon

the same ground, that honest men may not oppose robbers or pirates, because this may occasion disorder or bloodshed. If any mischief come in such cases, it is not to be charged upon him who defends his own right, but on him that invades his neighbor's. If the innocent honest man must quietly quit all he has for peace sake to him who will lay violent hands upon it, I desire it may be considered what a kind of peace there will be in the world which consists only in violence and rapine, and which is to be maintained only for the benefit of robbers and oppressors. Who would not think it an admirable peace betwixt the mighty and the mean, when the lamb, without resistance, yielded his throat to be torn by the imperious wolf? Polyphemus's den gives us a perfect pattern of such a peace.* Such a government wherein Ulysses and his companions had nothing to do but quietly to suffer themselves to be devoured. And no doubt Ulysses, who was a prudent man, preached up passive obedience, and exhorted them to a quiet submission by representing to them of what concernment peace was to mankind, and by showing the inconveniencies might happen if they should offer to resist Polyphemus, who had now the power over them.

229. The end of government is the good of mankind; and which is best for mankind, that the people should be always exposed to the boundless will of tyranny, or that the rulers should be sometimes liable to be opposed when they grow exorbitant in the use of their power, and employ it for the destruction, and not the preservation, of the properties of their people?

*   *   *

240. Here it is like the common question will be made: Who shall be judge whether the prince or legislative act contrary to their trust? This, perhaps, ill-affected and factious men may spread amongst the people, when the prince only makes use of his due prerogative. To this I reply, The people shall be judge; for who shall be judge whether his trustee or deputy acts well and according to the trust reposed in him, but he who deputes him and must, by having deputed him, have still a power to discard him when he fails in his trust? If this be reasonable in particular cases of private men, why should it be otherwise in that of the greatest moment, where the welfare of millions is concerned and also where the evil, if not prevented, is greater, and the redress very difficult, dear, and dangerous?

241. But, farther, this question, Who shall be judge? cannot mean that

* Homer, *Odyssey*, Book IX.—EDITOR.

there is no judge at all. For where there is no judicature on earth to decide controversies amongst men, God in heaven is judge. He alone, it is true, is judge of the right. But every man is judge for himself, as in all other cases so in this, whether another hath put himself into a state of war with him, and whether he should appeal to the supreme Judge, as Jephtha did.*

242. If a controversy arise betwixt a prince and some of the people in a matter where the law is silent or doubtful, and the thing be of great consequence, I should think the proper umpire in such a case should be the body of the people. For in such cases where the prince hath a trust reposed in him, and is dispensed from the common, ordinary rules of the law, there, if any men find themselves aggrieved, and think the prince acts contrary to, or beyond that trust, who so proper to judge as the body of the people (who at first lodged that trust in him) how far they meant it should extend? But if the prince, or whoever they be in the administration, decline that way of determination, the appeal then lies nowhere but to Heaven. Force between either persons who have no known superior on earth, or which permits no appeal to a judge on earth, being properly a state of war, wherein the appeal lies only to Heaven; and in that state the injured party must judge for himself when he will think fit to make use of that appeal and put himself upon it.

243. To conclude. The power that every individual gave the society when he entered into it can never revert to the individuals again, as long as the society lasts, but will always remain in the community; because without this there can be no community—no commonwealth, which is contrary to the original agreement; so also when the society hath placed the legislative in any assembly of men, to continue in them and their successors, with direction and authority for providing such successors, the legislative can never revert to the people whilst that government lasts; because, having provided a legislative with power to continue for ever, they have given up their political power to the legislative, and cannot resume it. But if they have set limits to the duration of their legislative, and made this supreme power in any person or assembly only temporary; or else when, by the miscarriages of those in authority, it is forfeited; upon the forfeiture of their rulers, or at the determination of the time set, it reverts to the society, and the people have a right to act as supreme, and continue the legislative in themselves or place it in a new form, or new hands, as they think good.

* Judges xi. 27.—EDITOR.

5

JEFFERSON ON DEMOCRACY

[Thomas Jefferson (1743–1826) was a gentleman farmer, lawyer, social philosopher, and statesman. His epitaph, written by himself, was, "Here was buried Thomas Jefferson, author of the Declaration of American Independence, of the statute of Virginia for religious freedom, and father of the University of Virginia." He chose to omit the fact that he was President from 1801 to 1809. As President he had sought to pay off the public debt, had purchased from Napoleon the Louisiana territory, thus nearly doubling the area of his country, and had resorted to a commercial embargo to avoid entanglement in the Napoleonic wars.

The expressions of his political thought are scattered through his state papers and his private correspondence. S. K. Padover has made a convenient anthology of his views in *Democracy,* by Thomas Jefferson (New York, D. Appleton-Century Company, Inc.), from which the following passages (except the Declaration of Independence) are taken.

Jefferson himself makes the following comment on the Declaration of Independence: "When forced, therefore, to resort to arms for redress, an appeal to the tribunal of the world was deemed proper for our justification. This was the object of the Declaration of Independence. Not to find out new principles, or new arguments, never before thought of, not merely to say things which had never been said before; but to place before mankind the common sense of the subject, in terms so plain and firm as to command their assent, and to justify ourselves in the independent stand we are compelled to take. Neither aiming at originality of principle or sentiment, nor yet copied from any particular and previous writing, it was intended to be an expression of the American mind, and to give to that expression the proper tone and spirit called for by the occasion."—*To Henry Lee, 1825* (Padover, pp. 21–22).]

The Declaration of Independence *
(1776)

When in the Course of human events, it becomes necessary for one people to dissolve the political bands which have connected them with another, and to assume among the Powers of the earth, the separate and equal station to which the Laws of Nature and of Nature's God entitle them, a decent respect to the opinions of mankind requires that they should declare the causes which impel them to the separation.

We hold these truths to be self-evident, that all men are created equal, that they are endowed by their Creator with certain unalienable Rights, that among these are Life, Liberty, and the pursuit of Happiness. That to secure these rights, Governments are instituted among Men, deriving their just powers from the consent of the governed, That whenever any Form of Government becomes destructive of these ends, it is the Right of the People to alter or to abolish it, and to institute new Government, laying its foundation on such principles and organizing its powers in such form, as to them shall seem most likely to effect their Safety and Happiness. Prudence, indeed, will dictate that Governments long established should not be changed for light and transient causes; and accordingly all experience hath shown, that mankind are more disposed to suffer, while evils are sufferable, than to right themselves by abolishing the forms to which they are accustomed. But when a long train of abuses † and usurpations, pursuing invariably the same Object evinces a design to reduce them under absolute Despotism, it is their right, it is their duty, to throw off such Government, and to provide new Guards for their future security.—Such has been the patient sufferance of these Colonies; and such is now the necessity which constrains them to alter their former Systems of Government. The history of the present King of Great Britain is a history of repeated injuries and usurpations, all having in direct object the establishment of an absolute Tyranny over these States. To prove this, let Facts be submitted to a candid world.

He has refused his Assent to Laws, the most wholesome and necessary for the public good.

He has forbidden his Governors to pass Laws of immediate and pressing importance, unless suspended in their operation till his Assent should

---

* From the Harvard Classics, vol. 43, P. F. Collier & Son Co.
† Compare Locke, above, section 225, "But if a long train of abuses. . . ."—Editor.

be obtained; and when so suspended, he has utterly neglected to attend to them.

He has refused to pass other Laws for the accommodation of large districts of people, unless those people would relinquish the right of Representation in the Legislature, a right inestimable to them and formidable to tyrants only.

He has called together legislative bodies at places unusual, uncomfortable, and distant from the depository of their Public Records, for the sole purpose of fatiguing them into compliance with his measures.

He has dissolved Representative Houses repeatedly, for opposing with manly firmness his invasions on the rights of the people.

He has refused for a long time, after such dissolutions, to cause others to be elected; whereby the Legislative Powers, incapable of Annihilation, have returned to the People at large for their exercise; the State remaining in the mean time exposed to all the dangers of invasion from without, and convulsions within.

He has endeavored to prevent the population of these States; for that purpose obstructing the Laws of Naturalization of Foreigners; refusing to pass others to encourage their migration hither, and raising the conditions of new Appropriations of Lands.

He has obstructed the Administration of Justice, by refusing his Assent to Laws for establishing Judiciary Powers.

He has made Judges dependent on his Will alone, for the tenure of their offices, and the amount and payment of their salaries.

He has erected a multitude of New Offices, and sent hither swarms of Officers to harass our People, and eat out their substance.

He has kept among us, in times of peace, Standing Armies without the Consent of our legislature.

He has affected to render the Military independent of and superior to the Civil Power.

He has combined with others to subject us to a jurisdiction foreign to our constitution, and unacknowledged by our laws; giving his Assent to their acts of pretended legislation:

For quartering large bodies of armed troops among us:

For protecting them, by a mock Trial, from Punishment for any Murders which they should commit on the Inhabitants of these States:

For cutting off our Trade with all parts of the world:

For imposing taxes on us without our Consent:

For depriving us in many cases, of the benefits of Trial by Jury:

For transporting us beyond Seas to be tried for pretended offenses:

For abolishing the free System of English Laws in a neighboring Province, establishing therein an Arbitrary government, and enlarging its Boundaries so as to render it at once an example and fit instrument for introducing the same absolute rule into these Colonies:

For taking away our Charters, abolishing our most valuable Laws, and altering fundamentally the Forms of our Governments:

For suspending our own Legislature, and declaring themselves invested with Power to legislate for us in all cases whatsoever.

He has abdicated Government here, by declaring us out of his Protection and waging War against us.

He has plundered our seas, ravaged our Coasts, burnt our towns, and destroyed the lives of our people.

He is at this time transporting large armies of foreign mercenaries to complete the works of death, desolation and tyranny, already begun with circumstances of Cruelty & perfidy scarcely paralleled in the most barbarous ages, and totally unworthy the Head of a civilized nation.

He has constrained our fellow Citizens taken Captive on the high Seas to bear Arms against their Country, to become the executioners of their friends and Brethren, or to fall themselves by their Hands.

He has excited domestic insurrections amongst us, and has endeavored to bring on the inhabitants of our frontiers, the merciless Indian Savages, whose known rule of warfare, is an undistinguished destruction of all ages, sexes and conditions.

In every stage of these Oppressions We have Petitioned for Redress in the most humble terms: Our repeated Petitions have been answered only by repeated injury. A Prince, whose character is thus marked by every act which may define a Tyrant, is unfit to be the ruler of a free People.

Nor have We been wanting in attention to our British brethren. We have warned them from time to time of attempts by their legislature to extend an unwarrantable jurisdiction over us. We have reminded them of the circumstances of our emigration and settlement here. We have appealed to their native justice and magnanimity, and we have conjured them by the ties of our common kindred to disavow these usurpations, which would inevitably interrupt our connections and correspondence. They too have been deaf to the voice of justice and of consanguinity. We must, therefore, acquiesce in the necessity, which denounces our Separation, and hold them, as we hold the rest of mankind, Enemies in War, in Peace Friends.

We, therefore, the Representatives of the United States of America, in General Congress, Assembled, appealing to the Supreme Judge of the world for the rectitude of our intentions, do, in the Name, and by Authority of the good People of these Colonies, solemnly publish and declare, That these United Colonies are, and of Right ought to be Free and Independent States; that they are Absolved from all Allegiance to the British Crown, and that all political connection between them and the State of Great Britain, is and ought to be totally dissolved; and that as Free and Independent States, they have full Power to levy War, conclude Peace, contract Alliances, establish Commerce, and to do all other Acts and Things which Independent States may of right do. And for the support of this Declaration, with a firm reliance on the Protection of Divine Providence, we mutually pledge to each other our Lives, our Fortunes and our sacred Honor.

If we are made in some degree for others, yet in a greater, are we made for ourselves. It were contrary to feeling, and indeed ridiculous to suppose that a man had less rights in himself than one of his neighbors, or indeed all of them put together. This would be slavery, and not that liberty which the bill of rights has made inviolable, and for the preservation of which our government has been charged. Nothing could so completely divest us of that liberty as the establishment of the opinion, that the State has a perpetual right to the services of all its members. This, to men of certain ways of thinking, would be to annihilate the blessings of existence, and to contradict the Giver of life, who gave it for happiness and not for wretchedness. And certainly, to such it were better that they had never been born.—To Monroe, 1782 (Padover, pp. 22–23).

I believe . . . that morality, compassion, generosity, are innate elements of the human constitution; that there exists a right independent of force; that a right to property is founded in our natural wants, in the means with which we are endowed to satisfy these wants, and the right to what we acquire by those means without violating the similar rights of other sensible beings; that no one has a right to obstruct another, exercising his faculties innocently for the relief of sensibilities made a part of his nature;

that justice is the fundamental law of society; that the majority, oppressing an individual, is guilty of a crime, abuses its strength, and by acting on the law of the strongest breaks up the foundations of society; that action by the citizens in person, in affairs within their reach and competence, and in all others by representatives, chosen immediately, and removable by themselves, constitutes the essence of a republic; that all governments are more or less republican in proportion as this principle enters more or less into their composition; and that a government by representation is capable of extension over a greater surface of country than one of any other form. —*To Dupont de Nemours, 1816* (Padover, pp. 28–29).

Societies exist under three forms, sufficiently distinguishable. 1. Without government, as among our Indians. 2. Under governments, wherein the will of every one has a just influence; as is the case in England, in a slight degree, and in our States, in a great one. 3. Under governments of force; as is the case in all other monarchies, and in most of the other republics. To have an idea of the curse of existence under these last, they must be seen. It is a government of wolves over sheep. It is a problem, not clear in my mind, that the first condition is not the best. But I believe it to be inconsistent with any great degree of population. The second state has a great deal of good in it. The mass of mankind under that, enjoys a precious degree of liberty and happiness. It has its evils, too; the principal of which is the turbulence to which it is subject. But weigh this against the oppressions of monarchy, and it becomes nothing. *Malo periculosam libertatem quam quietam servitutem.** Even this evil is productive of good. It prevents the degeneracy of government, and nourishes a general attention to the public affairs. I hold it, that a little rebellion, now and then, is a good thing, and as necessary in the political world as storms in the physical. Unsuccessful rebellions, indeed, generally establish the encroachments on the rights of the people, which have produced them. An observation of this truth should render honest republican governors so mild in their punishment of rebellions, as not to discourage them too much. It is a medicine necessary for the sound health of government.—*To Madison, 1787* (Padover, pp. 30–31).

---

* "I prefer freedom with danger to servitude with tranquillity."—EDITOR.

God forbid we should ever be twenty years without such a rebellion. The people cannot be all, and always, well informed. The part which is wrong will be discontented, in proportion to the importance of the facts they misconceive. If they remain quiet under such misconceptions, it is a lethargy, the forerunner of death to the public liberty. We have had thirteen States independent for eleven years. There has been one rebellion. That comes to one rebellion in a century and a half, for each State. What country before, ever existed a century and a half without a rebellion? And what country can preserve its liberties, if its rulers are not warned from time to time, that this people preserve the spirit of resistance? Let them take arms. The remedy is to set them right as to facts, pardon and pacify them. What signify a few lives lost in a century or two? The tree of liberty must be refreshed from time to time, with the blood of patriots and tyrants. It is its natural manure.—*To Wm. S. Smith, 1787* (Padover, pp. 31–32).

[Referring to the French Revolution]

In the struggle which was necessary, many guilty persons fell without the forms of trial, and with them some innocent. These I deplore as much as any body, and shall deplore some of them to the day of my death. But I deplore them as I should have done had they fallen in battle. It was necessary to use the arm of the people, a machine not quite so blind as balls and bombs, but blind to a certain degree. A few of their cordial friends met at their hands the fate of enemies. But time and truth will rescue and embalm their memories, while their posterity will be enjoying that very liberty for which they would never have hesitated to offer up their lives. The liberty of the whole earth was depending on the issue of the contest, and was ever such a prize won with so little innocent blood? My own affections have been deeply wounded by some of the martyrs to this cause, but rather than it should have failed I would have seen half the earth desolated; were there but an Adam and Eve left in every country, and left free, it would be better than as it now is.—*To Short, 1793* (Padover, p. 32).

We exist, and are quoted, as standing proofs that a government, so modeled as to rest continually on the will of the whole society, is a practicable government. Were we to break to pieces, it would damp the hopes and the efforts of the good, and give triumph to those of the bad through the whole enslaved world.* As members, therefore, of the universal society of mankind, and standing in high and responsible relation with them, it is our sacred duty to suppress passions among ourselves, and not to blast the confidence we have inspired of proof that a government of reason is better than one of force.—*To R. Rush, 1820* (Padover, pp. 43–44).

Let us, then, with courage and confidence pursue our own federal and republican principles, our attachment to our union and representative government. Kindly separated by nature and a wide ocean from the exterminating havoc of one quarter of the globe; too high-minded to endure the degradations of the others; possessing a chosen country, with room enough for our descendants to the hundredth and thousandth generation; entertaining a due sense of our equal right to the use of our own faculties, to the acquisitions of our industry, to honor and confidence from our fellow citizens, resulting not from birth but from our actions and their sense of them; enlightened by a benign religion, professed, indeed, and practised in various forms, yet all of them including honesty, truth, temperance, gratitude, and the love of man; acknowledging and adoring an overruling Providence, which by all its dispensations proves that it delights in the happiness of man here and his greater happiness hereafter; with all these blessings, what more is necessary to make us a happy and prosperous people?

*   *   *

About to enter, fellow citizens, on the exercise of duties which comprehend everything dear and valuable to you, it is proper that you should understand what I deem the essential principles of our government, and consequently those which ought to shape its administration. I will compress them within the narrowest compass they will bear, stating the general principle, but not all its limitations.

Equal and exact justice to all men, of whatever state or persuasion, religious or political;

peace, commerce, and honest friendship, with all nations—entangling alliances with none;

* Compare Lincoln's Gettysburg address, printed later in this volume.—EDITOR.

the support of the state governments in all their rights, as the most competent administrations for our domestic concerns and the surest bulwarks against anti-republican tendencies;

the preservation of the general government in its whole constitutional vigor, as the sheet anchor of our peace at home and safety abroad;

a jealous care of the right of election by the people—a mild and safe corrective of abuses which are lopped by the sword of the revolution where peaceable remedies are unprovided;

absolute acquiescence in the decisions of the majority—the vital principle of republics, from which there is no appeal but to force, the vital principle and immediate parent of despotism;

a well-disciplined militia—our best reliance in peace and for the first moments of war, till regulars may relieve them;

the supremacy of the civil over the military authority;

economy in the public expense, that labor may be lightly burdened;

the honest payment of our debts and sacred preservation of the public faith;

encouragement of agriculture, and of commerce as its handmaid;

the diffusion of information and the arraignment of all abuses at the bar of public reason;

freedom of religion;

freedom of the press;

freedom of person under the protection of the *habeas corpus;*

and trial by jury impartially selected—

these principles form the bright constellation which has gone before us, and guided our steps through an age of revolution and reformation. The wisdom of our sages and the blood of our heroes have been devoted to their attainment. They should be the creed of our political faith—the text of civil instruction—the touchstone by which to try the services of those we trust; and should we wander from them in moments of error or alarm, let us hasten to retrace our steps and to regain the road which alone leads to peace, liberty and safety.—*First Inaugural, March 4, 1801* (Padover, pp. 44, 49-51).

In every free and deliberating society, there must, from the nature of man, be opposite parties, and violent dissensions and discords; and one of these, for the most part, must prevail over the other for a longer or shorter time. Perhaps this party division is necessary to induce each to watch and relate to the people the proceedings of the other. But if on a temporary superiority of the one party, the other is to resort to a scission of the Union, no federal government can ever exist.—*To J. Taylor, 1798* (Padover, p. 65).

I tolerate with the utmost latitude the right of others to differ from me in opinion without imputing to them criminality. I know too well the weakness and uncertainty of human reason to wonder at its different results. Both of our political parties, at least the honest part of them, agree conscientiously in the same object—the public good; but they differ essentially in what they deem the means of promoting that good. One side . . . fears most the ignorance of the people; the other, the selfishness of rulers independent of them. Which is right, time and experience will prove. We think that one side of this experiment has been long enough tried, and proved not to promote the good of the many; and that the other has not been fairly and sufficiently tried. Our opponents think the reverse. With whichever opinion the body of the nation concurs, that must prevail. My anxieties on this subject will never carry me beyond the use of fair and honorable means, of truth and reason; nor have they ever lessened my esteem for moral worth, nor alienated my affections from a single friend, who did not first withdraw himself.—*To Abigail Adams, 1804* (Padover, p. 67).

It has long, however, been my opinion, and I have never shrunk from its expression (although I do not choose to put it into a newspaper, nor, like a Priam in armor, offer myself its champion), that the germ of dissolution of our federal government is in the constitution of the federal judiciary; an irresponsible body (for impeachment is scarcely a scare-crow) working like gravity by night and by day, gaining a little to-day and little to-morrow, and advancing its noiseless step like a thief, over the field of jurisdiction, until all shall be usurped from the States, and the government of all be consolidated into one. To this I am opposed; because, when all government, domestic and foreign, in little as in great things, shall be drawn to Washington as the center of all power, it will render powerless the checks provided of one government or another, and will become as venal and oppressive as the government from which we separated. It will be as in Europe, where every man must be either pike or gudgeon, hammer or anvil.—*To C. Hammond, 1821* (Padover, p. 99).

If ever this vast country is brought under a single government, it will be one of the most extensive corruption, indifferent and incapable of a wholesome care over so wide a spread of surface. This will not be borne, and you will have to choose between reformation and revolution. If I know the spirit of this country, the one or the other is inevitable. Before the canker is become inveterate, before its venom has reached so much of the body politic as to get beyond control, remedy should be applied. Let the future appointments of judges be for four or six years, and renewable by the President and Senate. This will bring their conduct, at regular periods, under revision and probation, and may keep them in equipoise between the general and special governments. We have erred in this point, by copying England, where certainly it is a good thing to have the judges independent of the King. But we have omitted to copy their caution also, which makes a judge removable on the address of both legislative Houses. That there should be public functionaries independent of the nation, whatever may be their demerit, is a solecism in a republic, of the first order of absurdity and inconsistency.—*To W. T. Barry, 1822* (Padover, p. 101).

To consider the judges as the ultimate arbiters of all constitutional questions [is] a very dangerous doctrine indeed, and one which would place us under the despotism of an oligarchy. . . . The Constitution has erected no such single tribunal—*To W. C. Jarvis, 1820* (Padover, p. 236).

The judiciary of the United States is the subtle corps of sappers and miners constantly working under ground to undermine the foundations of our confederate fabric.

A judiciary independent of a king or executive alone, is a good thing; but independence of the will of the nation is a solecism, at least in a republican government.—*To Ritchie, 1820* (Padover, p. 235).

[Jefferson's opinion of John Marshall]

A crafty chief judge.—*To Ritchie, 1820.*

His twistifications in the case of Marbury, in that of Burr, and the Yazoo case show how dexterously he can reconcile law to his personal biases.— *To Madison, 1810.*

Marshall bears [rancorous hatred] to the government of his country.— *Ibid.* (All from Padover, p. 275.)

If a nation expects to be ignorant and free, in a state of civilization, it expects what never was and never will be. The functionaries of every government have propensities to command at will the liberty and property of their constituents. There is no safe deposit for these but with the people themselves; nor can they be safe with them without information. Where the press is free, and every man able to read, all is safe.—*To Colonel Yancey, 1816* (Padover, p. 137).

I look to the diffusion of light and education as the resource most to be relied on for ameliorating the condition, promoting the virtue, and advancing the happiness of man. That every man shall be made virtuous, by any process whatever, is, indeed, no more to be expected, than that every tree shall be made to bear fruit, and every plant nourishment. The brier and bramble can never become the vine and olive; but their asperities may be softened by culture, and their properties improved to usefulness in the order and economy of the world. And I do hope that, in the present spirit of extending to the great mass of mankind the blessings of instruction, I see a prospect of great advancement in the happiness of the human race; and that this may proceed to an indefinite, although not to an infinite degree.— *To C. C. Blatchly, 1822* (Padover, pp. 141–142).

In every State, probably, in the Union, the press has exerted a freedom in canvassing the merits and measures of public men, of every description, which has not been confined to the strict limits of the common law. . . . Some degree of abuse is inseparable from the proper use of every thing; and in no instance is this more true, than in that of the press. It has accordingly been decided by the practice of the States, that it is better to leave a few of its noxious branches, to their luxuriant growth, than by pruning them away, to injure the vigor of those yielding the proper fruits. And can the wisdom of this policy be doubted by any who reflect, that to the press alone, chequered as it is with abuses, the world is indebted for all the triumphs which have been gained by reason and humanity, over error and oppression; who reflect, that to the same beneficent source, the United States owe much of the lights which conducted them to the rank of a free and independent nation; and which have improved their political system into a shape so auspicious to their happiness. Had 'Sedition Acts,' forbidding every publication that might bring the constituted agents into contempt or disrepute, or that might excite the hatred of the people against the authors of unjust or pernicious measures, been uniformly enforced against the press; might not the United States have been languishing at this day, under the infirmities of a sickly confederation: might they not possibly be miserable colonies, groaning under a foreign yoke?—*Virginia and Kentucky Resolutions, 1799* * (Padover, pp. 144–145).

Man may be governed by reason and truth. Our first object should therefore be to leave open to him all the avenues to truth. The most effectual hitherto found is the freedom of the press.—*To Judge Tyler, 1804* (Padover, p. 253).

They [Federalists] fill their newspapers with falsehoods, calumnies, and audacities. . . . We are going fairly through the experiment whether freedom of discussion, unaided by coercion, is not sufficient for the propagation and protection of truth, and for the maintenance of an administration pure and upright in its actions and views. No one ought to feel, under this experiment, more than myself. Nero wished all the necks of Rome united in one, that he might sever them at a blow. So our ex-federalists, wishing to have a single representative of all the objects of their hatred, honor me with that post, and exhibit against me such atrocities as no nation has ever before heard or endured. I shall protect them in the right of lying and calumniating, and still go on to merit the continuance of it, by pursuing steadily my object of proving that a people, easy in their circumstances as

* Madison was part author of this.

ours are, are capable of conducting themselves under a government founded not in the fears and follies of man, but on his reason, on the predominance of his social over his dissocial passions, so free as to restrain him from every moral wrong, which shall leave him, in short, in possession of all his natural rights.—*To Volney, 1802: N.Y. Pub. Lib., MS, II, 199* (Padover, p. 145).

Breaking men to military discipline, is breaking their spirits to principles of passive obedience.—*To J. Hay, 1788* (Padover, p. 261).

If there be one principle more deeply rooted than any other in the mind of every American, it is that we should have nothing to do with conquest.— *To Wm. Short, 1791* (Padover, p. 262).

Some men look at constitutions with sanctimonious reverence and deem them like the ark of the covenant, too sacred to be touched. . . . But I know also that laws and institutions must go hand in hand with the progress of the human mind.—*To Kercheval, 1816* (Padover, p. 237).

I would rather be exposed to the inconveniences attending too much liberty, than those attending too small a degree of it.—*To A. Stuart, 1791* (Padover, p. 238).

This ball of liberty, I believe most piously, is now so well in motion that it will roll round the globe, at least the enlightened part of it, for light and liberty go together.—*To T. Coxe, 1795* (Padover, p. 238).

To attain all this [liberty in European countries], rivers of blood must yet flow, and years of desolation pass over; yet the object is worth rivers of blood and years of desolation.—*To Adams, 1823* (Padover, p. 239).

[If a book] be false in its facts, disprove them; if false in its reasoning, refute it. But, for God's sake, let us freely hear both sides.—*To Dufief, 1814* (Padover, p. 240).

I fear nothing for our liberty from the assaults of force; but I have seen and felt much, and fear more from English books, English prejudices, English manners, and the apes, the dupes, and designs among our professional crafts.—*To Horatio G. Spafford, 1814* (Padover, p. 240).

Sole depositories of the remains of human liberty, our duty to ourselves, to posterity, and to mankind, call on us by every motive which is sacred or honorable, to watch over the safety of our beloved country during the troubles which agitate and convulse the residue of the world.—*To the Legislature of New York State, 1809* (Padover, p. 241).

Whenever the people are well-informed, they can be trusted with their own government; whenever things get so far wrong as to attract their notice, they may be relied on to set them to rights.—*To Dr. Price, 1789* (Padover, p. 248).

Trial by jury, I consider as the only anchor ever yet imagined by man, by which a government can be held to the principles of its constitution.—*To Thomas Paine, 1789* (Padover, p. 248).

He who would do his country the most good he can, must go quietly with the prejudices of the majority till he can lead them into reason.—*To Caesar Rodney, 1805: ibid., III, 164–165* (Padover, p. 249).

An aristocracy of wealth [is] of more harm and danger than benefit to society.—*Autobiography, 1821* (Padover, p. 233).

There is a natural aristocracy among men. The grounds of this are virtue and talents. . . . The natural aristocracy I consider as the most precious gift of nature, for the instruction, the trusts, and government of society.— *To Adams, 1813* (Padover, p. 233).

An industrious farmer occupies a more dignified place in the scale of beings . . . than a lazy lounger, valuing himself on his family, too proud to work, and drawing out a miserable existence by eating on that surplus of other men's labor, which is the sacred fund of the helpless poor.—*To De Meunier, 1786* (Padover, p. 233).

The insulated state in which nature has placed the American continent, should so far avail it that no spark of war kindled in the other quarters of the globe should be wafted across the wide oceans which separate us from them.—*To Baron von Humboldt, 1813* (Padover, p. 234).

I am not for linking ourselves by new treaties with the quarrels of Europe; entering that field of slaughter to preserve their balance, or joining in the confederacy of kings to war against the principles of liberty.—*To Elbridge Gerry, 1799* (Padover, p. 234).

I have ever deemed it fundamental for the United States, never to take active part in the quarrels of Europe. Their political interests are entirely distinct from ours. . . . They are nations of eternal war.—*To President Monroe, 1823* (Padover, pp. 234-235).

6

THE FRENCH DECLARATION OF RIGHTS

[The declaration of rights made in the midst of the French Revolution is closely akin to the doctrines of Locke and of the American Declaration of Independence. The following translation is taken from Thomas Paine, *The Rights of Man*, Everyman edition, E. P. Dutton and Company, Inc., pages 94–97.]

Declaration of the Rights of Man and of Citizens

BY THE NATIONAL ASSEMBLY OF FRANCE (1789)

The representatives of the people of France, formed into a National Assembly, considering that ignorance, neglect, or contempt of human rights, are the sole causes of public misfortunes and corruptions of Government, have resolved to set forth in a solemn declaration, these natural, imprescriptible, and inalienable rights; that this declaration being constantly present to the minds of the members of the body social, they may be ever kept attentive to their rights and their duties; that the acts of the legislative and executive powers of Government, being capable of being every moment compared with the end of political institutions, may be more respected; and also, that the future claims of the citizens, being directed by simple and incontestable principles, may always tend to the maintenance of the Constitution, and the general happiness.

For these reasons the National Assembly doth recognize and declare, in the presence of the Supreme Being, and with the hope of his blessing and favor, the following *sacred* rights of men and of citizens:

I. Men are born, and always continue, free and equal in respect of their rights. Civil distinctions, therefore, can be founded only on public utility.

II. The end of all political associations is the preservation of the natural and imprescriptible rights of man; and these rights are Liberty, Property, Security, and Resistance of Oppression.

III. The Nation is essentially the source of all sovereignty; nor can any individual, or any body of men, be entitled to any authority which is not expressly derived from it.

IV. Political Liberty consists in the power of doing whatever does not injure another. The exercise of the natural rights of every man, has no other limits than those which are necessary to secure to every *other* man the free exercise of the same rights; and these limits are determinable only by the law.

V. The law ought to prohibit only actions hurtful to society. What is not prohibited by the law should not be hindered; nor should any one be compelled to that which the law does not require.

VI. The law is an expression of the will of the community. All citizens have a right to concur, either personally or by their representatives, in its formation. It should be the same to all, whether it protects or punishes; and all being equal in its sight, are equally eligible to all honors, places, and employments, according to their different abilities, without any other distinction than that created by their virtues and talents.

VII. No man should be accused, arrested, or held in confinement, except in cases determined by the law, and according to the forms which it has prescribed. All who promote, solicit, execute, or cause to be executed, arbitrary orders, ought to be punished, and every citizen called upon, or apprehended by virtue of the law, ought immediately to obey, and renders himself culpable by resistance.

VIII. The law ought to impose no other penalties but such as are absolutely and evidently necessary; and no one ought to be punished, but in virtue of a law promulgated before the offense, and legally applied.

IX. Every man being presumed innocent till he has been convicted, whenever his detention becomes indispensable, all rigor to him, more than is necessary to secure his person, ought to be provided against by the law.

X. No man ought to be molested on account of his opinions, not even on account of his religious opinions, provided his avowal of them does not disturb the public order established by the law.

XI. The unrestrained communication of thoughts and opinions being one of the most precious Rights of Man, every citizen may speak, write, and publish freely, provided he is responsible for the abuse of this liberty, in cases determined by the law.

XII. A public force being necessary to give security to the Rights of Men and of citizens, that force is instituted for the benefit of the community and not for the particular benefit of the persons with whom it is intrusted.

XIII. A common contribution being necessary for the support of the public force, and for defraying the other expenses of Government, it ought to be divided equally among the members of the community, according to their abilities.

XIV. Every citizen has a right, either by himself or his representative, to a free voice in determining the necessity of public contributions, the appropriation of them, and their amount, mode of assessment, and duration.

XV. Every community has a right to demand of all its agents an account of their conduct.

XVI. Every community in which a separation of powers and a security of rights is not provided for, wants a Constitution.

XVII. The right to property being inviolable and sacred, no one ought to be deprived of it, except in cases of evident public necessity, legally ascertained, and on condition of a previous just indemnity.

7

"THE FEDERALIST" ON THE AMERICAN CONSTITUTION

[The papers collectively known as *The Federalist* are the chief expression in print of the more conservative forces that helped to form the American Constitution. The occasion of these papers was the campaign for ratification of the Constitution by the State of New York, and for that purpose they were printed anonymously in New York City newspapers in the winter of 1787–1788.

Their chief authors were Alexander Hamilton (1757–1804) and James Madison (1751–1836). Both men had been politically active throughout the Revolution and the period leading up to the formation of the Constitution.

The following passages show their concern for restraint upon "faction," and for the strength of the judiciary. Their viewpoint may be contrasted with Jefferson's faith in popular majorities and his distrust of the federal judiciary.

See V. L. Parrington, *Main Currents in American Thought,* New York, Harcourt, Brace and Company, 1927, Volume I, pages 267–307.]

The Federalist, No. X*
(MADISON)

To the People of the State of New York:
Among the numerous advantages promised by a well-constructed Union, none deserves to be more accurately developed than its tendency to break and control the violence of faction. The friend of popular governments never finds himself so much alarmed for their character and fate as when he contemplates their propensity to this dangerous vice. He will not fail, therefore, to set a due value on any plan which, without violating the principles to which he is attached, provides a proper cure for it. The insta-

---

* *The Federalist,* Everyman edition, E. P. Dutton and Company, Inc., pp. 41–48.

bility, injustice, and confusion introduced into the public councils, have, in truth, been the mortal diseases under which popular governments have everywhere perished; as they continue to be the favorite and fruitful topics from which the adversaries to liberty derive their most specious declamations. The valuable improvements made by the American constitutions on the popular models, both ancient and modern, cannot certainly be too much admired; but it would be an unwarrantable partiality, to contend that they have as effectually obviated the danger on this side, as was wished and expected. Complaints are everywhere heard from our most considerate and virtuous citizens, equally the friends of public and private faith, and of public and personal liberty, that our governments are too unstable, that the public good is disregarded in the conflicts of rival parties, and that measures are too often decided, not according to the rules of justice and the rights of the minor party, but by the superior force of an interested and overbearing majority. However anxiously we may wish that these complaints had no foundation, the evidence of known facts will not permit us to deny that they are in some degree true. It will be found, indeed, on a candid review of our situation, that some of the distresses under which we labor have been erroneously charged on the operation of our governments; but it will be found, at the same time, that other causes will not alone account for many of our heaviest misfortunes; and, particularly, for that prevailing and increasing distrust of public engagements, and alarm for private rights, which are echoed from one end of the continent to the other. These must be chiefly, if not wholly, effects of the unsteadiness and injustice with which a factious spirit has tainted our public administrations.

By a faction, I understand a number of citizens, whether amounting to a majority or minority of the whole, who are united and actuated by some common impulse of passion, or of interest, adverse to the rights of other citizens, or to the permanent and aggregate interests of the community.

There are two methods of curing the mischiefs of faction: the one, by removing its causes; the other, by controlling its effects.

There are again two methods of removing the causes of faction: the one, by destroying the liberty which is essential to its existence; the other, by giving to every citizen the same opinions, the same passions, and the same interests.

It could never be more truly said than of the first remedy, that it was worse than the disease. Liberty is to faction what air is to fire, an aliment without which it instantly expires. But it could not be less folly to abolish liberty, which is essential to political life, because it nourishes faction, than it would be to wish the annihilation of air, which is essential to animal life, because it imparts to fire its destructive agency.

The second expedient is as impracticable as the first would be unwise. As long as the reason of man continues fallible, and he is at liberty to exercise it, different opinions will be formed. As long as the connection subsists between his reason and his self-love, his opinions and his passions will have a reciprocal influence on each other; and the former will be objects to which the latter will attach themselves. The diversity in the faculties of men, from which the rights of property originate, is not less an insuperable obstacle to a uniformity of interests. The protection of these faculties is the first object of government. From the protection of different and unequal faculties of acquiring property, the possession of different degrees and kinds of property immediately results; and from the influence of these on the sentiments and views of the respective proprietors, ensues a division of the society into different interests and parties.

The latent causes of faction are thus sown in the nature of man; and we see them everywhere brought into different degrees of activity, according to the different circumstances of civil society. A zeal for different opinions concerning religion, concerning government, and many other points, as well of speculation as of practice; an attachment of different leaders ambitiously contending for pre-eminence and power; or to persons of other descriptions whose fortunes have been interesting to the human passions, have, in turn, divided mankind into parties, inflamed them with mutual animosity, and rendered them much more disposed to vex and oppress each other than to co-operate for their common good. So strong is this propensity of mankind to fall into mutual animosities, that where no substantial occasion presents itself, the most frivolous and fanciful distinctions have been sufficient to kindle their unfriendly passions and excite their most violent conflicts. But the most common and durable source of factions has been the various and unequal distribution of property. Those who hold and those who are without property have ever formed distinct interests in society. Those who are creditors, and those who are debtors, fall under a like discrimination. A landed interest, a manufacturing interest, a mercantile interest, a moneyed interest, with many lesser interests, grow up of necessity in civilized nations, and divide them into different classes, actuated by different sentiments and views. The regulation of these various and interfering interests forms the principal task of modern legislation, and involves the spirit of party and faction in the necessary and ordinary operations of the government.

No man is allowed to be a judge in his own cause, because his interest would certainly bias his judgment, and, not improbably, corrupt his integrity. With equal, nay, with greater reason, a body of men are unfit to be both judges and parties at the same time; yet what are many of the most important acts of legislation but so many judicial determinations, not indeed concerning the rights of single persons, but concerning the rights of large bodies of citizens? And what are the different classes of legislators but advocates and parties to the causes which they determine? Is a law proposed concerning private debts? It is a question to which the creditors are parties on one side and the debtors on the other. Justice ought to hold the balance between them. Yet the parties are, and must be, themselves the judges; and the most numerous party, or, in other words, the most powerful faction must be expected to prevail. Shall domestic manufactures be encouraged, and in what degree, by restrictions on foreign manufactures? are questions which would be differently decided by the landed and the manufacturing classes, and probably by neither with a sole regard to justice and the public good. The apportionment of taxes on the various descriptions of property is an act which seems to require the most exact impartiality; yet there is, perhaps, no legislative act in which greater opportunity and temptation are given to a predominant party to trample on the rules of justice. Every shilling with which they overburden the inferior number is a shilling saved to their own pockets.

It is in vain to say that enlightened statesmen will be able to adjust these clashing interests, and render them all subservient to the public good. Enlightened statesmen will not always be at the helm. Nor, in many cases, can such an adjustment be made at all without taking into view indirect and remote considerations, which will rarely prevail over the immediate interest which one party may find in disregarding the rights of another or the good of the whole.

The inference to which we are brought is, that the *causes* of faction cannot be removed, and that relief is only to be sought in the means of controlling its *effects*.

If a faction consists of less than a majority, relief is supplied by the republican principle, which enables the majority to defeat its sinister views by regular vote. It may clog the administration, it may convulse the society;

but it will be unable to execute and mask its violence under the forms of the Constitution. When a majority is included in a faction, the form of popular government, on the other hand, enables it to sacrifice to its ruling passion or interest both the public good and the rights of other citizens. To secure the public good and private rights against the danger of such a faction, and at the same time to preserve the spirit and the form of popular government, is then the great object to which our inquiries are directed. Let me add that it is the great desideratum by which this form of government can be rescued from the opprobrium under which it has so long labored, and be recommended to the esteem and adoption of mankind.

By what means is this object obtainable? Evidently by one of two only. Either the existence of the same passion or interest in a majority at the same time must be prevented, or the majority, having such co-existent passion or interest, must be rendered, by their number and local situation, unable to concert and carry into effect schemes of oppression. If the impulse and the opportunity be suffered to coincide, we well know that neither moral nor religious motives can be relied on as an adequate control. They are not found to be such on the injustice and violence of individuals, and lose their efficacy in proportion to the number combined together, that is, in proportion as their efficacy becomes needful.

From this view of the subject it may be concluded that a pure democracy, by which I mean a society consisting of a small number of citizens, who assemble and administer the government in person, can admit of no cure for the mischiefs of faction. A common passion or interest will, in almost every case, be felt by a majority of the whole; a communication and concert result from the form of government itself; and there is nothing to check the inducements to sacrifice the weaker party or an obnoxious individual. Hence it is that such democracies have ever been spectacles of turbulence and contention; have ever been found incompatible with personal security or the rights of property; and have in general been as short in their lives as they have been violent in their deaths. Theoretic politicians, who have patronized this species of government, have erroneously supposed that by reducing mankind to a perfect equality in their political rights, they would, at the same time, be perfectly equalized and assimilated in their possessions, their opinions, and their passions.

A republic, by which I mean a government in which the scheme of representation takes place, opens a different prospect, and promises the cure for which we are seeking. Let us examine the points in which it varies from pure democracy, and we shall comprehend both the nature of the cure and the efficacy which it must derive from the Union.

The two great points of difference between a democracy and a republic are: first, the delegation of the government, in the latter, to a small number of citizens elected by the rest; secondly, the greater number of citizens, and greater sphere of country, over which the latter may be extended.

The effect of the first difference is, on the one hand, to refine and enlarge the public views, by passing them through the medium of a chosen body of citizens, whose wisdom may best discern the true interest of their country, and whose patriotism and love of justice will be least likely to sacrifice it to temporary or partial considerations. Under such a regulation, it may well happen that the public voice, pronounced by the representatives of the people, will be more consonant to the public good than if pronounced by the people themselves, convened for the purpose. On the other hand, the effect may be inverted. Men of factious tempers, of local prejudices, or of sinister designs, may, by intrigue, by corruption, or by other means, first obtain the suffrages, and then betray the interests, of the people. The question resulting is, whether small or extensive republics are more favorable to the election of proper guardians of the public weal; and it is clearly decided in favor of the latter by two obvious considerations:

In the first place, it is to be remarked that, however small the republic may be, the representatives must be raised to a certain number, in order to guard against the cabals of a few; and that, however large it may be, they must be limited to a certain number, in order to guard against the confusion of a multitude. Hence the number of representatives in the two cases not being in proportion to that of the two constituents, and being proportionally greater in the small republic, it follows that, if the proportion of fit characters be not less in the large than in the small republic, the former will present a greater option, and consequently a greater probability of a fit choice.

In the next place, as each representative will be chosen by a greater number of citizens in the large than in the small republic, it will be more difficult for unworthy candidates to practise with success the vicious arts by which elections are too often carried; and the suffrages of the people being more free, will be more likely to center in men who possess the most attractive merit and the most diffusive and established character.

It must be confessed that in this, as in most other cases, there is a mean, on both sides of which inconveniences will be found to lie. By enlarging too much the number of electors, you render the representative too little acquainted with all their local circumstances and lesser interests; as by reducing it too much, you render him unduly attached to these, and too little fit to comprehend and pursue great and national objects. The federal Constitution forms a happy combination in this respect; the great and aggregate interests being referred to the national, the local and particular to the State legislatures.

The other point of difference is, the greater number of citizens and extent of territory which may be brought within the compass of republican than of democratic government; and it is this circumstance principally which renders factious combinations less to be dreaded in the former than in the latter. The smaller the society, the fewer probably will be the distinct parties and interests composing it; the fewer the distinct parties and interests, the more frequently will a majority be found of the same party; and the smaller the number of individuals composing a majority, and the smaller the compass within which they are placed, the more easily will they concert and execute their plans of oppression. Extend the sphere, and you take in a greater variety of parties and interests; you make it less probable that a majority of the whole will have a common motive to invade the rights of other citizens; or if such a common motive exists, it will be more difficult for all who feel it to discover their own strength, and to act in unison with each other. Besides other impediments, it may be remarked that, where there is a consciousness of unjust or dishonorable purposes, communication is always checked by distrust in proportion to the number whose concurrence is necessary.

Hence, it clearly appears, that the same advantage which a republic has over a democracy, in controlling the effects of faction, is enjoyed by a large over a small republic—is enjoyed by the Union over the States composing it. Does the advantage consist in the substitution of representatives whose enlightened views and virtuous sentiments render them superior to local prejudices and to schemes of injustice? It will not be denied that the representation of the Union will be most likely to possess these requisite endowments. Does it consist in the greater security afforded by a greater variety of parties, against the event of any one party being able to outnumber and oppress the rest? In an equal degree does the increased variety of parties comprised within the Union increase this security? Does it, in fine, consist in the greater obstacles opposed to the concert and accomplishment of the secret wishes of an unjust and interested majority? Here, again, the extent of the Union gives it the most palpable advantage.

The influence of factious leaders may kindle a flame within their particular States, but will be unable to spread a general conflagration through the other States. A religious sect may degenerate into a political faction in a part of the Confederacy; but the variety of sects dispersed over the entire face of it must secure the national councils against any danger from that source. A rage for paper money, for an abolition of debts, for an equal division of property, or for any other improper or wicked project, will be less apt to pervade the whole body of the Union than a particular member of it; in the same proportion as such a malady is more likely to taint a particular county or district, than an entire State.

In the extent and proper structure of the Union, therefore, we behold a republican remedy for the diseases most incident to republican government. And according to the degree of pleasure and pride we feel in being republicans, ought to be our zeal in cherishing the spirit and supporting the character of Federalists.   Publius.

The Federalist,* No. LI
(HAMILTON OR MADISON)

To the People of the State of New York:

To what expedient, then, shall we finally resort, for maintaining in practice the necessary partition of power among the several departments, as laid down in the Constitution? The only answer that can be given is, that as all these exterior provisions are found to be inadequate, the defect must be supplied, by so contriving the interior structure of the government as that its several constituent parts may, by their mutual relations, be the means of keeping each other in their proper places. Without presuming to undertake a full development of this important idea, I will hazard a few general observations, which may perhaps place it in a clearer light, and enable us to form a more correct judgment of the principles and structure of the government planned by the convention.

In order to lay a due foundation for that separate and distinct exercise of the different powers of government, which to a certain extent is admitted on all hands to be essential to the preservation of liberty, it is evident that each department should have a will of its own; and consequently should be so constituted that the members of each should have as little agency as pos-

* Everyman edition, pp. 263–265.

sible in the appointment of the members of the others. Were this principle rigorously adhered to, it would require that all the appointments for the supreme executive, legislative, and judiciary magistracies should be drawn from the same fountain of authority, the people, through channels having no communication whatever with one another. Perhaps such a plan of constructing the several departments would be less difficult in practice than it may in contemplation appear. Some difficulties, however, and some additional expense would attend the execution of it. Some deviations, therefore, from the principle must be admitted. In the constitution of the judiciary department in particular, it might be inexpedient to insist rigorously on the principle: first, because peculiar qualifications being essential in the members, the primary consideration ought to be to select that mode of choice which best secures these qualifications; secondly, because the permanent tenure by which the appointments are held in that department must soon destroy all sense of dependence on the authority conferring them.

It is equally evident, that the members of each department should be as little dependent as possible on those of the others, for the emoluments annexed to their offices. Were the executive magistrate, or the judges, not independent of the legislature in this particular, their independence in every other would be merely nominal.

But the great security against a gradual concentration of the several powers in the same department, consists in giving to those who administer each department the necessary constitutional means and personal motives to resist encroachments of the others. The provision for defense must in this, as in all other cases, be made commensurate to the danger of attack. Ambition must be made to counteract ambition. The interest of the man must be connected with the constitutional rights of the place. It may be a reflection on human nature that such devices should be necessary to control the abuses of government. But what is government itself but the greatest of all reflections on human nature? If men were angels, no government would be necessary. If angels were to govern men, neither external nor internal controls on government would be necessary. In framing a government which is to be administered by men over men, the great difficulty lies in this: you must first enable the government to control the governed; and in the next place oblige it to control itself. A dependence on the people is, no doubt, the primary control on the government; but experience has taught mankind the necessity of auxiliary precautions.

This policy of supplying, by opposite and rival interests, the defect of better motives, might be traced through the whole system of human affairs, private as well as public. We see it particularly displayed in all the subordinate distributions of power, where the constant aim is to divide and arrange the several offices in such a manner as that each may be a check on the other—that the private interest of every individual may be a sentinel over the public rights. These inventions of prudence cannot be less requisite in the distribution of the supreme powers of the State.

But it is not possible to give to each department an equal power of self-defense. In republican government, the legislative authority necessarily predominates. The remedy for this inconveniency is to divide the legislature into different branches; and to render them, by different modes of election and different principles of action, as little connected with each other as the nature of their common functions and their common dependence on the society will admit. It may even be necessary to guard against dangerous encroachments by still further precautions. As the weight of the legislative authority requires that it should be thus divided, the weakness of the executive may require, on the other hand, that it should be fortified.

The Federalist,* No. LXXVIII
(HAMILTON)

The complete independence of the courts of justice is peculiarly essential in a limited Constitution. By a limited Constitution I understand one which contains certain specified exceptions to the legislative authority; such, for instance, as that it shall pass no bills of attainder, no *ex post facto* laws, and the like. Limitations of this kind can be preserved in practice no other way than through the medium of courts of justice, whose duty it must be to declare all acts contrary to the manifest tenor of the Constitution void. Without this, all the reservations of particular rights or privileges would amount to nothing.

Some perplexity respecting the rights of the courts to pronounce legislative acts void, because contrary to the Constitution, has arisen from an imagination that the doctrine would imply a superiority of the judiciary to the legislative power. It is urged that the authority which can declare the acts of another void must necessarily be superior to the one whose acts may be declared void. As this doctrine is of great importance in all the American

* Everyman edition, pp. 396–399.

constitutions, a brief discussion of the ground on which it rests cannot be unacceptable.

There is no position which depends on clearer principles than that every act of a delegated authority, contrary to the tenor of the commission under which it is exercised, is void. No legislative act, therefore, contrary to the Constitution can be valid. To deny this would be to affirm that the deputy is greater than his principal; that the servant is above his master; that the representatives of the people are superior to the people themselves; that men acting by virtue of powers may do not only what their powers do not authorize, but what they forbid.

If it be said that the legislative body are themselves the constitutional judges of their own powers, and that the construction they put upon them is conclusive upon the other departments, it may be answered that this cannot be the natural presumption where it is not to be collected from any particular provisions in the Constitution. It is not otherwise to be supposed that the Constitution could intend to enable the representatives of the people to substitute their *will* to that of their constituents. It is far more rational to suppose that the courts were designed to be an intermediate body between the people and the legislature, in order, among other things, to keep the latter within the limits assigned to their authority. The interpretation of the laws is the proper and peculiar province of the courts. A constitution is, in fact, and must be regarded by the judges, as a fundamental law. It therefore belongs to them to ascertain its meaning, as well as the meaning of any particular act proceeding from the legislative body. If there should happen to be an irreconcilable variance between the two, that which has the superior obligation and validity ought, of course, to be preferred; or, in other words, the Constitution ought to be preferred to the statute, the intention of the people to the intention of their agents.

Nor does this conclusion by any means suppose a superiority of the judicial to the legislative power. It only supposes that the power of the people is superior to both; and that where the will of the legislature, declared in its statutes, stands in opposition to that of the people, declared in the Constitution, the judges ought to be governed by the latter rather than the former. They ought to regulate their decisions by the fundamental laws, rather than by those which are not fundamental.

This exercise of judicial discretion, in determining between two contradictory laws, is exemplified in a familiar instance. It not uncommonly happens that there are two statutes existing at one time, clashing in whole or in part with each other, and neither of them containing any repealing clause or expression. In such a case it is the province of the courts to liquidate and fix their meaning and operation. So far as they can, by any fair construction, be reconciled to each other, reason and law conspire to dictate that this should be done; where this is impracticable, it becomes a matter of necessity to give effect to one in exclusion to the other. The rule which has obtained in the courts for determining their relative validity is, that the last in order of time shall be preferred to the first. But this is a mere rule of construction, not derived from any positive law, but from the nature and reason of the thing. It is a rule not enjoined upon the courts by legislative provision, but adopted by themselves, as consonant to truth and propriety, for the direction of their conduct as interpreters of the law. They thought it reasonable that between the interfering acts of an *equal* authority, that which was the last indication of its will should have the preference.

But in regard to the interfering acts of a superior and subordinate authority, of an original and derivative power, the nature and reason of the thing indicate the converse of that rule as proper to be followed. They teach us that the prior act of a superior ought to be preferred to the subsequent act of an inferior and subordinate authority; and that accordingly, whenever a particular statute contravenes the Constitution, it will be the duty of the judicial tribunals to adhere to the latter and disregard the former.

It can be of no weight to say that the courts, on the pretense of a repugnancy, may substitute their own pleasure to the constitutional intentions of the legislature. This might as well happen in the case of two contradictory statutes; or it might as well happen in every adjudication upon any single statute. The courts must declare the sense of the law; and if they should be disposed to exercise WILL instead of JUDGMENT, the consequence would equally be the substitution of their pleasure to that of the legislative body. The observation, if it prove anything, would prove that there ought to be no judges distinct from that body.

If, then, the courts of justice are to be considered as the bulwarks of a limited Constitution against legislative encroachments, this consideration will afford a strong argument for the permanent tenure of judicial offices, since nothing will contribute so much as this to that independent spirit in the judges which must be essential to the faithful performance of so arduous a duty.

This independence of the judges is equally requisite to guard the Constitution and the rights of individuals from the effects of those ill humors, which the arts of designing men, or the influence of particular conjunctures, sometimes disseminate among the people themselves, and which, though they speedily give place to better information, and more deliberate reflection, have a tendency, in the meantime, to occasion dangerous innovations in the government, and serious oppressions of the minor party in the community. Though I trust the friends of the proposed Constitution will never concur with its enemies,* in questioning that fundamental principle of republican government which admits the right of the people to alter or abolish the established Constitution, whenever they find it inconsistent with their happiness, yet it is not to be inferred from this principle that the representatives of the people, whenever a momentary inclination happens to lay hold of a majority of their constituents, incompatible with the provisions in the existing constitution, would, on that account, be justifiable in a violation of those provisions; or that the courts would be under a greater obligation to connive at infractions in this shape than when they had proceeded wholly from the cabals of the representative body. Until the people have, by some solemn and authoritative act, annulled or changed the established form, it is binding upon themselves collectively, as well as individually; and no presumption, or even knowledge, of their sentiments, can warrant their representatives in a departure from it, prior to such an act. But it is easy to see that it would require an uncommon portion of fortitude in the judges to do their duty as faithful guardians of the Constitution where legislative invasions of it had been instigated by the major voice of the community.

But it is not with a view to infractions of the Constitution only that the independence of the judges may be an essential safeguard against the effects of occasional ill humors in the society. These sometimes extend no farther than to the injury of the private rights of particular classes of citizens by unjust and partial laws. Here also the firmness of the judicial magistracy is of vast importance in mitigating the severity and confining the operation of such laws. It not only serves to moderate the immediate mischiefs of those which may have been passed, but it operates as a check upon the legislative body in passing them; who, perceiving that obstacles to the success of iniquitous intention are to be expected from the scruples

* *Vide* "Protest of the Minority of the Convention of Pennsylvania," Martin's Speech, etc.—PUBLIUS [*i. e.,* Hamilton—EDITOR].

of the courts, are in a manner compelled, by the very motives of the injustice they meditate to qualify their attempts. This is a circumstance calculated to have more influence upon the character of our governments than but few may be aware of. The benefits of the integrity and moderation of the judiciary have already been felt in more States than one; and though they may have displeased those whose sinister expectations they may have disappointed, they must have commanded the esteem and applause of all the virtuous and disinterested. Considerate men, of every description, ought to prize whatever will tend to beget or fortify that temper in the courts; as no man can be sure that he may not be to-morrow the victim of a spirit of injustice, by which he may be a gainer to-day. And every man must now feel that the inevitable tendency of such a spirit is to sap the foundations of public and private confidence, and to introduce in its stead universal distrust and distress.

That inflexible and uniform adherence to the rights of the Constitution, and of individuals, which we perceive to be indispensable in the courts of justice, can certainly not be expected from judges who hold their offices by a temporary commission. Periodical appointments, however regulated, or by whomsoever made, would, in some way or other, be fatal to their necessary independence. If the power of making them was committed either to the Executive or legislature, there would be danger of an improper complaisance to the branch which possessed it; if to both, there would be an unwillingness to hazard the displeasure of either; if to the people, or to persons chosen by them for the special purpose, there would be too great a disposition to consult popularity, to justify a reliance that nothing would be consulted but the Constitution and the laws.

8

GEORGE WASHINGTON ON FREEDOM, UNITY, AND PEACE

[George Washington (1732–1799) was a gentleman farmer, surveyor, explorer, land speculator, soldier, revolutionist, and statesman, "first in war, first in peace, first in the hearts of his countrymen." He was a man of action, not of theory or propaganda, but that gave all the more force to the ideas which he saw fit to embody in his famous *Farewell Address*. His warnings against "parties" are rarely quoted, since a party-system, different from what he could foresee, is firmly established in our unwritten constitution. His warnings against European alliances, however, are often quoted under conditions which it was likewise impossible for Washington to foresee.

Washington's retirement at the end of his second term as President helped to establish the traditional objection to a third term for any President. The reader may search, if he chooses, for evidence that Washington intended his retirement to serve as a precedent.]

Washington's Farewell Address *
(1796)

Friends and Fellow-Citizens:

The period for a new election of a Citizen, to administer the Executive Government of the United States, being not far distant, and the time actually arrived, when your thoughts must be employed in designating the person, who is to be clothed with that important trust, it appears to me proper, especially as it may conduce to a more distinct expression of the public voice, that I should now apprize you of the resolution I have formed, to decline being considered among the number of those, out of whom a choice is to be made.

I beg you, at the same time, to do me the justice to be assured, that this

* From the Harvard Classics vol. 43, P. F. Collier & Son Co.

resolution has not been taken, without a strict regard to all the considerations appertaining to the relation, which binds a dutiful citizen to his country—and that, in withdrawing the tender of service which silence in my situation might imply, I am influenced by no diminution of zeal for your future interest, no deficiency of grateful respect for your past kindness; but am supported by a full conviction that the step is compatible with both.

The acceptance of, and continuance hitherto in, the office to which your suffrages have twice called me, have been a uniform sacrifice of inclination to the opinion of duty, and to a deference for what appeared to be your desire.—I constantly hoped that it would have been much earlier in my power, consistently with motives, which I was not at liberty to disregard, to return to that retirement, from which I had been reluctantly drawn. —The strength of my inclination to do this, previous to the last election, had even led to the preparation of an address to declare it to you; but mature reflection on the then perplexed and critical posture of our affairs with foreign Nations, and the unanimous advice of persons entitled to my confidence, impelled me to abandon the idea.—

I rejoice, that the state of your concerns, external as well as internal, no longer renders the pursuit of inclination incompatible with the sentiment of duty, or propriety; and am persuaded, whatever partiality may be retained for my services, that, in the present circumstances of our country, you will not disapprove my determination to retire.

The impressions, with which I first undertook the arduous trust, were explained on the proper occasion. In the discharge of this trust, I will only say, that I have, with good intentions, contributed towards the organization and administration of the government, the best exertions of which a very fallible judgment was capable.—Not unconscious, in the outset, of the inferiority of my qualifications, experience in my own eyes, perhaps still more in the eyes of others, has strengthened the motives to diffidence of myself; and every day the increasing weight of years admonishes me more and more, that the shade of retirement is as necessary to me as it will be welcome.—Satisfied, that, if any circumstances have given peculiar value to my services, they were temporary, I have the consolation to believe, that, while choice and prudence invite me to quit the political scene, patriotism does not forbid it.

In looking forward to the moment, which is intended to terminate the career of my public life, my feelings do not permit me to suspend the deep acknowledgment of that debt of gratitude, which I owe to my beloved country,—for the many honors it has conferred upon me; still more for the stedfast confidence with which it has supported me; and for the opportunities I have thence enjoyed of manifesting my inviolable attachment, by services faithful and persevering, though in usefulness unequal to my zeal.—If benefits have resulted to our country from these services, let it always be remembered to your praise, and as an instructive example in our annals, that under circumstances in which the Passions, agitated in every direction, were liable to mislead, amidst appearances sometimes dubious, vicissitudes of fortune often discouraging, in situations in which not unfrequently want of success has countenanced the spirit of criticism, the constancy of your support was the essential prop of the efforts, and a guarantee of the plans by which they were effected.—Profoundly penetrated with this idea, I shall carry it with me to my grave, as a strong incitement to unceasing vows that Heaven may continue to you the choicest tokens of its beneficence—that your union and brotherly affection may be perpetual—that the free constitution, which is the work of your hands, may be sacredly maintained—that its administration in every department may be stamped with wisdom and virtue—that, in fine, the happiness of the people of these States, under the auspices of liberty, may be made complete, by so careful a preservation and so prudent a use of this blessing, as will acquire to them the glory of recommending it to the applause, the affection, and adoption of every nation, which is yet a stranger to it.

Here, perhaps, I ought to stop.—But a solicitude for your welfare, which cannot end but with my life, and the apprehension of danger, natural to that solicitude, urge me on an occasion like the present, to offer to your solemn contemplation, and to recommend to your frequent review, some sentiments; which are the result of much reflection, of no inconsiderable observation and which appear to me all important to the permanency of your felicity as a People. These will be offered to you with the more freedom, as you can only see in them the disinterested warnings of a parting friend, who can possibly have no personal motive to bias his counsel.— Nor can I forget, as an encouragement to it, your indulgent reception of my sentiments on a former and not dissimilar occasion.

Interwoven as is the love of liberty with every ligament of your hearts, no recommendation of mine is necessary to fortify or confirm the attachment.—

The Unity of Government, which constitutes you one people, is also now dear to you.—It is justly so; for it is a main Pillar in the Edifice of your real independence; the support of your tranquillity at home; your peace abroad; of your safety; of your prosperity in every shape; of that very Liberty, which you so highly prize.—But as it is easy to foresee, that, from different causes, and from different quarters, much pains will be taken, many artifices employed, to weaken in your minds the conviction of this truth;—as this is the point in your political fortress against which the batteries of internal and external enemies will be most constantly and actively (though often covertly and insidiously) directed, it is of infinite moment, that you should properly estimate the immense value of your national Union to your collective and individual happiness;—that you should cherish a cordial, habitual, and immoveable attachment to it; accustoming yourselves to think and speak of it as of the Palladium of your political safety and prosperity; watching for its preservation with jealous anxiety; discountenancing whatever may suggest even a suspicion, that it can in any event be abandoned, and indignantly frowning upon the first dawning of every attempt to alienate any portion of our Country from the rest, or to enfeeble the sacred ties which now link together the various parts.

For this you have every inducement of sympathy and interest.—Citizens by birth or choice of a common country, that country has a right to concentrate your affections.—The name of AMERICAN, which belongs to you, in your national capacity, must always exalt the just pride of Patriotism, more than any appellation derived from local discriminations. With slight shades of difference, you have the same Religion, Manners, Habits, and Political Principles. You have in a common cause fought and triumphed together; the Independence and Liberty you possess are the work of joint counsels, and joint efforts—of common dangers, sufferings, and successes.—

But these considerations, however powerfully they address themselves to your sensibility, are greatly outweighed by those which apply more immediately to your Interest. Here every portion of our country finds the most commanding motives for carefully guarding and preserving the Union of the whole.

The *North*, in an unrestrained intercourse with the *South*, protected by the equal Laws of a common government, finds, in the productions of the latter, great additional resources of maritime and commercial enterprise—and precious materials of manufacturing industry.—The *South*, in the same intercourse, benefiting by the agency of the *North,* sees its agriculture grow and its commerce expand. Turning partly into its own channels the seamen of the *North,* it finds its particular navigation envigorated;—and, while it contributes, in different ways, to nourish and increase the general mass of the national navigation, it looks forward to the protection of a maritime strength to which itself is unequally adapted. The *East,* in a like intercourse with the *West,* already finds, and in the progressive improvement of interior communications, by land and water, will more and more find, a valuable vent for the commodities which it brings from abroad, or manufactures at home.—The *West* derives from the *East* supplies requisite to its growth and comfort, and—what is perhaps of still greater consequence, it must of necessity owe the *secure* enjoyment of indispensable *outlets* for its own productions to the weight, influence, and the future maritime strength of the Atlantic side of the Union, directed by an indissoluble community of interest as *one Nation.* —Any other tenure by which the *West* can hold this essential advantage, whether derived from its own separate strength, or from an apostate and unnatural connection with any foreign power, must be intrinsically precarious.

While then every part of our Country thus feels an immediate and particular interest in Union, all the parts combined in the united mass of means and efforts cannot fail to find greater strength, greater resource, proportionably greater security from external danger, a less frequent interruption of their Peace by foreign Nations; and, what is of inestimable value! they must derive from Union an exemption from those broils and wars between themselves, which so frequently afflict neighboring countries, not tied together by the same governments; which their own rivalships alone would be sufficient to produce; but which opposite foreign alliances, attachments, and intrigues would stimulate and embitter.— Hence likewise they will avoid the necessity of those overgrown Military establishments, which, under any form of government, are inauspicious to liberty, and which are to be regarded as particularly hostile to Republican Liberty. In this sense it is, that your Union ought to be considered as a main prop to your liberty, and that the love of the one ought to endear to you the preservation of the other.

These considerations speak a persuasive language to every reflecting and virtuous mind, and exhibit the continuance of the UNION as a primary object of Patriotic desire. Is there a doubt, whether a common government can embrace so large a sphere?—Let experience solve it. To listen to mere speculation in such a case were criminal.—We are authorized to hope that a proper organization of the whole, with the auxiliary agency of governments for the respective subdivisions, will afford a happy issue to the experiment. It is well worth a fair and full experiment. With such powerful and obvious motives to Union, affecting all parts of our country, while experience shall not have demonstrated its impracticability, there will always be reason to distrust the patriotism of those, who in any quarter may endeavor to weaken its bands.—

In contemplating the causes which may disturb our Union, it occurs as matter of serious concern, that any ground should have been furnished for characterizing parties by *geographical* discriminations—*Northern* and *Southern, Atlantic* and *Western;* whence designing men may endeavor to excite a belief, that there is a real difference of local interests and views. One of the expedients of Party to acquire influence, within particular districts, is to misrepresent the opinions and aims of other districts.—You cannot shield yourselves too much against the jealousies and heart burnings, which spring from these misrepresentations;—they tend to render alien to each other those, who ought to be bound together by fraternal affection.—The inhabitants of our Western country have lately had a useful lesson on this head—they have seen, in the negotiation by the Executive, and in the unanimous ratification by the Senate, of the treaty with Spain, and in the universal satisfaction at that event, throughout the United States, a decisive proof how unfounded were the suspicions propagated among them of a policy in the General Government and in the Atlantic States unfriendly to their interests in regard to the Mississippi—they have been witnesses to the formation of two Treaties, that with Great Britain, and that with Spain, which secure to them every thing they could desire, in respect to our Foreign Relations, towards confirming their prosperity.—Will it not be their wisdom to rely for the preservation of these advantages on the Union by which they were procured?—Will they not henceforth be deaf to those advisers, if such there are, who would sever them from their Brethren, and connect them with Aliens?—

To the efficacy and permanency of your Union, a Government for the whole is indispensable.—No alliances, however strict between the parts can be an adequate substitute.—They must inevitably experience the infractions and interruptions which all alliances in all times have experienced. Sensible of this momentous truth, you have improved upon your first essay, by the adoption of a Constitution of Government, better calculated than your former for an intimate Union, and for the efficacious management of your common concerns.—This government, the offspring of our own choice uninfluenced and unawed, adopted upon full investigation and mature deliberation, completely free in its principles, in the distribution of its powers, uniting security with energy, and containing within itself a provision for its own amendment, has a just claim to your confidence and your support.—Respect for its authority, compliance with its Laws, acquiescence in its measures, are duties enjoined by the fundamental maxims of true Liberty.—The basis of our political systems is the right of the people to make and to alter their Constitutions of Government. —But the Constitution which at any time exists, 'till changed by an explicit and authentic act of the whole People, is sacredly obligatory upon all.—The very idea of the power and the right of the People to establish Government presupposes the duty of every individual to obey the established Government.

All obstructions to the execution of the Laws, all combinations and associations, under whatever plausible character, with the real design to direct, control, counteract, or awe the regular deliberation and action of the constituted authorities, are destructive of this fundamental principle, and of fatal tendency.—They serve to organize faction, to give it an artificial and extraordinary force—to put in the place of the delegated will of the nation, the will of a party;—often a small but artful and enterprising minority of the community;—and, according to the alternate triumphs of different parties, to make the public administration the mirror of the ill-concerted and incongruous projects of faction, rather than the organ of consistent and wholesome plans digested by common councils, and modified by mutual interests.—However combinations or associations of the above descriptions may now and then answer popular ends, they are likely, in the course of time and things, to become potent engines, by which cunning, ambitious, and unprincipled men will be enabled to subvert the Power of the People, and to usurp for themselves the reins of Government; destroying afterwards the very engines, which have lifted them to unjust dominion.—

Towards the preservation of your Government, and the permanency of your present happy state, it is requisite, not only that you steadily discountenance irregular oppositions to its acknowledged authority, but also that you resist with care the spirit of innovation upon its principles, however specious the pretexts.—One method of assault may be to effect, in the forms of the Constitution, alterations which will impair the energy of the system, and thus to undermine what cannot be directly overthrown.—In all the changes to which you may be invited, remember that time and habit are at least as necessary to fix the true character of Governments, as of other human institutions—that experience is the surest standard, by which to test the real tendency of the existing Constitution of a Country—that facility in changes upon the credit of mere hypothesis and opinion exposes to perpetual change, from the endless variety of hypothesis and opinion:—and remember, especially, that, for the efficient management of your common interests, in a country so extensive as ours, a Government of as much vigor as is consistent with the perfect security of Liberty is indispensable.—Liberty itself will find in such a government, with powers properly distributed and adjusted, its surest Guardian.—It is, indeed, little else than a name, where the Government is too feeble to withstand the enterprise of faction, to confine each member of the society within the limits prescribed by the laws, and to maintain all in the secure and tranquil enjoyment of the rights of person and property.

I have already intimated to you the danger of parties in the State, with particular reference to the founding of them on Geographical discriminations.—Let me now take a more comprehensive view, and warn you in the most solemn manner against the baneful effects of the Spirit of Party, generally.

This Spirit, unfortunately, is inseparable from our nature, having its root in the strongest passions of the human mind.—It exists under different shapes in all Governments, more or less stifled, controlled, or repressed; but, in those of the popular form, it is seen in its greatest rankness, and is truly their worst enemy.—

The alternate domination of one faction over another, sharpened by the spirit of revenge, natural to party dissension, which in different ages and countries has perpetrated the most horrid enormities, is itself a frightful despotism.—But this leads at length to a more formal and permanent despotism.—The disorders and miseries, which result, gradually incline the minds of men to seek security and repose in the absolute power of an Individual; and sooner or later the chief of some prevailing faction, more able or more fortunate than his competitors, turns this disposition to the purposes of his own elevation, on the ruins of Public Liberty.

Without looking forward to an extremity of this kind, (which nevertheless ought not to be entirely out of sight), the common and continual mischiefs of the spirit of Party are sufficient to make it the interest and duty of a wise people to discourage and restrain it.—

It serves always to distract the Public Councils, and enfeeble the Public administration. It agitates the community with ill founded jealousies and false alarms, kindles the animosity of one part against another, foments occasionally riot and insurrection.—It opens the door to foreign influence and corruption, which find a facilitated access to the Government itself through the channels of party passions. Thus the policy and the will of one country, are subjected to the policy and will of another.

There is an opinion, that parties in free countries are useful checks upon the Administration of the Government, and serve to keep alive the spirit of Liberty.—This within certain limits is probably true—and in Governments of a Monarchical cast, Patriotism may look with indulgence, if not with favor, upon the spirit of party.—But in those of the popular character, in Governments purely elective, it is a spirit not to be encouraged. —From their natural tendency, it is certain there will always be enough of that spirit for every salutary purpose,—and there being constant danger of excess, the effort ought to be, by force of public opinion, to mitigate and assuage it.—A fire not to be quenched; it demands a uniform vigilance to prevent its bursting into a flame, lest, instead of warming, it should consume.

It is important, likewise, that the habits of thinking in a free country should inspire caution in those intrusted with its administration, to confine themselves within their respective constitutional spheres; avoiding in the exercise of the powers of one department to encroach upon another. The spirit of encroachment tends to consolidate the powers of all the departments in one, and thus to create, whatever the form of government, a real despotism.—A just estimate of that love of power, and proneness to abuse it, which predominates in the human heart, is sufficient to satisfy us of the truth of this position.—The necessity of reciprocal checks in the exercise of political power, by dividing and distributing it into different depositories, and constituting each the Guardian of the Public Weal against invasions by the others, has been evinced by experiments ancient and modern; some of them in our country and under our own eyes.—To preserve them must be as necessary as to institute them. If, in the opinion of the People, the distribution or modification of the Constitutional powers be in any particular wrong, let it be corrected by an amendment in the way which the constitution designates.—But let there be no change by usurpation; for though this, in one instance, may be the instrument of good, it is the customary weapon by which free governments are destroyed.—The precedent must always greatly overbalance in permanent evil any partial or transient benefit which the use can at any time yield.—

Of all the dispositions and habits, which lead to political prosperity, Religion, and Morality are indispensable supports.—In vain would that man claim the tribute of Patriotism, who should labor to subvert these great pillars of human happiness, these firmest props of the duties of Men and Citizens.—The mere Politician, equally with the pious man, ought to respect and to cherish them.—A volume could not trace all their connections with private and public felicity.—Let it simply be asked where is the security for property, for reputation, for life, if the sense of religious obligation *desert* the oaths, which are the instruments of investigation in Courts of Justice? And let us with caution indulge the supposition, that morality can be maintained without religion.—Whatever may be conceded to the influence of refined education on minds of peculiar structure —reason and experience both forbid us to expect, that national morality can prevail in exclusion of religious principle.—

'Tis substantially true, that virtue or morality is a necessary spring of popular government.—The rule indeed extends with more or less force to every species of Free Government.—Who that is a sincere friend to it can look with indifference upon attempts to shake the foundation of the fabric?—

Promote, then, as an object of primary importance, institutions for the general diffusion of knowledge. In proportion as the structure of a government gives force to public opinion, it is essential that public opinion should be enlightened.

As a very important source of strength and security, cherish public credit.—One method of preserving it is, to use it as sparingly as possible: —avoiding occasions of expense by cultivating peace, but remembering also that timely disbursements to prepare for danger frequently prevent much greater disbursements to repel it—avoiding likewise the accumulation of debt, not only by shunning occasions of expense, but by vigorous exertions in time of Peace to discharge the debts which unavoidable wars may have occasioned, not ungenerously throwing upon posterity the burthen which we ourselves ought to bear. The execution of these maxims belongs to your Representatives, but it is necessary that public opinion should co-operate.—To facilitate to them the performance of their duty, it is essential that you should practically bear in mind, that towards the payment of debts there must be Revenue—that to have Revenue there must be taxes—that no taxes can be devised, which are not more or less inconvenient and unpleasant—that the intrinsic embarrassment, inseparable from the selection of the proper objects (which is always a choice of difficulties) ought to be a decisive motive for a candid construction of the conduct of the Government in making it, and for a spirit of acquiescence in the measures for obtaining Revenue, which the public exigencies may at any time dictate.—

Observe good faith and justice towards all Nations. Cultivate peace and harmony with all.—Religion and Morality enjoin this conduct; and can it be, that good policy does not equally enjoin it?—It will be worthy of a free, enlightened, and, at no distant period, a great nation, to give to mankind the magnanimous and too novel example of a People always guided by an exalted justice and benevolence.—Who can doubt that in the course of time and things, the fruits of such a plan would richly repay any temporary advantages, which might be lost by a steady adherence to it? Can it be that Providence has not connected the permanent felicity of a Nation with its virtue? The experiment, at least, is recommended by every sentiment which ennobles human nature.—Alas! is it rendered impossible by its vices?

In the execution of such a plan nothing is more essential than that permanent, inveterate antipathies against particular nations and passionate attachments for others, should be excluded; and that, in place of them, just and amicable feelings towards all should be cultivated.—The Nation, which indulges towards another an habitual hatred or an habitual fondness, is in some degree a slave. It is a slave to its animosity or to its affection, either of which is sufficient to lead it astray from its duty and its interest.—Antipathy in one nation against another disposes each more readily to offer insult and injury, to lay hold of slight causes of umbrage, and to be haughty and intractable, when accidental or trifling occasions of dispute occur.—Hence frequent collisions, obstinate, envenomed and bloody contests.—The Nation prompted by ill-will and resentment, sometimes impels to War the Government, contrary to the best calculations of policy.—The Government sometimes participates in the national propensity, and adopts through passion what reason would reject;—at other times, it makes the animosity of the Nation subservient to projects of hostility instigated by pride, ambition, and other sinister and pernicious motives.—The peace often, sometimes perhaps the Liberty, of Nations has been the victim.—

So likewise a passionate attachment of one Nation for another produces a variety of evils.—Sympathy for the favorite nation, facilitating the illusion of an imaginary common interest in cases where no real common interest exists, and infusing into one the enmities of the other, betrays the former into a participation in the quarrels and wars of the latter, without adequate inducement or justification. It leads also to concessions to the favorite Nation of privileges denied to others, which is apt doubly to injure the Nation making the concessions; by unnecessarily parting with what ought to have been retained; and by exciting jealousy, ill-will, and a disposition to retaliate, in the parties from whom equal privileges are withheld; and it gives to ambitious, corrupted, or deluded citizens, (who devote themselves to the favorite Nation) facility to betray or sacrifice the interests of their own country, without odium, sometimes even with popularity:—gilding, with the appearances of a virtuous sense of obligation, a commendable deference for public opinion, or a laudable zeal for public good, the base or foolish compliances of ambition, corruption, or infatuation.—

As avenues to foreign influence in innumerable ways, such attachments are particularly alarming to the truly enlightened and independent Patriot.—How many opportunities do they afford to tamper with domestic factions, to practise the arts of seduction, to mislead public opinion, to influence or awe the public councils! Such an attachment of a small or weak, towards a great and powerful nation, dooms the former to be the satellite of the latter.

Against the insidious wiles of foreign influence, I conjure you to believe me, fellow-citizens, the jealousy of a free people ought to be *constantly* awake; since history and experience prove that foreign influence is one of the most baneful foes of republican Government.—But that jealousy, to be useful, must be impartial; else it becomes the instrument of the very influence to be avoided, instead of a defense against it.—Excessive partiality for one foreign nation, and excessive dislike of another, cause those whom they actuate to see danger only on one side, and serve to veil and even second the arts of influence on the other. Real Patriots, who may resist the intrigues of the favorite, are liable to become suspected and odious; while its tools and dupes usurp the applause and confidence of the people, to surrender their interests.—

The great rule of conduct for us, in regard to foreign Nations, is, in extending our commercial relations, to have with them as little *Political* connection as possible.—So far as we have already formed engagements, let them be fulfilled with perfect good faith.—Here let us stop.—

Europe has a set of primary interests, which to us have none, or a very remote relation.—Hence she must be engaged in frequent controversies, the causes of which are essentially foreign to our concerns.—Hence, therefore, it must be unwise in us to implicate ourselves, by artificial ties in the ordinary vicissitudes of her politics, or the ordinary combinations and collisions of her friendships, or enmities.

Our detached and distant situation invites and enables us to pursue a different course.—If we remain one People, under an efficient government, the period is not far off, when we may defy material injury from external annoyance; when we may take such an attitude as will cause the neutrality we may at any time resolve upon to be scrupulously respected. When belligerent nations, under the impossibility of making acquisitions upon us, will not lightly hazard the giving us provocation when we may choose peace or war, as our interest, guided by our justice, shall counsel.

Why forego the advantages of so peculiar a situation?—Why quit our own to stand upon foreign ground?—Why, by interweaving our destiny with that of any part of Europe, entangle our peace and prosperity in the toils of European ambition, rivalship, interest, humor, or caprice?—

'Tis our true policy to steer clear of permanent alliances, with any portion of the foreign world;—so far, I mean, as we are now at liberty to do it;—for let me not be understood as capable of patronizing infidelity to existing engagements. (I hold the maxim no less applicable to public than to private affairs, that honesty is always the best policy.)—I repeat it therefore let those engagements be observed in their genuine sense.—But in my opinion it is unnecessary and would be unwise to extend them.—

Taking care always to keep ourselves, by suitable establishments, on a respectable defensive posture, we may safely trust to temporary alliances for extraordinary emergencies.—

Harmony, liberal intercourse with all nations, are recommended by policy, humanity, and interest. But even our commercial policy should hold an equal and impartial hand:—neither seeking nor granting exclusive favors or preferences;—consulting the natural course of things;—diffusing and diversifying by gentle means the streams of commerce, but forcing nothing;—establishing with Powers so disposed—in order to give trade a stable course, to define the rights of our Merchants, and to enable the Government to support them—conventional rules of intercourse, the best that present circumstances and mutual opinion will permit; but temporary, and liable to be from time to time abandoned or varied, as experience and circumstances shall dictate; constantly keeping in view, that 'tis folly in one nation to look for disinterested favors from another;—that it must pay with a portion of its independence for whatever it may accept under that character—that by such acceptance, it may place itself in the condition of having given equivalents for nominal favors, and yet of being reproached with ingratitude for not giving more.—There can be no greater error than to expect or calculate upon real favors from Nation to Nation. 'Tis an illusion, which experience must cure, which a just pride ought to discard.

In offering to you, my Countrymen, these counsels of an old and affectionate friend, I dare not hope they will make the strong and lasting impression, I could wish,—that they will control the usual current of the passions, or prevent our Nation from running the course which has hitherto marked the destiny of Nations. But if I may even flatter myself, that they may be productive of some partial benefit; some occasional good; that they may now and then recur to moderate the fury of party spirit, to warn against the mischiefs of foreign intrigue, to guard against the impostures of pretended patriotism, this hope will be a full recompense for the solicitude for your welfare, by which they have been dictated.—

How far in the discharge of my official duties, I have been guided by the principles which have been delineated, the public Records and other evidences of my conduct must witness to You and to the world.—To myself the assurance of my own conscience is, that I have at least believed myself to be guided by them.

In relation to the still subsisting War in Europe, my Proclamation of the 22d of April 1793 is the index to my plan.—Sanctioned by your approving voice and by that of your Representatives in both Houses of Congress, the spirit of that measure has continually governed me:—uninfluenced by any attempts to deter or divert me from it.

After deliberate examination with the aid of the best lights I could obtain, I was well satisfied that our country, under all the circumstances of the case, had a right to take, and was bound in duty and interest to take, a Neutral position.—Having taken it, I determined, as far as should depend upon me, to maintain it, with moderation, perseverance, and firmness.—

The considerations which respect the right to hold this conduct, it is not necessary on this occasion to detail. I will only observe, that, according to my understanding of the matter, that right, so far from being denied by any of the Belligerent Powers, has been virtually admitted by all.—

The duty of holding a neutral conduct may be inferred, without any thing more, from the obligation which justice and humanity impose on every Nation, in cases in which it is free to act, to maintain inviolate the relations of Peace and Amity towards other Nations.—

The inducements of interest for observing that conduct will best be referred to your own reflections and experience.—With me, a predominant motive has been to endeavor to gain time to our country to settle and mature its yet recent institutions, and to progress without interruption to that degree of strength and consistency, which is necessary to give it, humanly speaking, the command of its own fortunes.

Though, in reviewing the incidents of my Administration, I am unconscious of intentional error—I am nevertheless too sensible of my defects not to think it probable that I may have committed many errors.—Whatever they may be, I fervently beseech the Almighty to avert or mitigate the evils to which they may tend.—I shall also carry with me the hope that my country will never cease to view them with indulgence; and that, after forty-five years of my life dedicated to its service with an upright zeal, the faults of incompetent abilities will be consigned to oblivion, as myself must soon be to the mansions of rest.

Relying on its kindness in this as in other things, and actuated by that fervent love towards it, which is so natural to a man, who views in it the native soil of himself and his progenitors for several generations;—I anticipate with pleasing expectation that retreat, in which I promise myself to realize, without alloy, the sweet enjoyment of partaking, in the midst of my fellow-citizens, the benign influence of good Laws under a free Government, the ever favorite object of my heart, and the happy reward, as I trust, of our mutual cares, labors, and dangers.

9

JOHN STUART MILL ON LIBERTY

[John Stuart Mill (1806–1873) was the son of James Mill, one of the leaders of the utilitarian and reformist movement. He was a precocious boy, and his father gave him an intensive education. For many years he served the East India Company in a position which gave him a share in the transactions of the Company with the native princes. Meanwhile he was active in the field of philosophy and political theory. He continued the tradition of his father and Jeremy Bentham, but with an increasing tendency to move from their extreme individualism toward more socialistic views, and from their over-simplified psychology of pleasure and pain to a recognition of the cultural needs and capacities of human nature.

Mill published his essay *On Liberty* in 1859. In it he defends a very high degree of individual liberty, not on the ground of "natural rights" as did Locke and the revolutionists of the eighteenth century, but on the ground of social utility. The essay has become a classic of liberal thought.]

On Liberty *
(1859)

* * *

The object of this Essay is to assert one very simple principle, as entitled to govern absolutely the dealings of society with the individual in the way of compulsion and control, whether the means used be physical force in the form of legal penalties, or the moral coercion of public opinion. That principle is, that the sole end for which mankind are warranted, individually or collectively, in interfering with the liberty of action of any of their number, is self-protection. That the only purpose for which power can be rightfully exercised over any member of a civilized community, against his will, is to prevent harm to others. His own good, either physical

* From *Utilitarianism, Liberty, Representative Government*, Everyman edition, E. P. Dutton and Company, Inc.

or moral, is not a sufficient warrant. He cannot rightfully be compelled to do or forbear because it will be better for him to do so, because it will make him happier, because, in the opinions of others, to do so would be wise, or even right. These are good reasons for remonstrating with him, or reasoning with him, or persuading him, or entreating him, but not for compelling him, or visiting him with any evil in case he do otherwise. To justify that, the conduct from which it is desired to deter him must be calculated to produce evil to some one else. The only part of the conduct of any one, for which he is amenable to society, is that which concerns others. In the part which merely concerns himself, his independence is, of right, absolute. Over himself, over his own body and mind, the individual is sovereign.

It is, perhaps, hardly necessary to say that this doctrine is meant to apply only to human beings in the maturity of their faculties. We are not speaking of children, or of young persons below the age which the law may fix as that of manhood or womanhood. Those who are still in a state to require being taken care of by others, must be protected against their own actions as well as against external injury. For the same reason, we may leave out of consideration those backward states of society in which the race itself may be considered as in its nonage. The early difficulties in the way of spontaneous progress are so great, that there is seldom any choice of means for overcoming them; and a ruler full of the spirit of improvement is warranted in the use of any expedients that will attain an end, perhaps otherwise unattainable. Despotism is a legitimate mode of government in dealing with barbarians, provided the end be their improvement, and the means justified by actually effecting that end. Liberty, as a principle, has no application to any state of things anterior to the time when mankind have become capable of being improved by free and equal discussion. Until then, there is nothing for them but implicit obedience to an Akbar or a Charlemagne, if they are so fortunate as to find one. But as soon as mankind have attained the capacity of being guided to their own improvement by conviction or persuasion (a period long since reached in all nations with whom we need here concern ourselves), compulsion, either in the direct form or in that of pains and penalties for non-compliance, is no longer admissible as a means to their own good, and justifiable only for the security of others.

It is proper to state that I forego any advantage which could be derived to my argument from the idea of abstract right, as a thing independent of utility. I regard utility as the ultimate appeal on all ethical questions; but it must be utility in the largest sense, grounded on the permanent interests of a man as a progressive being. Those interests, I contend, authorize the subjection of individual spontaneity to external control, only in respect to those actions of each, which concern the interest of other people. If any one does an act hurtful to others, there is a *prima facie* case for punishing him, by law, or, where legal penalties are not safely applicable, by general disapprobation. There are also many positive acts for the benefit of others, which he may rightfully be compelled to perform; such as to give evidence in a court of justice; to bear his fair share in the common defense, or in any other joint work necessary to the interest of the society of which he enjoys the protection; and to perform certain acts of individual beneficence, such as saving a fellow-creature's life, or interposing to protect the defenseless against ill-usage, things which whenever it is obviously a man's duty to do, he may rightfully be made responsible to society for not doing. A person may cause evil to others not only by his actions but by his inaction, and in either case he is justly accountable to them for the injury. The latter case, it is true, requires a much more cautious exercise of compulsion than the former. To make any one answerable for doing evil to others is the rule; to make him answerable for not preventing evil is, comparatively speaking, the exception. Yet there are many cases clear enough and grave enough to justify that exception. In all things which regard the external relations of the individual, he is *de jure* amenable to those whose interests are concerned, and, if need be, to society as their protector. There are often good reasons for not holding him to the responsibility; but these reasons must arise from the special expediencies of the case: either because it is a kind of case in which he is on the whole likely to act better, when left to his own discretion, than when controlled in any way in which society have it in their power to control him; or because the attempt to exercise control would produce other evils, greater than those which it would prevent. When such reasons as these preclude the enforcement of responsibility, the conscience of the agent himself should step into the vacant judgment seat, and protect those interests of others which have no external protection; judging himself all the more rigidly, because the case does not admit of his being made accountable to the judgment of his fellow-creatures.

But there is a sphere of action in which society, as distinguished from the individual, has, if any, only an indirect interest; comprehending all that portion of a person's life and conduct which affects only himself, or if it also affects others, only with their free, voluntary, and undeceived consent and participation. When I say only himself, I mean directly, and in the first instance; for whatever affects himself, may affect others through himself; and the objection which may be grounded on this contingency, will receive consideration in the sequel. This, then, is the appropriate region of human liberty. It comprises, first, the inward domain of consciousness; demanding liberty of conscience in the most comprehensive sense; liberty of thought and feeling; absolute freedom of opinion and sentiment on all subjects, practical or speculative, scientific, moral, or theological. The liberty of expressing and publishing opinions may seem to fall under a different principle, since it belongs to that part of the conduct of an individual which concerns other people; but, being almost of as much importance as the liberty of thought itself, and resting in great part on the same reasons, is practically inseparable from it. Secondly, the principle requires liberty of tastes and pursuits; of framing the plan of our life to suit our own character; of doing as we like, subject to such consequences as may follow: without impediment from our fellow-creatures, so long as what we do does not harm them, even though they should think our conduct foolish, perverse, or wrong. Thirdly, from this liberty of each individual, follows the liberty, within the same limits, of combination among individuals; freedom to unite, for any purpose not involving harm to others: the persons combining being supposed to be of full age, and not forced or deceived. [Pp. 72–75.]

* * *

. . . The disposition of mankind, whether as rulers or as fellow-citizens, to impose their own opinions and inclinations as a rule of conduct on others, is so energetically supported by some of the best and by some of the worst feelings incident to human nature, that it is hardly ever kept under restraint by anything but want of power; and as the power is not declining, but growing, unless a strong barrier of moral conviction can be raised against the mischief, we must expect, in the present circumstances of the world, to see it increase. [P. 77.]

* * *

[Regarding suppression of opinion Mill says:] . . . But I deny the right of the people to exercise such coercion, either by themselves or by their government. The power itself is illegitimate. The best government has no more title to it than the worst. It is as noxious, or more noxious, when exerted in accordance with public opinion, than when in opposition to it. If all mankind minus one were of one opinion, and only one person were of the contrary opinion, mankind would be no more justified in silencing that one person, than he, if he had the power, would be justified in silencing mankind. Were an opinion a personal possession of no value except to the owner; if to be obstructed in the enjoyment of it were simply a private injury, it would make some difference whether the injury was inflicted only on a few persons or on many. But the peculiar evil of silencing the expression of an opinion is, that it is robbing the human race; posterity as well as the existing generation; those who dissent from the opinion, still more than those who hold it. If the opinion is right, they are deprived of the opportunity of exchanging error for truth: if wrong, they lose, what is almost as great a benefit, the clearer perception and livelier impression of truth, produced by its collision with error. [P. 79.]

*   *   *

First: the opinion which it is attempted to suppress by authority may possibly be true. Those who desire to suppress it, of course deny its truth; but they are not infallible. They have no authority to decide the question for all mankind, and exclude every other person from the means of judging. To refuse a hearing to an opinion, because they are sure that it is false, is to assume that *their* certainty is the same thing as *absolute* certainty. All silencing of discussion is an assumption of infallibility. Its condemnation may be allowed to rest on this common argument, not the worse for being common. [P. 79.]

*   *   *

. . . Why is it, then, that there is on the whole a preponderance among mankind of rational opinions and rational conduct? If there really is this preponderance—which there must be unless human affairs are, and have always been, in an almost desperate state—it is owing to a quality of the human mind, the source of everything respectable in man either as an intellectual or as a moral being, namely, that his errors are corrigible. He is capable of rectifying his mistakes, by discussion and experience. Not by experience alone. There must be discussion, to show how experience is to be interpreted. Wrong opinions and practices gradually yield to fact and argument; but facts and arguments, to produce any effect on the mind, must be brought before it. Very few facts are able to tell their own story, without comments to bring out their meaning. The whole strength and value, then, of human judgment, depending on the one property, that it can be set right when it is wrong, reliance can be placed on it only when the means of setting it right are kept constantly at hand. In the case of any person whose judgment is really deserving of confidence, how has it become so? Because he has kept his mind open to criticism of his opinions and conduct. Because it has been his practice to listen to all that could be said against him; to profit by as much of it as was just, and expound to himself, and upon occasion to others, the fallacy of what was fallacious. Because he has felt, that the only way in which a human being can make some approach to knowing the whole of a subject, is by hearing what can be said about it by persons of every variety of opinion, and studying all modes in which it can be looked at by every character of mind. No wise man ever acquired his wisdom in any mode but this; nor is it in the nature of human intellect to become wise in any other manner. The steady habit of correcting and completing his own opinion by collating it with those of others, so far from causing doubt and hesitation in carrying it into practice, is the only stable foundation for a just reliance on it: for, being cognizant of all that can, at least obviously, be said against him, and having taken up his position against all gainsayers—knowing that he has sought for objections and difficulties, instead of avoiding them, and has shut out no light which can be thrown upon the subject from any quarter—he has a right to think his judgment better than that of any person, or any multitude, who have not gone through a similar process. [P. 82.]

*   *   *

. . . The beliefs which we have most warrant for have no safeguard to rest on, but a standing invitation to the whole world to prove them unfounded. If the challenge is not accepted, or is accepted and the attempt fails, we are far enough from certainty still; but we have done the best that the existing state of human reason admits of; we have neglected nothing that could give the truth a chance of reaching us: if the lists are kept open, we may hope that if there be a better truth, it will be found when the human mind is capable of receiving it; and in the meantime we may rely on having attained such approach to truth as is possible in our own day. This is the amount of certainty attainable by a fallible being, and this the sole way of attaining it.

Strange it is, that men should admit the validity of the arguments for free discussion, but object to their being "pushed to an extreme;" not seeing that unless the reasons are good for an extreme case, they are not good for any case. Strange that they should imagine that they are not assuming infallibility, when they acknowledge that there should be free discussion on all subjects which can possibly be *doubtful,* but think that some particular principle or doctrine should be forbidden to be questioned because it is so *certain,* that is, because *they are certain* that it is certain. To call any proposition certain, while there is any one who would deny its certainty if permitted, but who is not permitted, is to assume that we ourselves, and those who agree with us, are the judges of certainty, and judges without hearing the other side. [P. 83.]

*   *   *

Mankind can hardly be too often reminded, that there was once a man named Socrates, between whom and the legal authorities and public opinion of his time there took place a memorable collision. Born in an age and country abounding in individual greatness, this man has been handed down to us by those who best knew both him and the age, as the most virtuous man in it; while *we* know him as the head and prototype of all subsequent teachers of virtue, the source equally of the lofty inspiration of Plato and the judicious utilitarianism of Aristotle, *"i maëstri di color che sanno,"* * the two headsprings of ethical as of all other philosophy. This acknowledged master of all the eminent thinkers who have since lived—whose fame, still growing after more than two thousand years, all but outweighs the whole remainder of the names which make his native city illustrious —was put to death by his countrymen, after a judicial conviction, for impiety and immorality. Impiety, in denying the gods recognized by the State; indeed his accuser asserted (see the "Apologia" †) that he believed in no gods at all. Immorality, in being, by his doctrines and instructions, a "corruptor of youth." Of these charges the tribunal, there is every ground for believing, honestly found him guilty, and condemned the man who

* Dante calls Aristotle "master of those that know," *Inferno* iv, 131.—EDITOR.
† I. e., the "Apology" or "Defence" of Socrates included in Plato's works.—EDITOR.

probably of all then born had deserved best of mankind to be put to death as a criminal.

To pass from this to the only other instance of judicial iniquity, the mention of which, after the condemnation of Socrates, would not be an anticlimax: the event which took place on Calvary rather more than eighteen hundred years ago. The man who left on the memory of those who witnessed his life and conversation such an impression of his moral grandeur that eighteen subsequent centuries have done homage to him as the Almighty in person, was ignominiously put to death, as what? As a blasphemer. Men did not merely mistake their benefactor; they mistook him for the exact contrary of what he was, and treated him as that prodigy of impiety which they themselves are now held to be for their treatment of him. The feelings with which mankind now regard these lamentable transactions, especially the later of the two, render them extremely unjust in their judgment of the unhappy actors. These were, to all appearance, not bad men—not worse than men commonly are, but rather the contrary; men who possessed in a full, or somewhat more than a full measure, the religious, moral, and patriotic feelings of their time and people: the very kind of men who, in all times, our own included, have every chance of passing through life blameless and respected. The high-priest who rent his garments when the words were pronounced, which, according to all the ideas of his country, constituted the blackest guilt, was in all probability quite as sincere in his horror and indignation as the generality of respectable and pious men now are in the religious and moral sentiments they profess; and most of those who now shudder at his conduct, if they had lived in his time, and been born Jews, would have acted precisely as he did. Orthodox Christians who are tempted to think that those who stoned to death the first martyrs must have been worse men than they themselves are, ought to remember that one of those persecutors was Saint Paul.

Let us add one more example, the most striking of all, if the impressiveness of an error is measured by the wisdom and virtue of him who falls into it. If ever any one, possessed of power, had grounds for thinking himself the best and most enlightened among his contemporaries, it was the Emperor Marcus Aurelius. Absolute monarch of the whole civilized world, he preserved through life not only the most unblemished justice, but what was less to be expected from his Stoical breeding, the tenderest heart. The few failings which are attributed to him were all on the side of indulgence: while his writings, the highest ethical product of the ancient mind, differ scarcely perceptibly, if they differ at all, from the most characteristic teachings of Christ. This man, a better Christian in all but the dogmatic sense of the word than almost any of the ostensibly Christian sovereigns who have since reigned, persecuted Christianity. Placed at the summit of all the previous attainments of humanity, with an open, unfettered intellect, and a character which led him of himself to embody in his moral writings the Christian ideal, he yet failed to see that Christianity was to be a good and not an evil to the world, with his duties to which he was so deeply penetrated. Existing society he knew to be in a deplorable state. But such as it was, he saw, or thought he saw, that it was held together, and prevented from being worse, by belief and reverence of the received divinities. As a ruler of mankind, he deemed it his duty not to suffer society to fall in pieces; and saw not how, if its existing ties were removed, any others could be formed which could again knit it together. The new religion openly aimed at dissolving these ties: unless, therefore, it was his duty to adopt that religion, it seemed to be his duty to put it down. Inasmuch then as the theology of Christianity did not appear to him true or of divine origin; inasmuch as this strange history of a crucified God was not credible to him, and a system which purported to rest entirely upon a foundation to him so wholly unbelievable, could not be foreseen by him to be that renovating agency which, after all abatements, it has in fact proved to be; the gentlest and most amiable of philosophers and rulers, under a solemn sense of duty, authorized the persecution of Christianity. To my mind this is one of the most tragical facts in all history. It is a bitter thought, how different a thing the Christianity of the world might have been, if the Christian faith had been adopted as the religion of the empire under the auspices of Marcus Aurelius instead of those of Constantine. But it would be equally unjust to him and false to truth to deny, that no one plea which can be urged for punishing anti-Christian teaching was wanting to Marcus Aurelius for punishing, as he did, the propagation of Christianity. No Christian more firmly believes that Atheism is false, and tends to the dissolution of society, than Marcus Aurelius believed the same things of Christianity; he who, of all men then living, might have been thought the most capable of appreciating it. Unless any one who approves of punishment for the promulgation of opinions, flatters himself that he is a wiser and better man than Marcus Aurelius—more deeply versed in the wisdom of his time, more elevated in his intellect above it—

more earnest in his search for truth, or more single-minded in his devotion to it when found; let him abstain from that assumption of the joint infallibility of himself and the multitude, which the great Antoninus made with so unfortunate a result. [Pp. 86–88.]

*   *   *

But, indeed, the dictum that truth always triumphs over persecution is one of those pleasant falsehoods which men repeat after one another till they pass into commonplaces, but which all experience refutes. History teems with instances of truth put down by persecution. If not suppressed for ever, it may be thrown back for centuries. To speak only of religious opinions: the Reformation broke out at least twenty times before Luther, and was put down. Arnold of Brescia was put down. Fra Dolcino was put down. Savonarola was put down. The Albigeois were put down. The Vaudois were put down. The Lollards were put down. The Hussites were put down. Even after the era of Luther, wherever persecution was persisted in, it was successful. In Spain, Italy, Flanders, the Austrian empire, Protestantism was rooted out; and, most likely, would have been so in England, had Queen Mary lived, or Queen Elizabeth died. Persecution has always succeeded, save where the heretics were too strong a party to be effectually persecuted. No reasonable person can doubt that Christianity might have been extirpated in the Roman Empire. It spread, and became predominant, because the persecutions were only occasional, lasting but a short time, and separated by long intervals of almost undisturbed propagandism. It is a piece of idle sentimentality that truth, merely as truth, has any inherent power denied to error of prevailing against the dungeon and the stake. Men are not more zealous for truth than they often are for error, and a sufficient application of legal or even of social penalties will generally succeed in stopping the propagation of either. The real advantage which truth has consists in this, that when an opinion is true, it may be extinguished once, twice, or many times, but in the course of ages there will generally be found persons to rediscover it, until some one of its reappearances falls on a time when from favorable circumstances it escapes persecution until it has made such head as to withstand all subsequent attempts to suppress it. [Pp. 89–90.]

*   *   *

. . . Our merely social intolerance kills no one, roots out no opinions, but induces men to disguise them, or to abstain from any active effort for their diffusion. With us, heretical opinions do not perceptibly gain, or even lose, ground in each decade or generation; they never blaze out far and wide, but continue to smoulder in the narrow circles of thinking and studious persons among whom they originate, without ever lighting up the general affairs of mankind with either a true or a deceptive light. And thus is kept up a state of things very satisfactory to some minds, because, without the unpleasant process of fining or imprisoning anybody, it maintains all prevailing opinions outwardly undisturbed, while it does not absolutely interdict the exercise of reason by dissentients afflicted with the malady of thought. A convenient plan for having peace in the intellectual world, and keeping all things going on therein very much as they do already. But the price paid for this sort of intellectual pacification is the sacrifice of the entire moral courage of the human mind. A state of things in which a large portion of the most active and inquiring intellects find it advisable to keep the general principles and grounds of their convictions within their own breasts, and attempt, in what they address to the public, to fit as much as they can of their own conclusions to premises which they have internally renounced, cannot send forth the open, fearless characters, and logical, consistent intellects who once adorned the thinking world. The sort of men who can be looked for under it, are either mere conformers to common-place, or time-servers for truth, whose arguments on all great subjects are meant for their hearers, and are not those which have convinced themselves. Those who avoid this alternative, do so by narrowing their thoughts and interest to things which can be spoken of without venturing within the region of principles, that is, to small practical matters, which would come right of themselves, if but the minds of mankind were strengthened and enlarged, and which will never be made effectually right until then: while that which would strengthen and enlarge men's minds, free and daring speculation on the highest subjects, is abandoned. [Pp. 93–94.]

* * *

Never when controversy avoided the subjects which are large and important enough to kindle enthusiasm, was the mind of a people stirred up from its foundations, and the impulse given which raised even persons of the most ordinary intellect to something of the dignity of thinking beings. Of such we have had an example in the condition of Europe during the times immediately following the Reformation; another, though limited to the Continent and to a more cultivated class, in the speculative movement of the latter half of the eighteenth century; and a third, of still briefer duration, in the intellectual fermentation of Germany during the Goethean and Fichtean period. These periods differed widely in the particular opinions which they developed; but were alike in this, that during all three the yoke of authority was broken. In each, an old mental despotism had been thrown off, and no new one had yet taken its place. The impulse given at these three periods has made Europe what it now is. Every single improvement which has taken place either in the human mind or in institutions, may be traced distinctly to one or other of them. Appearances have for some time indicated that all three impulses are well nigh spent; and we can expect no fresh start until we again assert our mental freedom. [Pp. 94–95.]

*　*　*

He who lets the world, or his own portion of it, choose his plan of life for him, has no need of any other faculty than the ape-like one of imitation. He who chooses his plan for himself, employs all his faculties. He must use observation to see, reasoning and judgment to foresee, activity to gather materials for decision, discrimination to decide, and when he has decided, firmness and self-control to hold to his deliberate decision. And these qualities he requires and exercises exactly in proportion as the part of his conduct which he determines according to his own judgment and feelings is a large one. It is possible that he might be guided in some good path, and kept out of harm's way, without any of these things. But what will be his comparative worth as a human being? It really is of importance, not only what men do, but also what manner of men they are that do it. Among the works of man, which human life is rightly employed in perfecting and beautifying, the first in importance surely is man himself. Supposing it were possible to get houses built, corn grown, battles fought, causes tried, and even churches erected and prayers said, by machinery—by automatons in human form—it would be a considerable loss to exchange for these automatons even the men and women who at present inhabit the more civilized parts of the world, and who assuredly are but starved specimens of what nature can and will produce. Human nature is not a machine to be built after a model, and set to do exactly the work prescribed for it, but a tree, which requires to grow and develop itself on all sides, according to the tendency of the inward forces which make it a living thing.

It will probably be conceded that it is desirable people should exercise their understandings, and that an intelligent following of custom, or even occasionally an intelligent deviation from custom, is better than a blind and simply mechanical adhesion to it. To a certain extent it is admitted that our understanding should be our own: but there is not the same willingness to admit that our desires and impulses should be our own likewise; or that to possess impulses of our own, and of any strength, is anything but a peril and a snare. Yet desires and impulses are as much a part of a perfect human being as beliefs and restraints: and strong impulses are only perilous when not properly balanced; when one set of aims and inclinations is developed into strength, while others, which ought to co-exist with them, remain weak and inactive. It is not because men's desires are strong that they act ill; it is because their consciences are weak. There is no natural connection between strong impulses and a weak conscience. The natural connection is the other way. To say that one person's desires and feelings are stronger and more various than those of another, is merely to say that he has more of the raw material of human nature, and is therefore capable, perhaps of more evil, but certainly of more good. Strong impulses are but another name for energy. Energy may be turned to bad uses; but more good may always be made of an energetic nature, than of an indolent and impassive one. Those who have most natural feeling are always those whose cultivated feelings may be made the strongest. The same strong susceptibilities which make the personal impulses vivid and powerful, are also the source from whence are generated the most passionate love of virtue, and the sternest self-control. It is through the cultivation of these that society both does its duty and protects its interests: not by rejecting the stuff of which heroes are made, because it knows not how to make them. A person whose desires and impulses are his own—are the expression of his own nature, as it has been developed and modified by his own culture—is said to have a character. One whose desires and impulses are not his own, has no character, no more than a steam-engine has a character. If, in addition to being his own, his impulses are strong, and are under the government of a strong will, he has an energetic character. Whoever thinks that individuality of desires and impulses should not be encouraged to unfold itself, must maintain that society has no need of strong natures—is not the better for containing many persons who have much character—and that a high general average of energy is not desirable. [Pp. 117–118.]

*   *   *

It is not by wearing down into uniformity all that is individual in themselves, but by cultivating it, and calling it forth, within the limits imposed by the rights and interests of others, that human beings become a noble and beautiful object of contemplation; and as the works partake the character of those who do them, by the same process human life also becomes rich, diversified, and animating, furnishing more abundant aliment to high thoughts and elevating feelings, and strengthening the tie which binds every individual to the race, by making the race infinitely better worth belonging to. In proportion to the development of his individuality, each person becomes more valuable to himself, and is therefore capable of being more valuable to others. There is a greater fulness of life about his own existence, and when there is more life in the units there is more in the mass which is composed of them. As much compression as is necessary to prevent the stronger specimens of human nature from encroaching on the rights of others cannot be dispensed with; but for this there is ample compensation even in the point of view of human development. The means of development which the individual loses by being prevented from gratifying his inclinations to the injury of others, are chiefly obtained at the expense of the development of other people. And even to himself there is a full equivalent in the better development of the social part of his nature, rendered possible by the restraint put upon the selfish part. To be held to rigid rules of justice for the sake of others, develops the feelings and capacities which have the good of others for their object. But to be restrained in things not affecting their good, by their mere displeasure, develops nothing valuable, except such force of character as may unfold itself in resisting the restraint. If acquiesced in, it dulls and blunts the whole nature. To give any fair play to the nature of each, it is essential that different persons should be allowed to lead different lives. In proportion as this latitude has been exercised in any age, has that age been noteworthy to posterity. Even despotism does not produce its worst effects, so long as individuality exists under it; and whatever crushes individuality is despotism, by whatever name it may be called, and whether it professes to be enforcing the will of God or the injunctions of men. [Pp. 120–121.]

* * *

. . . No government by a democracy or a numerous aristocracy, either in its political acts or in the opinions, qualities, and tone of mind which it fosters, ever did or could rise above mediocrity, except in so far as the sovereign Many have let themselves be guided (which in their best times they always have done) by the counsels and influence of a more highly gifted and instructed One or Few. The initiation of all wise or noble things comes and must come from individuals; generally at first from some one individual. The honor and glory of the average man is that he is capable of following that initiative; that he can respond internally to wise and noble things, and be led to them with his eyes open. I am not countenancing the sort of "hero-worship" which applauds the strong man of genius for forcibly seizing on the government of the world and making it do his bidding in spite of itself. All he can claim is, freedom to point out the way. The power of compelling others into it is not only inconsistent with the freedom and development of all the rest, but corrupting to the strong man himself. [P. 124.]

* * *

. . . M. de Tocqueville, in his last important work, remarks how much more the Frenchmen of the present day resemble one another than did those even of the last generation. The same remark might be made of Englishmen in a far greater degree. In a passage already quoted from Wilhelm von Humboldt, he points out two things as necessary conditions of human development, because necessary to render people unlike one another; namely, freedom, and variety of situations. The second of these two conditions is in this country every day diminishing. The circumstances which surround different classes and individuals, and shape their characters, are daily becoming more assimilated. Formerly, different ranks, different neighborhoods, different trades and professions, lived in what might be called different worlds; at present to a great degree in the same. Comparatively speaking, they now read the same things, listen to the same things, see the same things, go to the same places, have their hopes and fears directed to the same objects, have the same rights and liberties, and the same means of asserting them. Great as are the differences of position which remain, they are nothing to those which have ceased. And the assimilation is still proceeding. All the political changes of the age promote it, since they all tend to raise the low and to lower the high. Every extension of education promotes it, because education brings people under common influences, and gives them access to the general stock of facts and sentiments. Improvement in the means of communication promotes it, by bringing the inhabitants of distant places into personal contact, and keeping up a rapid flow of changes of residence between one place and another. The increase of commerce and manufactures promotes it, by diffusing more widely the advantages of easy circumstances, and opening all objects of ambition, even the highest, to general competition, whereby the desire of rising becomes no longer the character of a particular class, but of all classes. A more powerful agency than even all these, in bringing about a general similarity among mankind, is the complete establishment, in this and other free countries, of the ascendancy of public opinion in the State. As the various social eminences which enabled persons entrenched on them to disregard the opinion of the multitude gradually become leveled; as the very idea of resisting the will of the public, when it is positively known that they have a will, disappears more and more from the minds of practical politicians; there ceases to be any social support for nonconformity—any substantive power in society which, itself opposed to the ascendancy of numbers, is interested in taking under its protection opinions and tendencies ·at variance with those of the public.

The combination of all these causes forms so great a mass of influences hostile to Individuality, that it is not easy to see how it can stand its ground. It will do so with increasing difficulty, unless the intelligent part of the public can be made to feel its value—to see that it is good there should be differences, even though not for the better, even though, as it may appear to them, some should be for the worse. If the claims of Individuality are ever to be asserted, the time is now, while much is still wanting to complete the enforced assimilation. It is only in the earlier stages that any stand can be successfully made against the encroachment. The demand that all other people shall resemble ourselves grows by what it feeds on. If resistance waits till life is reduced *nearly* to one uniform type, all deviations from that type will come to be considered impious, immoral, even monstrous and contrary to nature. Mankind speedily become unable to conceive diversity, when they have been for some time unaccustomed to see it. [Pp. 130–131.]

* * *

In this age, the mere example of non-conformity, the mere refusal to bend the knee to custom, is itself a service. Precisely because the tyranny of opinion is such as to make eccentricity a reproach, it is desirable, in order to break through that tyranny, that people should be eccentric. Eccentricity has always abounded when and where strength of character has abounded; and the amount of eccentricity in a society has generally been proportional to the amount of genius, mental vigor, and moral courage it contained. That so few now dare to be eccentric marks the chief danger of the time. [Pp. 124–125.]

* * *

[After stating some objections to government interference, Mill continues:] The third and most cogent reason for restricting the interference of government is the great evil of adding unnecessarily to its power. Every function superadded to those already exercised by the government causes its influence over hopes and fears to be more widely diffused, and converts, more and more, the active and ambitious part of the public into hangers-on of the government, or of some party which aims at becoming the government. If the roads, the railways, the banks, the insurance offices, the great joint-stock companies, the universities, and the public charities, were all of them branches of the government; if, in addition, the municipal corporations and local boards, with all that now devolves on them, became departments of the central administration; if the employés of all these different enterprises were appointed and paid by the government, and looked to the government for every rise in life; not all the freedom of the press and popular constitution of the legislature would make this or any other country free otherwise than in name. And the evil would be greater, the more efficiently and scientifically the administrative machinery was constructed—the more skilful the arrangements for obtaining the best qualified hands and heads with which to work it. In England it has of late been proposed that all the members of the civil service of government should be selected by competitive examination, to obtain for these employments the most intelligent and instructed persons procurable;

and much has been said and written for and against this proposal. One of the arguments most insisted on by its opponents is that the occupation of a permanent official servant of the State does not hold out sufficient prospects of emolument and importance to attract the highest talents, which will always be able to find a more inviting career in the professions, or in the service of companies and other public bodies. One would not have been surprised if this argument had been used by the friends of the proposition, as an answer to its principal difficulty. Coming from the opponents it is strange enough. What is urged as an objection is the safety-valve of the proposed system. If indeed all the high talent of the country *could* be drawn into the service of the government, a proposal tending to bring about that result might well inspire uneasiness. If every part of the business of society which required organized concert, or large and comprehensive views, were in the hands of the government, and if government offices were universally filled by the ablest men, all the enlarged culture and practised intelligence in the country, except the purely speculative, would be concentrated in a numerous bureaucracy, to whom alone the rest of the community would look for all things: the multitude for direction and dictation in all they had to do; the able and aspiring for personal advancement. To be admitted into the ranks of this bureaucracy, and when admitted, to rise therein, would be the sole objects of ambition. Under this *régime,* not only is the outside public ill-qualified, for want of practical experience, to criticize or check the mode of operation of the bureaucracy, but even if the accidents of despotic or the natural working of popular institutions occasionally raise to the summit a ruler or rulers of reforming inclinations, no reform can be effected which is contrary to the interest of the bureaucracy. Such is the melancholy condition of the Russian empire, as shown in the accounts of those who have had sufficient opportunity of observation. The Czar himself is powerless against the bureaucratic body; he can send any one of them to Siberia, but he cannot govern without them, or against their will. On every decree of his they have a tacit veto, by merely refraining from carrying it into effect. In countries of more advanced civilization and of a more insurrectionary spirit, the public, accustomed to expect everything to be done for them by the State, or at least to do nothing for themselves without asking from the State not only leave to do it, but even how it is to be done, naturally hold the State responsible for all evil which befalls them, and when the evil exceeds their amount of patience, they rise against the government, and make what is called a revolution; whereupon somebody else, with or without legitimate authority from the nation, vaults into the seat, issues his orders to the bureaucracy, and everything goes on much as it did before; the bureaucracy being unchanged, and nobody else being capable of taking their place.

A very different spectacle is exhibited among a people accustomed to transact their own business. In France, a large part of the people, having been engaged in military service, many of whom have held at least the rank of non-commissioned officers, there are in every popular insurrection several persons competent to take the lead, and improvise some tolerable plan of action. What the French are in military affairs, the Americans are in every kind of civil business; let them be left without a government, every body of Americans is able to improvise one, and to carry on that or any other public business with a sufficient amount of intelligence, order, and decision. This is what every free people ought to be: and a people capable of this is certain to be free; it will never let itself be enslaved by any man or body of men because these are able to seize and pull the reins of the central administration. No bureaucracy can hope to make such a people as this do or undergo anything that they do not like. But where everything is done through the bureaucracy, nothing to which the bureaucracy is really adverse can be done at all. The constitution of such countries is an organization of the experience and practical ability of the nation into a disciplined body for the purpose of governing the rest; and the more perfect that organization is in itself, the more successful in drawing to itself and educating for itself the persons of greatest capacity from all ranks of the community, the more complete is the bondage of all, the members of the bureaucracy included. For the governors are as much the slaves of their organization and discipline as the governed are of the governors. [Pp. 165–167.]

10

LINCOLN'S AMERICANISM

[Abraham Lincoln (1809–1865) expressed American ideals primarily in his life and policies. But in some of his utterances he gave classic expression to the spiritual side of American nationalism. In November, 1863, he spoke at the dedication of a soldiers' cemetery at Gettysburg, where the furthest northern advance of the Confederacy had been repulsed in the preceding July. In March, 1865, having been reëlected to the presidency after a difficult campaign in the midst of civil war, he delivered his Second Inaugural Address. These addresses contain no word of hate for the South, but stress the preservation of popular government and the restoration of national unity.]

The Gettysburg Address *

Fourscore and seven years ago our fathers brought forth upon this continent a new nation, conceived in liberty, and dedicated to the proposition that all men are created equal.

Now we are engaged in a great civil war, testing whether that nation, or any nation so conceived and so dedicated, can long endure. We are met on a great battle-field of that war. We have come to dedicate a portion of that field as a final resting-place for those who here gave their lives that that nation might live. It is altogether fitting and proper that we should do this.

But in a larger sense we cannot dedicate, we cannot consecrate, we cannot hallow this ground. The brave men, living and dead, who struggled here, have consecrated it far above our power to add or detract. The world will little note nor long remember what we say here, but it can never forget what they did here. It is for us, the living, rather, to be dedicated here to the unfinished work which they who fought here have thus far so

---

* From *The Speeches of Abraham Lincoln*, Everyman edition, E. P. Dutton and Company, Inc.

nobly advanced. It is rather for us to be here dedicated to the great task remaining before us; that from these honored dead we take increased devotion to that cause for which they gave the last full measure of devotion; that we here highly resolve that these dead shall not have died in vain; that this nation, under God, shall have a new birth of freedom; and that government of the people, by the people, and for the people, shall not perish from the earth.

Lincoln's Second Inaugural Address *

Fellow-Countrymen: At this second appearing to take the oath of the Presidential office, there is less occasion for an extended address than there was at first. Then, a statement, somewhat in detail, of a course to be pursued, seemed fitting and proper. Now, at the expiration of four years, during which public declarations have been constantly called forth on every point and phase of the great contest which still absorbs the attention and engrosses the energies of the nation, little that is new could be presented. The progress of our arms, upon which all else chiefly depends, is as well known to the public as to myself; and it is, I trust, reasonably satisfactory and encouraging to all. With high hope for the future, no prediction in regard to it is ventured.

On the occasion corresponding to this four years ago, all thoughts were anxiously directed to an impending civil war. All dreaded it—all sought to avert it. While the inaugural address was being delivered from this place, devoted altogether to saving the Union without war, insurgent agents were in the city seeking to destroy it without war—seeking to dissolve the Union, and divide effects, by negotiation. Both parties deprecated war; but one of them would make war rather than let the nation survive; and the other would accept war rather than let it perish. And the war came.

One-eighth of the whole population were colored slaves, not distributed generally over the Union, but localized in the Southern part of it. These slaves constituted a peculiar and powerful interest. All knew that this interest was, somehow, the cause of the war. To strengthen, perpetuate, and extend this interest was the object for which the insurgents would rend the Union, even by war; while the Government claimed no right to do more than to restrict the territorial enlargement of it. Neither party expected for the war the magnitude or the duration which it has already attained. Neither anticipated that the cause of the conflict might cease with, or even

* From the Harvard Classics, Vol. 43, P. F. Collier & Son Co.

before, the conflict itself should cease. Each looked for an easier triumph, and a result less fundamental and astounding. Both read the same Bible, and pray to the same God; and each invokes his aid against the other. It may seem strange that any men should dare to ask a just God's assistance in wringing their bread from the sweat of other men's faces; but let us judge not, that we be not judged. The prayers of both could not be answered—that of neither has been answered fully. The Almighty has his own purposes. "Woe unto the world because of offenses! for it must needs be that offenses come; but woe to that man by whom the offense cometh." If we shall suppose that American slavery is one of those offenses which, in the providence of God, must needs come, but which, having continued through his appointed time, he now wills to remove, and that he gives to both North and South this terrible war, as the woe due to those by whom the offense came, shall we discern therein any departure from those divine attributes which the believers in a living God always ascribe to him? Fondly do we hope—fervently do we pray—that this mighty scourge of war may speedily pass away. Yet, if God wills that it continue until all the wealth piled by the bondman's two hundred and fifty years of unrequited toil shall be sunk, and until every drop of blood drawn with the lash shall be paid by another drawn with the sword, as was said three thousand years ago, so still it must be said: "The judgments of the Lord are true and righteous altogether."

With malice toward none; with charity for all; with firmness in the right, as God gives us to see the right, let us strive on to finish the work we are in; to bind up the nation's wounds; to care for him who shall have borne the battle, and for his widow, and his orphan—to do all which may achieve and cherish a just and lasting peace among ourselves, and with all nations.

11

WHITMAN ON THE PROSPECTS OF DEMOCRACY

[Walt Whitman (1819–1892) was a newspaper man and editorial writer in Brooklyn in the 1840's and 1850's. The first edition of his *Leaves of Grass* appeared in 1855. In later editions, many new poems were added. For a time during the Civil War he served in hospitals caring for wounded soldiers. In the later 1860's he became a clerk in the office of the Attorney-General in Washington.

Referring to him as a poet of democracy, Thomas Mann says (in *The Coming Victory of Democracy*), "The world has probably never produced a master of words who has known so well as Whitman how to elevate and translate a social principle into intoxicating song, or how to endow it with such powerful emotional content, representing a magnificent fusion of spirituality and sensuousness."

Whitman's *Democratic Vistas* (1871), like his poems, unites sympathy for individual Americans as he finds them, faith in political and social democracy, and a grandiose vision of the future of these States.]

Democratic Vistas *

As the greatest lessons of Nature through the universe are perhaps the lessons of variety and freedom, the same present the greatest lessons also in New World politics and progress. If a man were asked, for instance, the distinctive points contrasting modern European and American political and other life with the old Asiatic cultus, as lingering-bequeathed yet in China and Turkey, he might find the amount of them in John Stuart Mill's profound essay on Liberty in the future, where he demands two main constituents, or sub-strata, for a truly grand nationality—1st, a large variety of character—and 2nd, full play for human nature to expand itself in numberless and even conflicting directions—(seems to be for general humanity much like the influences that make up, in their limit-

* From the Everyman edition of *Leaves of Grass and Democratic Vistas*, E. P. Dutton and Company, Inc.

less field, that perennial health-action of the air we call the weather—
an infinite number of currents and forces, and contributions, and tem-
peratures, and cross purposes, whose ceaseless play of counterpart upon
counterpart brings constant restoration and vitality). With this thought—
and not for itself alone, but all it necessitates, and draws after it—let me
begin my speculations. [P. 301.]

* * *

. . . I will not gloss over the appalling dangers of universal suffrage in
the United States. In fact, it is to admit and face these dangers I am writing. To him or her within whose thought rages the battle, advancing,
retreating, between democracy's convictions, aspirations, and the people's
crudeness, vice, caprices, I mainly write this essay. I shall use the words
America and democracy as convertible terms. Not an ordinary one is the
issue. The United States are destined either to surmount the gorgeous
history of feudalism, or else prove the most tremendous failure of time.
Not the least doubtful am I on any prospects of their material success.
The triumphant future of their business, geographic and productive
departments, on larger scales and in more varieties than ever, is certain.
In those respects the republic must soon (if she does not already) outstrip
all examples hitherto afforded, and dominate the world. [P. 302.]

* * *

Admitting all this, with the priceless value of our political institutions,
general suffrage (and fully acknowledging the latest, widest opening of
the doors), I say that, far deeper than these, what finally and only is to
make of our western world a nationality superior to any hither known,
and outtopping the past, must be vigorous, yet unsuspected Literatures,
perfect personalities and sociologies, original, transcendental, and expressing (what, in highest sense, are not yet expressed at all) democracy and
the modern. With these, and out of these, I promulgate new races of
Teachers, and of perfect Women, indispensable to endow the birth-stock
of a New World. For feudalism, caste, the ecclesiastic traditions, though
palpably retreating from political institutions, still hold essentially, by their
spirit, even in this country, entire possession of the more important fields,
indeed the very subsoil, of education, and of social standards and literature.

I say that democracy can never prove itself beyond cavil, until it

founds and luxuriantly grows its own forms of art, poems, schools, theology, displacing all that exists, or that has been produced anywhere in the
past, under opposite influences. . . . For know you not, dear, earnest
reader, that the people of our land may all read and write, and may all
possess the right to vote—and yet the main things may be entirely lacking?
—(and this to suggest them).

Viewed, to-day, from a point of view sufficiently over-arching, the problem of humanity all over the civilized world is social and religious, and is
to be finally met and treated by literature. The priest departs, the divine
literatus comes. Never was anything more wanted than, to-day, and here
in the States, the poet of the modern is wanted, or the great literatus of
the modern. At all times, perhaps, the central point in any nation, and
that whence it is itself really swayed the most, and whence it sways others,
is its national literature, especially its archetypal poems. Above all previous lands, a great original literature is surely to become the justification
and reliance (in some respects the sole reliance) of American democracy.

Few are aware how the great literature penetrates all, gives hue to all,
shapes aggregates and individuals, and, after subtle ways, with irresistible
power, constructs, sustains, demolishes at will. Why tower, in reminis-
cence, above all the nations of the earth, two special lands, petty in themselves, yet inexpressibly gigantic, beautiful, columnar? Immortal Judah
lives, and Greece immortal lives, in a couple of poems. [Pp. 303–304.]

*   *   *

. . . Painting, sculpture, and the dramatic theater, it would seem, no
longer play an indispensable or even important part in the workings and
mediumship of intellect, utility, or even high esthetics. Architecture remains, doubtless with capacities, and a real future. Then music, the com-
biner, nothing more spiritual, nothing more sensuous, a god, yet completely human, advances, prevails, holds highest place; supplying in certain
wants and quarters what nothing else could supply. Yet in the civilization
of to-day it is undeniable that, over all the arts, literature dominates, serves
beyond all—shapes the character of church and school—or, at any rate, is
capable of doing so. Including the literature of science, its scope is indeed
unparalleled.

Before proceeding further, it were perhaps well to discriminate on certain points. Literature tills its crops in many fields, and some may flourish,
while others lag. What I say in these Vistas has its main bearing on

imaginative literature, especially poetry, the stock of all. In the department
of science, and the specialty of journalism, there appear, in these States,
promises, perhaps fulfilments, of highest earnestness, reality and life.
These, of course, are modern. But in the region of imaginative, spinal
and essential attributes, something equivalent to creation is, for our age
and lands, imperatively demanded. For not only is it not enough that the
new blood, new frame of democracy shall be vivified and held together
merely by political means, superficial suffrage, legislation, etc., but it is
clear to me that, unless it goes deeper, gets at least as firm and as warm
a hold in men's hearts, emotions and belief, as, in their days, feudalism
or ecclesiasticism, and inaugurates its own perennial sources, welling from
the center for ever, its strength will be defective, its growth doubtful, and
its main charm wanting. [P. 306.]

* * *

For my part, I would alarm and caution even the political and business
reader, and to the utmost extent, against the prevailing delusion that the
establishment of free political institutions, and plentiful intellectual smart-
ness, with general good order, physical plenty, industry, etc. (desirable and
precious advantages as they all are), do, of themselves, determine and
yield to our experiment of democracy the fruitage of success. With such
advantages at present fully, or almost fully, possessed—the Union just
issued, victorious, from the struggle with the only foes it need ever
fear (namely, those within itself, the interior ones), and with unprece-
dented materialistic advancement—society, in these States, is cankered,
crude, superstitious and rotten. Political, or law-made society is, and private, or voluntary society, is also. In any vigor, the element of the moral
conscience, the most important, the verteber to State or man, seems to me
either entirely lacking, or seriously enfeebled or ungrown. [P. 308.]

* * *

Let me illustrate further, as I write, with current observations, localities,
etc. The subject is important, and will bear repetition. After an absence,
I am now again (September, 1870) in New York city and Brooklyn, on
a few weeks' vacation. The splendor, picturesqueness, and oceanic ampli-
tude and rush of these great cities, the unsurpassed situation, rivers and
bay, sparkling sea-tides, costly and lofty new buildings, façades of marble
and iron, of original grandeur and elegance of design, with the masses of

gay color, the preponderance of white and blue, the flags flying, the end-less ships, the tumultuous streets, Broadway, the heavy, low, musical roar, hardly ever intermitted, even at night; the jobbers' houses, the rich shops, the wharves, the great Central Park, and the Brooklyn Park of hills (as I wander among them this beautiful fall weather, musing, watching, absorb-ing)—the assemblages of the citizens in their groups, conversations, trades, evening amusements, or along the by-quarters—these, I say, and the like of these, completely satisfy my senses of power, fulness, motion, etc., and give me, through such senses and appetites, and through my esthetic conscience, a continued exaltation and absolute fulfilment. Always and more and more, as I cross the East and North rivers, the ferries, or with the pilots in their pilot-houses, or pass an hour in Wall Street, or the Gold Exchange, I realize (if we must admit such partialisms) that not Nature alone is great in her fields of freedom and the open air, in her storms, the shows of night and day, the mountains, forests, seas—but in the artificial, the work of man too is equally great—in this profusion of teeming humanity—in these ingenuities, streets, goods, houses, ships—these hurrying, feverish, electric crowds of men, their complicated business genius (not least among the geniuses), and all this mighty, many-threaded wealth and industry concentrated here.

But sternly discarding, shutting our eyes to the glow and grandeur of the general superficial effect, coming down to what is of the only real importance, Personalities, and examining minutely, we question, we ask, Are there, indeed, *men* here worthy the name? Are there athletes? Are there perfect women, to match the generous material luxuriance? Is there a pervading atmosphere of beautiful manners? Are there crops of fine youths, and majestic old persons? Are there arts worthy freedom and a rich people? Is there a great moral and religious civilization—the only justification of a great material one? Confess that to severe eyes, using the moral microscope upon humanity, a sort of dry and flat Sahara ap-pears, these cities, crowded with petty grotesques, malformations, phan-toms, playing meaningless antics. Confess that everywhere, in shop, street, church, theater, bar-room, official chair, are pervading flippancy and vulgarity, low cunning, infidelity—everywhere the youth puny, impu-dent, foppish, prematurely ripe—everywhere an abnormal libidinousness, unhealthy forms, male, female, painted, padded, dyed, chignoned, muddy complexions, bad blood, the capacity for good motherhood decreasing or deceased, shallow notions of beauty, with a range of manners, or rather lack of manners (considering the advantages enjoyed), probably the meanest to be seen in the world. [Pp. 309–310.]

*   *   *

The political history of the past may be summed up as having grown out of what underlies the words, order, safety, caste, and especially out of the need of some prompt deciding authority, and of cohesion at all cost. Leaping time, we come to the period within the memory of people now living, when, as from some lair where they had slumbered long, accumulating wrath, sprang up and are yet active (1790, and on even to the present, 1870), those noisy eructations, destructive iconoclasms, a fierce sense of wrongs, amid which moves the form, well known in modern history, in the old world, stained with much blood, and marked by savage reactionary clamors and demands. These bear, mostly, as on one inclosing point of need.

For after the rest is said—after the many time-honored and really true things for subordination, experience, rights of property, etc., have been listened to and acquiesced in—after the valuable and well-settled statement of our duties and relations in society is thoroughly conned over and exhausted—it remains to bring forward and modify everything else with the idea of that Something a man is (last precious consolation of the drudging poor), standing apart from all else, divine in his own right, and a woman in hers, sole and untouchable by any canons of authority, or any rule derived from precedent, state-safety, the acts of legislatures, or even from what is called religion, modesty, or art. The radiation of this truth is the key of the most significant doings of our immediately preceding three centuries, and has been the political genesis and life of America. Advancing visibly, it still more advances invisibly. Underneath the fluctuations of the expressions of society, as well as the movements of the politics of the leading nations of the world, we see steadily pressing ahead and strengthening itself, even in the midst of immense tendencies toward aggregation, this image of completeness in separation, of individual personal dignity, of a single person, either male or female, characterized in the main, not from extrinsic acquirements or position, but in the pride of himself or herself alone; and, as an eventual conclusion and summing up (or else the entire scheme of things is aimless, a cheat, a crash), the simple idea that the last, best dependence is to be upon humanity itself, and its own inherent, normal, full-grown qualities without any superstitious support whatever.

This idea of perfect individualism it is indeed that deepest tinges and gives character to the idea of the aggregate. For it is mainly or altogether to serve independent separatism that we favor a strong generalization, consolidation. As it is to give the best vitality and freedom to the rights of the States (every bit as important as the right of nationality, the union), that we insist on the identity of the Union at all hazards. [Pp. 312–313.]

*   *   *

Literature, strictly considered, has never recognized the People, and, whatever may be said, does not to-day. Speaking generally, the tendencies of literature, as hitherto pursued, have been to make mostly critical and querulous men. It seems as if, so far, there were some natural repugnance between a literary and professional life, and the rude rank spirit of the democracies. There is, in later literature, a treatment of benevolence, a charity business, rife enough it is true; but I know nothing more rare, even in this country, than a fit scientific estimate and reverent appreciation of the People —of their measureless wealth of latent power and capacity, their vast, artistic contrasts of lights and shades—with, in America, their entire reliability in emergencies, and a certain breadth of historic grandeur, of peace or war, far surpassing all the vaunted samples of book-heroes, or any *haut ton* coteries, in all the records of the world.

The movements of the late secession war, and their results, to any sense that studies well and comprehends them, show that popular democracy, whatever its faults and dangers, practically justifies itself beyond the proudest claims and wildest hopes of its enthusiasts. Probably no future age can know, but I well know, how the gist of this fiercest and most resolute of the world's war-like contentions resided exclusively in the unnamed, unknown rank and file; and how the brunt of its labor of death was, to all essential purposes, volunteered. The People, of their own choice, fighting, dying for their own idea, insolently attacked by the secession-slave-power, and its very existence imperiled. Descending to detail, entering any of the armies, and mixing with the private soldiers, we see and have seen august spectacles. We have seen the alacrity with which the American-born populace, the peaceablest and most good-natured race in the world, and the most personally independent and intelligent, and the least fitted to submit to the irksomeness and exasperation of regimental discipline, sprang, at the first tap of the drum, to arms—not for gain, nor even glory, nor to repel invasion—but for an emblem, a mere abstraction—for the life, *the safety of the flag*. We have seen the unequaled docility and obedience of these soldiers. We have seen them tried long and long by hopelessness, mismanagement, and by defeat; have seen the incredible slaughter toward or through which the armies (as first at Fredericksburg, and afterward at the Wilderness), still unhesitatingly obey'd orders to advance. We have seen them in trench, or crouching behind breastwork, or tramping in deep mud, or amid pouring rain or thick-falling snow, or under forced marches in hottest summer (as on the road to get to Gettysburg)—vast suffocating swarms, divisions, corps, with every single man so grimed and black with sweat and dust, his own mother would not have known him—his clothes all dirty, stained and torn, with sour, accumulated sweat for perfume—many a comrade, perhaps a brother, sun-struck, staggering out, dying, by the roadside, of exhaustion—yet the great bulk bearing steadily on, cheery enough, hollow bellied from hunger, but sinewy with unconquerable resolution.

We have seen this race proved by wholesale, by drearier, yet more fearful tests—the wound, the amputation, the shattered face or limb, the slow hot fever, long impatient anchorage in bed, and all the forms of maiming, operation, and disease. Alas! America have we seen, though only in her early youth, already to hospital brought. There have we watched these soldiers, many of them only boys in years—marked their decorum, their religious nature and fortitude, and their sweet affection. Wholesale, truly. For at the front, and through the camps, in countless tents, stood the regimental, brigade, and division hospitals; while everywhere amid the land, in or near cities, rose clusters of huge, white-washed, crowded, one-story wooden barracks; and there ruled agony with bitter scourge, yet seldom brought a cry; and there stalked death by day and night along the narrow aisles between the rows of cots, or by the blankets on the ground, and touched lightly many a poor sufferer, often with blessed, welcome touch. [Pp. 314–316.]

*   *   *

. . . We believe the ulterior object of political and all other government (having, of course, provided for the police, the safety of life, property, and for the basic statute and common law, and their administration, always first in order), to be among the rest, not merely to rule, to repress disorder, etc., but to develop, to open up to cultivation, to encourage the possibilities of all beneficent and manly outcroppage, and of that aspiration for independence, and the pride and self-respect latent in all characters. (Or, if there be exceptions, we cannot, fixing our eyes on them alone, make theirs the rule for all.)

I say the mission of government, henceforth, in civilized lands, is not repression alone, and not authority alone, not even of law, nor by that favorite standard of the eminent writer, the rule of the best men, the born heroes and captains of the race (as if such ever, or one time out of a hundred, get into the big places, elective or dynastic)—but higher than the highest arbitrary rule, to train communities through all their grades, beginning with individuals and ending there again, to rule themselves. [P. 317.]

*   *   *

. . . To be a voter with the rest is not so much; and this, like every institute, will have its imperfections. But to become an enfranchised man, and now, impediments removed, to stand and start without humiliation, and equal with the rest; to commence, or have the road cleared to commence, the grand experiment of development, whose end (perhaps requiring several generations), may be the forming of a full-grown man or woman—that *is* something. To ballast the State is also secured, and in our times is to be secured, in no other way.

We do not (at any rate I do not), put it either on the ground that the People, the masses, even the best of them, are, in their latent or exhibited qualities, essentially sensible and good—nor on the ground of their rights; but that good or bad, rights or no rights, the democratic formula is the only safe and preservative one for coming times. [P. 318.]

*   *   *

And, topping democracy, this most alluring record, that it alone can bind, and ever seeks to bind, all nations, all men, of however various and distant lands, into a brotherhood, a family. It is the old, yet ever-modern dream of earth, out of her eldest and her youngest, her fond philosophers and poets. Not that half only, individualism, which isolates. There is another half, which is adhesiveness or love, that fuses, ties, and aggregates, making the races comrades, and fraternizing all. Both are to be vitalized by religion (sole worthiest elevator of man or State), breathing into the proud, material tissues, the breath of life. For I say at the core of democracy, finally, is the religious element. All the religions, old and new, are there. Nor may the scheme step forth, clothed in resplendent beauty and command, till these, bearing the best, the latest fruit, the spiritual, shall fully appear.

The true gravitation-hold of liberalism in the United States will be a more universal ownership of property, general homesteads, general comfort—a vast, inter-twining reticulation of wealth. As the human frame, or, indeed, any object in this manifold universe, is best kept together by the simple miracle of its own cohesion, and the necessity, exercise, and profit thereof, so a great and varied nationality, occupying millions of square miles, were firmest held and knit by the principle of the safety and endurance of the aggregate of its middling property owners. So that, from another point of view, ungracious as it may sound, and a paradox after what we have been saying, democracy looks with suspicious, ill-satisfied eye upon the very poor, the ignorant, and on those out of business. She asks for men and women with occupations, well-off, owners of houses and acres, and with cash in the bank —and with some cravings for literature, too; and must have them, and hastens to make them. Luckily, the seed is already well-sown, and has taken ineradicable root.

[Whitman adds the following paragraph as a note:] For fear of mistake, I may as well distinctly specify, as cheerfully included in the model and standard of these Vistas, a practical, stirring, worldly, money-making, even materialistic character. It is undeniable that our farms, stores, offices, dry-goods, coal and groceries, enginery, cash-accounts, trades, earnings, markets, etc., should be attended to in earnest, and actively pursued, just as if they had a real and permanent existence. I perceive clearly that the extreme business energy, and this almost maniacal appetite for wealth prevalent in the United States, are parts of amelioration and progress, indispensably needed to prepare the very results I demand. My theory includes riches, and the getting of riches, and the amplest products, power, activity, inventions, movements, etc. Upon them, as upon substrata, I raise the edifice designed in these Vistas. [Pp. 319–321.]

* * *

Political democracy, as it exists and practically works in America, with all its threatening evils, supplies a training-school for making first-class men. It is life's gymnasium, not of good only, but of all. We try often, though we fall back often. A brave delight, fit for freedom's athletes, fills these arenas, and fully satisfies, out of the action in them, irrespective of success. Whatever we do not attain, we at any rate attain the experiences of the fight, the hardening of the strong campaign, and throb with currents of attempt at least. Time is ample. Let the victors come after us. Not for nothing does evil play its part among us. Judging from the main portions of the history of the world, so far, justice is always in jeopardy, peace walks amid hourly pitfalls, and of slavery, misery, meanness, the craft of tyrants and the credulity of the populace, in some of their protean forms, no voice can at any time say, They are not. The clouds break a little, and the sun shines out—but soon and certain the lowering darkness falls again, as if to last for ever. Yet is there an immortal courage and prophecy in every sane soul that cannot, must not, under any circumstances, capitulate. *Vive,* the attack—the perennial assault! *Vive,* the unpopular cause—the spirit that audaciously aims—the never-abandoned efforts, pursued the same amid opposing proofs and precedents. [P. 322.]

*   *   *

Did you, too, O friend, suppose democracy was only for elections, for politics, and for a party name? I say democracy is only of use there that it may pass on and come to its flower and fruits in manners, in the highest forms of interaction between men, and their beliefs—in religion, literature, colleges, and schools—democracy in all public and private life, and in the army and navy.

[Whitman adds the following paragraph as a note:] The whole present system of the officering and *personnel* of the army and navy of these States, and the spirit and letter of their trebly-aristocratic rules and regulations, is a monstrous exotic, a nuisance and revolt, and belong here just as much as orders of nobility, or the Pope's council of cardinals. I say if the present theory of our army and navy is sensible and true, then the rest of America is an unmitigated fraud. [P. 325.]

*   *   *

America has yet morally and artistically originated nothing. She seems singularly unaware that the models of persons, books, manners, etc., appropriate for former conditions and for European lands, are but exiles and exotics here. No current of her life, as shown on the surfaces of what is authoritatively called her society, accepts or runs into social or esthetic democracy; but all the currents set squarely against it. Never, in the Old World, was thoroughly upholstered exterior appearance and show, mental and other, built entirely on the idea of caste, and on the sufficiency of mere outside acquisition—never were glibness, verbal intellect more the test, the emulation—more loftily elevated as head and sample—than they are on the surface of our republican States this day. The writers of a time hint the mottoes of its gods. The word of the modern, say these voices, is the word Culture.

We find ourselves abruptly in close quarters with the enemy. This word Culture, or what it has come to represent, involves, by contrast, our whole theme, and has been, indeed, the spur, urging us to engagement. Certain questions arise. As now taught, accepted and carried out, are not the processes of culture rapidly creating a class of supercilious infidels, who believe in nothing? Shall a man lose himself in countless masses of adjustments, and be so shaped with reference to this, that, and the other, that the simply good and healthy and brave parts of him are reduced and clipped away, like the bordering of box in a garden? [P. 330.]

*   *   *

I do not so much object to the name, or word, but I should certainly insist, for the purposes of these States, on a radical change of category, in the distribution of precedence. I should demand a program of culture, drawn out, not for a single class alone, or for the parlors or lecture-rooms, but with an eye to practical life, the west, the working-men, the facts of farms and jack-planes and engineers, and of the broad range of the women also of the middle and working strata, and with reference to the perfect equality of women, and of a grand and powerful motherhood. I should demand of this program or theory a scope generous enough to include the widest human area. It must have for its spinal meaning the formation of a typical personality of character, eligible to the uses of the high average of men— and *not* restricted by conditions ineligible to the masses. The best culture will always be that of the manly and courageous instincts, and loving perceptions, and of self-respect—aiming to form, over this continent, an idiocrasy of universalism, which, true child of America, will bring joy to its mother, returning to her in her own spirit, recruiting myriads of offspring, able, natural, perceptive, tolerant, devout believers in her, America, and with some definite instinct why and for what she has arisen, most vast, most formidable of historic births, and is, now and here, with wonderful step, journeying through Time.

The problem, as it seems to me, presented to the New World, is, under permanent law and order, and after preserving cohesion (ensemble-Individuality), at all hazards, to vitalize man's free play of special Personalism, recognizing in it something that calls ever more to be considered, fed, and adopted as the substratum for the best that belongs to us (government indeed is for it), including the new esthetics of our future. [P. 331.]

* * *

. . . To our model, a clear-blooded, strong-fibered physique is indispensable; the questions of food, drink, air, exercise, assimilation, digestion, can never be intermitted. Out of these we descry a well-begotten selfhood—in youth, fresh, ardent, emotional, aspiring, full of adventure; at maturity, brave, perceptive, under control, neither too talkative nor too reticent, neither flippant nor somber; of the bodily figure, the movements easy, the complexion showing the best blood, somewhat flushed, breast expanded, an erect attitude, a voice whose sound outvies music, eyes of calm and steady gaze, yet capable also of flashing—and a general presence that holds its own in the company of the highest. (For it is native personality, and that alone, that endows a man to stand before presidents or generals, or in any distinguished collection, with *aplomb*—and *not* culture, or any knowledge or intellect whatever.) [P. 332.]

* * *

. . . Manners, costumes, too, though important, we need not dwell upon here. Like beauty, grace of motion, etc., they are results. Causes, original things, being attended to, the right manners unerringly follow. Much is said, among artists, of "the grand style," as if it were a thing by itself. When a man, artist or whoever, has health, pride, acuteness, noble aspirations, he has the motive-elements of the grandest style. The rest is but manipulation (yet that is no small matter).

Leaving still unspecified several sterling parts of any model fit for the future personality of America, I must not fail, again and ever, to pronounce myself on one, probably the least attended to in modern times—a hiatus, indeed, threatening its gloomiest consequences after us. I mean the simple, unsophisticated Conscience, the primary moral element. If I were asked to specify in what quarter lie the grounds of darkest dread, respecting the America of our hopes, I should have to point to this particular. I should demand the invariable application to individuality, this day and any day, of that old, ever-true plumb-rule of persons, eras, nations. [P. 332.]

* * *

The ripeness of Religion is doubtless to be looked for in this field of individuality, and is a result that no organization or church can ever achieve. [P. 333.]

* * *

Personalism fuses this, and favors it. I should say, indeed, that only in the perfect uncontamination and solitariness of individuality may the spirituality of religion positively come forth at all. Only here, and on such terms, the meditation, the devout ecstasy, the soaring flight. Only here, communion with the mysteries, the eternal problems, whence? whither? Alone, and identity, and the mood—and the soul emerges, and all statements, churches, sermons, melt away like vapors. Alone, and silent thought and awe, and aspiration—and then the interior consciousness, like a hitherto unseen inscription, in magic ink, beams out its wondrous lines to the sense. Bibles may convey, and priests expound, but it is exclusively for the noiseless operation of one's isolated Self, to enter the pure ether of veneration, reach the divine levels, and commune with the unutterable. [P. 333.]

* * *

. . . America, it may be, is doing very well upon the whole, notwithstanding these antics of the parties and their leaders, these half-brained nominees, and many ignorant ballots, and many elected failures and blatherers. It is the dilettanti, and all who shirk their duty, who are not doing well. As for you, I advise you to enter more strongly yet into politics. I advise every young man to do so. Always inform yourself; always do the best you can; always vote. Disengage yourself from parties. They have been useful, and to some extent remain so; but the floating, uncommitted electors, farmers, clerks, mechanics, the masters of parties—watching aloof, inclining victory this side or that side—such are the ones most needed, present and future. For America, if eligible at all to downfall and ruin, is eligible within herself, not without; for I see clearly that the combined foreign world could not beat her down. But these savage, wolfish parties alarm me. Owning no law but their own will, more and more combative, less and less tolerant of the idea of ensemble and of equal brotherhood, the perfect equality of the States, the ever-overarching American ideas, it behooves you to convey yourself implicitly to no party, nor submit blindly to their dictators, but steadily hold yourself judge and master over all of them. [P. 334.]

* * *

For us, along the great highways of time, those monuments stand—those forms of majesty and beauty. For us those beacons burn through all the nights. Unknown Egyptians, graving hieroglyphs; Hindus, with hymn and apothegm and endless epic; Hebrew prophet, with spirituality, as in flashes of lightning, conscience like red-hot iron, plaintive songs and screams of vengeance for tyrannies and enslavement; Christ, with bent head, brooding love and peace, like a dove; Greek, creating eternal shapes of physical and esthetic proportion! Roman, lord of satire, the sword, and the codex;—of the figures, some far off and veiled, others nearer and visible; Dante, stalking with lean form, nothing but fiber, not a grain of superfluous flesh; Angelo, and the great painters, architects, musicians; rich Shakespeare, luxuriant as the sun, artist and singer of feudalism in its sunset, with all the gorgeous colors, owner thereof, and using them at will; and so to such as German Kant and Hegel, where they, though near us, leaping over the ages, sit again, impassive, imperturbable, like the Egyptian gods. Of these, and the like of these, is it too much, indeed, to return to our favorite figure, and view them as orbs and systems of orbs, moving in free paths in the spaces of that other heaven, the cosmic intellect, the soul?

Ye powerful and resplendent ones! ye were, in your atmospheres, grown not for America, but rather for her foes, the feudal and the old—while our genius is democratic and modern. Yet could ye, indeed, but breathe your breath of life into our New World's nostrils—not to enslave us, as now, but, for our needs, to breed a spirit like your own—perhaps (dare we to say it?) to dominate, even destroy, what you yourselves have left! On your plane, and no less, but even higher and wider, must we mete and measure for to-day and here. I demand races of orbic bards, with unconditional, uncompromising sway. Come forth, sweet democratic despots of the west! [Pp. 340–341.]

* * *

The old men, I remember as a boy, were always talking of American independence. What is independence? Freedom from all laws or bonds except those of one's own being, controlled by the universal ones. To lands, to man, to woman, what is there at last to each, but the inherent soul, nativity, idiocrasy, free, highest-poised, soaring its own flight, following out itself?

At present, these States, in their theology and social standards (of greater importance than their political institutions) are entirely held possession of by foreign lands. We see the sons and daughters of the New World, ignorant of its genius, not yet inaugurating the native, the universal, and the near still importing the distant, the partial, and the dead. We see London, Paris, Italy—not original, superb, as where they belong—but second-hand here, where they do not belong. We see the shreds of Hebrews, Romans, Greeks; but where, on her own soil, do we see, in any faithful, highest, proud expression, America herself? I sometimes question whether she has a corner in her own house.

Not but that in one sense, and a very grand one, good theology, good art, or good literature, has certain features shared in common. The combination fraternizes, ties the races—is, in many particulars, under laws applicable indifferently to all, irrespective of climate or date, and, from whatever source, appeals to emotions, pride, love, spirituality, common to humankind. Nevertheless, they touch a man closest (perhaps only actually touch him), even in these, in their expression through autochthonic lights and shades, flavors, fondnesses, aversions, specific incidents, illustrations, out of his own nationality, geography, surroundings, antecedents, etc. The spirit and the form are one, and depend far more on association, identity, and place, than is supposed. Subtly interwoven with the materiality and personality of a land, a race—Teuton, Turk, Californian, or what not—there is always something —I can hardly tell what it is—history but describes the results of it—it is the same as the untellable look of some human faces. Nature, too, in her stolid forms, is full of it—but to most it is there a secret. This something is rooted in the invisible roots, the profoundest meanings of that place, race, or nationality; and to absorb and again effuse it, uttering words and products as from its midst, and carrying it into highest regions, is the work, or a main part of the work, of any country's true author, poet, historian, lecturer, and perhaps even priest and philosoph. Here, and here only, are the foundations for our really valuable and permanent verse, drama, etc. [Pp. 344-345.]

* * *

. . . America demands a poetry that is bold, modern, and all-surrounding and cosmical, as she is herself. It must in no respect ignore science or the modern, but inspire itself with science and the modern. It must bend its vision toward the future, more than the past. [P. 346.]

* * *

Long ere the second centennial arrives, there will be some forty to fifty great States, among them Canada and Cuba. When the present century closes, our population will be sixty or seventy millions. The Pacific will be ours, and the Atlantic mainly ours. There will be daily electric communication with every part of the globe. What an age! What a land! Where, elsewhere, one so great? The individuality of one nation must then, as always, lead the world. Can there be any doubt who the leader ought to be? Bear in mind, though, that nothing less than the mightiest original non-subordinated SOUL has ever really, gloriously led, or ever can lead. (This Soul—its other name, in these Vistas, is LITERATURE.)

In fond fancy leaping those hundred years ahead let us survey America's works, poems, philosophies, fulfilling prophecies, and giving form and decision to best ideals. Much that is now undreamed of, we might then perhaps see established, luxuriantly cropping forth, richness, vigor of letters and of artistic expression, in whose products character will be a main requirement, and not merely erudition or elegance.

Intense and loving comradeship, the personal and passionate attachment of man to man—which, hard to define, underlies the lessons and ideals of the profound saviors of every land and age, and which seems to promise, when thoroughly developed, cultivated, and recognized in manners and literature, the most substantial hope and safety of the future of these States, will then be fully expressed.

[Whitman adds the following paragraph as a note:] It is to the development, identification, and general prevalence of that fervid comradeship (the adhesive love, at least rivaling the amative love hitherto possessing imaginative literature, if not going beyond it), that I look for the counterbalance and offset of our materialistic and vulgar American democracy, and for the spiritualization thereof. Many will say it is a dream, and will not follow my inferences: but I confidently expect a time when there will be seen, running like a half-hid warp through all the myriad audible and visible worldly interests of America, threads of manly friendship, fond and loving, pure and sweet, strong and life-long, carried to degrees hitherto unknown—not only giving tone to individual character, and making it unprecedently emotional, muscular, heroic, and refined, but having the deepest relations to general politics. I say democracy infers such loving comradeship, as its most inevitable twin or counterpart, without which it will be incomplete, in vain, and incapable of perpetuating itself.

A strong-fibered joyousness and faith, and the sense of health *al fresco*, may well enter into the preparation of future noble American authorship. Part of the test of a great literatus shall be the absence in him of the idea of the covert, the lurid, the maleficent, the devil, the grim estimates inherited from the Puritans, hell, natural depravity, and the like. The great literatus will be known, among the rest, by his cheerful simplicity, his adherence to natural standards, his limitless faith in God, his reverence, and by the absence in him of doubt, ennui, burlesque, persiflage, or any strained and temporary fashion.

Nor must I fail, again and yet again, to clinch, reiterate more plainly still (O that indeed such survey as we fancy may show in time this part completed also!) the lofty aim, surely the proudest and the purest, in whose service the future literatus of whatever field, may gladly labor. As we have intimated, offsetting the material civilization of our race, our nationality, its wealth, territories, factories, population, products, trade, and military and naval strength, and breathing breath of life into all these, and more, must be its moral civilization—the formulation, expression, aidancy whereof, is the very highest height of literature. The climax of this loftiest range of civilization, rising above all the gorgeous shows and results of wealth, intellect, power, and art, as such—above even theology and religious fervor—is to be its development, from the eternal bases, and the fit expression, of absolute Conscience, moral soundness, Justice. Even in religious fervor there is a touch of animal heat. But moral conscientiousness, crystalline, without flaw, not Godlike only, entirely human, awes and enchants for ever. Great is emotional love, even in the order of the rational universe. But, if we must make gradations, I am clear there is something greater. Power, love, veneration, products, genius, esthetics, tried by subtlest comparisons, analyses, and in serenest moods, somewhere fail, somehow become vain. Then noiseless, with flowing steps, the lord, the sun, the last ideal comes. By the names right, justice, truth, we suggest, but do not describe it. To the world of men it remains a dream, an idea as they call it. But no dream is it to the wise— but the proudest, almost only solid lasting thing of all. Its analogy in the material universe is what holds together this world, and every object upon it, and carries its dynamics on for ever sure and safe. Its lack, and the persistent shirking of it, as in life, sociology, literature, politics, business, and even sermonizing, these times, or any times, still leaves the abysm, the mortal flaw and smutch, mocking civilization to-day, with all its unquestioned triumphs, and all the civilization so far known. [Pp. 347–349.]

* * *

. . . A fitly born and bred race, growing up in right conditions of out-door as much as in-door harmony, activity and development, would probably, from and in those conditions, find it enough merely *to live*—and would, in their relations to the sky, air, water, trees, etc., and to the countless common shows, and in the fact of life itself, discover and achieve happiness—with Being suffused night and day by wholesome ecstasy, surpassing all the pleasures that wealth, amusement, and even gratified intellect, erudition, or the sense of art, can give. [Pp. 349–350.]

*   *   *

I hail with joy the oceanic, variegated, intense practical energy, the demand for facts, even the business materialism of the current age, our States. But woe to the age and land in which these things, movements, stopping at themselves, do not tend to ideas. As fuel to flame, and flame to the heavens, so must wealth, science, materialism—even this democracy of which we make so much—unerringly feed the highest mind, the soul. Infinitude the flight: fathomless the mystery. Man, so diminutive, dilates beyond the sensible universe, competes with, outcopes space and time, meditating even one great idea. Thus, and thus only, does a human being, his spirit, ascend above, and justify, objective Nature, which, probably nothing in itself, is incredibly and divinely serviceable, indispensable, real, here. And as the purport of objective Nature is doubtless folded, hidden, somewhere here— as somewhere here is what this globe and its manifold forms, and the light of day, and night's darkness, and life itself, with all its experiences, are for— it is here the great literature, especially verse, must get its inspiration and throbbing blood. Then may we attain to a poetry worthy the immortal soul of man, and which, while absorbing materials, and, in their own sense, the shows of Nature, will, above all, have, both directly and indirectly, a freeing, fluidizing, expanding, religious character, exulting with science, fructifying the moral elements, and stimulating aspirations, and meditations on the unknown.

The process, so far, is indirect and peculiar, and though it may be suggested, cannot be defined. Observing, rapport, and with intuition, the shows and forms presented by Nature, the sensuous luxuriance, the beautiful in living men and women, the actual play of passions, in history and life—and, above all, from those developments either in Nature or human personality in which power (dearest of all to the sense of the artist) transacts itself— out of these, and seizing what is in them, the poet, the esthetic worker in any field, by the divine magic of his genius, projects them, their analogies, by curious removes, indirections, in literature and art. (No useless attempt to repeat the material creation, by daguerreotyping the exact likeness by mortal mental means.) This is the image-making faculty, coping with material creation, and rivaling, almost triumphing over it. This alone, when all the other parts of a specimen of literature or art are ready and waiting, can breathe into it the breath of life, and endow it with identity.

"The true question to ask," says the librarian of Congress in a paper read before the Social Science Convention at New York, October 1869, "The true question to ask respecting a book, is, *has it helped any human soul?*" This is the hint, statement, not only of the great literatus, his book, but of every great artist. It may be that all works of art are to be first tried by their art qualities, their image-forming talent, and their dramatic, pictorial, plot-constructing, euphonious and other talents. Then, whenever claiming to be first-class works, they are to be strictly and sternly tried by their foundation in, and radiation, in the highest sense and always indirectly, of, the ethic principles, and eligibility to free, arouse, dilate. [Pp. 352–353.]

* * *

And still, providing for contingencies, I fain confront the fact, the need of powerful native philosophs and orators and bards, these States, as rallying points to come, in times of danger, and to fend off ruin and defection. For history is long, long, long. Shift and turn the combinations of the statement as we may, the problem of the future of America is in certain respects as dark as it is vast. Pride, competition, segregation, vicious wilfulness, and licence beyond example, brood already upon us. Unwieldy and immense, who shall hold in behemoth? who bridle leviathan? Flaunt it as we choose, athwart and over the roads of our progress loom huge uncertainty, and dreadful, threatening gloom. It is useless to deny it: Democracy grows rankly up the thickest, noxious, deadliest plants and fruits of all—brings worse and worse invaders—needs newer, larger, stronger, keener compensations and compellers. [P. 355.]

* * *

Even to-day, amid these whirls, incredible flippancy, and blind fury of parties, infidelity, entire lack of first-class captains and leaders, added to the plentiful meanness and vulgarity of the ostensible masses—that problem, the labor question, beginning to open like a yawning gulf, rapidly widening every year—what prospect have we? We sail a dangerous sea of seething currents, cross and under-currents, vortices—all so dark, untried—and whither shall we turn? It seems as if the Almighty had spread before this nation charts of imperial destinies, dazzling as the sun, yet with many a deep intestine difficulty, and human aggregate of cankerous imperfection—saying, lo! the roads, the only plans of development, long and varied with all terrible balks and ebullitions. You said in your soul, I will be empire of empires, overshadowing all else, past and present, putting the history of old-world dynasties, conquests behind me, as of no account—making a new history, a history of democracy, making old history a dwarf—I alone inaugurating largeness, culminating time. If these, O lands of America, are indeed the prizes, the determinations of your soul, be it so. But behold the cost, and already specimens of the cost. Thought you greatness was to ripen for you like a pear? If you would have greatness, know that you must conquer it through ages, centuries—must pay for it with a proportionate price. For you too, as for all lands, the struggle, the traitor, the wily person in office, scrofulous wealth, the surfeit of prosperity, the demonism of greed, the hell of passion, the decay of faith, the long postponement, the fossil-like lethargy, the ceaseless need of revolutions, prophets, thunderstorms, deaths, births, new projections and invigorations of ideas and men. [Pp. 355–356.]

*   *   *

We see our land, America, her literature, esthetics, etc., as, substantially, the getting in form, or effusement and statement, of deepest basic elements and loftiest final meanings, of history and man—and the portrayal (under the eternal laws and conditions of beauty) of our own physiognomy, the subjective tie and expression of the objective, as from our own combination, continuation, and points of view—and the deposit and record of the national mentality, character, appeals, heroism, wars, and even liberties—where these, and all, culminate in native literary and artistic formulation, to be perpetuated; and not having which native, first-class formulation, she will flounder about, and her other, however imposing, eminent greatness, prove merely a passing gleam; but truly having which, she will understand herself, live nobly, nobly contribute, emanate, and, swinging, poised safely on herself, illumined and illuming, become a full-formed world, and divine Mother not only of material but spiritual worlds, in ceaseless succession through time—the main thing being the average, the bodily, the concrete, the democratic, the popular, on which all the superstructures of the future are to permanently rest. [Pp. 358–359.]

12

HOOVER ON AMERICAN INDIVIDUALISM

[Herbert Hoover (born 1874) became wealthy as a mining engineer prac-
tising in many parts of the world. This experience helped him to become a
valuable administrator of relief in Europe during and after the World War.
Later he became active in politics and served as President from 1929 to
1933. His little book *American Individualism* was published in 1922.]

American Individualism *

* * *

Our individualism differs from all others because it embraces these great
ideals: *that while we build our society upon the attainment of the individual,
we shall safeguard to every individual an equality of opportunity to take
that position in the community to which his intelligence, character, ability,
and ambition entitle him; that we keep the social solution free from frozen
strata of classes; that we shall stimulate effort of each individual to achievement; that through an enlarging sense of responsibility and understanding
we shall assist him to this attainment; while he in turn must stand up to the
emery wheel of competition.*

Individualism cannot be maintained as the foundation of a society if
it looks to only legalistic justice based upon contracts, property, and
political equality. Such legalistic safeguards are themselves not enough.
In our individualism we have long since abandoned the laissez faire of
the 18th Century—the notion that it is "every man for himself and the
devil take the hindmost." We abandoned that when we adopted the ideal
of equality of opportunity—the fair chance of Abraham Lincoln. We
have confirmed its abandonment in terms of legislation, of social and
economic justice,—in part because we have learned that it is the hindmost who throws the bricks at our social edifice, in part because we have

---

* From *American Individualism,* by Herbert Hoover, copyright, 1922, by Doubleday, Doran and Company, Inc.

learned that the foremost are not always the best nor the hindmost the worst—and in part because we have learned that social injustice is the destruction of justice itself. We have learned that the impulse to production can only be maintained at a high pitch if there is a fair division of the product. We have also learned that fair division can only be obtained by certain restrictions on the strong and the dominant. We have indeed gone even further in the 20th Century with the embracement of the necessity of a greater and broader sense of service and responsibility to others as a part of individualism. [Pp. 9–11.]

*   *   *

If we examine the impulses that carry us forward, none is so potent for progress as the yearning for individual self-expression, the desire for creation of something. Perhaps the greatest human happiness flows from personal achievement. Here lies the great urge of the constructive instinct of mankind. But it can only thrive in a society where the individual has liberty and stimulation to achievement. Nor does the community progress except through its participation in these multitudes of achievements.

Furthermore, the maintenance of productivity and the advancement of the things of the spirit depend upon the ever-renewed supply from the mass of those who can rise to leadership. Our social, economic, and intellectual progress is almost solely dependent upon the creative minds of those individuals with imaginative and administrative intelligence who create or who carry discoveries to widespread application. No race possesses more than a small percentage of these minds in a single generation. But little thought has ever been given to our racial dependency upon them. Nor that our progress is in so large a measure due to the fact that with our increased means of communication these rare individuals are to-day able to spread their influence over so enlarged a number of lesser capable minds as to have increased their potency a million-fold. In truth, the vastly greater productivity of the world with actually less physical labor is due to the wider spread of their influence through the discovery of these facilities. And they can arise solely through the selection that comes from the free-running mills of competition. They must be free to rise from the mass; they must be given the attraction of premiums to effort. [Pp. 21–23.]

*   *   *

That high and increasing standards of living and comfort should be the first of considerations in public mind and in government needs no apology. We have long since realized that the basis of an advancing civilization must be a high and growing standard of living for all the people, not for a single class; that education, food, clothing, housing, and the spreading use of what we so often term non-essentials, are the real fertilizers of the soil from which spring the finer flowers of life. The economic development of the past fifty years has lifted the general standard of comfort far beyond the dreams of our forefathers. The only road to further advance in the standard of living is by greater invention, greater elimination of waste, greater production and better distribution of commodities and services, for by increasing their ratio to our numbers and dividing them justly we each will have more of them.

The superlative value of individualism through its impulse to production, its stimulation to invention, has, so far as I know, never been denied. Criticism of it has lain in its wastes but more importantly in its failures of equitable sharing of the product. In our country these contentions are mainly over the division to each of his share of the comforts and luxuries, for none of us is either hungry or cold or without a place to lay his head —and we have much besides. In less than four decades we have added electric lights, plumbing, telephones, gramophones, automobiles, and what not in wide diffusion to our standards of living. Each in turn began as a luxury, each in turn has become so commonplace that seventy or eighty per cent. of our people participate in them.

To all practical souls there is little use in quarreling over the share of each of us until we have something to divide. So long as we maintain our individualism we will have increasing quantities to share and we shall have time and leisure and taxes with which to fight out proper sharing of the "surplus." The income tax returns show that this surplus is a minor part of our total production after taxes are paid. Some of this "surplus" must be set aside for rewards to saving, for stimulation of proper effort to skill, to leadership and invention—therefore the dispute is in reality over much less than the total of such "surplus." While there should be no minimizing of a certain fringe of injustices in sharing the results of production or in the wasteful use made by some of their share, yet there is vastly wider field for gains to all of us through cheapening the costs of production and distribution through the eliminating of their wastes, from increasing the volume of product by each and every one doing his utmost, than will ever come to us even if we can think out a method of abstract justice in sharing which did not stifle production of the total product. [Pp. 32–35.]

*　　*　　*

The domination by arbitrary individual ownership is disappearing because the works of to-day are steadily growing more and more beyond the resources of any one individual, and steadily taxation will reduce relatively excessive individual accumulations. The number of persons in partnership through division of ownership among many stockholders is steadily increasing—thus 100,000 to 200,000 partners in a single concern are not uncommon. The overwhelmingly largest portion of our mobile capital is that of our banks, insurance companies, building and loan associations, and the vast majority of all this is the aggregated small savings of our people. Thus large capital is steadily becoming more and more a mobilization of the savings of the small holder—the actual people themselves—and its administration becomes at once more sensitive to the moral opinions of the people in order to attract their support. The directors and managers of large concerns, themselves employees of these great groups of individual stockholders, or policy holders, reflect a spirit of community responsibility.

Large masses of capital can only find their market for service or production to great numbers of the same kind of people that they employ and they must therefore maintain confidence in their public responsibilities in order to retain their customers. In times when the products of manufacture were mostly luxuries to the average of the people, the condition of their employees was of no such interest to their customers as when they cater to employees in general. Of this latter, no greater proofs need exist than the efforts of many large concerns directly dependent upon public good will to restrain prices in scarcity—and the very general desire to yield a measure of service with the goods sold. Another phase of this same development in administration of capital is the growth of a sort of institutional sense in many large business enterprises. The encouragement of solidarity in all grades of their employees in the common service and common success, the sense of mutuality with the prosperity of the community are both vital developments in individualism. [Pp. 39–41.]

*　　*　　*

A great test of the soundness of a social system must be its ability to evolve within itself those orderly shifts in its administration that enable it to apply the new tools of social, economic, and intellectual progress, and to eliminate the malign forces that may grow in the application of these tools. When we were almost wholly an agricultural people our form of organization and administration, both in the governmental and economic fields, could be simple. With the enormous shift in growth to industry and commerce we have erected organisms that each generation has denounced as Frankensteins, yet the succeeding generation proves them to be controllable and useful. The growth of corporate organizations, of our banking systems, of our railways, of our electrical power, of our farm coöperatives, of our trade unions, of our trade associations, and of a hundred others indeed develops both beneficent and malign forces. The timid become frightened. But our basic social ideas march through the new things in the end. Our demagogues, of both radical and standpat breed, thrive on demands for the destruction of one or another of these organizations as the only solution for their defects, yet progress requires only a guardianship of the vital principles of our individualism with its safeguard of true equality of opportunity in them. [Pp. 46–47.]

*   *   *

Looked at as the umpire in our social system, our Government has maintained an equality before the law and a development of legal justice and an authority in restraint of evil instincts that support this social system and its ideals so far as the imperfections of developing human institutions permit. It has gone the greatest distance of any government toward maintaining an equality of franchise; an equality of entrance to public office, and government by the majority. It has succeeded far beyond all others in those safeguards of equality of opportunity through education, public information, and the open channels of free speech and free press. It is, however, much easier to chart the course of progress to government in dealing with the abstract problems of order, political liberty, and stimulation to intellectual and moral advancement than it is to chart its relations to the economic seas. These seas are new and only partly discovered or explored.

Our Government's greatest troubles and failures are in the economic field. Forty years ago the contact of the individual with the Government had its largest expression in the sheriff or policeman, and in debates over political equality. In those happy days the Government offered but small interference with the economic life of the citizen. But with the vast development of industry and the train of regulating functions of the national and municipal government that followed from it; with the recent vast increase in taxation due to the war;—the Government has become through its relations to economic life the most potent force for maintenance or destruction of our American individualism.

The entrance of the Government began strongly three decades ago, when our industrial organization began to move powerfully in the direction of consolidation of enterprise. We found in the course of this development that equality of opportunity and its corollary, individual initiative, was being throttled by the concentration of control of industry and service, and thus an economic domination of groups builded over the nation. At this time, particularly, we were threatened with a form of autocracy of economic power. Our mass of regulation of public utilities and our legislation against restraint of trade is the monument to our intent to preserve an equality of opportunity. This regulation is itself proof that we have gone a long way toward the abandonment of the "capitalism" of Adam Smith.

Day by day we learn more as to the practical application of restrictions against economic and political domination. We sometimes lag behind in the correction of those forces that would override liberty, justice, and equality of opportunity, but the principle is so strong within us that domination of the few will not be tolerated. These restraints must keep pace with the growing complexity of our economic organization, but they need tuning to our social system if they would not take us into great dangers. As we build up our powers of production through the advancing application of science we create new forces with which men may dominate—railway, power, oil, and what not. They may produce temporary blockades upon equality of opportunity.

To curb the forces in business which would destroy equality of opportunity and yet to maintain the initiative and creative faculties of our people are the twin objects we must attain. To preserve the former we must regulate that type of activity that would dominate. To preserve the latter, the Government must keep out of production and distribution of commodities and services. This is the deadline between our system and socialism. Regulation to prevent domination and unfair practices, yet preserving rightful initiative, are in keeping with our social foundations. Nationalization of industry or business is their negation. [Pp. 51-55.]

* * *

The primary safeguard of American individualism is an understanding of it; of faith that it is the most precious possession of American civilization, and a willingness courageously to test every process of national life upon the touchstone of this basic social premise. Development of the human institutions and of science and of industry have been long chains of trial and error. Our public relations to them and to other phases of our national life can be advanced in no other way than by a willingness to experiment in the remedy of our social faults. The failures and unsolved problems of economic and social life can be corrected; they can be solved within our social theme and under no other system. The solution is a matter of will to find a solution; of a sense of duty as well as of a sense of right and citizenship. No one who buys "bootleg" whiskey can complain of gunmen and hoodlumism.

Humanity has a long road to perfection, but we of America can make sure progress if we will preserve our individualism, if we will preserve and stimulate the initiative of our people, if we will build up our insistence and safeguards to equality of opportunity, if we will glorify service as a part of our national character. Progress will march if we hold an abiding faith in the intelligence, the initiative, the character, the courage, and the divine touch in the individual. [Pp. 70-71.]

13

JOHN DEWEY ON PROGRESSIVE DEMOCRACY

[John Dewey (born 1859) has published a steady stream of books and articles on philosophy, education, and social problems since 1882, besides being an influential teacher at the University of Michigan, the University of Chicago and Columbia University. His major concern has been to replace submission, external control, and competition by spontaneity, self-control, and coöperation, and to replace rigid traditional dogmas by progressive intelligent experimentation. He has emphasized democracy, which he conceives not as a fixed set of individual rights coördinated by a fixed constitution, but as a progressive, experimental, coöperative effort to meet developing human needs.

The following passages contain some of Dewey's criticism of the rigid dogmas of communism on the one hand and of the competitive individualism of Hoover on the other, and include some expression of his own democratic ideal.]

Freedom and Culture *
(1939)

* * *

Important social movements develop some sort of philosophy by which to guide, nominally, at least, their practical efforts and also to justify them *ex post facto*. German culture has been especially ardent and prolific in this direction, all attempts to deal with actual conditions on any other basis being regarded as proof that those engaged in them are mere "empiricists," a term of condemnation about equivalent to calling them quacks. In Marxism those who accepted any law except one having exclusively material support were utopian dreamers. The fact then that the dialectical formula was borrowed from the most metaphysical, in a non-scientific sense, of all modern philosophers was no deterrent to the vogue

* From *Freedom and Culture* by John Dewey (G. P. Putnam's Sons, New York, 1939).

of the Marxist synthesis, since its practical character seemed to be vouched for not only by actual economic conditions and by Marx's predictions, but in particular by the increase in class conflict that was taking place.

The idea of class war took on a peculiarly timely quality because of its teaching that the then existing class struggle was that of bourgeoisie capitalists with the proletariat, the class of factory wage-workers having neither land nor any form of reserve capital. Moreover, Marx's study of the concrete facts of the factory system in Great Britain backed up his general theory with a considerable number of economic generalizations which proved sound on any theory:—such as the existence of economic cycles with crises of increasing severity, a tendency toward combination and concentration, etc. The simplified Romanticism of the principle of a negation of negations taught that class war would, through the mediation of a temporary dictatorship of the proletariat, finally usher in a classless society. In the latter the state as a political coercive power would wither away, all political agencies becoming organs of democratic administration of affairs of common interest. Even the anarchist with his opposition to all coercive power could find satisfaction in contemplation of this ultimate outcome.

Marxists object vigorously and naturally to any suggestion of an identification of their creed with theological systems of the past. But all absolutisms tend to assume a theological form and to arouse the kind of emotional ardor that has accompanied crusading religions in the past. The theological concerns and conflicts of the earlier centuries of our era involved, moreover, contemporary interests not now recoverable in imagination. That is, they were more "practical" in fact than they now appear in retrospect. Similarly the monolithic and in itself speculative Marxist doctrine took on immediate practical coloring in connection with existing economic conditions and new forms of oppressions they had produced. There is nothing novel or peculiar in a combination of theory and practice in which practical events give definite color to an abstract theory, while the theory serves as a fountainhead of inspiration to action, providing also rallying cries and slogans. Exegesis can always serve to bridge gaps and inconsistencies; and every absolutistic creed demonstrates that no limits can be put to exegetical ingenuity. What actually happens can, accordingly, be brought into harmony with dogma while the latter is covertly accommodated to events.

There is no need to go into the full scope of Marxist philosophy upon its theoretical side. What is of concern here is the support alleged to be given by it to a strictly *scientific* form of social development, one which is inevitable *because* scientific. As is said of literary products, Marxism is "dated" in the matter of its claims to be peculiarly scientific. For just as *necessity* and search for a *single* all-comprehensive law was typical of the intellectual atmosphere of the forties of the last century, so *probability* and *pluralism* are the characteristics of the present state of science. That the older interpretation of the idea of causal necessity has undergone a shock does not need to be told to those acquainted with recent developments. It is not necessary, however, to go to the point of throwing the idea entirely overboard to make the point which is significant for the present topic.

There is a worldwide difference between the idea that causal sequences will be found in any given set of events taken for investigation, and the idea that *all* sets of events are linked together into a *single* whole by *one* causal law. Even if it be admitted that the former principle is a necessary postulate of scientific inquiry, the latter notion is metaphysical and *extra*-scientific. When natural science was first struggling to achieve its independence, and later when an attempt was made to take social phenomena out of the domain of arbitrary free-will, those who wanted to promote the new struggles borrowed from dominant theology the idea which the latter had made familiar, that of a single all-embracing causal force. The nature of the force and the way it worked were radically altered in the new apologetics for science. But the requirements of habit were satisfied in maintaining the old forms of thought—just as the first "horseless carriages" kept the shape of the carriages they displaced. The void left by surrender first of a supernatural force, and then of Nature (which had replaced Deity during the periods of deistic rationalism) is thus made good. Only gradually did the work of science and the specific conclusions it reached make it clear that science was not a competitor with theology for a single ultimate explanation, so that the justification was no longer resorted to.

The surrender does not mean that search for broad generalizations has been given up. It means that the nature and function of these generalizations have changed. They are now, in effect and function, formulae for effecting transformations from one field to another, the qualitative difference of the fields being maintained. The doctrine of the conservation of energy represents, for example, an exceedingly comprehensive generalization. In terms of the now discarded philosophy of science, it would be said to set up a force which is at once electrical, mechanical, thermal, etc., and yet none of them, but a kind of nondescript Thing-in-itself back of all of them. In actual scientific procedure, it is a formula for converting any one of these forms of energy into any other, provided certain conditions are satisfied.

The same principle holds good of the recently discovered transmutation of chemical elements. It does not wipe out the differences of quality that mark off phenomena from one another but sets forth the conditions under which one kind is changed into another kind. Differences in the practical operations that are based upon science correspond with the change that has come about in theory—as the techniques of modern chemical industry are different from the dreams of the alchemists. No one today would think of undertaking a definite invention, the heavier-than-air flying boat, the internal combustion engine, and so on, by setting out from an alleged universal law of the working of some single ultimate force. The inventor who translates an idea into a working technological device starts from examination of special materials and tries special methods for combining them.

The practical techniques derived from the Marxist single all-embracing law of a single causative force follow the pattern discarded in scientific inquiry and in scientific engineering. What is necessary according to it is to promote class war in as great a variety of ways and on as many occasions as possible. For the essence of the theory, according to the dialectical method, is not recognition of class conflicts as *facts*—in which respect it provided a needed correction of the early nineteenth century notion of universal harmony and universal interdependence. Its distinguishing trait is that social progress is made by intensifying the conflict between the capitalistic employing classes and the proletarian employed class, so that the supreme principle of morals is to strengthen the power of the latter class.

The physical analogy is about like this: suppose that there had once been a theory that "nature abhors friction." It is then discovered that no mechanical work is done without resistance, and that there is no resistance without friction. It is then concluded that by abolishing lubrication and magnifying friction, a state of universal friction will by its own inner dialectic result in an adjustment of energies to one another which will provide the best possible conditions for doing useful work. Society *is* marked by conflict and friction of interests; interests may by some stretching and more consolidation be used to define classes. It may also be admitted that the conflict between them has under certain conditions served as a stimulus to social progress; it might even be admitted that a society in which there was no opposition of interests would be sunk in a condition of hopeless lethargy. But the idea of obtaining universal harmony by the greatest possible intensification of conflicts would remain analogous to the physical illustration given. Persons who are not Marxists often identify the proposition that serious strife of economic interests exists with the genuine Marxist thesis that it is the sole agency by which social change is effected in the desirable direction of a classless society.

The criticism made is not directed then to any generalization made by Marx on the basis of observation of actual conditions. On the contrary, the implication of the criticism is the necessity for *continued* observation of actual conditions, with testing and revision of all earlier generalization on the basis of what is now observed. The inherent theoretical weakness of Marxism is that it supposed a generalization that was made at a particular date and place (and made even then only by bringing observed facts under a premise drawn from a metaphysical source) can obviate the need for continued resort to observation, and to continual revision of generalizations in their office of working hypotheses. In the name of science, a thoroughly anti-scientific procedure was formulated, in accord with which a generalization is made having the nature of ultimate "truth," and hence holding good at all times and places.

Laissez-faire individualism indulged in the same kind of sweeping generalization but in the opposite direction. Doubtless, in accordance with the law of the union of opposites, this background played its part in creating a cultural atmosphere favorable to Marxism. But two opposite errors do not constitute one truth, especially when both errors have the same root. With some disregard for historic facts, the Marxist doctrine might even be regarded as a generalized version of that aspect of classic economic theory which held that completely free competition in the open market would automatically produce universal harmony of persons and nations, Marx converting competition of individuals into war of classes.

Marxism has, then, been selected as an illustration of the monistic block-universe theory of social causation. A few years ago the laissez-faire view, developed out of ideas of Adam Smith when they were wedded to ideas of utilitarian morals and psychology, would have been appropriately taken. The Russian Revolution is chiefly accountable for having brought Marxism to the foreground. Being conducted in the name of Marx, it claimed to be a large scale demonstration of the validity of the Marxist theory. The Union of Socialist Soviet Republics has fastened attention upon the theory as no idea ever succeeds on its own account in obtaining notice. It caused Marxism to be a terrifying menace in some quarters while giving it enormous prestige in other quarters. It led to a disruption of old socialist parties, as the Russian Revolution was held up in other countries as proof of the Marxist theory of class war and the dictatorship of the proletariat. The issue raised by events in Russia gave actuality to Marxist doctrine in every country of the globe.

An event of this sort cannot occur without arousing intense feeling, and corresponding conflicts of interpretation. In the present case, the division extends not only to the theory but to the facts of the situation. One can find data, real or alleged, to support almost any view as to the actual situation in the U.S.S.R., according to the source one takes to be authoritative. Facts, including statistics, are cited to show that extraordinary progress has been made in industrialization of the country and mechanization of agricultural pursuits, with an immense gain in productivity, and, what is more important, in creation of a genuine workers' republic, attended with striking rise in the material and cultural standards of living of the great mass of the population. But one may also find evidence to support the view that the dictatorship of the proletariat became first that of a party over the proletariat and then the dictatorship of a small band of bureaucrats over the party, until the latter, to maintain power, has adopted, with greatly improved technical skill in execution, all the repressive measures of the overthrown Czarist despotism. One can find evidence that, under a regime of governmental, instead of social, control, economic classes marked by great inequality of income are growing up. Such questions of fact are not settled by argument. Hence though there is no doubt in my own mind as to the conclusion available evidence points to, I shall not here attempt to take a stand on the particular issues of fact which are involved.

Certain facts that are not denied suffice as far as the present topic and problem are concerned. A monistic theory is accompanied in its practical execution by one-party control of press, schools, radio, the theater and every means of communication, even to effective restrictions imposed on private gatherings and private conversations. One of the reasons for the great difference in opinion about the state of facts—the point just mentioned—is the fact that effective dictatorship (and an ineffective dictatorship is not a dictatorship at all) exercises complete command over the press, over travel, over letters and personal communications. In consequence, only a few have access to the sources of information about political methods, and that few is just the group with the greatest interest in preventing free inquiry and report.

This suppression of freedom of belief and of speech, press and assembly is not among the facts in dispute for it is of the essence of the dictatorship, which in turn is of the essence of the doctrine the Revolution claims to have put in force. Nor is ruthless persecution and punishment of all dissenters one of the disputed facts. A succession of trials has eliminated from life (as well as from political action) every one of the men and women who brought on the Revolution, save a few relatively minor characters. The *justification* of the action is one of the things in controversy, but not the fact of the exile, imprisonment or execution of every important earlier leader. As a criterion for judging the theory back of revolutionary method of class war, it would not seem to make a great deal of difference whether we decide these men were traitors to their own cause of the liberation of humanity, or are victims of the desire of a clique to keep in their hands a monopoly of all power—great as will be the difference in our judgment about the character of the persons involved.

Events not in dispute confirm the conclusion drawn from other historical instances that absolute principles are intolerant of dissent, for dissent from "The Truth" is more than an intellectual error. It is proof of an evil and dangerous will. When the dominant dogma is definitely theological, the evil will is described in one set of terms; when it is political, the phraseology is different, "counter-revolution" taking the place of "heresy."

The psychological and moral dispositions stimulated and the kind of activities in which they are expressed are extraordinarily similar. No general theory, moreover, is self-translating in application to particular events. Some body of persons must exist to state just what its significance is in its bearing upon this and that situation, and a body that merely interprets is impotent unless it has power to enforce decisions. The extreme danger of giving any body of persons power for whose exercise they are not accountable is a commonplace in a democracy. Arbitrary irresponsibility varies in direct ratio to the claim for absoluteness on the part of the principle in behalf of which power is exercised. To sustain the principle against heresy, or counter-revolutionary action, it finally becomes necessary to clothe the human officials that are supposed to represent the principle with the finality of the professed end. Divinity once hedged about kings. An earlier repudiation in Russia of glorification of individual persons, because of the immensely superior importance of collective action, gives way to Byzantine adulation of the Leader. [Pp. 82–91.]

*   *   *

The experimental method of science is the exemplification of empirical method when experience has reached maturity. It is opposed equally to "vulgar" empiricism which recognizes only rule-of-thumb action, depending upon a succession of trial-and-error acts that are unregulated by connection with an idea which is both expressed and tested, and to that absolutism which insists there is but one Truth and that truth one already revealed and possessed by some group or party. Mr. John Strachey, an Englishman, not a Russian, may be quoted upon the extent to which present "Communist" thought is authoritarian and monistic—that is, ruled by an ideal of uniformity. For he says that communistic parties even outside of Russia, e. g., in this country, in "refusal to tolerate the existence of incompatible opinions . . . are simply asserting the claim that Socialism is scientific." * It would be difficult, probably impossible, to find a more direct and elegantly finished denial of all the qualities that make ideas and theories either scientific or democratic than is contained in this statement. It helps explain why literary persons have been chiefly the ones in this country who have fallen for Marxist theory, since they are the ones who, having the least amount of scientific attitude, swallow most readily the notion that "science" is a new kind of infallibility.

To repeat a statement already made in another connection, no generalization which, like Marxism, claims to state the final truth about changes (whether physical or social), can set forth the significance of the general idea that is accepted in connection with actual events as they happen. For the purpose of day by day *action,* the sole value of a theory is the significance given to concrete events, when they are viewed in the light of the theory, in the concrete relations they sustain to one another. It is no accident that the final effect of uniformity of ideas is to set up

* *What Are We to Do?,* New York, Random House, 1938, p. 235.—EDITOR.

some selected body of persons above the theoretical generalization. Those who determine what the theory signifies in terms of the one important thing—namely, *what should be done*—are supreme over the theory even when they claim to act in subjection to it. The demand for uniformity of opinion, "the refusal to tolerate the existence of incompatible opinions," demands first that there be a party and then a select council of persons within the party, to decide just what after all is The Truth with respect to events as they arise—together with a truly theological technique of exegesis to explain the perfect consistency existing among a succession of inconsistent policies. Thus there has been the change from the earlier denunciation of democracy as identical with middle class capitalism and the labeling of all other socialists as Social-Fascists, to the present policy of a Popular Front, and to the presentation of Bolshevism as twentieth century democracy. And, again, change from denunciation of Nazi Germany to the beginnings of a virtual alliance with it, but now in the wholly praiseworthy interest of world peace, following upon the former orthodox doctrine that only communism can institute peace after a succession of wars international and civil.* Scientific method in operating with working hypotheses instead of with fixed and final Truth is not forced to have an Inner Council to declare just what is the Truth nor to develop a system of exegesis which rivals the ancient theological way of explaining away apparent inconsistencies. It welcomes a clash of "incompatible opinions" as long as they can produce observed facts in their support.

Since Marxism has been taken as the example of a uniformitarian theory, basing itself upon "objective" factors of the environment in separation from their interaction with the factors of human nature, something will be said in closing about the ignoring of human qualities. For it contradicts the statement sometimes made that the essence of Marxism, at least as a practical doctrine, is appeal to the motive of self-interest. This statement is made as an accusation by non-Marxists, while it sometimes appears in what profess to be Marxist documents. But actually it comes close to reversing actual Marxist doctrine—the doctrine that the state of the forces of production is the sole causal force. For according to this view, all the factors of human nature are shaped from without by "materialistic," that is economic, forces. To give independent validity to any com-

---

* Now—July, 1940—the alliance is more than virtual and Russia's zeal for peace is at least questionable.—EDITOR.

ponent of human nature would be, from the Marxist standpoint, a relapse into the "idealistic" type of theory that Marxism came to destroy.

A much juster criticism would be that Marxism systematically neglects everything on the side of human nature with respect to its being a factor having efficacy, save as it is previously determined by the state of the forces of production. In claiming to replace "Utopian" socialisms, Marxism throws out psychological as well as moral considerations. Whether the theory is in fact able to live up to this claim—without which its "materialism" is meaningless—is another matter. For it would seem as if certain organic needs and appetites at least were required to set the "forces of production" moving. But if this bio-psychological factor is admitted, then it must *interact* with "external" factors, and there is no particular point at which its operation can be said to cease.

The point involved has a practical as well as theoretical force. Take for example the matter of classes and of class-*consciousness,* the latter being an imperatively required condition in the Marxist theory. According to orthodox Marxism, the class consciousness of the proletariat is generated by the fact that the state of economic forces represented by large-scale factory production throws wage-workers closely together with little or no direct intercourse with employers—such as existed, for example, in shops where hand tools were used. Physical conditions thus demarcate economic classes, and throw into relief the conflict of interests between employers and employees, together with the community of interests, if only in misery, that bind together the latter. Now as an observation there is an undeniable element of truth in this position—especially in contrast with the favorite editorial exhortation that there can be no conflict between "Capital" and "Labor" since each depends on the other. But the facts involved in the observation are not compatible with the ultimate theory. The formation of a class, especially of class consciousness, depends upon the operation of psychological factors which are not mentioned—and which the theory rules out. [Pp. 96–99.]

* * *

Mere general ideas can be argued for and against without the necessity of recourse to observation. The arguments are saved from being a mere matter of words only because there are certain emotional attitudes involved. When general ideas are not capable of being continuously checked and revised by observation of what actually takes place, they are, as a mere truism, in the field of opinion. Clash of opinions is in that case the occasion for controversy, not, as is now the case in natural science, a location of a problem and an occasion for making further observations. If any generalization can be safely laid down about intellectual matters and their consequences, it is that the reign of opinion, and of controversial conflicts, is a function of absence of methods of inquiry which bring new facts to light and by so doing establish the basis for consensus of beliefs.

Social events are sufficiently complex in any case so that the development of effective methods of observation, yielding generalization about correlation of events, is difficult. The prevailing type of theory adds the further handicap of making such observation unnecessary—save as this and that arbitrarily selected event is used in argumentative controversy. The prime necessity is to frame general ideas, first, to promote search for problems—as against the assumption of a ready-made solution in view of which there are no problems; and, secondly, to solve these problems by generalizations that state interactions between analytically observed events.

I return to the particular social philosophy which associates the economic regime actuated by effort to make private profit with the essential conditions of free and democratic institutions. It is not necessary to go back to the theory in its early English formulation at the hands of laissez-faire liberals. For in spite of the discrediting of the philosophy by events, efforts put forth in this country to establish so-called social control of business have led at present to its revival in an extremely naked form. One does not need to endorse the measures for control that are used to be aware of the fallacy of the theory upon which current objections to them are based. The theory is that capitalism, interpreted as the maximum range of free personal opportunity for production and exchange of goods and services is the Siamese twin of democracy. For the former is identical, so it is claimed, with the personal qualities of initiative, independence, vigor, that are the basic conditions of free political institutions. Hence, so it is argued, the check given to the operation of these personal qualities by governmental regulation of business activities is at the same time an attack upon the practical and moral conditions for the existence of political democracy.*

I am not concerned here with the merits of the special arguments put

* Compare Herbert Hoover's *American Individualism* and his *Challenge to Liberty.*—Editor.

forth in behalf and against the measures employed. The point is that appeal to certain alleged human motivations in a wholesale way, such as "initiative, independence, enterprise" at large, obscures the need for observation of events in the concrete. If and when special events are observed, interpretation of them is predestined instead of growing out of what is observed. By keeping the issues in the realm of opinion, appeal to equally general wholesale views on the other side is promoted. Then we get a kind of head-on conflict between something called "individualism" on one side and "socialism" on the other. Examination of concrete conditions might disclose certain specifiable conditions under which both of the methods vaguely pointed at by these words would operate to advantage.

The current use of the word *enterprise* as an honorific term is especially instructive with regard to the attempt to draw support for policies from a reference to general inherent traits of human nature. For the only legitimate signification of "enterprise" is a neutral one, an *undertaking* the desirability of which is a matter of actual results produced, which accordingly need to be studied in the concrete. But *enterprise* is given the significance of a certain desirable trait of human nature, so that the issue is taken out of the field of observation into that of opinion plus a eulogistic emotion. "Enterprise" like "initiative" and like "industry" can be exerted in behalf of an indefinite number of objects; the words may designate the activities of an Al Capone or a racketeering labor union as well as a socially useful industrial undertaking.

The case is cited in some detail because it provides a striking example, first, of the conversion of an existing mode of social behavior into a psychological property of human nature; and, secondly, conversion of an alleged matter of psychological fact into a principle of value—a moral matter. Social problems that are set by conditions having definite spatial and temporal boundaries—which have to be determined by observation—are made into matters capable of absolute determination without reference to conditions of place and date. Hence they become matters of opinion and controversial argument—and as the latter decides nothing, the final tendency is to appeal to force as the ultimate arbiter.

The theory of the components of human nature used by the intellectual radicals of Great Britain to justify popular government and freedom included more than the self-interest motivation. It was officially held that sympathy with the gains and losses, the pleasures and pains of others, is a native part of the human endowment. The two components, self-interest and sympathy, opposite in quality, were ingeniously linked together in the complete doctrine—occasionally with explicit reference to the supposedly analogous centripetal and centrifugal components of Newtonian celestial mechanics. The self-interest phase supplied the foundation of the theory of public and governmental action; the sympathetic phase took care of the relations of individuals to one another in their private capacities. The doctrine taught that if political institutions were reformed to do away with special privileges and unfair favoritisms, the sympathetic motive would have a vastly enlarged field of effective and successful operation, since bad institutions were the chief cause that led men to find their personal advantage in acts injurious to others.

The theory was even more important in the reaction it called out than in itself. For "organic idealistic" philosophies developed in Germany during the nineteenth century, and now form the theoretical background and justification of totalitarianism. They took their clew and point of departure from the weaknesses of the theories that based politics and morals, in theory and in practice, upon alleged components of human nature. An adequate account of the form and substance of the reaction would take us into matters which cannot be set forth without going into technicalities. But its basis is simple.

The attempt to locate the source of authority of politics and morals in human nature was regarded as the source of anarchy, disorder, and conflict;—an attempt to build social institutions and personal relationships upon the most unstable of shifting quicksands. At the same time, the philosophers who formulated the new view were Protestants and Northerners. Hence their reaction did not move them to urge acceptance of the doctrines of the Roman Church as the bulwark against the dissolving tendencies of ultra-individualistic ideas and policies.

The French Revolution, with its excesses, was uniformly regarded in German thought as the logical outcome of the attempt to locate authority where nothing binding could be found. It was thus taken to be a practical large scale demonstration of the weakness inherent in the position. The most that could be said for the doctrine was what could be said in defense of the French Revolution—it helped to get rid of abuses that had grown up. As a positive and constructive principle, it was a tragic delusion. The statement of the Rights of Man setting forth the official creed of the Revolution was said to be a summary of the false doctrines that had produced all the characteristic evils of the age. The protest, as just said, refused to accept the doctrines of the Church as the basis for its criticisms and for the constructive measures it proposed. It was itself too deeply influenced by the conditions which had produced the individualism against which it revolted. The extent of this influence is why the movement is criticized by representatives of the Hellenic-medieval ideas as itself intensely "subjectivistic." It found the way to "reconcile" freedom and authority, individuality and law, by setting up an Absolute Self, Mind, Spirit, of which human beings are individually partial manifestations, a "truer" and fuller manifestation being found in social institutions, the state and the course of history. Since history is the final court of judgment and since it represents the movement of absolute Spirit, appeal to force to settle issues between nations is not "really" an appeal to force, but rather to the ultimate logic of absolute reason. The individualistic movement was a necessary transitional movement to bring men to recognition of the primacy and ultimacy of Spirit and Personality in the constitution of nature, man, and society. German organic idealism was to save all that is true in the movement, while eliminating its errors and dangers by lifting it up to the plane of absolute Self and Spirit. There is much that is technical in the movement; much of its detail can be explained only on the ground of special intellectual events. But its heart and core is found in its attempt to find a "higher" justification for individuality and freedom where the latter are merged with law and authority, which *must* be rational since they are manifestations of Absolute Reason. Contemporary totalitarianism has no difficulty in discovering that the Germanic racial spirit embodied in the German state is an adequate substitute, for all practical purposes, for the Hegelian Absolute Spirit.

Rousseau is usually, and in many respects properly, regarded as the prophet and intellectual progenitor of the French Revolution. But by one of those ironies with which history abounds he was also a stepfather of the theory that came to full expression in Germany. He served in this capacity partly indirectly by his attack on culture which, as previously said, was the challenge that resulted in glorification of culture over against human nature. But he also acted positively and directly. For in his political writings he advanced the idea that a Common Will is the source of legitimate political institutions; that freedom and law are one and the same thing in the operations of the Common Will, for it must act for the Common Good and hence for the "real" or true Good of every individual.

If the latter set up their purely personal desires against the General Will, it was accordingly legitimate (indeed necessary) to "*force* them to be free." Rousseau intended his theory to state the foundation of self-governing institutions and majority rule. But his premise was employed to prove that the Common—or Universal—Will and Reason was embodied in the national state. Its most adequate incarnation was in those states in which the authority of law, order, and discipline had not been weakened by democratic heresies:—a view which was used in Germany after the Napoleonic conquest to create an aggressive national spirit in that country, one which provided the basis for systematic depreciation of French "materialistic" civilization as over against German *Kultur*—a depreciation later extended to condemnation of democratic institutions in any country.

While this brief exposition of the reaction against the individualistic theory of human nature suggests the ground pattern of National Socialism, it also throws some light upon the predicament in which democratic countries find themselves. The fact that the individualistic theory was used a century and more ago to justify political self-government and then aided promotion of its cause does not constitute the theory a present trustworthy guide of democratic action. It is profitable to read today the bitterly vivid denunciations of Carlyle on the theory as it was originally put forth. He denounced with equal fierceness the attempt to erect political authority upon the basis of self-interest and private morals upon the exercise of sympathy. The latter was sentimentalism run riot and the former was "Anarchy plus the Constable"—the latter being needed to preserve even a semblance of outward order. His plea for discipline and order included even a plea for leadership by select persons.

The present predicament may be stated as follows: Democracy does involve a belief that political institutions and law should be such as to take fundamental account of human nature. They must give it freer play than any non-democratic institutions. At the same time, the theory, legalistic and moralistic, about human nature that has been used to expound and justify this reliance upon human nature has proved inadequate. Upon the legal and political side, during the nineteenth century it was progressively overloaded with ideas and practices which have more to do with business carried on for profit than with democracy. On the moralistic side, it has tended to substitute emotional exhortation to act in accord with the Golden Rule for the discipline and the control afforded by incorporation of democratic ideals into *all* the relations of life. Because of lack of an adequate theory of human nature in its relations to democracy, attachment to democratic ends and methods has tended to become a matter of tradition and habit—an excellent thing as far as it goes, but when it becomes routine is easily undermined when change of conditions changes other habits.

Were I to say that democracy needs a new psychology of human nature, one adequate to the heavy demands put upon it by foreign and domestic conditions, I might be taken to utter an academic irrelevancy. But if the remark is understood to mean that democracy has always been allied with humanism, with faith in the potentialities of human nature, and that the present need is vigorous reassertion of this faith, developed in relevant ideas and manifested in practical attitudes, it but continues the American tradition. For belief in the "common man" has no significance save as an expression of belief in the intimate and vital connection of democracy and human nature.

We cannot continue the idea that human nature when left to itself, when freed from external arbitrary restrictions, will tend to the production of democratic institutions that work successfully. We have now to state the issue from the other side. We have to see that democracy means the belief that humanistic culture *should* prevail; we should be frank and open in our recognition that the proposition is a moral one—like any idea that concerns what *should* be.

Strange as it seems to us, democracy is challenged by totalitarian states of the Fascist variety on moral grounds just as it is challenged by totalitarianisms of the left on economic grounds. We may be able to defend democracy on the latter score, as far as comparative conditions are involved, since up to the present at least the Union of Socialist Republics has not "caught up" with us, much less "surpassed" us, in material affairs. But defense against the other type of totalitarianism (and perhaps in the end against also the Marxist type) requires a positive and courageous constructive awakening to the significance of faith in human nature for development of every phase of our culture:—science, art, education, morals and religion, as well as politics and economics. No matter how uniform and constant human nature is in the abstract, the conditions within which and upon which it operates have changed so greatly since political democracy was established among us, that democracy cannot now depend upon or be expressed in political institutions alone. We cannot even be certain that they and their legal accompaniments are actually democratic at the present time—for democracy is expressed in the attitudes of human beings and is measured by consequences produced in their lives.

The impact of the humanist view of democracy upon all forms of culture, upon education, science and art, morals and religion, as well as upon industry and politics, saves it from the criticism passed upon moralistic exhortation. For it tells us that we need to examine every one of the phases of human activity to ascertain what effects it has in release, maturing and fruition of the potentialities of human nature. It does not tell us to "re-arm morally" and all social problems will be solved. It says, Find out how all the constituents of our existing culture are operating and then see to it that whenever and wherever needed they be modified in order that their workings may release and fulfill the possibilities of human nature.

It used to be said (and the statement has not gone completely out of fashion) that democracy is a by-product of Christianity, since the latter teaches the infinite worth of the individual human soul. We are now told by some persons that since belief in the soul has been discredited by science, the moral basis for democracy supposed to exist must go into the discard. We are told that if there are reasons for preferring it to other arrangements of the relations of human beings to one another, they must be found in specialized external advantages which outweigh the advantages of other social forms. From a very different quarter, we are told that weakening of the older theological doctrine of the soul is one of the reasons for the eclipse of faith in democracy. These two views at opposite poles give depth and urgency to the question whether there are adequate grounds for faith in the potentialities of human nature and whether they can be accompanied by the intensity and ardor once awakened by religious ideas upon a theological basis. Is human nature intrinsically such a poor thing that the idea is *absurd*? I do not attempt to give any answer, but the word *faith* is intentionally used. For in the long run democracy will stand or fall with the possibility of maintaining the faith and justifying it by works.

Take, for example, the question of intolerance. Systematic hatred and suspicion of any human group, "racial," sectarian, political, denotes deep-seated scepticism about the qualities of human nature. From the standpoint of a faith in the possibilities of human nature possessing religious quality it is blasphemous. It may start by being directed at a particular group, and be supported in name by assigning special reasons why that group is not worthy of confidence, respect, and decent human treatment. But the underlying attitude is one of fundamental distrust of human nature. Hence it spreads from distrust and hatred of a particular group until it may undermine the conviction that any group of persons has any intrinsic right for esteem or recognition—which, then, if it be given, is for some special and external grounds, such as usefulness to our particular interests and ambitions. There is no physical acid which has the corrosive power possessed by intolerance directed against persons because they belong to a group that bears a certain name. Its corrosive potency gains with what it feeds on. An anti-humanist attitude is the essence of every form of intolerance. Movements that begin by stirring up hostility against a group of people end by denying to them all human qualities.

The case of intolerance is used as an illustration of the intrinsic connection between the prospects of democracy and belief in the potentialities of human nature—not for its own sake, important as it is on its own account. How much of our past tolerance was positive and how much of it a toleration equivalent to "standing" something we do not like, "putting up" with something because it involves too much trouble to try to change it? For a good deal of the present reaction against democracy is probably simply the disclosure of a weakness that was there before; one that was covered up or did not appear in its true light. Certainly racial prejudice against negroes, Catholics, and Jews is no new thing in our life. Its presence among us is an intrinsic weakness and a handle for the accusation that we do not act differently from Nazi Germany.

The greatest practical inconsistency that would be revealed by searching our own habitual attitudes is probably one between the democratic method of forming opinions in political matters and the methods in common use in forming beliefs in other subjects. In theory, the democratic method is persuasion through public discussion carried on not only in legislative halls but in the press, private conversations and public asemblies. The substitution of ballots for bullets, of the right to vote for the lash, is an expression of the will to substitute the method of discussion for the method of coercion. With all its defects and partialities in determination of political decisions, it has worked to keep factional disputes within bounds, to an extent that was incredible a century or more ago. While Carlyle could bring his gift of satire into play in ridiculing the notion that men by talking to and at each other in an assembly hall can settle what is true in social affairs any more than they can settle what is true in the multiplication table, he failed to see that if men had been using clubs to maim and kill one another to decide the product of 7 times 7, there would have been sound reasons for appealing to discussion and persuasion even in the latter case. The fundamental reply is that social "truths" are so unlike mathematical truths that unanimity of uniform belief is possible in respect to the former only when a dictator has the power to tell others what they must believe—or profess they believe. The adjustment of interests demands that diverse interests have a chance to articulate themselves.

The real trouble is that there is an intrinsic split in our habitual attitudes when we profess to depend upon discussion and persuasion in politics and then systematically depend upon other methods in reaching conclusions in matters of morals and religion, or in anything where we depend upon a person or group possessed of "authority." We do not have to go to theological matters to find examples. In homes and in schools, the places where the essentials of character are supposed to be formed, the usual procedure is settlement of issues, intellectual and moral, by appeal to the "authority" of a parent, teacher, or textbook. Dispositions formed under such conditions are so inconsistent with the democratic method that in a crisis they may be aroused to act in positively anti-democratic ways for anti-democratic ends; just as resort to coercive force and suppression of civil liberties are readily palliated in nominally democratic communities when the cry is raised that "law and order" are threatened.

It is no easy matter to find adequate authority for action in the demand, characteristic of democracy, that conditions be such as will enable the potentialities of human nature to reach fruition. Because it is not easy the democratic road is the hard one to take. It is the road which places the greatest burden of responsibility upon the greatest number of human beings. Backsets and deviations occur and will continue to occur. But that which is its weakness at particular times is its strength in the long course of human history. Just because the cause of democratic freedom is the cause of the fullest possible realization of human potentialities, the latter when they are suppressed and oppressed will in time rebel and demand an opportunity for manifestation. With the founders of American democracy, the claims of democracy were inherently one with the demands of a just and equal morality. We cannot now well use their vocabulary.

Changes in knowledge have outlawed the significations of the words they commonly used. But in spite of the unsuitability of much of their language for present use, what they asserted was that self-governing institutions are the means by which human nature can secure its fullest realization in the greatest number of persons. The question of what is involved in self-governing methods is now much more complex. But for this very reason, the task of those who retain belief in democracy is to revive and maintain in full vigor the original conviction of the intrinsic moral nature of democracy, now stated in ways congruous with present conditions of culture. We have advanced far enough to say that democracy is a way of life. We have yet to realize that it is a way of personal life and one which provides a moral standard for personal conduct. [Pp. 116–130.]

14

THE COMMUNIST MANIFESTO

[The founders of Communism were Karl Marx (1818–1883) and Friedrich Engels (1820–1895). Marx had a university education and was influenced by the philosophy of Hegel. He had some experience as an editor of radical publications in Germany, and took part in the uprisings of 1848–1849. But from 1844 to 1848 he had been studying economics in Paris, and from 1849 until his death he spent most of his time in the British Museum in London, engaged in vast economic researches and writing enormous manuscripts. The first volume of his *Capital* (1867) is the main work published in his lifetime; other publications have been based on his manuscripts.

Engels, although of German birth and education, had an early apprenticeship in business in a Manchester firm in which his father owned some stock. He first met Marx in Paris in 1844, and from that time on they collaborated in developing the theories of Communism. He took somewhat more extensive part in revolutionary activities than Marx in Germany, France, and Belgium, in 1845–1850. From 1850 to 1869 he was active as a business man in England, which enabled him to give financial support to Marx in his researches. After the death of Marx, Engels was active in editing his works.

The Communist Manifesto is the joint work of Marx and Engels, authorized by a meeting of the "Communist League" in London, November 1847, drawn up in January 1848, published in German and French in 1848 and in English in 1850. It is the first, best-known, and most influential expression of Communist theory.]

The Communist Manifesto *
(1848)

A specter is haunting Europe—the specter of Communism. All the powers of old Europe have entered into a holy alliance to exorcise this specter;

---

* From the authorized English translation of 1888 edited by Engels.

Pope and Czar, Metternich and Guizot, French radicals and German police spies.

Where is the party in opposition that has not been decried as Communistic by its opponents in power? Where the opposition that has not hurled back the branding reproach of Communism, against the more advanced opposition parties, as well as against its reactionary adversaries?

Two things result from this fact.

I. Communism is already acknowledged by all European powers to be in itself a power.

II. It is high time that Communists should openly, in the face of the whole world, publish their views, their aims, their tendencies, and meet this nursery tale of the Specter of Communism with a Manifesto of the party itself.

To this end the Communists of various nationalities have assembled in London, and sketched the following manifesto to be published in the English, French, German, Italian, Flemish and Danish languages.

I

BOURGEOIS AND PROLETARIANS *

The history of all hitherto existing society † is the history of class struggles.

Freeman and slave, patrician and plebeian, lord and serf, guild master ‡ and journeyman, in a word, oppressor and oppressed, stood in constant opposition to one another, carried on an uninterrupted, now hidden, now

* By bourgeoisie is meant the class of modern Capitalists, owners of the means of social production and employers of wage-labor. By proletariat, the class of modern wage-laborers who, having no means of production of their own, are reduced to selling their labor-power in order to live.

† That is, all *written* history. In 1847, the pre-history of society, the social organization existing previous to recorded history, was all but unknown. Since then, Haxthausen discovered common ownership of land in Russia, Maurer proved it to be the social foundation from which all Teutonic races started in history, and by and by village communities were found to be, or to have been the primitive form of society everywhere from India to Ireland. The inner organization of this primitive Communistic society was laid bare, in its typical form, by Morgan's crowning discovery of the true nature of the *Gens* and its relation to the *Tribe*. With the dissolution of these primæval communities society begins to be differentiated into separate and finally antagonistic classes. I have attempted to retrace this process of dissolution in: "Der Ursprung der Familie, des Privateigenthums und des Staats," 2nd edit., Stuttgart, 1886.

‡ Guild master, that is a full member of a guild, a master within, not a head of a guild.

open fight, that each time ended, either in the revolutionary reconstitution of society at large, or in the common ruin of the contending classes.

In the earlier epochs of history we find almost everywhere a complicated arrangement of society into various orders, a manifold gradation of social rank. In ancient Rome we have patricians, knights, plebeians, slaves; in the middle ages, feudal lords, vassals, guild masters, journeymen, apprentices, serfs; in almost all of these classes, again, subordinate gradations.

The modern bourgeois society that has sprouted from the ruins of feudal society, has not done away with class antagonisms. It has but established new classes, new conditions of oppression, new forms of struggle in place of the old ones.

Our epoch, the epoch of the bourgeois, possesses, however, this distinctive feature: it has simplified the class antagonisms. Society as a whole is more and more splitting up into two great hostile camps, into two great classes directly facing each other: Bourgeoisie and Proletariat.

From the serfs of the middle ages sprang the chartered burghers of the earliest towns. From these burgesses the first elements of the bourgeoisie were developed.

The discovery of America, the rounding of the Cape, opened up fresh ground for the rising bourgeoisie. The East Indian and Chinese markets, the colonization of America, trade with the colonies, the increase in the means of exchange and in commodities generally, gave to commerce, to navigation, to industry, an impulse never before known, and thereby, to the revolutionary element in the tottering feudal society, a rapid development.

The feudal system of industry, under which industrial production was monopolized by close guilds, now no longer sufficed for the growing wants of the new markets. The manufacturing system took its place. The guild masters were pushed on one side by the manufacturing middle class; division of labor between the different corporate guilds vanished in the face of division of labor in each single workshop.

Meantime the markets kept ever growing, the demand ever rising. Even manufacture no longer sufficed. Thereupon steam and machinery revolutionized industrial production. The place of manufacture * was taken by the giant, Modern Industry, the place of the industrial middle class, by industrial millionaires, the leaders of whole industrial armies, the modern bourgeois.

* In the literal sense of "Making by hand."—EDITOR.

Modern industry has established the world's market, for which the discovery of America paved the way. The market has given an immense development to commerce, to navigation, to communication by land. This development has, in its turn, reacted on the extension of industry; and in proportion as industry, commerce, navigation and railways extended, in the same proportion the bourgeoisie developed, increased its capital, and pushed into the background every class handed down from the middle ages.

We see, therefore, how the modern bourgeoisie is itself the product of a long course of development, of a series of revolutions in the modes of production and of exchange.

Each step in the development of the bourgeoisie was accompanied by a corresponding political advance of that class. An oppressed class under the sway of the feudal nobility, an armed and self-governing association in the mediæval commune,* here independent urban republic (as in Italy and Germany), there taxable "third estate" of the monarchy (as in France), afterwards, in the period of manufacture proper, serving either the semi-feudal or the absolute monarchy as a counterpoise against the nobility, and, in fact, corner-stone of the great monarchies in general, the bourgeoisie has at last, since the establishment of Modern Industry and of the world's market, conquered for itself, in the modern representative State, exclusive political sway. The executive of the modern State is but a committee for managing the common affairs of the whole bourgeoisie.

The bourgeoisie, historically, has played a most revolutionary part.

The bourgeoisie, wherever it has got the upper hand, has put an end to all feudal, patriarchal, idyllic relations. It has pitilessly torn asunder the motley feudal ties that bound man to his "natural superiors," and has left remaining no other nexus between man and man than naked self-interest, callous "cash payment." It has drowned the most heavenly ecstasies of religious fervor, of chivalrous enthusiasm, of philistine sentimentalism, in the icy water of egotistical calculation. It has resolved personal worth into exchange value, and in place of the numberless indefeasible chartered freedoms, has set up that single, unconscionable freedom—Free Trade. In one word, for exploitation, veiled by religious and political illusions, it has substituted naked, shameless, direct, brutal exploitation.

* "Commune" was the name taken, in France, by the nascent towns even before they had conquered from their feudal lords and masters, local self-government and political rights as the "Third Estate." Generally speaking, for the economical development of the bourgeoisie, England is here taken as the typical country; for its political development, France.

The bourgeoisie has stripped of its halo every occupation hitherto honored and looked up to with reverent awe. It has converted the physician, the lawyer, the priest, the poet, the man of science, into its paid wage laborers.

The bourgeoisie has torn away from the family its sentimental veil, and has reduced the family relation to a mere money relation.

The bourgeoisie has disclosed how it came to pass that the brutal display of vigor in the middle ages, which Reactionists so much admire, found its fitting complement in the most slothful indolence. It has been the first to show what man's activity can bring about. It has accomplished wonders far surpassing Egyptian pyramids, Roman aqueducts, and Gothic cathedrals; it has conducted expeditions that put in the shade all former Exoduses of nations and crusades.

The bourgeoisie cannot exist without constantly revolutionizing the instruments of production, and thereby the relations of production, and with them the whole relations of society. Conservation of the old modes of production in unaltered forms, was, on the contrary, the first condition of existence for all earlier industrial classes. Constant revolutionizing of production, uninterrupted disturbance of all social conditions, everlasting uncertainty and agitation, distinguish the bourgeois epoch from all earlier ones. All fixed, fast-frozen relations, with their train of ancient and venerable prejudices and opinions, are swept away; all new-formed ones become antiquated before they can ossify. All that is solid melts into air, all that is holy is profaned, and man is at last compelled to face with sober senses his real conditions of life and his relations with his kind.

The need of a constantly expanding market for its products chases the bourgeoisie over the whole surface of the globe. It must nestle everywhere, settle everywhere, establish connections everywhere.

The bourgeoisie has through its exploitation of the world's market given a cosmopolitan character to production and consumption in every country. To the great chagrin of Reactionists, it has drawn from under the feet of industry the national ground on which it stood. All old-established national industries have been destroyed or are daily being destroyed. They are dislodged by new industries, whose introduction becomes a life and death question for all civilized nations, by industries that no longer work up indigenous raw material, but raw material drawn from the remotest zones, industries whose products are consumed, not only at home, but in every quarter of the globe. In place of the old wants, satisfied by the productions of the country, we find new wants, requiring for their satisfaction the products of distant lands and climes. In place of the old local and national seclusion and self-sufficiency, we have intercourse in every direction, universal inter-dependence of nations. And as in material, so also in intellectual production. The intellectual creations of individual nations become common property. National one-sidedness and narrow-mindedness become more and more impossible, and from the numerous national and local literatures, there arises a world literature.

The bourgeoisie, by the rapid improvement of all instruments of production, by the immensely facilitated means of communication, draws all, even the most barbarian, nations into civilization. The cheap prices of its commodities are the heavy artillery with which it batters down all Chinese walls, with which it forces the barbarians' intensely obstinate hatred of foreigners to capitulate. It compels all nations, on pain of extinction, to adopt the bourgeois mode of production; it compels them to introduce what it calls civilization into their midst, i. e., to become bourgeois themselves. In one word, it creates a world after its own image.

The bourgeoisie has subjected the country to the rule of the towns. It has created enormous cities, has greatly increased the urban population as compared with the rural, and has thus rescued a considerable part of the population from the idiocy of rural life. Just as it has made the country dependent on the towns, so it has made barbarian and semi-barbarian countries dependent on the civilized ones, nations of peasants on nations of bourgeois, the East on the West.

The bourgeoisie keeps more and more doing away with the scattered state of the population, of the means of production, and of property. It has agglomerated population, centralized means of production, and has concentrated property in a few hands. The necessary consequence of this was political centralization. Independent, or but loosely connected provinces, with separate interests, laws, governments and systems of taxation, became lumped together into one nation, with one government, one code of laws, one national class interest, one frontier, and one customs tariff.

The bourgeoisie, during its rule of scarce one hundred years, has created more massive and more colossal productive forces than have all preceding generations together. Subjection of Nature's forces to man, machinery, application of chemistry to industry and agriculture, steam navigation, railways, electric telegraphs, clearing of whole continents for cultivation, canalization of rivers, whole populations conjured out of the ground—what earlier century had even a presentiment that such productive forces slumbered in the lap of social labor?

We see then: the means of production and of exchange on whose foundation the bourgeoisie built itself up, were generated in feudal society. At a certain stage in the development of these means of production and of exchange, the conditions under which feudal society produced and exchanged, the feudal organization of agriculture and manufacturing industry, in one word, the feudal relations of property, became no longer compatible with the already developed productive forces; they became so many fetters. They had to be burst asunder.

Into their place stepped free competition, accompanied by a social and political constitution adapted to it, and by the economical and political sway of the bourgeois class.

A similar movement is going on before our own eyes. Modern bourgeois society with its relations of production, of exchange, and of property, a society that has conjured up such gigantic means of production and of exchange, is like the sorcerer, who is no longer able to control the powers of the nether world whom he has called up by his spells. For many a decade past the history of industry and commerce is but the history of the revolt of modern productive forces against modern conditions of production, against the property relations that are the conditions for the existence of the bourgeoisie and of its rule. It is enough to mention the commercial crises that by their periodical return put on its trial, each time more threateningly, the existence of the bourgeois society. In these crises a great part not only of the existing products, but also of the previously created productive forces, is periodically destroyed. In these crises there breaks out an epidemic that, in all earlier epochs, would have seemed an absurdity— the epidemic of overproduction. Society suddenly finds itself put back into a state of momentary barbarism; it appears as if a famine, a universal war of devastation had cut off the supply of every means of subsistence; industry and commerce seem to be destroyed; and why? because there is too much civilization, too much means of subsistence, too much industry, too much commerce. The productive forces at the disposal of society no longer tend to further the development of the conditions of bourgeois property; on the contrary, they have become too powerful for these conditions, by which they are fettered, and so soon as they overcome these fetters, they bring disorder into the whole of bourgeois society, endanger the existence of bourgeois property. The conditions of bourgeois society are too narrow to comprise the wealth created by them. And how does the bourgeoisie get over these crises? On the one hand by enforced destruction of a mass of productive forces; on the other, by the conquest of new markets, and by the more thorough exploitation of the old ones. That is to say, by paving the way for more extensive and more destructive crises, and by diminishing the means whereby crises are prevented.

The weapons with which the bourgeoisie felled feudalism to the ground are now turned against the bourgeoisie itself.

But not only has the bourgeoisie forged the weapons that bring death to itself; it has also called into existence the men who are to wield those weapons—the modern working class—the proletarians.

In proportion as the bourgeoisie, i. e., capital, is developed, in the same proportion is the proletariat, the modern working class, developed; a class of laborers, who live only so long as they find work, and who find work only so long as their labor increases capital. These laborers, who must sell themselves piecemeal, are a commodity, like every other article of commerce, and are consequently exposed to all the vicissitudes of competition, to all the fluctuations of the market.

Owing to the extensive use of machinery and to division of labor, the work of the proletarians has lost all individual character, and, consequently, all charm for the workman. He becomes an appendage of the machine, and it is only the most simple, most monotonous, and most easily acquired knack, that is required of him. Hence, the cost of production of a workman is restricted almost entirely to the means of subsistence that he requires for his maintenance, and for the propagation of his race. But the price of a commodity, and therefore also of labor, is equal, in the long run, to its cost of production. In proportion, therefore, as the repulsiveness of the work increases, the wage decreases. Nay, more, in proportion as the use of machinery and division of labor increase, in the same proportion the burden of toil also increases, whether by prolongation of the working hours, by increase of the work exacted in a given time, or by increased speed of the machinery, etc.

Modern industry has converted the little workshop of the patriarchal master into the great factory of the industrial capitalist. Masses of laborers, crowded into the factory, are organized like soldiers. As privates of the industrial army they are placed under the command of a perfect hierarchy of officers and sergeants. Not only are they slaves of the bourgeois class, and of the bourgeois State, they are daily and hourly enslaved by the machine, by the over-seer, and, above all, by the individual bourgeois manu-facturer himself. The more openly this despotism proclaims gain to be its end and aim, the more petty, the more hateful and the more embittering it is.

The less skill and exertion of strength is implied in manual labor, in other words, the more modern industry becomes developed, the more is the labor of men superseded by that of women. Differences of age and sex have no longer any distinctive social validity for the working class. All are instruments of labor, more or less expensive to use, according to age and sex.

No sooner is the exploitation of the laborer by the manufacturer so far at an end that he receives his wages in cash, than he is set upon by the other portions of the bourgeoisie, the landlord, the shopkeeper, the pawnbroker, etc.

The lower strata of the middle class—the small tradespeople, shopkeep-ers, and retired tradesmen generally, the handicraftsmen and peasants—all these sink gradually into the proletariat, partly because their diminutive capital does not suffice for the scale on which modern industry is carried on, and is swamped in the competition with the large capitalists, partly because their specialized skill is rendered worthless by new methods of pro-duction. Thus the proletariat is recruited from all classes of the population.

The proletariat goes through various stages of development. With its birth begins its struggle with the bourgeoisie. At first the contest is carried on by individual laborers, then by the workpeople of a factory, then by the operatives of one trade, in one locality, against the individual bourgeois who directly exploits them. They direct their attacks not against the bour-geois conditions of production, but against the instruments of production themselves; they destroy imported wares that compete with their labor, they smash to pieces machinery, they set factories ablaze, they seek to re-store by force the vanished status of the workman of the middle ages.

At this stage the laborers still form an incoherent mass scattered over the whole country, and broken up by their mutual competition. If anywhere they unite to form more compact bodies, this is not yet the consequence of their own active union, but of the union of the bourgeoisie, which class, in order to attain its own political ends, is compelled to set the whole proletariat in motion, and is moreover yet, for a time, able to do so. At this stage, therefore, the proletarians do not fight their enemies, but the enemies of their enemies, the remnants of absolute monarchy, and land owners, the non-industrial bourgeois, the petty bourgeoisie. Thus the whole historical movement is concentrated in the hands of the bourgeoisie; every victory so obtained is a victory for the bourgeoisie.

But with the development of industry the proletariat not only increases in number; it becomes concentrated in greater masses, its strength grows and it feels that strength more. The various interests and conditions of life within the ranks of the proletariat are more and more equalized, in proportion as machinery obliterates all distinctions of labor, and nearly everywhere reduces wages to the same low level. The growing competition among the bourgeois, and the resulting commercial crises, make the wages of the workers ever more fluctuating. The unceasing improvement of machinery, ever more rapidly developing, makes their livelihood more and more precarious; the collisions between individual workman and individual bourgeois take more and more the character of collisions between two classes. Thereupon the workers begin to form combinations (Trades' Unions) against the bourgeois; they club together in order to keep up the rate of wages; they found permanent associations in order to make provision beforehand for these occasional revolts. Here and there the contest breaks out into riots.

Now and then the workers are victorious, but only for a time. The real fruit of their battles lies not in the immediate result but in the ever improved means of communication that are created in modern industry and that place the workers of different localities in contact with one another. It was just this contact that was needed to centralize the numerous local struggles, all of the same character, into one national struggle between classes. But every class struggle is a political struggle. And that union, to attain which the burghers of the middle ages, with their miserable highways, required centuries, the modern proletarians, thanks to railways, achieve in a few years.

This organization of the proletarians into a class and consequently into a political party, is continually being upset again by the competition between the workers themselves. But it ever rises up again; stronger, firmer, mightier. It compels legislative recognition of particular interests of the workers, by taking advantage of the divisions among the bourgeoisie itself. Thus the ten-hours bill in England was carried.

Altogether collisions between the classes of the old society further, in many ways, the course of the development of the proletariat. The bourgeoisie finds itself involved in a constant battle. At first with the aristocracy;

later on, with those portions of the bourgeoisie itself whose interests have become antagonistic to the progress of industry; at all times with the bourgeoisie of foreign countries. In all these countries it sees itself compelled to appeal to the proletariat, to ask for its help, and thus to drag it into the political arena. The bourgeoisie itself, therefore, supplies the proletariat with weapons for fighting the bourgeoisie.

Further, as we have already seen, entire sections of the ruling classes are, by the advance of industry, precipitated into the proletariat, or are at least threatened in their conditions of existence. These also supply the proletariat with fresh elements of enlightenment and progress.

Finally, in times when the class struggle nears the decisive hour, the process of dissolution going on within the ruling class, in fact within the whole range of old society, assumes such a violent, glaring character, that a small section of the ruling class cuts itself adrift, and joins the revolutionary class, the class that holds the future in its hands. Just as, therefore, at an earlier period, a section of the nobility went over to the bourgeoisie, so now a portion of the bourgeoisie goes over to the proletariat, and in particular, a portion of the bourgeois ideologists, who have raised themselves to the level of comprehending theoretically the historical movement as a whole.

Of all the classes that stand face to face with the bourgeoisie to-day, the proletariat alone is a really revolutionary class. The other classes decay and finally disappear in the face of modern industry; the proletariat is its special and essential product.

The lower middle class, the small manufacturer, the shopkeeper, the artisan, the peasant, all these fight against the bourgeoisie to save from extinction their existence as fractions of the middle class. They are therefore not revolutionary, but conservative. Nay, more, they are reactionary, for they try to roll back the wheel of history. If by chance they are revolutionary, they are so only in view of their impending transfer into the proletariat; they thus defend not their present, but their future interests, they desert their own standpoint to place themselves at that of the proletariat.

The "dangerous class," the social scum, that passively rotting class thrown off by the lowest layers of old society, may, here and there, be swept into the movement by a proletarian revolution; its conditions of life, however, prepare it far more for the part of a bribed tool of reactionary intrigue.

In the conditions of the proletariat, those of old society at large are already virtually swamped. The proletarian is without property; his relation to his wife and children has no longer anything in common with the bourgeois family relations; modern industrial labor, modern subjection to capital, the same in England as in France, in America as in Germany, has stripped him of every trace of national character. Law, morality, religion, are to him so many bourgeois prejudices, behind which lurk in ambush just as many bourgeois interests.

All the preceding classes that got the upper hand sought to fortify their already acquired status by subjecting society at large to their conditions of appropriation. The proletarians cannot become masters of the productive forces of society, except by abolishing their own previous mode of appropriation, and thereby also every other previous mode of appropriation. They have nothing of their own to secure and to fortify; their mission is to destroy all previous securities for, and insurances of, individual property.

All previous historical movements were movements of minorities, or in the interest of minorities. The proletarian movement is the self-conscious, independent movement of the immense majority, in the interest of the immense majority. The proletariat, the lowest stratum of our present society, cannot stir, cannot raise itself up, without the whole superincumbent strata of official society being sprung into the air.

Though not in substance, yet in form, the struggle of the proletariat with the bourgeoisie is at first a national struggle. The proletariat of each country must, of course, first of all settle matters with its own bourgeoisie.

In depicting the most general phases of the development of the proletariat, we traced the more or less veiled civil war, raging within existing society, up to the point where that war breaks out into open revolution, and where the violent overthrow of the bourgeoisie lays the foundation for the sway of the proletariat.

Hitherto every form of society has been based, as we have already seen, on the antagonism of oppressing and oppressed classes. But in order to oppress a class certain conditions must be assured to it under which it can, at least, continue its slavish existence. The serf, in the period of serfdom, raised himself to membership in the commune, just as the petty bourgeois, under the yoke of feudal absolutism, managed to develop into a bourgeois. The modern laborer, on the contrary, instead of rising with the progress of industry, sinks deeper and deeper below the conditions of existence of his own class. He becomes a pauper, and pauperism develops more rapidly than population and wealth. And here it becomes evident that the bourgeoisie is unfit any longer to be the ruling class in society and to impose its conditions of existence upon society as an over-riding law. It is unfit to rule because it is incompetent to assure an existence to its slave within his slavery, because it cannot help letting him sink into such a state that it has to feed him instead of being fed by him. Society can no longer live under this bourgeoisie; in other words, its existence is no longer compatible with society.

The essential condition for the existence, and for the sway of the bourgeois class, is the formation and augmentation of capital; the condition for capital is wage-labor. Wage-labor rests exclusively on competition between the laborers. The advance of industry, whose involuntary promoter is the bourgeoisie, replaces the isolation of the laborers, due to competition, by their revolutionary combination, due to association. The development of modern industry, therefore, cuts from under its feet the very foundation on which the bourgeoisie produces and appropriates products. What the bourgeoisie therefore produces, above all, are its own grave diggers. Its fall and the victory of the proletariat are equally inevitable.

II

Proletarians and Communists

In what relation do the Communists stand to the proletarians as a whole?

The Communists do not form a separate party opposed to other working class parties.

They have no interests separate and apart from those of the proletariat as a whole.

They do not set up any sectarian principles of their own by which to shape and mould the proletarian movement.

The Communists are distinguished from the other working class parties by this only: 1. In the national struggles of the proletarians of the different countries, they point out and bring to the front the common interests of the entire proletariat, independently of all nationality. 2. In the various stages of development which the struggle of the working class against the bourgeoisie has to pass through, they always and everywhere represent the interests of the movement as a whole.

The Communists, therefore, are on the one hand, practically, the most advanced and resolute section of the working class parties of every country, that section which pushes forward all others; on the other hand, theoretically, they have over the great mass of the proletariat the advantage of clearly understanding the line of march, the conditions, and the ultimate general results of the proletarian movement.

The immediate aim of the Communists is the same as that of all the other proletarian parties: formation of the proletariat into a class, overthrow of the bourgeois supremacy, conquest of political power by the proletariat.

The theoretical conclusions of the Communists are in no way based on ideas or principles that have been invented, or discovered, by this or that would-be universal reformer.

They merely express, in general terms, actual relations springing from an existing class struggle, from a historical movement going on under our very eyes. The abolition of existing property relations is not at all a distinctive feature of Communism.

All property relations in the past have continually been subject to historical change, consequent upon the change in historical conditions.

The French revolution, for example, abolished feudal property in favor of bourgeois property.

The distinguishing feature of Communism is not the abolition of property generally, but the abolition of bourgeois property. But modern bourgeois private property is the final and most complete expression of the system of producing and appropriating products, that is based on class antagonisms, on the exploitation of the many by the few.

In this sense the theory of the Communists may be summed up in the single sentence: Abolition of private property.

We Communists have been reproached with the desire of abolishing the right of personally acquiring property as the fruit of a man's own labor, which property is alleged to be the ground work of all personal freedom, activity and independence.

Hard-won, self-acquired, self-earned property! Do you mean the property of the petty artisan and of the small peasant, a form of property that preceded the bourgeois form? There is no need to abolish that; the development of industry has to a great extent already destroyed it, and is still destroying it daily.

Or do you mean modern bourgeois private property?

But does wage labor create any property for the laborer? Not a bit. It creates capital, i. e., that kind of property which exploits wage-labor, and which cannot increase except upon condition of begetting a new supply of wage-labor for fresh exploitation. Property, in its present form, is based on the antagonism of capital and wage labor. Let us examine both sides of this antagonism.

To be a capitalist, is to have not only a purely personal, but a social *status* in production. Capital is a collective product, and only by the united action of many members, nay, in the last resort, only by the united action of all members of society, can it be set in motion.

Capital is therefore not a personal, it is a social power.

When, therefore, capital is converted into common property, into the property of all members of society, personal property is not thereby transformed into social property. It is only the social character of the property that is changed. It loses its class character.

Let us now take wage-labor.

The average price of wage-labor is the minimum wage, i. e., that quantum of the means of subsistence, which is absolutely requisite to keep the laborer in bare existence as a laborer. What, therefore, the wage-laborer appropriates by means of his labor, merely suffices to prolong and reproduce a bare existence. We by no means intend to abolish this personal appropriation of the products of labor, an appropriation that is made for the maintenance and reproduction of human life, and that leaves no surplus wherewith to command the labor of others. All that we want to do away with, is the miserable character of this appropriation, under which the laborer lives merely to increase capital, and is allowed to live only in so far as the interest of the ruling class requires it.

In bourgeois society living labor is but a means to increase accumulated labor. In Communist society accumulated labor is but a means to widen, to enrich, to promote the existence of the laborer.

In bourgeois society, therefore, the past dominates the present; in Communist society, the present dominates the past. In bourgeois society capital is independent and has individuality, while the living person is dependent and has no individuality.

And the abolition of this state of things is called by the bourgeois: abolition of individuality and freedom! And rightly so. The abolition of bourgeois individuality, bourgeois independence, and bourgeois freedom is undoubtedly aimed at.

By freedom is meant, under the present bourgeois conditions of production, free trade, free selling and buying.

But if selling and buying disappears, free selling and buying disappears also. This talk about free selling and buying, and all the other "brave words" of our bourgeoisie about freedom in general, have a meaning, if any, only in contrast with restricted selling and buying, with the fettered traders of the middle ages, but have no meaning when opposed to the Communistic abolition of buying and selling, of the bourgeois conditions of production, and of the bourgeoisie itself.

You are horrified at our intending to do away with private property. But in your existing society private property is already done away with for nine-tenths of the population; its existence for the few is solely due to its non-existence in the hands of those nine-tenths. You reproach us, therefore, with intending to do away with a form of property, the necessary condition for whose existence is the non-existence of any property for the immense majority of society.

In one word, you reproach us with intending to do away with your property. Precisely so: that is just what we intend.

From the moment when labor can no longer be converted into capital, money, or rent, into a social power capable of being monopolized, i. e., from the moment when individual property can no longer be transformed into bourgeois property, into capital, from that moment, you say, individuality vanishes!

You must, therefore, confess that by "individual" you mean no other person than the bourgeois, than the middle class owner of property. This person must, indeed, be swept out of the way, and made impossible.

Communism deprives no man of the power to appropriate the products of society: all that it does is to deprive him of the power to subjugate the labor of others by means of such appropriation.

It has been objected, that upon the abolition of private property all work will cease, and universal laziness will overtake us.

According to this, bourgeois society ought long ago to have gone to the dogs through sheer idleness; for those of its members who work, acquire nothing, and those who acquire anything, do not work. The whole of this objection is but another expression of tautology, that there can no longer be any wage-labor when there is no longer any capital.

All objections against the Communistic mode of producing and appropriating material products, have, in the same way, been urged against the Communistic modes of producing and appropriating intellectual products. Just as, to the bourgeois the disappearance of class property is the disappearance of production itself, so the disappearance of class culture is to him identical with the disappearance of all culture.

That culture, the loss of which he laments, is, for the enormous majority, a mere training to act as a machine.

But don't wrangle with us so long as you apply to our intended abolition of bourgeois property, the standard of your bourgeois notions of freedom, culture, law, etc. Your very ideas are but the outgrowth of the conditions of your bourgeois production and bourgeois property, just as your jurisprudence is but the will of your class made into a law for all, a will, whose essential character and direction are determined by the economical conditions of existence of your class.

The selfish misconception that induces you to transform into eternal laws of nature and of reason, the social forms springing from your present mode of production and form of property—historical relations that rise and disappear in the progress of production—the misconception you share with every ruling class that has preceded you. What you see clearly in the case of ancient property, what you admit in the case of feudal property, you are of course forbidden to admit in the case of your own bourgeois form of property.

Abolition of the family! Even the most radical flare up at this infamous proposal of the Communists.

On what foundation is the present family, the bourgeois family, based? On capital, on private gain. In its completely developed form this family exists only among the bourgeoisie. But this state of things finds its complement in the practical absence of the family among the proletarians, and in public prostitution.

The bourgeois family will vanish as a matter of course when its complement vanishes, and both will vanish with the vanishing of capital.

Do you charge us with wanting to stop the exploitation of children by their parents? To this crime we plead guilty.

But, you will say, we destroy the most hallowed of relations, when we replace home education by social.

And your education! Is not that also social, and determined by the social conditions under which you educate, by the intervention, direct or indirect, of society by means of schools, etc.? The Communists have not invented the intervention of society in education; they do but seek to alter the character of that intervention, and to rescue education from the influence of the ruling class.

The bourgeois clap-trap about the family and education, about the hallowed co-relation of parent and child become all the more disgusting, as, by the action of modern industry, all family ties among the proletarians are torn asunder, and their children transformed into simple articles of commerce and instruments of labor.

But you Communists would introduce community of women, screams the whole bourgeoisie in chorus.

The bourgeois sees in his wife a mere instrument of production. He hears that the instruments of production are to be exploited in common, and, naturally, can come to no other conclusion than that the lot of being common to all will likewise fall to the women.

He has not even a suspicion that the real point aimed at is to do away with the status of women as mere instruments of production.

For the rest nothing is more ridiculous than the virtuous indignation of our bourgeois at the community of women which, they pretend, is to be openly and officially established by the Communists. The Communists have no need to introduce community of women; it has existed almost from time immemorial.

Our bourgeois, not content with having the wives and daughters of their proletarians at their disposal, not to speak of common prostitutes, take the greatest pleasure in seducing each other's wives.

Bourgeois marriage is in reality a system of wives in common, and thus, at the most, what the Communists might possibly be reproached with, is that they desire to introduce, in substitution for a hypocritically concealed, an openly legalized community of women. For the rest it is self-evident that the abolition of the present system of production must bring with it the abolition of the community of women springing from that system, i. e., of prostitution both public and private.

The Communists are further reproached with desiring to abolish countries and nationality.

The workingmen have no country. We cannot take from them what they have not got. Since the proletariat must first of all acquire political supremacy, must rise to be the leading class of the nation, must constitute itself *the* nation, it is, so far, itself national, though not in the bourgeois sense of the word.

National differences and antagonisms between peoples are daily more and more vanishing, owing to the development of the bourgeoisie, to freedom of commerce, to the world's market, to uniformity in the mode of production and in the conditions of life corresponding thereto.

The supremacy of the proletariat will cause them to vanish still faster. United action, of the leading civilized countries at least, is one of the first conditions for the emancipation of the proletariat.

In proportion as the exploitation of one individual by another is put an end to, the exploitation of one nation by another will also be put an end to. In proportion as the antagonism between classes within the nation vanishes, the hostility of one nation to another will come to an end.

The charges against Communism made from a religious, a philosophical, and, generally, from an ideological standpoint are not deserving of serious examination.

Does it require deep intuition to comprehend that man's ideas, views, and conceptions, in one word, man's consciousness changes with every change in the conditions of his material existence, in his social relations and in his social life?

What else does the history of ideas prove, than that intellectual production changes its character in proportion as material production is changed? The ruling ideas of each age have ever been the ideas of its ruling class.

When people speak of ideas that revolutionize society they do but express the fact that within the old society the elements of a new one have been created, and that the dissolution of the old ideas keeps even pace with the dissolution of the old conditions of existence.

When the ancient world was in its last throes the ancient religions were overcome by Christianity. When Christian ideas succumbed in the eighteenth century to rationalist ideas, feudal society fought its death battle with the then revolutionary bourgeoisie. The ideas of religious liberty and freedom of conscience merely gave expression to the sway of free competition within the domain of knowledge.

"Undoubtedly," it will be said, "religious, moral, philosophical and juridical ideas have been modified in the course of historical development. But religion, morality, philosophy, political science, and law, constantly survived this change.

"There are besides, eternal truths, such as Freedom, Justice, etc., that are common to all states of society. But Communism abolishes eternal truths, it abolishes all religion and all morality, instead of constituting them on a new basis; it therefore acts in contradiction to all past historical experience."

What does this accusation reduce itself to? The history of all past society has consisted in the development of class antagonisms, antagonisms that assumed different forms at different epochs.

But whatever form they may have taken, one fact is common to all past ages, viz., the exploitation of one part of society by the other. No wonder, then, that the social consciousness of past ages, despite all the multiplicity and variety it displays, moves within certain common forms, or general ideas, which cannot completely vanish except with the total disappearance of class antagonisms.

The Communist revolution is the most radical rupture with traditional property relations; no wonder that its development involves the most radical rupture with traditional ideas.

But let us have done with the bourgeois objections to Communism.

We have seen above that the first step in the revolution by the working class is to raise the proletariat to the position of the ruling class; to win the battle of democracy.

The proletariat will use its political supremacy to wrest, by degrees, all capital from the bourgeoisie; to centralize all instruments of production in the hands of the State, i. e., of the proletariat organized as the ruling class; and to increase the total of productive forces as rapidly as possible.

Of course, in the beginning this cannot be effected except by means of despotic inroads on the rights of property and on the conditions of bourgeois production; by means of measures, therefore, which appear economically insufficient and untenable, but which, in the course of the movement, outstrip themselves, necessitate further inroads upon the old social order and are unavoidable as a means of entirely revolutionizing the mode of production.

These measures will, of course, be different in different countries.

Nevertheless in the most advanced countries the following will be pretty generally applicable:

1. Abolition of property in land and application of all rents of land to public purposes.

2. A heavy progressive or graduated income tax.

3. Abolition of all right of inheritance.

4. Confiscation of the property of all emigrants and rebels.

5. Centralization of credit in the hands of the State, by means of a national bank with State capital and an exclusive monopoly.

6. Centralization of the means of communication and transport in the hands of the State.

7. Extension of factories and instruments of production owned by the State; the bringing into cultivation of waste lands, and the improvement of the soil generally in accordance with a common plan.

8. Equal liability of all to labor. Establishment of industrial armies, especially for agriculture.

9. Combination of agriculture with manufacturing industries: gradual abolition of the distinction between town and country, by a more equable distribution of the population over the country.

10. Free education for all children in public schools. Abolition of children's factory labor in its present form. Combination of education with industrial production, etc., etc.

When, in the course of development, class distinctions have disappeared and all production has been concentrated in the hands of a vast association of the whole nation, the public power will lose its political character. Political power, properly so called, is merely the organized power of one class for oppressing another. If the proletariat during its contest with the bourgeoisie is compelled, by the force of circumstances, to organize itself as a class, if, by means of a revolution, it makes itself the ruling class, and, as such, sweeps away by force the old conditions of production then it will, along with these conditions, have swept away the conditions for the existence of class antagonisms, and of classes generally, and will thereby have abolished its own supremacy as a class.

In place of the old bourgeois society with its classes and class antagonisms we shall have an association in which the free development of each is the condition for the free development of all.

[Part III deals with the relation to other types of socialist theory current in 1848, and is here omitted.—EDITOR.]

IV

POSITION OF THE COMMUNISTS IN RELATION TO THE VARIOUS EXISTING OPPOSITION PARTIES

Section II has made clear the relations of the Communists to the existing working class parties, such as the Chartists in England and the Agrarian Reformers in America.

The Communists fight for the attainment of the immediate aims, for the enforcement of the momentary interests of the working class; but in the movement of the present, they also represent and take care of the future of that movement. In France the Communists ally themselves with the Social-Democrats,* against the conservative and radical bourgeoisie, reserving, however, the right to take up a critical position in regard to phrases and illusions traditionally handed down from the great Revolution.

In Switzerland they support the Radicals, without losing sight of the fact that this party consists of antagonistic elements, partly of Democratic Socialists, in the French sense, partly of radical bourgeois.

In Poland they support the party that insists on an agrarian revolution, as the prime condition for national emancipation, that party which fomented the insurrection of Cracow in 1846.

In Germany they fight with the bourgeoisie whenever it acts in a revolutionary way against the absolute monarchy, the feudal squirearchy, and the petty bourgeoisie.

But they never cease, for a single instant, to instil into the working class the clearest possible recognition of the hostile antagonism between bourgeoisie and proletariat, in order that the German workers may straightway use, as so many weapons against the bourgeoisie, the social and political conditions that the bourgeoisie must necessarily introduce along with its supremacy, and in order that, after the fall of the reactionary classes in Germany, the fight against the bourgeoisie itself may immediately begin.

The Communists turn their attention chiefly to Germany, because that country is on the eve of a bourgeois revolution that is bound to be carried out under more advanced conditions of European civilization, and with a much more developed proletariat, than that of England was in the seventeenth, and of France in the eighteenth century, and because the bourgeois revolution in Germany will be but the prelude to an immediately following proletarian revolution.

In short, the Communists everywhere support every revolutionary movement against the existing social and political order of things.

In all these movements they bring to the front, as the leading question in each, the property question, no matter what its degree of development at the time.

* The party then represented in parliament by Ledru-Rollin, in literature by Louis Blanc, in the daily press by the Reforme. The name of Social-Democracy signified, with these its inventors, a section of the Democratic or Republican party more or less tinged with Socialism.

Finally, they labor everywhere for the union and agreement of the democratic parties of all countries.

The Communists disdain to conceal their views and aims. They openly declare that their ends can be attained only by the forcible overthrow of all existing social conditions. Let the ruling classes tremble at a Communistic revolution. The proletarians have nothing to lose but their chains. They have a world to win.

Workingmen of all countries, unite!

———

[*Capital* by Karl Marx is the Bible of the Communist movement, but it is too complicated to be satisfactorily represented by such a selection as could be printed here. Extensive selections from this and other Communist literature may be found in a *Handbook of Marxism*, edited by Emile Burns, New York, International Publishers, 1935.]

15

LENIN AND STALIN: MARXISM IN THE TWENTIETH CENTURY

[Both Lenin and Stalin have made Communism their entire career, first as revolutionists and afterwards as administrators. In their writings they have also defended the validity of Marxism and defined its applications in the twentieth century in Russia and in the world at large. The real name of Nicolai Lenin was Vladimir I. Ulyanov (1870–1924). The real name of Stalin ("Man of Steel") was Iosif Vissarionovich Djugashvili (born 1879); since the death of Lenin he has had the position of highest power in Russia.

In the first of the following passages Lenin discusses the interrelations of Communism, the state, revolution, and democracy. In the second, Stalin enumerates Lenin's contributions to Marxist theory. In the third, Stalin's own contributions to Marxist theory are described. The fourth passage presents the declaration of the rights and duties of citizens in the Soviet Constitution adopted in 1936, with comments by Stalin and others.]

Lenin on Democracy and Communism *

In capitalist society, under the conditions most favorable to its development, we have a more or less complete democracy in the form of a democratic republic. But this democracy is always bound by the narrow framework of capitalist exploitation, and consequently always remains, in reality, a democracy only for the minority, only for the possessing classes, only for the rich. Freedom in capitalist society always remains more or less the same as it was in the ancient Greek republics, that is, freedom for the slave owners. The modern wage-slaves, in virtue of the conditions of capitalist exploitation, remain to such an extent crushed by want and poverty that they "cannot be bothered with democracy," have "no time for politics";

* From N. Lenin, *The State and Revolution,* New York, The Vanguard Press, 1926, pp. 191–206; written in Switzerland shortly before the Revolution of 1917, and first published in 1918.

that, in the ordinary peaceful course of events, the majority of the population is debarred from participating in public political life.

The accuracy of this statement is perhaps most clearly proved by Germany, just because in this State constitutional legality has lasted and remained stable for a remarkably long time—for nearly half a century (1871-1914); and the Social-Democracy during this time has been able, far better than has been the case in other countries, to make use of "legality" in order to organize into a political party a larger proportion of the working class than has occurred anywhere else in the world.

What, then, is this highest proportion of politically conscious and active wage-slaves that has so far been observed in capitalist society? One million members of the Social-Democratic Party out of fifteen millions of wage-workers! Three millions industrially organized out of fifteen millions!

Democracy for an insignificant minority, democracy for the rich—that is the democracy of capitalist society. If we look more closely into the mechanism of capitalist democracy, everywhere—in the so-called "petty" details of the suffrage (the residential qualification, the exclusion of women, etc.), in the technique of the representative institutions, in the actual obstacles to the right of meeting (public buildings are not for the "poor"), in the purely capitalist organization of the daily press, etc., etc.—on all sides we shall see restrictions upon restrictions of democracy. These restrictions, exceptions, exclusions, obstacles for the poor, seem slight—especially in the eyes of one who has himself never known want, and has never lived in close contact with the oppressed classes in their hard life, and nine-tenths, if not ninety-nine hundredths, of the bourgeois publicists and politicians are of this class! But in their sum these restrictions exclude and thrust out the poor from politics and from an active share in democracy. Marx splendidly grasped the *essence* of capitalist democracy, when, in his analysis of the experience of the Commune, he said that the oppressed are allowed, once every few years to decide which particular representatives of the oppressing class are to represent and repress them in Parliament!

But from this capitalist democracy—inevitably narrow, stealthily thrusting aside the poor, and therefore, to its core, hypocritical and treacherous—progress does not march along a simple, smooth and direct path to "greater and greater democracy," as the Liberal professors and the lower middle class opportunists would have us believe. No, progressive development—that is, towards Communism—marches through the dictatorship of the proletariat; and cannot do otherwise, for there is no one else who can *break the resistance* of the exploiting capitalists, and no other way of doing it.

And the dictatorship of the proletariat—that is, the organization of the advance-guard of the oppressed as the ruling class, for the purpose of crushing the oppressors—cannot produce merely an expansion of democracy. *Together* with an immense expansion of democracy—for the first time becoming democracy for the poor, democracy for the people, and not democracy for the rich folk—the dictatorship of the proletariat will produce a series of restrictions of liberty in the case of the oppressors, exploiters and capitalists. We must crush them in order to free humanity from wage-slavery; their resistance must be broken by force. It is clear that where there is suppression there must also be violence, and there cannot be liberty or democracy.

Engels expressed this splendidly in his letter to Bebel when he said, as the reader will remember, that "the proletariat needs the State, not in the interests of liberty, but for the purpose of crushing its opponents; and, when one will be able to speak of freedom, the State will have ceased to exist."

Democracy for the vast majority of the nation, and the suppression by force—that is, the exclusion from democracy—of the exploiters and oppressors of the nation; this is the modification of democracy which we shall see during the *transition* from capitalism to Communism.

Only in Communist society, when the resistance of the capitalists has finally been broken, when the capitalists have disappeared, when there are no longer any classes (that is, when there is no difference between the members of society in respect of their social means of production) *only then* "does the State disappear *and one can speak of freedom.*" Only then will be possible and will be realized a really full democracy, a democracy without any exceptions. And only then will democracy itself begin to wither away in virtue of the simple fact that, free from capitalist slavery, from the innumerable horrors, savagery, absurdities and infamies of capitalist exploitation, people will gradually *become accustomed* to the observation of the elementary rules of social life, known for centuries, repeated for thousands of years in all sermons. They will become accustomed to their observance without force, without constraint, without subjection, without the *special apparatus* for compulsion which is called the State.

The expression "the State withers away," is very well chosen, for it indicates the gradual and elemental nature of the process. Only habit can, and undoubtedly will, have such an effect: for we see around us millions of times how readily people get accustomed to observe the necessary rules of life in common, if there is no exploitation, if there is nothing that causes indignation, that calls forth protest and revolt and has to be suppressed.

Thus, in capitalist society, we have a democracy that is curtailed, wretched, false; a democracy only for the rich, for the minority. The dictatorship of the proletariat, the period of transition to Communism, will, for the first time, produce a democracy for the people, for the majority, side by side with the necessary suppression of the minority constituted by the exploiters. Communism alone is capable of giving a really complete democracy, and the fuller it is the more quickly will it become unnecessary and wither away of itself. In other words, under capitalism we have a State in the proper sense of the word: that is, a special instrument for the suppression of one class by another, and of the majority by the minority at that. Naturally, for the successful discharge of such a task as the systematic suppression by the minority of exploiters of the majority of exploited, the greatest ferocity and savagery of suppression is required, and seas of blood are needed, through which humanity has to direct its path, in a condition of slavery, serfdom and wage labor.

Again, during the *transition* from capitalism to Communism, suppression is *still* necessary; but in this case it is suppression of the minority of exploiters by the majority of exploited. A special instrument, a special machine for suppression—that is, the "State"—is necessary, but this is now a transitional State, no longer a State in the ordinary sense of the term. For the suppression of the minority of exploiters, by the majority of those who were *but yesterday* wage-slaves, is a matter comparatively so easy, simple and natural that it will cost far less bloodshed than the suppression of the risings of the slaves, serfs or wage laborers, and will cost the human race far less. And it is compatible with the diffusion of democracy over such an overwhelming majority of the nation that the need for any *special machinery* for *suppression* will gradually cease to exist. The exploiters are unable, of course, to suppress the people without a most complex machine for performing this duty; but *the people* can suppress the exploiters even with a very simple "machine"—almost without any "machine" at all, without any special apparatus—by the simple *organization of the armed masses* (such as the Councils of Workers' and Soldiers' Deputies, we may remark, anticipating a little).

Finally, only under Communism will the State become quite unnecessary, for there will be *no one* to suppress—"no one" in the sense of a *class,* in the sense of a systematic struggle with a definite section of the population. We are not utopians, and we do not in the least deny the possibility and inevitability of excesses by *individual persons,* and equally the need to suppress such excesses. But, in the first place, for this no special machine, no special instrument of repression is needed. This will be done by the armed nation itself, as simply and as readily as any crowd of civilized people, even in modern society, parts a pair of combatants or does not allow a woman to be outraged. And, secondly, we know that the fundamental social cause of excesses which violate the rules of social life is the exploitation of the masses, their want and their poverty. With the removal of this chief cause, excesses will inevitably begin to "wither away." We do not know how quickly and in what stages, but we know that they will be withering away. With their withering away, the State will also wither away. Marx, without plunging into Utopia, defined more fully what can *now* be defined regarding this future epoch: namely, the difference between the higher and lower phases (degrees, stages) of Communist society.

The First Phase of Communist Society

In the *Criticism of the Gotha Programme,* Marx disproves in detail the Lassallean * idea of the receipt by the workers under Socialism of the "undiminished" or "full product of their labor." Marx shows that out of the whole of the social labor of society, it will be necessary to deduct a reserve fund, a fund for the expansion of industry, the replacement of "worn-out" machinery, and so on; then, also, out of the collective product a fund for the expenses of management, for schools, hospitals, homes for the aged, and so forth.

Instead of the hazy, obscure, general phrase of Lassalle—"the full product of his labor for the worker"—Marx gives a sober estimate as to how exactly a Socialist society will have to manage its affairs. Marx takes up a *concrete* analysis of the conditions of life of a society in which there will be no capitalism, and says: "We have to deal here" (analyzing the program of the Party), "not with a Communist society which has *developed* on its own foundations, but with one which has just *issued* actually from capitalist society, and which, in consequence, in all respects—economic, moral and intellectual—still bears the stamp of the old society, from the womb of which it came." And it is this Communist society—a society which has just come into the world out of the womb of capitalism, and which, in all re-

* See article in Encyc. of Social Sciences on Ferdinand Lassalle, 1825–1864.—EDITOR.

spects, bears the stamp of the old society—that Marx terms the first, or lower, phase of Communist society.

The means of production are now no longer the private property of individuals. The means of production belong to the whole of society. Every member of society, performing a certain part of socially-necessary labor, receives a certificate from society that he has done such and such a quantity of work. According to this certificate, he receives from the public stores of articles of consumption a corresponding quantity of products. After the deduction of that proportion of labor which goes to the public fund, every worker, therefore, receives from society as much as he has given it.

"Equality" seems to reign supreme. But when Lassalle, having in view such a social order (generally called "Socialism," but termed by Marx the first phase of Communism) speaks of this as "just distribution," and says that this is "the equal right of each to an equal share of the products of labor," Lassalle is mistaken, and Marx explains his error.

"Equal right [says Marx], we indeed have here; but it is *still* a 'bourgeois right' which, like every right, *pre-supposes inequality*. Every 'right' is an application of the *same* measure to *different* people who, as a matter of fact, are not similar and are not equal to one another; and, therefore, 'equal right' is really a violation of equality, and an injustice. In effect, every man having done as much social labor as every other, receives an equal share of the social products (with the above-mentioned deductions). Notwithstanding this, different people are not equal to one another. One is strong, another is weak; one is married, the other is not. One has more children, another has less, and so on.

"With equal labor [Marx concludes] and, therefore, with an equal share in the public stock of articles of consumption, one will, in reality, receive more than another, will find himself richer, and so on. To avoid all this, 'rights,' instead of being equal, should be unequal."

The first phase of Communism, therefore, still cannot produce justice and equality; differences and unjust differences in wealth will still exist, but the *exploitation* of one man by many, will have become impossible, because it will be impossible to seize as private property the *means of production,* the factories, machines, land, and so on. While tearing to tatters Lassalle's small bourgeois, confused phrase about "equality" and "justice" *in general,* Marx at the same time shows the *line of development* of Communist society, which is forced at first to destroy *only* the "injustice" that the means of production are in the hands of private individuals. *It is not capable* of destroying at once the further injustice which is constituted by the distribution of the articles of consumption according to "work performed" (and not according to need).

The vulgar economists, including the bourgeois professors (such as "our" Tugan-Baranowsky *), constantly reproach the Socialists with forgetting the inequality of mankind and with "dreaming" of destroying this inequality. Such a reproach, as we see, only proves the extreme ignorance of the bourgeois ideologists.

Marx not only, with the greatest care, takes into account the inevitable inequalities of men; he also takes cognizance of the fact that the mere conversion of the means of production into the common property of the whole society—"Socialism" in the generally accepted sense of the word—*does not remove* the shortcomings of distribution and the inequality of "bourgeois justice," which continue to exist as long as the products are divided according to the quantity of "work performed."

"But these defects [Marx continues] are unavoidable in the first phase of Communist society, in the form in which it comes forth, after the prolonged travail of birth, from capitalist society. Justice can never be in advance of its stage of economic development, and of the cultural development of society conditioned by the latter."

And so, in the first phase of Communist society (generally called Socialism) "bourgeois justice is *not* abolished in its entirety, but only in part, only in proportion to the economic transformation so far attained, that is, only in respect of the means of production." "Bourgeois law" recognizes them as the private property of separate individuals. Socialism converts them into common property, and to that extent, and only to that extent, does "bourgeois law" die out. But it continues to live as far as its other part is concerned, in the capacity of regulator or adjuster dividing labor and allotting the products amongst the members of society.

"He who does not work neither shall he eat"—this Socialist principle is *already* realized. "For an equal quantity of labor an equal quantity of products"—this Socialist principle is also already realized. Nevertheless, this is not yet Communism, and this does not abolish "bourgeois law," which gives to unequal individuals, in return for an unequal (in reality) amount of work, an equal quantity of products.

This is a "defect," says Marx, but it is unavoidable during the first phase

* See article in Encyc. of Social Sciences on M. I. Tugan-Baronovsky, 1865–1919. —EDITOR.

of Communism; for, if we are not to land in Utopia, we cannot imagine that, having overthrown capitalism, people will at once learn to work for society *without any regulations by law;* indeed, the abolition of capitalism does not *immediately* lay the economic foundations for such a change.

And there is no other standard yet than that of "bourgeois law." To this extent, therefore, a form of State is still necessary, which, whilst maintaining the public ownership of the means of production, preserves the equality of labor and equality in the distribution of the products. The State is withering away in so far as there are no longer any capitalists, any classes, and, consequently, any *class* whatever to suppress. But the State is not yet dead altogether, since there still remains the protection of "bourgeois law," which sanctifies actual inequality. For the complete extinction of the State complete Communism is necessary.

The Highest Phase of Communist Society

Marx continues:

"In the highest phase of Communist society, after the disappearance of the enslavement of man caused by his subjection to the principle of division of labor; when, together with this, the opposition between brain and manual work will have disappeared; when labor will have ceased to be a mere means of supporting life and will itself have become one of the first necessities of life; when with the all-round development of the individual, the productive forces, too, will have grown to maturity, and all the forces of social wealth will be pouring an uninterrupted torrent—only then will it be possible wholly to pass beyond the narrow horizon of bourgeois laws, and only then will society be able to inscribe on its banner: 'From each according to his ability; to each according to his needs.' "

Only now can we appreciate the full justice of Engels' observations when he mercilessly ridiculed all the absurdity of combining the words "freedom" and "State." While the State exists there can be no freedom. When there is freedom there will be no State.

The economic basis for the complete withering away of the State is that high stage of development of Communism when the distinction between brain and manual work disappears; consequently, when one of the principal sources of modern *social* inequalities will have vanished—a source, moreover, which it is impossible to remove immediately by the mere conversion of the means of production into public property, by the mere expropriation of the capitalists.

This expropriation will make it possible gigantically to develop the forces of production. And seeing how incredibly, even now, capitalism *retards* this development, how much progress could be made even on the basis of modern technique at the level it has reached, we have a right to say, with the fullest confidence, that the expropriation of the capitalists will result inevitably in a gigantic development of the productive forces of human society. But how rapidly this development will go forward, how soon it will reach the point of breaking away from the division of labor, of the destruction of the antagonism between brain and manual work, of the transformation of work into a "first necessity of life"—this we do not and *cannot* know.

Consequently, we are right in speaking solely of the inevitable withering away of the State, emphasizing the protracted nature of this process, and its dependence upon the rapidity of development of the *higher phase* of Communism; leaving quite open the question of lengths of time, or the concrete forms of this withering away, since material for the solution of such questions is not available.

The State will be able to wither away completely when society has realized the formula: "From each according to his ability; to each according to his needs"; that is when people have become accustomed to observe the fundamental principles of social life, and their labor is so productive, that they will voluntarily work *according to their abilities.* "The narrow horizon of bourgeois law," which compels one to calculate, with the pitilessness of a Shylock, whether one has not worked half-an-hour more than another, whether one is not getting less pay than another—this narrow horizon will then be left behind. There will then be no need for any exact calculation by society of the quantity of products to be distributed to each of its members; each will take freely "according to his needs."

From the capitalist point of view, it is easy to declare such a social order "a pure Utopia," and to sneer at the Socialists for promising each the right to receive from society, without any control of the labor of the individual citizens, any quantity of truffles, motor cars, pianos, and so forth. Even now, most bourgeois "savants" deliver themselves of such sneers, but thereby they only display at once their ignorance and their material interest in defending capitalism. Ignorance—for it has never entered the head of any Socialist "to promise" that the highest phase of Communism will actually arrive, while the *anticipation* of the great Socialists that it *will* arrive, assumes *neither the present* productive powers of labor, *nor the present* unthinking "man in the street" capable of spoiling, without reflection, the stores of social wealth and of demanding the impossible. As long as the "highest" phase of Communism has not arrived, the Socialists demand the *strictest* control, *by society and by the State,* of the quantity of labor and the quantity of consumption; only this control must *start* with the expropriation of the capitalists, with the control of the workers over the capitalists, and must be carried out, not by a government of bureaucrats, but by a government of the *armed workers.*

The interested defense of capitalism by the capitalist ideologists (and their hangers-on like Tseretelli, Tchernoff & Co.) consists just in that they *substitute* their disputes and discussions about the far future for the essential, imperative questions *of the day:* the expropriation of the capitalists, the conversion of *all* citizens into workers and employees of *one* huge "syndicate"—the whole State—and the complete subordination of the whole of the work of this syndicate to a really democratic State—to the *State consisting of the Councils of Workers' and Soldiers' Deputies.* In reality, when a learned professor, and in his train, some philistine, and in his wake, Messrs. Tseretelli and Tchernoff, talk of unreasonable Utopias, of the demagogic promises of the Bolsheviks, of the impossibility of "bringing in" Socialism, it is the higher stage or phase of Communism which they have in mind, and which no one has not only promised, but ever even thought of trying to "bring in," because, in any case, it is altogether impossible to "bring it in."

And here we come to that question of the scientific difference between Socialism and Communism, upon which Engels touched in his discussion cited above on the incorrectness of the name "Social-Democrat." The political difference between the first, or lower, and the higher phase of Communism will in time, no doubt, be tremendous; but it would be ridiculous to emphasize it now, under capitalism, and only, perhaps, some isolated anarchist could invest it with primary importance—that is, if there are still people amongst the anarchists who have learned nothing from the Plekanoff-like conversion of the Kropotkins,* the Graves, the Cornelisens, and other "leading lights" of anarchism to Social-Chauvinism or Anarcho-"Jusquauboutism" as one of the few anarchists still preserving their honor (Gay) has expressed it.

But the scientific difference between Socialism and Communism is

---

* See articles in Encyc. of Social Sciences on G. V. Plekhanov, 1857–1918, and P. E. Kropotkin, 1842–1921.—EDITOR.

clear. That which is generally called Socialism is termed by Marx the first or lower phase of Communist society. In so far as the means of production become public property, the word Communism is also applicable here, providing that we do not forget that it is not full Communism. The great importance of Marx's explanation is this: that here, too, he consistently applies materialist dialectics, the theory of evolution, looking upon Communism as something which evolves *out of* capitalism.

Instead of artificially elaborate and scholastic definitions and profitless disquisitions on the meanings of words ("what Socialism is," "what Communism is"), Marx gives us an analysis of what may be called the stages in the economic growth of Communism.

In its first phase or first stage Communism *cannot* as yet be economically mature and quite free of all tradition and of all taint of capitalism. Hence we see the interesting phenomenon of the first phase of Communism retaining "the narrow horizon of bourgeois law." Bourgeois law, in respect of the distribution of articles of consumption, presupposes inevitably the capitalist State, for law is nothing without the organization for *forcing* people to obey it. Consequently, for a certain time not only bourgeois law, but even the capitalist State may remain under Communism without the capitalist class.

This may appear to some a paradox, a piece of intellectual subtlety of which Marxism is often accused by people who would not put themselves out to study its extraordinarily profound teachings. But, as a matter of fact, the Old surviving in the New confronts us in life at every step in nature as well as in Society. It is not Marx's own sweet will which smuggled a scrap of bourgeois law into Communism; he simply indicated what is economically and politically inevitable in a society issuing from the *womb of capitalism*.

Democracy is of great importance in the working class struggle for freedom against the capitalists. But democracy is not a limit one may not overstep; it is merely one of the stages in the course of development from feudalism to capitalism, and from capitalism to Communism.

Democracy implies equality. The immense significance of the struggle of the proletariat for equality and the power of attraction of such a battlecry are obvious, if we but rightly interpret it as meaning the *annihilation of classes*. But the equality of democracy is *formal* equality—no more; and immediately after the attainment of the equality of all members of society in respect of the ownership of the means of production, that is, of equality of labor and equality of wages, there will inevitably arise before humanity the question of going further from equality which is formal to equality which is real, and of realizing in life the formula, "From each according to his ability; to each according to his needs." By what stages, by means of what practical measures humanity will proceed to this higher aim—this we do not and cannot know. But it is important that one should realize how infinitely mendacious is the usual capitalist representation of Socialism as something lifeless, petrified, fixed once for all. In reality, it is only with Socialism that there will commence a rapid, genuine, real mass advance, in which first the majority and then the *whole* of the population will take part—an advance in all domains of social and individual life.

Democracy is a form of the State—one of the varieties of the State, and, consequently, like every State, it stands as an organized, systematic application of force against mankind. That is its one aspect. But, on the other hand, it is the formal recognition of the equality of all citizens, the equal right of all to determine the structure and administration of the State. Out of this formal recognition there arises, in its turn, a stage in the development of democracy, when it first rallies the proletariat as a revolutionary class against capitalism, and gives it an opportunity to crush, to break to atoms, to wipe off the face of the earth the capitalist government machine —even the republican variety: the standing army, police, and bureaucracy. Second, it enables it to substitute for all this a more democratic, but still a *State* machinery in the shape of armed masses of the working class, which then become transformed into a universal participation of the people in a militia.

Here "quantity passes into quality." Such a degree of democracy carries with it the abandonment of the framework of capitalist society, and the beginning of its Socialist reconstruction. If *everyone* really takes part in the administration of the State, capitalism cannot retain its hold. As a matter of fact, capitalism, as it develops, itself prepares the ground for everyone to be able really to take part in the administration of the State.

We may class as part of this preparation of the ground the universal literacy of the population, already realized in most of the more progressive capitalist countries, then the education and discipline inculcated upon millions of workers by the huge, complex, and socialized apparatus of the post, railways, big factories, large-scale commerce, banking and so on, and so forth.

With such an economic groundwork it is quite possible, immediately, within twenty-four hours, to pass to the overthrow of the capitalists and bureaucrats, and to replace them, in the control of production and distribution, in the business of apportioning labor and products, by the armed workers, or the people in arms. The question of control and bookkeeping must not be confused with the question of the scientifically educated staff of engineers, agriculturists and so on. These gentlemen work to-day owing allegiance to the capitalists: they will work even better to-morrow, owing it to the armed workers. Bookkeeping and control—these are the chief things necessary for the smooth and correct functioning of the *first phase* of Communist society. *All* the citizens are here transformed into the hired employees of the State, which then is the armed workers. *All* the citizens become the employees and workers of *one* national State "syndicate." It simply resolves itself into a question of all working to an equal extent, of all carrying out regularly the measure of work apportioned to them, and of all receiving equal pay.

The bookkeeping and control necessary for this have been simplified by capitalism to the utmost, till they have become the extraordinarily simple operations of watching, recording and issuing receipts, within the reach of anybody who can read and write and knows the first four arithmetical rules.* When the majority of the citizens themselves begin everywhere to keep such accounts and maintain such control over the capitalists, now converted into employees, and over the intellectual gentry, who still retain capitalist habits, this control will, indeed, become universal, pervading, rational: it will be ubiquitous, and there will be no way of escaping it.

The whole of society will have become one office and one factory, with equal work and equal pay. But this "factory" discipline, which the proletariat will extend to the whole of society on the defeat of capitalism and the overthrow of the exploiters, is by no means our ideal, and is far from our final aim. It is but a foothold as we press on to the radical cleansing of society from all the brutality and foulness of capitalist exploitation: we leave it behind as we move on.

When all, or be it even only the greater part of society, have learned how to govern the State, have taken this business into their own hands, have established a control over the insignificant minority of capitalists, over

* When most of the functions of the State are reduced to this bookkeeping and control by the workers themselves, it ceases to be a "political" State. Then "the public functions are converted from political into simple administrative functions" (cf. above, chap. iv, par. 2, on the dispute of Engels with the anarchists).

the gentry with capitalist leanings, and workers thoroughly demoralized by capitalism—from this moment the need for any government begins to vanish. The more complete the democracy, the nearer the moment when it ceases to be necessary. The more democratic the "State" consisting of armed workers, which is "no longer really a State in the ordinary sense of the term," the more rapidly does every form of the State begin to decay. For when all have learned to manage, and really do manage, socialized production, when all really do keep account and control of the idlers, gentlefolk, swindlers and such like "guardians of capitalist traditions," the escape from such general registration and control will inevitably become so increasingly difficult, so much the exception, and will probably be accompanied by such swift and severe punishment (for the armed workers are very practical people, not sentimental intellectuals, and they will scarcely allow anyone to trifle with them), that very soon the *necessity* of observing the simple, fundamental rules of any kind of social life will become a habit. The door will then be wide open for the transition from the first phase of Communist society to its second higher phase, and along with it to the complete withering away of the State.

Stalin on Lenin's Contribution to Marxism *

I think that Lenin "added" no "new principles" to Marxism nor did Lenin abolish any of the "old" principles of Marxism. Lenin always was and remained a loyal and consistent pupil of Marx and Engels, and wholly and entirely based himself on the principles of Marxism. But Lenin did not merely carry out the doctrines of Marx and Engels. He developed these doctrines further. What does that mean? It means that he developed the doctrines of Marx and Engels in accordance with the new conditions of development, with the new phase of capitalism, with imperialism. This means that in developing further the doctrines of Marx in the new conditions of the class struggle, Lenin contributed to the general treasury of Marxism something new as compared with what was created by Marx and Engels and with what they could create in the pre-imperialist period of capitalism. Moreover, Lenin's contribution to Marxism is based wholly and entirely on the principles laid down by Marx and Engels. In that sense we speak of Leninism as Marxism of the epoch of imperialism and proletarian revolutions. Here, for example, are a number of questions in

* From Joseph Stalin, "Interview with the First American Labor Delegation in Russia" [Sept. 9, 1927], in *What is Leninism?*, "compiled and arranged by V. Bystryansky and M. Mishin," New York, International Publishers, 1936, pp. 41–46.

the sphere of which Lenin contributed something new in developing further the doctrines of Marx:

First: the question of monopolistic capitalism—of imperialism as the new phase of capitalism. In *Capital* Marx and Engels analyzed the basis of capitalism. But Marx and Engels lived in the pre-monopolistic period of capitalism, in the period of the smooth evolution of capitalism and its "peaceful" expansion throughout the whole world. This old phase of capitalism came to a close towards the end of the nineteenth and the beginning of the twentieth centuries, when Marx and Engels had already passed away. Clearly Marx and Engels could only guess at the new conditions of the development of capitalism which arose out of the new phase of capitalism which succeeded the old phase. In the imperialistic, monopolistic phase of development the smooth evolution of capitalism gave way to spasmodic, cataclysmic development, the unevenness of development and the contradictions of capitalism emerged with particular force; the struggle for markets and spheres for the investment of capital conducted amidst conditions of extreme unevenness of development made periodical imperialist wars for a periodical redistribution of the world and of spheres of influence inevitable. The service Lenin rendered, and, consequently, his new contribution, was that on the basis of the main postulates enunciated in *Capital* he made a fundamental Marxian analysis of imperialism as the final phase of capitalism, he exposed its ulcers and the conditions of its inevitable doom. On the basis of this analysis arose Lenin's well-known postulate that the conditions of imperialism made possible the victory of socialism in separate capitalist countries.

Second: The question of the dictatorship of the proletariat. The fundamental idea of the dictatorship of the proletariat as the political domination of the proletariat and as a method of overthrowing the reign of capital by violence was created by Marx and Engels. Lenin's new contribution in this field was that (a) utilizing the experience of the Paris Commune and the Russian Revolution, he discovered the Soviet form of government as the state form of the dictatorship of the proletariat; (b) he deciphered the formula of the dictatorship of the proletariat from the point of view of the problem of the allies of the proletariat, and defined the dictatorship of the proletariat as a special form of class alliance between the proletariat, which is the leader, and the exploited masses of the non-proletarian classes (the peasantry, etc.) who are led; (c) he particularly emphasized the fact that the dictatorship of the proletariat is a higher type of democracy in class society, *i. e., proletarian* democracy, which expresses the interest of the majority (the exploited) as against capitalist democracy which expresses the interests of the minority (the exploiters).

Third: the question of the forms and methods of the successful building up of socialism in the period of dictatorship of the proletariat, in the period of transition from capitalism to socialism in a country encircled by capitalist states. Marx and Engels regarded the period of the dictatorship of the proletariat as a more or less prolonged period replete with revolutionary conflicts and civil wars in the course of which the proletariat in power would take the economic, political, cultural and organizational measures necessary for the purpose of establishing a new socialist society, a society without classes and without a state, in place of the old capitalist society. Lenin wholly and entirely based himself on these fundamental postulates of Marx and Engels. Lenin's new contribution in this field was: (a) he proved that it was possible to construct complete socialist society in a land of the dictatorship of the proletariat encircled by imperialist states provided the country is not crushed by the military intervention of the surrounding capitalist states; (b) he outlined the concrete path of economic policy (the "New Economic Policy") by which the proletariat, being in command of the economic key positions (industry, land, transport, the banks, etc.), links up socialized industry with agriculture ("linking up industry with peasant agriculture") and thus leads the whole of national economy towards socialism; (c) he outlined the concrete channels by which the bulk of the peasantry is gradually brought into the line of socialist construction through the medium of the coöperative societies, which, in the hands of the proletarian dictatorship, represent a powerful instrument for the transformation of petty-peasant economy and for the reëducation of the main masses of the peasantry in the spirit of socialism.

Fourth: the question of the hegemony of the proletariat in revolution, in all popular revolutions—in the revolution against tsarism as well as in the revolution against capitalism. Marx and Engels presented the main outlines of the idea of the hegemony of the proletariat. Lenin's new contribution in this field was that he further developed and expanded these outlines into a symmetrical system of the hegemony of the proletariat, into a symmetrical system of proletarian leadership of the masses of the toilers in town and country not only in the fight for the overthrow of tsarism and capitalism, but also in the work of building up socialism under the dictatorship of the proletariat. It is well known that, thanks to Lenin and his

Party, the idea of the hegemony of the proletariat was skillfully applied in Russia. This, in passing, explains why the revolution in Russia brought the proletariat to power. In previous revolutions it usually happened that the workers did all the fighting at the barricades, shed their blood and overthrew the old order, but power passed into the hands of the bourgeoisie, which oppressed and exploited the workers. That was the case in England and in France. That was the case in Germany. In Russia, however, things took a different turn. In Russia, the workers did not merely represent the shock troops of the revolution. While serving as the shock troops of the revolution, the Russian proletariat at the same time strove for hegemony, for the political leadership of all the exploited masses of town and country, rallying them around itself, detaching them from the bourgeoisie and politically isolating the bourgeoisie. Being the leader of the exploited masses, the Russian proletariat all the time waged a fight to seize power in its own hands and utilize it in its own interests against the bourgeoisie and against capitalism. This explains why every powerful outbreak of the revolution in Russia, as in October 1905, and in February 1917, gave rise to Soviets of Workers' Deputies as the embryo of the new apparatus of power—the function of which would be to crush the bourgeoisie—as against the bourgeois parliament, the old apparatus of power —the function of which was to crush the proletariat. On two occasions the bourgeoisie in Russia tried to restore the bourgeois parliament and put an end to the Soviets: In August 1917, at the time of the "Preliminary Parliament" prior to the capture of power by the Bolsheviks, and in January 1918, at the time of the "Constituent Assembly" after power had been seized by the proletariat. On both occasions these efforts failed. Why? Because the bourgeoisie was already politically isolated. The vast masses of the toilers regarded the proletariat as the sole leader of the revolution and the soviets had already been tried and tested by the masses as their own workers' government. For the proletariat to have replaced these soviets by a bourgeois parliament would have been tantamount to committing suicide. It is not surprising, therefore, that bourgeois parliamentarism did not take root in Russia. That is why the revolution in Russia led to the establishment of the rule of the proletariat. These were the results of the application of the Leninist system of the hegemony of the proletariat in revolution.

Fifth: the national and colonial question. In analyzing the events in Ireland, India, China and the Central European countries like Poland

and Hungary, in their time Marx and Engels developed the basic, initial ideas of the national and colonial question. In his works Lenin based himself on these ideas. Lenin's new contribution in this field was: (a) that he gathered these ideas into one symmetrical system of views on national and colonial revolutions in the epoch of imperialism; (b) that he connected the national and colonial question with the question of overthrowing imperialism, and (c) that he declared the national and colonial question to be a component part of the general question of international proletarian revolution.

Finally: the question of the Party of the proletariat. Marx and Engels gave the main outlines of the idea of the Party as being the vanguard of the proletariat, without which (the Party) the proletariat could not achieve its emancipation, could not capture power or reconstruct capitalist society. Lenin's new contribution to this theory was that he developed these outlines further and applied them to the new conditions of the proletarian struggle in the period of imperialism and showed: (a) that the Party is a higher form of the class organization of the proletariat as compared with the other forms of proletarian organization (labor unions, coöperative societies, state organization) and, moreover, its function was to generalize and direct the work of these organizations; (b) that the dictatorship of the proletariat may be realized only through the Party as its directing force; (c) that the dictatorship of the proletariat can be complete only if it is led by a single party, the Communist Party, which does not and must not share leadership with any other party; and (d) that without iron discipline in the Party, the tasks of the dictatorship of the proletariat to crush the exploiters and to transform class society into socialist society cannot be fulfilled.*

This, in the main, is the new contribution which Lenin made in his works; he developed and made more concrete the doctrines of Marx in a manner applicable to the new conditions of the proletarian struggle in the period of imperialism.

That is why we say that Leninism is Marxism of the epoch of imperialism and proletarian revolutions.

---

* Compare the expansion and application of this conception of "party" by John Strachey in *What Are We to Do?*, Random House, 1938, Chapters XIV–XVIII, and Dewey's criticism, pages 143–145 of this volume. Compare also Hitler's conception of "party," pages 218–219, 220–221 of this volume.—EDITOR.

[*The Further Development of Leninism by Stalin* *]

The theory of Marxism-Leninism is being concretized and developed by Stalin, the comrade-in-arms and disciple of Lenin, the best continuer of his cause.

Stalin developed the Marxist-Leninist doctrine of the *proletarian dictatorship,* worked out the question of the forms of the class struggle of the proletariat at the various stages of socialist construction, of the ways of destroying the capitalist elements and classes in general. Stalin concretized the Marxist-Leninist doctrine of the transitional period from capitalism to communism. Stalin developed the doctrine of Lenin *concerning the possibility of building socialism in our country.* On this basis Stalin developed the general plan of the offensive of socialism on the entire front, concretized the methods, forms and ways of building classless, socialist society.

Stalin developed the Leninist doctrine of *industrialization* as a condition of the victory of socialism in our country. Stalin made a most valuable contribution to Marxist-Leninist theory by working out the question of the concrete ways of the *socialist remolding of the peasantry* under the leadership of the proletariat, the question of the production bond,† of the conditions and methods of *collectivizing agriculture* and liquidating the kulaks as a class on the basis of mass collectivization.

Stalin developed the Marxist-Leninist theory in the *national and colonial question* as part of the general question of the international revolution.

Stalin developed the doctrine of Lenin *concerning the Party and its rôle in the system of the proletarian dictatorship;* he brilliantly worked out the *strategy and tactics* of the proletarian Party. Stalin developed the Leninist

---

* From Marx-Engels-Lenin Institute, *Karl Marx, The Fiftieth Anniversary of His Death,* 1933, printed in *What Is Leninism?,* International Publishers Co., 1936, pp. 54–55.

† From the introduction of the New Economic Policy in 1921 to the beginning of the first Five-Year Plan period, the principal form of intercourse between town and country was the bond (*smychka*) *based on trade,* when in exchange for agricultural produce the industries supplied the peasants with goods mainly for the satisfaction of their personal needs (cloth, boots, kerosene, sugar, etc.).

With the beginning of the first Five-Year Plan the main form of intercourse between town and country became the *bond based on production, i.e.,* the working class directs its efforts in production towards serving the production requirements of the countryside, which it supplies with agricultural machinery, tractors, fertilizers, etc.—*Ed.* [of *What Is Leninism?*].

analysis of the social and ideological roots of *opportunism*, having disclosed the peculiar features of its manifestations at the various stages of the class struggle.

On the basis of Lenin's doctrine of imperialism Stalin made an accurate analysis of the *struggle of the two systems* in the conditions of the general crisis of capitalism and the growing international proletarian revolution.

With Leninist firmness and irreconcilability Stalin guides the struggle on two fronts against every manifestation of opportunism within the Party or the Communist International, against Trotskyism, which later became counter-revolutionary, and against Right opportunism, the product of the counter-revolutionary kulak resistance to the victorious proletariat. As a theoretician and leader of the Party and the Communist International, Stalin, by his entire activity, affords a splendid example of the union of revolutionary theory and practice, and enriches *materialist dialectics*, the revolutionary method of Marxism-Leninism. *Stalin's name is on a par with the names of the great theoreticians and leaders of the world proletariat, Marx, Engels and Lenin.*

Constitution (Fundamental Law) of the Union of Soviet Socialist Republics *

CHAPTER X

FUNDAMENTAL RIGHTS AND DUTIES OF CITIZENS

ARTICLE 118

Citizens of the U.S.S.R. have the right to work, that is, are guaranteed the right to employment and payment for their work in accordance with its quantity and quality.

The right to work is ensured by the socialist organization of the national economy, the steady growth of the productive forces of Soviet society, the elimination of the possibility of economic crises, and the abolition of unemployment.

ARTICLE 119

Citizens of the U.S.S.R. have the right to rest and leisure.

The right to rest and leisure is ensured by the reduction of the working day to seven hours for the overwhelming majority of the workers, the

---

* Published under the imprint of Ogiz, State Publishing House of Political Literature, 1938.

institution of annual vacations with full pay for workers and employees and the provision of a wide network of sanatoria, rest homes and clubs for the accommodation of the working people.

ARTICLE 120

Citizens of the U.S.S.R. have the right to maintenance in old age and also in case of sickness or loss of capacity to work.

This right is ensured by the extensive development of social insurance of workers and employees at state expense, free medical service for the working people and the provision of a wide network of health resorts for the use of the working people.

ARTICLE 121

Citizens of the U.S.S.R. have the right to education.

This right is ensured by universal, compulsory elementary education; by education, including higher education, being free of charge; by the system of state stipends for the overwhelming majority of students in the universities and colleges; by instruction in schools being conducted in the native language, and by the organization in the factories, state farms, machine and tractor stations and collective farms of free vocational, technical and agronomic training for the working people.

ARTICLE 122

Women in the U.S.S.R. are accorded equal rights with men in all spheres of economic, state, cultural, social and political life.

The possibility of exercising these rights is ensured to women by granting them an equal right with men to work, payment for work, rest and leisure, social insurance and education, and by state protection of the interests of mother and child, pre-maternity and maternity leave with full pay, and the provision of a wide network of maternity homes, nurseries and kindergartens.

ARTICLE 123

Equality of rights of citizens of the U.S.S.R., irrespective of their nationality or race, in all spheres of economic, state, cultural, social and political life, is an indefeasible law.

Any direct or indirect restriction of the rights of, or, conversely, any establishment of direct or indirect privileges for, citizens on account of their race or nationality, as well as any advocacy of racial or national exclusiveness or hatred and contempt, is punishable by law.

ARTICLE 124

In order to ensure to citizens freedom of conscience, the church in the U.S.S.R. is separated from the state, and the school from the church. Freedom of religious worship and freedom of anti-religious propaganda is recognized for all citizens. [No freedom of pro-religious propaganda is recognized.—EDITOR.]

ARTICLE 125

In conformity with the interests of the working people, and in order to strengthen the socialist system, the citizens of the U.S.S.R. are guaranteed by law:

a) freedom of speech;
b) freedom of the press;
c) freedom of assembly, including the holding of mass meetings;
d) freedom of street processions and demonstrations.

These civil rights are ensured by placing at the disposal of the working people and their organizations printing presses, stocks of paper, public buildings, and streets, communications facilities and other material requisites for the exercise of these rights. [See comment below, by Anna Louise Strong.—EDITOR.]

ARTICLE 126

In conformity with the interests of the working people, and in order to develop the organizational initiative and political activity of the masses of the people, citizens of the U.S.S.R. are ensured the right to unite in public organizations—trade unions, coöperative associations, youth organizations, sport and defense organizations, cultural, technical and scientific societies; and the most active and politically most conscious citizens in the ranks of the working class and other sections of the working people unite in the Communist Party of the Soviet Union (Bolsheviks), which is the vanguard of the working people in their struggle to strengthen and develop the socialist system and is the leading core of all organizations of the working people, both public and state. [Obviously no rights are ensured to any organization which would not let Bolsheviks function as its "leading core." See comment below by Stalin.—EDITOR.]

ARTICLE 127

Citizens of the U.S.S.R. are guaranteed inviolability of the person. No person may be placed under arrest except by decision of a court or with the sanction of a procurator. [Articles 114, 115, and 116 provide that the Supreme Soviet appoints the Procurator of the U.S.S.R., who appoints the Procurators of the various republics, who in turn appoint the local procurators. Article 117 reads: "The organs of the Procurator's Office perform their functions independently of any local organs whatsoever, being subordinate solely to the Procurator of the U.S.S.R."—EDITOR.]

ARTICLE 128

The inviolability of the homes of citizens and privacy of correspondence are protected by law.

ARTICLE 129

The U.S.S.R. affords the right of asylum to foreign citizens persecuted for defending the interests of the working people, or for their scientific activities, or for their struggle for national liberation.

ARTICLE 130

It is the duty of every citizen of the U.S.S.R. to abide by the Constitution of the Union of Soviet Socialist Republics, to observe the laws, to maintain labor discipline, honestly to perform public duties, and to respect the rules of socialist intercourse.

ARTICLE 131

It is the duty of every citizen of the U.S.S.R. to safeguard and strengthen public, socialist property as the sacred and inviolable foundation of the Soviet system, as the source of the wealth and might of the country, as the source of the prosperous and cultured life of all the working people.

Persons committing offenses against public, socialist property are enemies of the people.

ARTICLE 132

Universal military service is law.

Military service in the Workers' and Peasants' Red Army is an honorable duty of the citizens of the U.S.S.R.

ARTICLE 133

To defend the fatherland is the sacred duty of every citizen of the U.S.S.R. Treason to the country—violation of the oath of allegiance, desertion to the enemy, impairing the military power of the state, espionage

—is punishable with all the severity of the law as the most heinous of crimes.

Stalin on the Soviet Constitution *

[Stalin, after mentioning several groups of critics, continues as follows.]

Finally, there is one more group of critics. Whereas the preceding group charges that the draft Constitution renounced the dictatorship of the working class, this group, on the contrary, charges that the draft makes no change in the existing position of the U.S.S.R.; that it leaves the dictatorship of the working class intact, does not provide for freedom of political parties, and preserves the present leading position of the Communist Party of the U.S.S.R. And, at the same time, this group of critics believes that the absence of freedom for parties in the U.S.S.R. is an indication of the violation of the fundamental principles of democracy.

I must admit the draft of the new Constitution really does leave in force the regime of the dictatorship of the working class, and also leaves unchanged the present leading position of the Communist Party of the U.S.S.R. (*Loud applause.*)

If our venerable critics regard this as a shortcoming of the draft Constitution, this can only be regretted. We Bolsheviks, however, consider this as a merit of the draft Constitution. (*Loud applause.*) As for freedom for various political parties, we here adhere to somewhat different views.

The party is part of the class, its vanguard section. Several parties and consequently freedom of parties can only exist in a society where antagonistic classes exist whose interests are hostile and irreconcilable, where there are capitalists and workers, landlords and peasants, kulaks and poor peasants.

But in the U.S.S.R. there are no longer such classes as capitalists, landlords, kulaks, etc. In the U.S.S.R. there are only two classes, workers and peasants, whose interests not only are not antagonistic but, on the contrary, amicable. Consequently there are no grounds for the existence of several parties, and therefore for the existence of freedom of such parties in the U.S.S.R. There are grounds for only one party, the Communist Party, in the U.S.S.R. Only one party can exist, the Communist Party, which boldly defends the interests of the workers and peasants to the

---

* From his Report to the Eighth Congress of Soviets, Nov. 25, 1936, printed in *Stalin on the New Soviet Constitution*, New York, International Publishers, pp. 22–23.

very end. And there can hardly be any doubt about the fact that it defends the interests of these classes. (*Loud applause.*)

They talk about democracy. But what is democracy? Democracy in capitalist countries where there are antagonistic classes is in the last analysis the democracy for the strong, democracy for the propertied minority. Democracy in the U.S.S.R., on the contrary, is democracy for all. But from this it follows that the principles of democracy are violated not by the draft of the new Constitution of the U.S.S.R. but by the bourgeois constitutions.

That is why I think that the Constitution of the U.S.S.R. is the only thoroughly democratic constitution in the world.

Comment on Article 125

[In *The New Soviet Constitution* (New York, Henry Holt and Company, 1937) Anna Louise Strong, long known as a friendly interpreter of the Soviet régime, refers to the words "in accordance with the interests of working people and in the interests of strengthening the socialist system" as "the clause which qualifies freedom" (p. 111). She adds a comment by the Commissar for Justice, Krylenko, "We don't wish to be hypocrites. No worker, collective farmer or any other working person will object to the fact that any persons who might wish to bring back the capitalist system are not given either free speech or free press by our constitution" (*ibid.*).]

16

MUSSOLINI ON FASCISM

[Benito Mussolini was born in 1883. At first a Socialist agitator, he broke with his party in 1914 to urge intervention in World War I. In the Italian army he rose no higher than the rank of corporal. He led the Fascist party to power in 1922, and gradually turned Italy into a dictatorship. He conquered Ethiopia in 1935-36. In April, 1939, he seized Albania; in May, he concluded a military alliance with Hitler. In June, 1940, he invaded France; in October, he unsuccessfully invaded Greece. After the loss of North Africa and Sicily, he was deposed from power in July, 1943, but was soon rescued by the Germans. He was seized and killed by partisan forces in April, 1945.

Mussolini's journalistic talent and experience enabled him to express his views with vigor and clarity. He contributed two sections to the article on Fascism in the *Enciclopedia Italiana* in 1932. The second section, here presented, is the classic statement of Fascist doctrine. The translation used is the "authorized translation" by Jane Soames, printed in "Day to Day Pamphlets" No. 18, published by L. and V. Woolf at the Hogarth Press, London, 1933; also printed in "International Conciliation," No. 306, New York, Carnegie Endowment for International Peace, January, 1935, and in Alfred Zimmern's *Modern Political Doctrines,* London and New York, Oxford University Press, 1939.]

The Political and Social Doctrine of Fascism

When, in the now distant March of 1919, I summoned a meeting at Milan through the columns of the *Popolo d'Italia* of the surviving members of the Interventionist Party who had themselves been in action, and who had followed me since the creation of the Fascist Revolutionary Party (which took place in the January of 1915), I had no specific doctrinal attitude in my mind. I had a living experience of one doctrine only— that of Socialism, from 1903-4 to the winter of 1914—that is to say, about a decade: and from Socialism itself, even though I had taken part in the movement first as a member of the rank and file and then later as a leader, yet I had no experience of its doctrine in practice. My own doctrine, even in this period, had always been a doctrine of action. A unanimous universally accepted theory of Socialism did not exist after 1905, when the revisionist movement began in Germany under the leadership of Bernstein, while under pressure of the tendencies of the time, a Left Revolutionary movement also appeared, which though never getting further than talk in Italy, in Russian Socialistic circles laid the foundations of Bolshevism. Reformation, Revolution, Centralization—already the echoes of these terms are spent—while in the great stream of Fascism are to be found ideas which began with Sorel, Péguy,* with Lagardelle in the "Mouvement Socialiste," and with the Italian trades-union movement which throughout the period 1904–14 was sounding a new note in Italian Socialist circles (already weakened by the betrayal of Giolitti) through Olivetti's *Pagine Libere,* Orano's *La Lupa,* and Enrico Leone's *Divenire Sociale.*†

After the War, 1919, Socialism was already dead as a doctrine: it existed only as a hatred. There remained to it only one possibility of action, especially in Italy, reprisals against those who had desired the War and who must now be made to "expiate" its results. The *Popolo d'Italia* was then given the sub-title of "The newspaper of ex-service men and producers," and the word "producers" was already the expression of a mental attitude. Fascism was not the nursling of a doctrine worked out beforehand with detailed elaboration; it was born of the need for action and it was itself from the beginning practical rather than theoretical; it was not merely another political party but, even in the first two years, in opposition to all political parties as such, and itself a living movement. The name which I then gave to the organization fixed its character. And yet, if one were to re-read, in the now dusty columns of that date, the report of the meeting in which the *Fasci Italiani di combattimento* were constituted, one would there find no ordered expression of doctrine, but a series of aphorisms, anticipations, and aspirations which, when refined by time from the original ore, were destined after some years to develop into an ordered series of doctrinal concepts, forming the Fascist political doc-

* See articles in Encyc. of Social Sciences on Georges Sorel, 1847–1922, and Charles Péguy, 1873–1914.—EDITOR.
† These are three radical periodicals of the period.—EDITOR.

trine—different from all others either of the past or the present day.

"If the bourgeoisie," I said then, "think that they will find lightning-conductors in us, they are the more deceived; we must start work at once. . . . We want to accustom the working-class to real and effectual leadership, and also to convince them that it is no easy thing to direct an industry or a commercial enterprise successfully. . . . We shall combat every retrograde idea, technical or spiritual. . . . When the succession to the seat of government is open, we must not be unwilling to fight for it. We must make haste; when the present régime breaks down, we must be ready at once to take its place. It is we who have the right to the succession, because it was we who forced the country into the War, and led her to victory. The present method of political representation cannot suffice, we must have a representation direct from the individuals concerned. It may be objected against this program that it is a return to the conception of the corporation, but that is no matter. . . . Therefore, I desire that this assembly shall accept the claim of national trades-unionism from the economic point of view. . . ."

Now is it not a singular thing that even on this first day in the Piazza San Sepolcro that word "corporation" arose, which later, in the course of the Revolution, came to express one of the creations of social legislation at the very foundation of the régime?

Fascism is now a completely individual thing, not only as a régime but as a doctrine. And this means that to-day Fascism exercising its critical sense upon itself and upon others, has formed its own distinct and peculiar point of view, to which it can refer and upon which, therefore, it can act in the face of all problems, practical or intellectual, which confront the world.

And above all, Fascism, the more it considers and observes the future and the development of humanity quite apart from political considerations of the moment, believes neither in the possibility nor the utility of perpetual peace. It thus repudiates the doctrine of Pacifism—born of a renunciation of the struggle and an act of cowardice in the face of sacrifice. War alone brings up to its highest tension all human energy and puts the stamp of nobility upon the peoples who have the courage to meet it. All other trials are substitutes, which never really put men into the position where they have to make the great decision—the alternative of life or death. Thus a doctrine which is founded upon this harmful postulate of peace is hostile to Fascism. And thus hostile to the spirit of Fascism,

though accepted for what use they can be in dealing with particular political situations, are all the international leagues and societies which, as
history will show, can be scattered to the winds when once strong national
feeling is aroused by any motive—sentimental, ideal or practical. This
anti-pacifist spirit is carried by Fascism even into the life of the individual;
the proud motto of the *Squadrista,* "Me ne frego" ["I don't give a damn"],
written on the bandage of the wound, is an act of philosophy not only
stoic, the summary of a doctrine not only political—it is the education to
combat, the acceptation of the risks which combat implies, and a new
way of life for Italy. Thus the Fascist accepts life and loves it, knowing
nothing of and despising suicide: he rather conceives of life as duty and
struggle and conquest, life which should be high and full, lived for oneself, but above all for others—those who are at hand and those who are far
distant, contemporaries, and those who will come after.

Such a conception of life makes Fascism the complete opposite of that
doctrine, the base of so-called scientific and Marxian Socialism, the materialist conception of history; according to which the history of human
civilization can be explained simply through the conflict of interests
among the various social groups and by the change and development in
the means and instruments of production. That the changes in the economic field—new discoveries of raw materials, new methods of working
them, and the inventions of science—have their importance no one can
deny; but that these factors are sufficient to explain the history of humanity excluding all others is an absurd delusion. Fascism, now and
always, believes in holiness and in heroism; that is to say, in actions influenced by no economic motive, direct or indirect. And if the economic
conception of history be denied, according to which theory men are no
more than puppets, carried to and fro by the waves of chance, while the
real directing forces are quite out of their control, it follows that the
existence of an unchangeable and unchanging class-war is also denied—
the natural progeny of the economic conception of history. And above all
Fascism denies that class-war can be the preponderant force in the transformation of society. These two fundamental concepts of Socialism being
thus refuted, nothing is left of it but the sentimental aspiration—as old
as humanity itself—towards a social system in which the sorrows and
sufferings of the humblest shall be alleviated. But here again Fascism repudiates the conception of "economic" happiness, to be realized by Socialism and, as it were, at a given moment in economic evolution to assure to

everyone the maximum of well-being. Fascism denies the materialist conception of happiness as a possibility, and abandons it to its inventors, the economists of the first half of the nineteenth century: that is to say, Fascism denies the validity of the equation, well-being=happiness, which would reduce men to the level of animals, caring for one thing only—to be fat and well fed—and would thus degrade humanity to a purely physical existence.

After Socialism, Fascism combats the whole complex system of democratic ideology, and repudiates it, whether in its theoretical premises or in its practical application. Fascism denies that the majority, by the simple fact that it is a majority, can direct human society; it denies that numbers alone can govern by means of a periodical consultation, and it affirms the immutable, beneficial, and fruitful inequality of mankind, which can never be permanently leveled through the mere operation of a mechanical process such as universal suffrage. The democratic régime may be defined as from time to time giving the people the illusion of sovereignty, while the real effective sovereignty lies in the hands of other concealed and irresponsible forces. Democracy is a régime nominally without a king, but it is ruled by many kings—more absolute, tyrannical, and ruinous than one sole king, even though a tyrant. This explains why Fascism, having first in 1922 (for reasons of expediency) assumed an attitude tending towards republicanism, renounced this point of view before the march to Rome; being convinced that the question of political form is not to-day of prime importance, and after having studied the examples of monarchies and republics past and present reached the conclusion that monarchy or republicanism are not to be judged, as it were, by an absolute standard; but that they represent forms in which the evolution—political, historical, traditional, or psychological—of a particular country has expressed itself. Fascism supersedes the antithesis of monarchy or republicanism, while democracy still tarries beneath the domination of this idea, forever pointing out the insufficiency of the first and forever praising the second as the perfect régime. To-day, it can be seen that there are republics innately reactionary and absolutist, and also monarchies which incorporate the most ardent social and political hopes of the future.

But the Fascist negation of Socialism, Democracy, and Liberalism must not be taken to mean that Fascism desires to lead the world back to the state of affairs before 1789, the date which seems to be indicated as the opening year of the succeeding semi-Liberal century: we do not desire to turn back; Fascism has not chosen De Maistre * for its high priest. Absolute monarchy has been and can never return, any more than blind acceptance of ecclesiastical authority.

So, too, the privileges of the feudal system "have passed away," and the division of society into castes impenetrable from outside, and with no intercommunication among themselves: the Fascist conception of authority has nothing to do with such a polity. A party which entirely governs a nation is a fact entirely new to history, there are no possible references or parallels. Fascism uses in its construction whatever elements in the Liberal, Social, or Democratic doctrines still have a living value; it maintains what may be called the certainties which we owe to history, but it rejects all the rest—that is to say, the conception that there can be any doctrine of unquestioned efficacy for all times and all peoples. Given that the nineteenth century was the century of Socialism, of Liberalism, and of Democracy, it does not necessarily follow that the twentieth century must also be a century of Socialism, Liberalism, and Democracy: political doctrines pass, but humanity remains; and it may rather be expected that this will be a century of authority, a century of the Left, a century of Fascism. For if the nineteenth century was a century of individualism (Liberalism always signifying individualism) it may be expected that this will be the century of collectivism, and hence the century of the State. It is a perfectly logical deduction that a new doctrine can utilize all the still vital elements of previous doctrines.

The foundation of Fascism is the conception of the State, its character, its duty, and its aim. Fascism conceives of the State as an absolute, in comparison with which all individuals or groups are relative, only to be conceived of in their relation to the State. The conception of the Liberal State is not that of a directing force, guiding the play and development, both material and spiritual, of a collective body, but merely a force limited to the function of recording results: on the other hand, the Fascist State is itself conscious, and has itself a will and a personality—thus it may be called the "ethical" State.

From 1929 until to-day, evolution, both political and economic, has everywhere gone to prove the validity of these doctrinal premises. Of such gigantic importance is the State. It is the force which alone can provide a solution to the dramatic contradiction of capitalism, and that state of

* See article in Encyc. of Social Sciences on Joseph de Maistre, 1753–1821.—EDITOR.

affairs which we call the crisis can only be dealt with by the State, as
between other States. Where is the shade of Jules Simon, who in the
dawn of Liberalism proclaimed that, "The State must labor to make
itself unnecessary, and prepare the way for its own dismissal"? Or of Mc-
Culloch, who, in the second half of the last century, affirmed that the State
must guard against the danger of governing too much? What would
the Englishman, Bentham, say to-day to the continual and inevitably-
invoked intervention of the State in the sphere of economics, while according to his theories industry should ask no more of the State than to
be left in peace? Or the German, Humboldt, according to whom the
"lazy" State should be considered the best? It is true that the second wave
of Liberal economists were less extreme than the first, and Adam Smith *
himself opened the door—if only very cautiously—which leads to State
intervention in the economic field: but whoever says Liberalism implies
individualism, and whoever says Fascism implies the State. Yet the Fascist
State is unique, and an original creation. It is not reactionary, but revolutionary, in that it anticipates the solution of the universal political problems which elsewhere have to be settled in the political field by the rivalry
of parties, the excessive power of the parliamentary régime and the irresponsibility of political assemblies; while it meets the problems of the
economic field by a system of syndicalism which is continually increasing
in importance, as much in the sphere of labor as of industry: and in
the moral field enforces order, discipline, and obedience to that which
is the determined moral code of the country. Fascism desires the State to
be a strong and organic body, at the same time reposing upon broad and
popular support. The Fascist State has drawn into itself even the economic activities of the nation, and, through the corporative social and
educational institutions created by it, its influence reaches every aspect of
the national life and includes, framed in their respective organizations,
all the political, economic and spiritual forces of the nation. A State which
reposes upon the support of millions of individuals who recognize its
authority, are continually conscious of its power and are ready at once to
serve it, is not the old tyrannical State of the medieval lord nor has it
anything in common with the absolute governments either before or after
1789. The individual in the Fascist State is not annulled but rather multi-

* See articles in Encyc. of Social Sciences on Jules Simon, 1814–1896, John R. Mc-
Culloch, 1789–1864, Jeremy Bentham, 1748–1832, Wilhelm von Humboldt, 1767–
1835, Adam Smith, 1723–1790.—Editor.

plied, just in the same way that a soldier in a regiment is not diminished but rather increased by the number of his comrades. The Fascist State organizes the nation, but leaves a sufficient margin of liberty to the individual; the latter is deprived of all useless and possibly harmful freedom, but retains what is essential; the deciding power in this question cannot be the individual, but the State alone.

The Fascist State is not indifferent to the fact of religion in general, or to that particular and positive faith which is Italian Catholicism. The State professes no theology, but a morality, and in the Fascist State religion is considered as one of the deepest manifestations of the spirit of man, thus it is not only respected but defended and protected. The Fascist State has never tried to create its own God, as at one moment Robespierre * and the wildest extremists of the Convention tried to do; nor does it vainly seek to obliterate religion from the hearts of men as does Bolshevism: Fascism respects the God of the ascetics, the saints and heroes, and equally, God as He is perceived and worshipped by simple people.

The Fascist State is an embodied will to power and government: the Roman tradition is here an ideal of force in action. According to Fascism, government is not so much a thing to be expressed in territorial or military terms as in terms of morality and the spirit. It must be thought of as an empire—that is to say, a nation which directly or indirectly rules other nations, without the need for conquering a single square yard of territory. For Fascism, the growth of empire, that is to say the expansion of the nation, is an essential manifestation of vitality, and its opposite a sign of decadence. Peoples which are rising, or rising again after a period of decadence, are always imperialist; any renunciation is a sign of decay and of death. Fascism is the doctrine best adapted to represent the tendencies and the aspirations of a people, like the people of Italy, who are rising again after many centuries of abasement and foreign servitude. But empire demands discipline, the coördination of all forces and a deeply felt sense of duty and sacrifice: this fact explains many aspects of the practical working of the régime, the character of many forces in the State, and the necessarily severe measures which must be taken against those who would oppose this spontaneous and inevitable movement of Italy in the twentieth century, and would oppose it by recalling the outworn ideology of the nineteenth century—repudiated wheresoever there has

* See article in Encyc. of Social Sciences on Maximilian Robespierre, 1758–1794. —Editor.

been the courage to undertake great experiments of social and political transformation: for never before has the nation stood more in need of authority, of direction, and of order. If every age has its own characteristic doctrine, there are a thousand signs which point to Fascism as the characteristic doctrine of our time. For if a doctrine must be a living thing, this is proved by the fact that Fascism has created a living faith; and that this faith is very powerful in the minds of men, is demonstrated by those who have suffered and died for it.

Fascism has henceforth in the world the universality of all those doctrines which, in realizing themselves, have represented a stage in the history of the human spirit.

[Mussolini claimed a kind of universality for fascism. His view was supported by the emergence of nationalist dictatorships in Germany (Hitler), in Spain (Franco), in Portugal (Salazar), and in Argentina (Peron). Great Britain had its British Fascist movement between wars. The United States had the Ku Klux Klan, Huey Long, Father Coughlin, the German Bund, and many other anti-democratic movements. Such movements in the United States exploit pre-existing anti-foreign, anti-Negro, anti-Jewish, or anti-Catholic sentiments, and intensify them. They exploit anti-Communist sentiment by representing our government as pro-Communist or unable to combat Communism. Such movements have not been taken very seriously, but Hitler also was not taken seriously until he became too powerful to stop.

On American anti-democratic movements, see John M. Mecklin, *The Ku Klux Klan*, New York, Harcourt, Brace and Company, 1924; George Seldes, *Facts and Fascism*, In Fact, Inc., 1943; John Roy Carlson (Arthur Derounian), *Under Cover*, 1943, and *The Plotters*, 1946, both New York, E. P. Dutton & Co., Inc.; Raymond Gram Swing, *Forerunners of American Fascism*, New York, Julian Messner, Inc., 1935; Harold Lavine, *Fifth Column in America*, New York, Doubleday and Company, Inc., 1940.]

17

HITLER ON NAZI METHODS AND ASPIRATIONS

[Adolf Hitler was born in a small Austrian town in 1889. After some years of poverty in Vienna, he moved to Munich in 1912. He served in the German army during the war, but rose no higher than the rank of corporal. From 1919 onward he was active in the National Socialist (Nazi) Party and became its leader. For his part in the uprising of November 23, 1923, in Munich, he was confined for a year in the fortress of Landsberg, beginning April 1, 1924. Here he wrote the first volume of *Mein Kampf*, which appeared in 1925; the second volume appeared in 1927. In these volumes he clearly proclaimed his program of destroying representative government in Germany, persecuting the Jews, crushing France, and annexing a large part of Russia.

Hitler came into power as chancellor Jan. 30, 1933. After the death of President Hindenburg in 1934, he made Germany a totalitarian state, and began rearming the country. In 1936 he reoccupied the Rhineland. He annexed Austria in March, 1938. In September of the same year he gained a foothold in Czechoslovakia through the negotiations at Munich, and seized complete control of the nation in March, 1939. On August 24, 1939, a nonaggression pact with Russia was signed. On Sept. 1, 1939, he launched World War II by invading Poland. In June, 1940, France fell and Hitler attacked Russia. When Japan's attack on Pearl Harbor in December, 1941, brought America into the conflict, Hitler declared war on the United States. By the end of 1942, Hitler's power extended from the English Channel and the Pyrenees to Stalingrad and the Black Sea; the program of *Mein Kampf* seemed almost realized. After that, his enemies fought back with increasing effectiveness until he was isolated with a handful of followers in a bombshelter under Berlin, where he shot himself April 30, 1945. It had required the "blood, toil, tears and sweat" of England, Russia, the United States, and many smaller nations to crush him.

Owing to copyright restrictions it is impossible to reprint any extensive selection from *Mein Kampf*. The editor has therefore summarized in his own words (with brief quotations) some of the chief passages dealing with race, party, propaganda, state, education, and foreign policy. In this there is both gain and loss. Hitler's style is diffuse and rambling, so that his main ideas may emerge more clearly in a condensed version. On the other hand a summary, however conscientiously made, lacks the authority of the original text, and readers may suspect the editor of false emphasis and bias. The present editor has supplied references to the English version of the passages summarized, and occasionally to the German text as well. He invites his readers to pass on from this summary to more extensive reading in Hitler's book; in that way they will get a fuller comprehension of Hitler's personality, methods, and aims.

The text on which the summary is based, and from which quotations are drawn, is *Mein Kampf* by Adolf Hitler, New York, Reynal & Hitchcock, 1940, published by arrangement with Houghton Mifflin Company, Boston, Mass., copyright, 1939, by Houghton Mifflin Company, copyright, 1925 and 1927 by Verlag Frz. Eher Nachf. G.m.b.H. The translations and annotations were made under the editorial sponsorship of John Chamberlain, Sidney B. Fay, John Gunther, Carlton J. H. Hayes, Graham Hutton, Alvin Johnson, William L. Langer, Walter Millis, R. Roussy de Sales, and George N. Shuster; this group includes some of the leading journalists, editors, and historical writers of the United States.

The German text to which references are made is *Mein Kampf* von Adolf Hitler, 400–404 Auflage 1939 Zentralverlag der NSDAP. Frz. Eher Nachf. München.]

"Every animal mates only with a representative of the same species" (p. 389). In the exceptional cases of breeding with another species the offspring are sterile or else through lack of vitality succumb to disease or other dangers. Thus bastard forms are eliminated and uniformity is maintained in each species (pp. 389–390). Therefore it is silly not to recognize that any mixing of Aryans with lower human races is disastrous. In Central and South America there has been more race mixture than in North America, which accounts for their inferior culture (p. 392).

The higher aspects of culture, such as science, engineering, and the fine arts, cannot be advanced or even maintained unless the superior race that creates them is preserved. Therefore the higher race must not seek peace with its rivals, but must fight for its own purity and power. It must not trust that the spread of ideas among miscellaneous racial elements will promote civilization. Let the right race dominate and high ideals will be realized. Even universal peace might be achieved if the highest race should become "the only master of the globe" (*"Tatsächlich ist die pazifistisch-humane Idee vielleicht ganz gut dann, wenn der höchststehende Mensch sich vorher die Welt in einem Umfange erobert und unterworfen hat, der ihn zum alleinigen Herrn dieser Erde macht"*) (pp. 393–397; German quotation from p. 315).

Only the Aryan is a culture-creator (*"Kulturbegründer," "kulturschöpferisch"*). Other races may be culture-bearers (*"Kulturträger"*) when guided by the Aryan. Still others are culture-destroyers (*"Kulturzerstörer"*). The Japanese are an example of culture-bearers under Aryan influence; but if that influence were withdrawn, their culture would soon decline (pp. 397–399).

The following is the typical cycle of culture-history: A few Aryans conquer a larger population of an inferior race. Using the latter as tools, they develop a culture suited to the land and to the capacities of the conquered people. All goes well so long as the conquerors retain their racial purity, but when race-mixture begins the culture declines. At last nothing remains to indicate the Aryans' achievement except some traces of blondness in the population and some surviving products of their culture. Occasionally such a decadent nation is again touched by Aryan influence, and a revival of culture is achieved without violent conquest, through the spontaneous response of the surviving Aryan elements. History should be rewritten from this standpoint (pp. 400–401).

Since the early Aryans had no machinery they had to utilize inferior men as slaves. They gave their slaves something better than their former freedom, namely participation in such culture as only the Aryan can create. But to preserve this culture the Aryan must preserve the purity of his blood (pp. 404–406). "All that is not race in this world is trash" (p. 406) (German, p. 324: *"Was nicht gute Rasse ist auf dieser Welt ist Spreu."*—"What is not good race . . . is chaff").

The superiority of the Aryan does not lie in any superior intensity of the will to live, or in any superior mental talents, but in the individual's willingness to devote his labor to the community and even to risk his life for it. This is *idealism* as opposed to egoism (pp. 407–408, 410).

The lack of this idealistic disposition places the Jew at the opposite pole from the Aryan (pp. 412, 414). "The Jew remains united only if forced by a common danger or attracted by a common booty" (p. 416) (German, p. 330, does not mention booty in this sentence). If there were only Jews in the world, their egoism would drive them to destroy one another (p. 416). They have never had a culture of their own (p. 413), but their tenacious will to live has enabled them to persist as parasites on other cultures (pp. 414, 420), and, like other parasites, they ultimately destroy their host (p. 420).

To secure toleration for their parasitic activities the Jews present themselves as adherents of a religion rather than as members of an alien race, but this is an "infamous deception" (pp. 420–421, German p. 335). Their activities follow approximately the following cycle, especially in Germany (pp. 425–451):

Jews first enter other communities as importers and exporters. Then they become middlemen for internal production. They tend to monopolize trade and finance. They become bankers to the monarchy. They lure monarchs into extravagances to make them dependent on Jewish money-lenders. They accept baptism in order to secure full civic rights. When they see the power of the monarchs declining and are impelled to seek the favor of the general public, they pretend in various ways to "become Germans." They seek popularity by a show of philanthropy and political liberalism. They promote democracy and humanitarianism. They promote the development of joint-stock companies, stock speculation, and trade-unions. They develop the Marxist philosophy, which weakens the nation by internationalism, pacifism, and class warfare. By control of the press they create turmoil. Both international finance and international Communism are Jewish tricks to weaken the national spirit and make possible the degradation of the Aryan race by admixture of Jewish blood. The seduction of Aryan girls by Jews, and the bringing of Negroes to the Rhine, are Jewish devices to weaken the Aryan race and attain mastery of the world for themselves. "For a racially pure people, conscious of its blood, can never be enslaved by the Jew. He will forever only be the master of bastards in this world" (p. 449, German p. 357).

* * *

No view of life (*"Weltanschauung"*), however correct and however valuable to mankind, can become effective in the life of a nation unless it is adopted by a group willing to fight for it until it becomes the acknowledged and enforced principle of the whole national life. The searcher for truth may formulate a lofty general ideal; but a leader who senses the limitations and passions of the popular mind must reduce this ideal to a specific program and secure for this program the uniform, unwavering, and uncompromising allegiance of a militant party. The program may fall short of the ideal, but only in this way can actual progress toward the ideal be made. Only through the leadership of one man can the necessary unity of program and fighting faith be secured. It is necessary that some one should lead, and the individual proves his right to leadership by achieving it (pp. 575–577).

* * *

It is a mistake to think of the state as deserving reverence just because it *is* a state, or to think that its main function is to preserve law and order, or to promote a certain economic system (pp. 584–587). The German state gains nothing by spreading the German language to peoples of non-German blood (pp. 588–591). Rather the function of the state is to promote human culture by preserving the culture-creating Aryan race and leading it to a position of dominance (pp. 595–601). This aim cannot be achieved without "a period of fighting" (p. 601). Germanic states should prevent further race-mixture (p. 606). The state should prevent parenthood on the part of persons with inherited diseases and should remove the financial obstacles to large families for healthy mothers (p. 608).

These eugenic measures must be supplemented by educational reforms. Education should aim at vigorous physical health, without which a vigorous spirit is rarely to be found. Education should aim at "the development of character, especially the promotion of will power and determination, connected with education for joyfully assuming responsibility" (p. 613). Knowledge and intellectual training are of secondary importance (*ibid.*). Clothing should reveal the man's physique, so that he may take pride in improving it, and so that Aryan girls may be attracted to worthy mates, instead of being seduced by "bow-legged, disgusting Jewish bastards" (p. 619, German p. 458).

The time given in school to foreign languages (p. 627) and natural sciences (p. 631) should be reduced. History too should be abbreviated and the emphasis laid on the main outline (pp. 628–630). Roman history and the Greek ideal of culture should be stressed, for they are phases of the same culture as the German (p. 631). Less emphasis should be placed on training in technical knowledge which merely enhances the earning power of the selfish individual (pp. 631–632).

The youth should be developed into a genuine German, ready to make sacrifices for his nationality. But he cannot be proud of a nation half of which is in misery (pp. 635–636). "The intimate coupling of nationalism and feeling of social justice must be planted in the young heart. Then there will some day arise a people of State citizens, bound to one another and forged together by a common love and a common pride, unshakable and invincible for all times" (p. 636, German 475). The current dislike of strong national passions is a sign of weakness. "It is certain, however, that this world approaches a great change. And there can only be the sole question whether it turns out for the benefit of Aryan mankind or for the profit of the eternal Jew" (*ibid.*).

* * *

Just as the superior race should rule over inferior races, so within the superior race power should be given to superior individuals. Not majorities but personal merit should be decisive (pp. 660–661). Social organization should be such as to facilitate the emergence of superior leaders (pp. 665, 669). Marxism and parliamentary government stress masses and majorities, submerging human differences (pp. 666–668). Instead of this there should be a hierarchy of leaders on the military model, each with absolute authority over his subordinates and absolute responsibility to his superiors. There should be a parliament, and councils at various levels, but these should merely advise their respective leaders, never make decisions by majority vote. Only the leader at each level should make decisions (pp. 669–671).

* * *

The truly national German state must be brought into being by a fighting party, which is not willing merely to remain one party among other parties, but demands the complete reorganization of national life in accord with its views (pp. 674–675). It must not compromise with its opponents like ordinary parties, nor coöperate to maintain existing conditions which it condemns, but must use all available means to break up those conditions. It must unite the most energetic and courageous elements of the nation into a compact fighting group (pp. 676–677).

It is not necessary that every member of the group be instructed in the whole system of thought conceived by its leader, any more than all the soldiers in an army need to be instructed in the theory of strategy. In both cases it is enough that the followers have a few definite ideas and a fanatical devotion to them (pp. 677–678). "The very nature of *organization* implies that it can only exist if the broad masses, motivated by sentiment, serve a highest intellectual leadership. A company of two hundred men, mentally all equally able, could in the long run be disciplined only with greater difficulty than a company of one hundred and ninety mentally less able and ten who are more highly educated" (p. 678, German 509).

The twenty-five articles constituting the program of the National Socialist movement [summarized and discussed by the American editors on pp. 686–694] are not a complete expression of the ideas and aims of its leadership, but a fighting creed to unite the mass of its followers (pp. 680–683).

* * *

A political movement requires theorists to elaborate its ideals and programs, organizers to develop a compact, disciplined, militant group, and leaders to attract by propaganda the widest possible approval from the masses. Persons who excel in one of these functions do not necessarily excel in the others (pp. 847–852). "However, the combination of theorist, organizer, and leader in one person is the rarest thing to be found on this globe; this combination makes the great man" (p. 849, German p. 651). [Of whom could Hitler be thinking?—EDITOR.]

It is the function of propaganda to influence the masses, not to give scientific instruction to the few who can grasp it. Therefore it must be adapted to the comprehension of the least intelligent, and must appeal more to feeling than to reason (pp. 230–233).

The Jews, in accusing Ludendorff of responsibility for losing the World War, made "the very correct assumption that in the size of the lie there is always contained a certain factor of credibility, since the great masses of a people may be more corrupt in the bottom of their hearts than they will be consciously and intentionally bad, therefore with the primitive simplicity of their minds they will more easily fall victims to a great lie than to a small one, since they themselves perhaps also lie sometimes in little things, but would certainly still be too much ashamed of too great lies." In such cases refutation is never wholly effective, and "some part of the most impudent lie will remain and stick; a fact which all great lying artists and societies of the world know only too well and therefore also villainously employ" (p. 313, German pp. 252–253).

There must be a distinction between the followers and the members of a movement. The numerous followers are won by propaganda to passive acquiescence in the movement. The relatively few members participate actively in spreading the movement, make sacrifices and take risks for it (pp. 849–851). When the movement achieves success, it must limit its membership still more strictly, so that the original nucleus of the organization may continue to dominate the process of applying its ideas and realizing its aims throughout the nation. The founders of the movement must become the masters of the state (pp. 854–855).

"A movement which during a time of majority rule orients itself essentially in all and everything towards the leader idea and towards the responsibility conditioned by this will some day conquer the previous condition with mathematical certainty and will emerge victorious" (p. 859, German, pp. 661–662).

* * *

The only question regarding any policy toward foreign nations is, "Does it benefit our nation now or in the future? . . . Partisan, religious, humanitarian and all other points of view in general are completely beside the point" (p. 888, German p. 687). No foreign statesman can be expected to be "pro-German." The problem of alliances is to find nations whose interests coincide with ours [Germany's] in important respects, at least for a limited time, instead of conflicting with ours. With such nations we can coöperate as allies (pp. 901–902). "National fates are solidly welded together only through a perspective [prospect] of a common triumph in the sense of common gains, conquests, in short, a joint expansion of power" (p. 901, German p. 697).

The only available allies for Germany are England and Italy. It is against English interests that either France or Germany should attain such military dominance in Europe that it could compete with England as a world power. It is therefore possible for England and Germany to coöperate in restraining the power of France. France and Italy are rivals in the Mediterranean, and a German-Italian alliance against France is therefore practicable (pp. 902–903). France is "the German people's irreconcilable mortal enemy" (*"der unerbittliche Todfeind"*) (p. 902, German p. 699). She inevitably seeks, whatever her temporary government may be, to keep her frontier on the Rhine and to weaken Germany by dismemberment (p. 902).

The problem is made more complex and in the highest degree dangerous by the ambitions of the Jews for world-dominion. The international Jews incite England to go beyond her national interest (which is merely to prevent Germany from becoming a world-power) and to seek the economic and political destruction of Germany (pp. 905–906). In France there is *"unanimity* between the *plans of the Jew-controlled stock exchange* and the desires of a *chauvinistically oriented national statecraft"* [Italics in American translation.—Editor.] (p. 907). The French people "which is constantly becoming more negrofied constitutes, by its tie with the aims of Jewish world dominion, a grim danger for the existence of the European white race" (*"Dieses an sich immer mehr der Vernegerung anheimfallende Volk bedeutet in seiner Bindung an die Ziele der jüdischen Weltbeherrschung eine lauernde Gefahr für den Bestand der weissen Rasse Europas"*) (pp. 907–908, German p. 704). Italy, by taking measures against the Masons, the super-national press, and international Marxism, tends to free itself from Jewish influence (pp. 927–928). National Socialism must inspire the German people to unite with other Aryans to fight the Jewish menace (pp. 931–933).

* * *

German foreign policy must seek for the German people sufficient land so that it can nourish itself by the products of its own soil. "Only a sufficiently extensive area on this globe guarantees a nation freedom of existence" (p. 935, German p. 728). We can justify the shedding of our sons' blood only if it secures land on which some day German peasants may beget sons (pp. 947–948). A victory over France will have little value unless it enables us to get more land in Europe (p. 949). "But if we talk about new soil and territory in Europe to-day, we can think primarily only of *Russia* and its vassal border states" (pp. 950–951, German p. 742). It is a stroke of luck for us that Jews now control Russia; since Jews are culture-destroyers, not culture-creators, they cannot in the long run hold that empire together (pp. 951–952).

The idea of an alliance with Russia is absurd. If Germany and Russia together fought against western Europe, the struggle would occur on German soil, with no effective aid from Russia. "Its outcome would be the end of Germany" (". . . *das Ergebnis wäre die unabwendbare Nie-derlage*") (p. 959, German p. 749). [Remember that Hitler is writing of the situation in 1923–1926.—EDITOR.] The present rulers of Russia are criminals who cannot be trusted to keep an alliance (pp. 959–960). Moreover, international Jewry, which rules Russia through the Bolshevists, aspires to conquer Germany too by bolshevization (pp. 959–961).

The right foreign policy for Germany is to bring its recurrent struggle with France to a decisively victorious conclusion, and then conquer in eastern Europe the territory needed for German expansion. "That foreign policy will be acknowledged as correct only if, a bare century from now, two hundred and fifty million Germans are living on this continent, and then not squeezed together as factory coolies for the rest of the world, but: as peasants and workers mutually guaranteeing each other's life by their productivity" (p. 979, German p. 767).

[On Hitler's rise to power, see Konrad Heiden, *Der Fuehrer,* Boston, Houghton Mifflin Company, 1944. Alfred Rosenberg's *Mythus des 20. Jahrhunderts* (*The Myth of the Twentieth Century*), 1930, stands next to *Mein Kampf* in importance as an expression of Nazi ideology, but no English translation has appeared. Rosenberg also issued the German edition of the *Protocols of Zion,* a spurious document widely used in Anti-Semitic propaganda in many countries, including the United States. Albert R. Chandler has discussed the *Myth* and the *Protocols* in *Rosenberg's Nazi Myth,* Ithaca, Cornell University Press, 1945. Further references: Rohan D'O. Butler, *The Roots of National Socialism,* New York, E. P. Dutton & Co., Inc., 1942; M. F. Ashley Montagu, *Man's Most Dangerous Myth: The Fallacy of Race,* New York, Columbia University Press, 1942; Lee J. Levinger, *Anti-Semitism Yesterday and Tomorrow,* New York, The Macmillan Company, 1936; John S. Curtiss, *An Appraisal of the Protocols of Zion,* New York, Columbia University Press, 1942. The results of Anti-Semitism are shown in the destruction of six million Jews in Europe between 1939 and 1945, reducing the total Jewish population of the world from seventeen million to eleven million (*The Palestine Year Book,* Washington, D.C., Zionist Organization of America, 1945, page 23). H. R. Trevor-Roper, in *The Last Days of Hitler,* New York, The Macmillan Company, 1947, throws light on the character of Hitler and his associates.]

18

THE SPIRIT OF JAPAN

[When Japan attacked Pearl Harbor her imperialist leaders could rely on the fanatical devotion of their people to the national cause and their complete submission to a quasi-divine monarch. The main reasons for this may be expressed in two words—Mikado and Bushido. The Mikado, as lineal descendant of the sun goddess, reigned by divine right, and was destined sooner or later to bring all the world "under one roof." Bushido is the traditional moral code which demands loyalty, honor, courage, and iron self-control.

The position of the Mikado is concisely described by H. R. Spencer in the following passage from his *Government and Politics Abroad*, New York, Henry Holt and Company, 1936, pages 502–503.]

The position of the emperor is unique in the modern world. By the design of the nation's leading minds, the public is led to think of this exalted personage as divine, of transcendent, super-human quality. This conception fits into the ancient national worship system, called *Shinto*, and in the public mind it links the living occupant of the throne with his revered imperial ancestors (theoretically an unbroken line since 660 B. C.), and also bases men's loyalty on the strong family feeling of the Japanese race.

This attitude is hardly declining at all with the lapse of time and the dawn of the modern western spirit in Japan. In contrast, on this point, with the general practice in modern Japan of imitating western ways, the present system of public education is rearing a generation who are taught to regard the occupant of the throne, not as a puppet in the hands of ministers, nor even as an exalted, dignified adviser of the governing group, but as the actual personification of the nation, the incarnation of the nation's spirit; and that, too, in a degree infinitely more pervasive and intense than is to be alleged of the English Edward VIII or any European king. For the purposes of a policy of imperialism, this emperor-worship makes possible the inculcation of religious devotion, to sanctify (literally) the political purposes of the men around the throne. Patriotism and religion are made one. The soldier is taught that there is no limit, spiritually, to the obligation he owes to his supreme commander. A certain Maj. Kogi committed suicide in 1932 because he felt that (although rendered insensible by his wounds) he had been eternally disgraced by the fact that he was actually taken prisoner by the Chinese in the course of military operations. His spirited deed, symbolizing purification of the army's service by his personal self-sacrifice, was exalted by the minister of war (Araki) as a sample of soldierly conduct that ought to be regarded as the normal expected thing, not the quixotic exception. Officers and soldiers are required to make of themselves the devoted slaves of their divine emperor.

Taking this mystical popular attitude as a background, we are prepared to observe that while the emperor reigns, he does not rule. As in centuries past, the monarch's powers are exercised in actual government by the will of a small oligarchy, mainly bureaucratic, at times in varying degree militaristic, yet tending in recent decades (at least until the present crisis) to be somewhat influenced by popular currents of opinion as expressed by Parliament. As in England, every act of government is performed in the name of the emperor. But he performs no act except upon advice. Reciprocally, it may be presumed that the decision upon governmental matters is subject also to the emperor's advice. But beyond that, there is no generally recognized responsibility of ministers to Parliament, for making clear to the public mind the public's appreciation, whether of praise or blame.

[At the beginning of the twentieth century Professor Inazo Nitobe of the University of Kyoto wrote a little book called Bushido, the Soul of Japan.* In it he expounded the ideal of Japanese chivalry which was developed long ago by a class of warring nobles, but which in modern times has permeated all classes of the population. A study of this ideal will help us to comprehend the spirit in which Japan develops her national life and fights her battles.

Bushido, "the way of the military knight" required the virtues of rectitude, courage, benevolence, politeness, veracity, honor, loyalty, and self-

* G. P. Putnam's Sons, ed. 10, 1905.

control. In the following pages, Nitobe's treatment of courage, loyalty, and self-control is given nearly in full, with brief indications regarding the other virtues.

Rectitude was defined by one famous warrior as "the power of deciding upon a certain course of conduct in accordance with reason, without wavering;—to die when it is right to die, to strike when to strike is right" (page 23). Although "reason" is mentioned, no systematically thought-out code of ethics or law is meant, but rather the sense of duty which the demands of society and tradition develop in the individual.

The following is a transcription of Nitobe's chapter on courage:]

Courage was scarcely deemed worthy to be counted among virtues, unless it was exercised in the cause of Righteousness. In his *Analects* Confucius defines Courage by explaining, as is often his wont, what its negative is. "Perceiving what is right," he says, "and doing it not, argues lack of courage." Put this epigram into a positive statement, and it runs, "Courage is doing what is right." To run all kinds of hazards, to jeopard one's self, to rush into the jaws of death—these are too often identified with Valor, and in the profession of arms such rashness of conduct— what Shakespeare calls "valor misbegot"—is unjustly applauded; but not so in the Precepts of Knighthood. Death for a cause unworthy of dying for, was called a "dog's death." "To rush into the thick of battle and to be slain in it," says a Prince of Mito, "is easy enough, and the merest churl is equal to the task; but," he continues, "it is true courage to live when it is right to live, and to die only when it is right to die"—and yet the prince had not even heard of the name of Plato, who defines courage as "the knowledge of things that a man should fear and that he should not fear." A distinction which is made in the West between moral and physical courage has long been recognized among us. What samurai youth has not heard of "Great Valor" and the "Valor of a Villain"?

Valor, Fortitude, Bravery, Fearlessness, Courage, being the qualities of soul which appeal most easily to juvenile minds, and which can be trained by exercise and example, were, so to speak, the most popular virtues, early emulated among the youth. Stories of military exploits were repeated almost before boys left their mother's breast. Does a little booby cry for any ache? The mother scolds him in this fashion: "What a coward to cry for a trifling pain! What will you do when your arm is cut off in battle?

What when you are called upon to commit *hara-kiri?*" We all know the
pathetic fortitude of a famished little boy-prince of Sendai, who in the
drama is made to say to his little page, "Seest thou those tiny sparrows in
the nest, how their yellow bills are opened wide, and now see! there
comes their mother with worms to feed them. How eagerly and happily
the little ones eat! but for a samurai, when his stomach is empty, it is a
disgrace to feel hungry." Anecdotes of fortitude and bravery abound in
nursery tales, though stories of this kind are not by any means the only
method of early imbuing the spirit with daring and fearlessness. Parents,
with sternness sometimes verging on cruelty, set their children to tasks that
called forth all the pluck that was in them. "Bears hurl their cubs down
the gorge," they said. Samurai's sons were let down to steep valleys of
hardship, and spurred to Sisyphus-like tasks. Occasional deprivation of
food or exposure to cold was considered a highly efficacious test for inur-
ing them to endurance. Children of tender age were sent among utter
strangers with some message to deliver, were made to rise before the sun,
and before breakfast attend to their reading exercises, walking to their
teachers with bare feet in the cold of winter; they frequently—once or
twice a month, as on the festival of a god of learning,—came together in
small groups and passed the night without sleep, in reading aloud by
turns. Pilgrimages to all sorts of uncanny places—to execution grounds, to
graveyards, to houses reputed of being haunted, were favorite pastimes
of the young. In the days when decapitation was public, not only were
small boys sent to witness the ghastly scene, but they were made to visit
alone the place in the darkness of night and there to leave a mark of
their visit on the trunkless head.

The spiritual aspect of valor is evidenced by composure—calm presence
of mind. Tranquillity is courage in repose. It is a statical manifestation of
valor, as daring deeds are a dynamical. A truly brave man is ever serene;
he is never taken by surprise; nothing ruffles the equanimity of his
spirit. In the heat of battle he remains cool; in the midst of catastrophes
he keeps level his mind. Earthquakes do not shake him, he laughs at
storms. We admire him as truly great, who, in the menacing presence of
danger or death, retains his self-possession; who, for instance, can compose a poem under impending peril, or hum a strain in the face of death.
Such indulgence betraying no tremor in the writing or in the voice is
taken as an infallible index of a large nature—of what we call a capacious

mind (*yoyu*), which, far from being pressed or crowded, has always room for something more.

It passes current among us as a piece of authentic history, that as Ota Dokan, the great builder of the castle of Tokyo, was pierced through with a spear, his assassin, knowing the poetical predilection of his victim, accompanied his thrust with this couplet:

> "Ah! how in moments like these
> Our heart doth grudge the light of life";

whereupon the expiring hero, not one whit daunted by the mortal wound in his side, added the lines:

> "Had not in hours of peace,
> It learned to lightly look on life."

There is even a sportive element in a courageous nature. Things which are serious to ordinary people, may be but play to the valiant. Hence in old warfare it was not at all rare for the parties to a conflict to exchange repartee or to begin a rhetorical contest. Combat was not solely a matter of brute force; it was, as well, an intellectual engagement.

Of such character was the battle fought on the banks of the Koromo River, late in the eleventh century. The eastern army routed, its leader, Sadato, took to flight. When the pursuing general pressed him hard and called aloud, "It is a disgrace for a warrior to show his back to the enemy," Sadato reined his horse; upon this the conquering chief shouted an impromptu verse:

> "Torn into shreds is the warp of the cloth" (*koromo*).

Scarcely had the words escaped his lips when the defeated warrior, undismayed, completed the couplet:

> "Since age has worn its threads by use."

Yoshiie, whose bow had all the while been bent, suddenly unstrung it and turned away, leaving his prospective victim to do as he pleased. When asked the reason of his strange behavior, he replied that he could not bear to put to shame one who had kept his presence of mind while hotly pursued by his enemy.

The sorrow which overtook Antony and Octavius at the death of Brutus, has been the general experience of brave men. Kenshin, who fought for fourteen years with Shingen, when he heard of the latter's death, wept aloud at the loss of "the best of enemies." It was this same Kenshin who had set a noble example for all time in his treatment of Shingen, whose provinces lay in a mountainous region quite away from the sea, and who had consequently depended upon the Hōjō provinces of the Tokaido for salt. The Hōjō prince wishing to weaken him, although not openly at war with him, had cut off from Shingen all traffic in this important article. Kenshin, hearing of his enemy's dilemma and able to obtain his salt from the coast of his own dominions, wrote Shingen that in his opinion the Hōjō lord had committed a very mean act, and that although he (Kenshin) was at war with him (Shingen) he had ordered his subjects to furnish him with plenty of salt—adding, "I do not fight with salt, but with the sword," affording more than a parallel to the words of Camillus, "We Romans do not fight with gold, but with iron." Nietzsche spoke for the samurai heart when he wrote, "You are to be proud of your enemy; then the success of your enemy is your success also." Indeed, valor and honor alike require that we should own as enemies in war only such as prove worthy of being friends in peace. When valor attains this height, it becomes akin to Benevolence.

[Benevolence, on the authority of Confucius and Mencius, was regarded as the highest requirement of a ruler of men. Nitobe remarks:]

Under the regime of feudalism, which could easily degenerate into militarism, it was to benevolence that we owed our deliverance from despotism of the worst kind [page 37]. A feudal prince, although unmindful of owing reciprocal obligations to his vassals, felt a higher sense of responsibility to his ancestors and to Heaven. He was a father to his subjects, whom Heaven entrusted to his care [page 38].

Fortunately mercy was not so rare as it was beautiful, for it is universally true that "The bravest are the tenderest, the loving are the daring." "Bushi no nasaké"—the tenderness of a warrior—had a sound which appealed at once to whatever was noble in us; [Nitobe is recalling the childhood of his own generation of Japanese] not that the mercy of a samurai was generically different from the mercy of any other being, but because it implied mercy was not a blind impulse, but where it recognized due regard to justice, and where mercy did not remain merely a certain state of mind, but where it was backed with power to save or kill. As economists speak of demand as being effectual or ineffectual, similarly we may call the mercy of Bushi effectual, since it implied the power of acting for the good or detriment of the recipient.

Priding themselves as they did in their brute strength and privileges to turn it into account, the samurai gave full consent to what Mencius taught concerning the power of love. "Benevolence," he says, "brings under its sway whatever hinders its power, just as water subdues fire: they only doubt the power of water to quench flames who try to extinguish with a cupful a whole wagon of burning fagots." He also says that "the feeling of distress is the root of benevolence," therefore a benevolent man is ever mindful of those who are suffering and in distress. Thus did Mencius long anticipate Adam Smith, who founds his ethical philosophy on sympathy [pages 41–43].

[In regard to politeness, Nitobe points out that foreign observers have stressed its prevalence among the Japanese. He continues:]

Politeness is a poor virtue, if it is actuated only by a fear of offending good taste, whereas it should be the outward manifestation of a sympathetic regard for the feelings of others. It also implies a due regard for the fitness of things, therefore due respect to social positions; for these latter express no plutocratic distinctions, but were originally distinctions for actual merit [page 50].

I have said that etiquette was elaborated into the finest niceties, so much so that different schools, advocating different systems, came into existence. But they all united in the ultimate essential, and this was put by a great exponent of the best-known school of etiquette, the Ogasawara, in the following terms: "The end of all etiquette is to so cultivate your mind that even when you are quietly seated, not the roughest ruffian can dare make onset on your person." It means, in other words, that by constant exercise in correct manners, one brings all the parts and faculties of the body into perfect order and into such harmony with itself and its environment as to express the mastery of spirit over the flesh [page 54].

As to veracity, the samurai prided himself upon it. His word carried such weight with it that promises were generally made and fulfilled without a written pledge, which would have been deemed quite beneath his dignity. Many thrilling anecdotes were told of those who atoned by death for *ni-gon,* a double tongue [page 62].

[As to honor, Nitobe remarks:]

The sense of honor, implying a vivid consciousness of personal dignity and worth, could not fail to characterize the samurai, born and bred to value the duties and privileges of their profession. . . . A good name . . . assumed as a matter of course, any infringement upon its integrity was felt as shame, and the sense of shame (*Ren-chi-shin*) was one of the earliest to be cherished in juvenile education. "You will be laughed at," "It will disgrace you," "Are you not ashamed?" were the last appeal to correct behavior on the part of a youthful delinquent. Such a recourse to his honor touched the most sensitive spot in the child's heart, as though he had been nursed on honor while he was in his mother's womb; for most truly is honor a pre-natal influence, being closely bound up with strong family consciousness [pages 72–73].

[Although the code of honor was sometimes carried to morbid excess, it was "strongly counterbalanced by preaching magnanimity and patience" (page 76).
The following is Nitobe's account of the virtue of loyalty, given nearly in full:]

Feudal morality shares other virtues in common with other systems of ethics, with other classes of people, but this virtue—homage and fealty to a superior—is its distinctive feature. I am aware that personal fidelity is a moral adhesion existing among all sorts and conditions of men,—a gang of pickpockets owe allegiance to a Fagin; but it is only in the code of chivalrous honor that loyalty assumes paramount importance.

In spite of Hegel's criticism * that the fidelity of feudal vassals, being an obligation to an individual and not to a commonwealth, is a bond established on totally unjust principles, a great compatriot of his made it his boast that personal loyalty was a German virtue. Bismarck had good reasons to do so, not because the *Treue* he boasts of was the monopoly of his Fatherland or of any single nation or race, but because this favored fruit of chivalry lingers latest among the people where feudalism has

---

* *Philosophy of History* (Eng. trans. by Sibree), Pt. IV., sec. ii., ch. i.

lasted longest. In America, where "everybody is as good as anybody else," and, as the Irishman added, "better too," such exalted ideas of loyalty as we feel for our sovereign may be deemed "excellent within certain bounds," but preposterous as encouraged among us. Montesquieu complained long ago that right on one side of the Pyrenees was wrong on the other, and the recent Dreyfus trial proved the truth of his remark, save that the Pyrenees were not the sole boundary beyond which French justice finds no accord. Similarly, loyalty as we conceive it may find few admirers elsewhere, not because our conception is wrong, but because it is, I am afraid, forgotten, and also because we carry it to a degree not reached in any other country. Griffis * was quite right in stating that whereas in China Confucian ethics made obedience to parents the primary human duty, in Japan precedence was given to loyalty. At the risk of shocking some of my good readers, I will relate of one "who could endure to follow a fall'n lord" and who thus, as Shakespeare assures, "earned a place i' the story."

The story is of one of the greatest characters of our history, Michizané, who, falling a victim to jealousy and calumny, is exiled from the capital. Not content with this, his unrelenting enemies are now bent upon the extinction of his family. Strict search for his son—not yet grown—reveals the fact of his being secreted in a village school kept by one Genzo, a former vassal of Michizané. When orders are dispatched to the schoolmaster to deliver the head of the juvenile offender on a certain day, his first idea is to find a suitable substitute for it. He ponders over his school-list, scrutinizes with careful eyes all the boys, as they stroll into the classroom, but none among the children born of the soil bears the least resemblance to his protégé. His despair, however, is but for a moment; for, behold, a new scholar is announced—a comely boy of the same age as his master's son, escorted by a mother of noble mien.

No less conscious of the resemblance between infant lord and infant retainer, were the mother and the boy himself. In the privacy of home both had laid themselves upon the altar; the one his life—the other her heart, yet without sign to the outer world. Unwitting of what had passed between them, it is the teacher from whom comes the suggestion.

Here, then, is the scapegoat!—The rest of the narrative may be briefly told.—On the day appointed, arrives the officer commissioned to identify and receive the head of the youth. Will he be deceived by the false head?

* *Religions of Japan.*

The poor Genzo's hand is on the hilt of the sword, ready to strike a blow either at the man or at himself, should the examination defeat his scheme. The officer takes up the gruesome object before him, goes calmly over each feature, and in a deliberate, business-like tone, pronounces it genuine.—That evening in a lonely home awaits the mother we saw in the school. Does she know the fate of her child? It is not for his return that she watches with eagerness for the opening of the wicket. Her father-in-law has been for a long time a recipient of Michizané's bounties, but since his banishment, circumstances have forced her husband to follow the service of the enemy of his family's benefactor. He himself could not be untrue to his own cruel master; but his son could serve the cause of the grandsire's lord. As one acquainted with the exile's family, it was he who had been entrusted with the task of identifying the boy's head. Now the day's—yea, the life's—hard work is done, he returns home and as he crosses its threshold, he accosts his wife, saying: "Rejoice, my wife, our darling son has proved of service to his lord!"

"What an atrocious story!" I hear my readers exclaim. "Parents deliberately sacrificing their own innocent child to save the life of another man's!" But this child was a conscious and willing victim: it is a story of vicarious death—as significant as, and not more revolting than, the story of Abraham's intended sacrifice of Isaac. In both cases was obedience to the call of duty, utter submission to the command of a higher voice, whether given by a visible or an invisible angel, or heard by an outward or an inward ear;—but I abstain from preaching.

The individualism of the West, which recognizes separate interests for father and son, husband and wife, necessarily brings into strong relief the duties owed by one to the other; but Bushido held that the interest of the family and of the members thereof is intact,—one and inseparable. This interest is bound up with affection—natural, instinctive, irresistible; hence, if we die for one we love with natural love (which animals themselves possess), what is that? "For if ye love them that love you, what reward have ye? Do not even the publicans the same?"

In his great history, Sanyo relates in touching language the heart struggle of Shigemori concerning his father's rebellious conduct. "If I be loyal, my father must be undone; if I obey my father, my duty to my sovereign must go amiss." Poor Shigemori! We see him afterward praying with all his soul that kind Heaven may visit him with death, that he may be released from this world where it is hard for purity and righteousness to dwell.

Many a Shigemori has his heart torn by the conflict between duty and affection. Indeed, neither Shakespeare nor the Old Testament itself contains an adequate rendering of *ko,* our conception of filial piety, and yet in such conflicts Bushido never wavered in its choice of loyalty. Women, too, encouraged their offspring to sacrifice all for the king. Even as resolute as Widow Windham and her illustrious consort, the samurai matron stood ready to give up her boys for the cause of loyalty.

Since Bushido, like Aristotle and some modern sociologists, conceived the state as antedating the individual,—the latter being born into the former as part and parcel thereof,—he must live and die for it or for the incumbent of its legitimate authority. Readers of Crito will remember the argument with which Socrates represents the laws of the city as pleading with him on the subject of his escape. Among others he makes them (the laws or the state) say: "Since you were begotten and nurtured and educated under us, dare you once to say you are not our offspring and servant, you and your fathers before you?" These are words which do not impress us as anything extraordinary; for the same thing has long been on the lips of Bushido, with this modification, that the laws and the state were represented with us by a personal being. Loyalty is an ethical outcome of this political theory.

*   *   *

Bushido did not require us to make our conscience the slave of any lord or king. Thomas Mowbray was a veritable spokesman for us when he said:

> "Myself I throw, dread sovereign, at thy foot.
> My life thou shalt command, but not my shame;
> The one my duty owes; but my fair name,
> Despite of death that lives upon my grave,
> To dark dishonor's use, thou shalt not have."

A man who sacrificed his own conscience to the capricious will or freak of fancy of a sovereign was accorded a low place in the estimate of the Precepts. Such an one was despised as *nei-shin,* a cringeling, who makes court by unscrupulous fawning, or as *chô-shin,* a favorite who steals his master's affections by means of servile compliance; these two species of subjects corresponding exactly to those which Iago describes,—the one, a duteous and knee-crooking knave, doting on his own obsequious bondage, wearing out his time much like his master's ass; the other trimming in forms and visages of duty, keeping yet his heart attending on himself. When a subject differed from his master, the loyal path for him to pursue was to use every available means to persuade him of his error, as Kent did to King Lear. Failing in this, let the master deal with him as he wills. In cases of this kind, it was quite a usual course for the samurai to make the last appeal to the intelligence and conscience of his lord by demonstrating the sincerity of his words with the shedding of his own blood.

Life being regarded as the means whereby to serve his master, and its ideal being set upon honor, the whole education and training of a samurai were conducted accordingly.

[The demands of Bushido were evidently so exacting as to require a high degree of self-control. Some of the aspects of this virtue are treated in the following paragraphs:]

The discipline of fortitude on the one hand, inculcating endurance without a groan, and the teaching of politeness on the other, requiring us not to mar the pleasure or serenity of another by expressions of our own sorrow or pain, combined to engender a stoical turn of mind, and eventually to confirm it into a national trait of apparent stoicism. I say apparent stoicism, because I do not believe that true stoicism can ever become the characteristic of a whole nation, and also because some of our national manners and customs may seem to a foreign observer hard-hearted. Yet we are really as susceptible to tender emotion as any race under the sky.

I am inclined to think that in one sense we have to feel more than others—yes, doubly more—since the very attempt to restrain natural promptings entails suffering. Imagine boys—and girls, too—brought up not to resort to the shedding of a tear or the uttering of a groan for the relief of their feelings,—and there is a physiological problem whether such effort steels their nerves or makes them more sensitive.

It was considered unmanly for a samurai to betray his emotions on his face. "He shows no sign of joy or anger," was a phrase used, in describing a great character. The most natural affections were kept under control. A father could embrace his son only at the expense of his dignity; a husband would not kiss his wife,—no, not in the presence of other people, whatever he might do in private! There may be some truth in the remark of a witty youth when he said, "American husbands kiss their wives in public and beat them in private; Japanese husbands beat theirs in public and kiss them in private."

Calmness of behavior, composure of mind, should not be disturbed by passion of any kind. I remember when, during the late war with China, a regiment left a certain town, a large concourse of people flocked to the station to bid farewell to the general and his army. On this occasion an American resident resorted to the place, expecting to witness loud demonstrations, as the nation itself was highly excited and there were fathers, mothers, wives, and sweethearts of the soldiers in the crowd. The American was strangely disappointed; for as the whistle blew and the train began to move, the hats of thousands of people were silently taken off and their heads bowed in reverential farewell; no waving of handkerchiefs, no word uttered, but deep silence in which only an attentive ear could catch a few broken sobs. In domestic life, too, I know of a father who spent whole nights listening to the breathing of a sick child, standing behind the door that he might not be caught in such an act of parental weakness! I know of a mother who, in her last moments, refrained from sending for her son, that he might not be disturbed in his studies. Our history and everyday life are replete with examples of heroic matrons who can well bear comparison with some of the most touching pages of Plutarch. Among our peasantry an Ian Maclaren would be sure to find many a Marget Howe.

*   *   *

It is not altogether perverseness of oriental minds that the instant our emotions are moved, we try to guard our lips in order to hide them. Speech is very often with us, as the Frenchman defines it, "the art of concealing thought."

Call upon a Japanese friend in time of deepest affliction and he will invariably receive you laughing, with red eyes or moist cheeks. At first you may think him hysterical. Press him for explanation and you will get a few broken commonplaces—"Human life has sorrow"; "They who meet must part"; "He that is born must die"; "It is foolish to count the years of a child that is gone, but a woman's heart will indulge in follies"; and the like. So the noble words of a noble Hohenzollern—"Lerne zu leiden ohne klagen"—had found many responsive minds among us long before they were uttered.

Indeed, the Japanese have recourse to risibility whenever the frailties of human nature are put to severest test. I think we possess a better reason than Democritus himself for our Abderian * tendency, for laughter with us oftenest veils an effort to regain balance of temper when disturbed by any untoward circumstance. It is a counterpoise of sorrow or rage.

The suppression of feelings being thus steadily insisted upon, they find their safety-valve in poetical aphorisms. A poet of the tenth century writes: "In Japan and China as well, humanity, when moved by sorrow, tells its bitter grief in verse." A mother who tries to console her broken heart by fancying her departed child absent on his wonted chase after the dragon-fly hums,

> "How far to-day in chase, I wonder,
> Has gone my hunter of the dragon-fly!"

I refrain from quoting other examples, for I know I could do only scant justice to the pearly gems of our literature, were I to render into a foreign tongue the thoughts which were wrung drop by drop from bleeding hearts and threaded into beads of rarest value. I hope I have in a measure shown that inner working of our minds which often presents an appearance of callousness or of an hysterical mixture of laughter and dejection, and whose sanity is sometimes called in question.

[There are crises in which a Japanese can maintain his honor only through the ceremonial form of suicide called *hara-kiri* or *seppuku*. In this act etiquette, courage, and self-control are brought to their highest pitch. Any reader who desires to understand this custom should turn to Chapter XII of Nitobe's book.]

* From Abdera, the birthplace of Democritus, called "the laughing philosopher." —EDITOR.

19

PIUS XI ON RECONSTRUCTING THE SOCIAL ORDER

[Pope Leo XIII (Gioacchino Pecci, 1810–1893, Pope from 1878) published in 1891 an encyclical referred to as *Rerum Novarum,* from its opening words, or *The Condition of the Working Classes,* from its contents. The English version of this may be found in *The Great Encyclical Letters of Pope Leo XIII,* New York, Benziger Brothers, 1903. In this letter he condemned both the injustice from which the working classes suffered and the remedy proposed by Socialism. He defended private property as a natural right in conformity with God's will. He called for the solution of the problem in a coöperative spirit under the guidance of church and state.

On the fortieth anniversary of this encyclical, Pope Pius XI published an encyclical called *Quadrigesimo Anno (Forty Years After)* or *On the Reconstruction of the Social Order.* The English version is published by the America Press, New York. Pius XI (Achille Ratti), 1857–1939, Pope from 1929, had been a librarian, diplomat, and mountain-climber as well as a clergyman before he succeeded to the papacy. In this encyclical he first reviewed the contents and influence of *Rerum Novarum;* then he outlined his own solution of the economic problem in the passage here reproduced; in a later section he reviewed the changes in Socialism since 1891 and found that neither the extreme form (Communism) nor the more moderate forms were compatible with Catholicism. In conclusion he declared that "this longed-for social reconstruction must be preceded by a profound renewal of the Christian spirit" and exhorted the clergy to strive toward that end.]

On the Reconstruction of the Social Order *

II. Leo's Teaching Vindicated and Developed

In the course of these years, however, doubts have arisen concerning the correct interpretation of certain passages of the Encyclical or their inferences, and these doubts have led to controversies even among Catholics, not always of a peaceful character. On the other hand, the new needs of our age and the changed conditions of society have rendered necessary a more precise application and amplification of Leo's doctrine. We, therefore, gladly seize this opportunity of answering their doubts, so far as in Us lies, and of satisfying the demands of the present day. This we do in virtue of Our Apostolic office, by which We are a debtor to all.†

The Moral Law and Economics. But before proceeding to discuss these problems We lay down the principle long since clearly established by Leo XIII, that We have the right and duty of judging, by Our supreme authority, social and economic problems.‡ It is not, of course, for the Church to lead men to transient and perishable happiness only, but to that which is eternal. Indeed "the Church believes that it would be wrong for her to interfere without just cause in such earthly concerns." § But she never can relinquish her God-given task of interposing her authority, not indeed in technical matters, for which she has neither the suitable equipment nor the mission, but in all those that have a bearing on moral conduct. For the deposit of truth entrusted to Us by God, and Our weighty office of propagating, interpreting and urging in season and out of season the entire moral law, demand that both social and economic questions be brought within Our supreme jurisdiction, insofar as they refer to moral issues.

For, though economic science and moral discipline are guided each by its own principles in its own sphere, it is false that the two orders are so distinct and alien that the former in no way depends on the latter. The so-called laws of economics, derived from the nature of earthly goods and from the qualities of human body and soul, determine what aims are unattainable or attainable in economic matters and what means are thereby necessary, while reason itself clearly deduces from the nature of

* New York, The America Press, 1938.
† Rom. i, 14.
‡ Encycl. *Rerum Novarum*, p. 9.
§ Encycl. *Ubi Arcano*, Dec. 23, 1922.

things and from the individual and social character of man, what is the end and object of the whole economic order assigned by God the Creator.

For it is the moral law alone which commands us to seek in all our conduct our supreme and final end, and to strive directly in our specific actions for those ends which nature, or rather, the Author of Nature, has established for them, duly subordinating the particular to the general. If this law be faithfully obeyed, the result will be that particular economic aims, whether of society as a body or of individuals, will be intimately linked with the universal teleological order, and as a consequence we shall be led by progressive stages to the final end of all, God Himself, our highest and lasting good.

Ownership. Descending now to details, We commence with ownership, or the right of property. You are aware, Venerable Brethren and beloved children, how strenuously Our Predecessor, of happy memory, defended the right of property against the teachings of the Socialists of his time, showing that the abolition of private ownership would prove to be not beneficial, but grievously harmful to the working classes. Yet, since there are some who falsely and unjustly accuse the Supreme Pontiff and the Church as upholding, both then and now, the wealthier classes against the proletariat, and since controversy has arisen among Catholics as to the true sense of Pope Leo's teaching, We have thought it well to defend from calumny the Leonine doctrine in this matter, which is also the Catholic doctrine, and to safeguard it against false interpretations.

Individual and Social. First, let it be made clear beyond all doubt that neither Leo XIII, nor those theologians who have taught under the guidance and direction of the Church, have ever denied or called in question the twofold aspect of ownership, which is individual or social accordingly as it regards individuals or concerns the common good. Their unanimous contention has always been that the right to own private property has been given to man by nature or rather by the Creator Himself, not only in order that individuals may be able to provide for their own needs and those of their families, but also that by means of it, the goods which the Creator has destined for the human race may truly serve this purpose. Now these ends cannot be secured unless some definite and stable order is maintained.

There is, therefore, a double danger to be assiduously avoided. On the one hand, if the social and public aspect of ownership be denied or minimized, we fall into Individualism, as it is called, or something akin to it; on the other hand, the rejection or diminution of its private and individual character necessarily leads one into Collectivism, or at least compels one to adopt its tenets. To disregard these dangers would be to rush headlong into the quicksands of Modernism with its moral, juridical and social order, which We condemned in the Encyclical Letter issued at the beginning of Our Pontificate.*

Let this be noted particularly by those seekers after novelties who launch against the Church the odious calumny that she has allowed a pagan concept of ownership to creep into the teachings of her theologians and that another concept must be substituted, which in their astounding ignorance they call Christian.

Possession and Use. That We may keep within bounds the controversies which have arisen concerning ownership and the duties attaching to it, We reassert in the first place the fundamental principle laid down by Leo XIII, that the right of property must be distinguished from its use.† That justice, which is called commutative justice, commands us faithfully to respect the possessions of others, not encroaching on the rights of another and thus exceeding the rights of ownership. The putting of one's own possessions to proper use, however, does not fall under this form of justice, but under certain other virtues, and therefore it is "a duty not enforced by courts of justice." ‡ Hence it is false to contend that the right of ownership and its proper use are bounded by the same limits; and it is even less true that the very misuse or even the non-use of ownership destroys or forfeits the right itself.

Most helpful therefore and worthy of all praise are the efforts of those who, in a spirit of harmony and with due regard for the traditions of the Church, seek to determine the precise nature of these duties and to define the boundaries imposed by the requirements of social life upon the right of ownership itself or upon its use. On the contrary, it is a grievous error so to weaken the individual character of ownership as actually to destroy it.

The State and Ownership. It follows from the twofold character of ownership, which We have termed individual and social, that men must take into account in this matter not only their own advantage but also

---

* Encycl. *Ubi Arcano,* Dec. 23, 1922.
† Encycl. *Rerum Novarum,* p. 13.
‡ *Ibid.,* p. 14.

the common good. To define in detail these duties, when the need occurs and when the natural law does not do so, is the function of the Government. Provided that the natural and Divine law be observed, the public authority, in view of the common good, may specify more accurately what is licit and what is illicit for property owners in the use of their possessions. Moreover, Leo XIII had wisely taught that "the defining of private possession has been left by God to man's industry and to the laws of individual peoples." *

History proves that the right of ownership, like other elements of social life, is not absolutely rigid, and this doctrine We Ourselves have given utterance to on a previous occasion in the following terms: "How varied are the forms which the right of property has assumed! First, the primitive form used amongst rude and savage peoples, which still exists in certain localities even in our own day; then, that of the patriarchal age; later came various tyrannical types (We use the word in its classical meaning); finally, the feudal and monarchic systems down to the varieties of more recent times." †

It is plain, however, that the State may not discharge this duty in an arbitrary manner. Man's natural right of possessing and transmitting property by inheritance must be kept intact and cannot be taken away by the State from man. For "man is older than the State," ‡ and "the domestic household is antecedent, as well in idea as in fact, to the gathering of men into a civil union." §

The prudent Pontiff had already declared it unlawful for the State to exhaust the means of individuals by crushing taxes and tributes: "The right to possess private property is derived from nature, not from man; and the State has by no means the right to abolish it, but only to control its use and bring it into harmony with the interests of the public good." ||

However, when civil authority adjusts ownership to meet the needs of the public good it acts not as an enemy, but as the friend of private owners; for thus it effectively prevents the possession of private property, intended by Nature's Author in His wisdom for the sustaining of human life, from creating intolerable burdens and so rushing to its own de-

* *Ibid.*, p. 5.
† Allocution to Azione Cattolica Italiana, May 16, 1926.
‡ Encycl. *Rerum Novarum*, p. 4.
§ *Ibid.*, p. 7.
|| *Ibid.*, pp. 27, 28.

struction. It does not therefore abolish, but protects private ownership, and, far from weakening the right of private property, it gives it new strength.

Use of One's Surplus. At the same time a man's superfluous income is not left entirely to his own discretion. We speak of that portion of his income which he does not need in order to live as becomes his station. On the contrary, the grave obligations of charity, beneficence, and liberality, which rest upon the wealthy are constantly insisted upon in telling words by Holy Scripture and the Fathers of the Church.

However, the investment of superfluous income in order that opportunities for gainful employment may abound, provided the labor employed produces results which are really useful, is to be considered, according to the teaching of the Angelic Doctor,* an act of real liberality particularly appropriate to the needs of our time.

Labor as a Title. The original acquisition of property takes place by first occupation and by industry, or, as it is called, specification. This is the universal teaching of tradition and the doctrine of Our Predecessor, for, despite unreasonable assertions to the contrary, no wrong is done to any man by the occupation of goods unclaimed or which belong to nobody. The only form of labor, however, which gives the workingman a title to its fruits is that which a man exercises as his own master, and by which some new form or new value is produced.

Altogether different is the labor one man hires out to another, and which is expended on the property of another. To it apply appositely the words of Leo XIII: "Most time it is that only by the labor of workingmen that States grow rich." † Is it not indeed apparent that the huge possessions which constitute human wealth are begotten by and flow from the hands of the workingman, toiling either unaided or with the assistance of tools and machinery which wonderfully intensify his efficiency?

Universal experience teaches us that no nation has ever yet risen from want and poverty to a better and loftier station without the unremitting toil of all its citizens, both employers and employed. But it is no less self-evident that these ceaseless labors would have remained ineffective, indeed could never have been attempted, had not God, the Creator of all things, in His goodness bestowed in the first instance the wealth and resources of nature, its treasures and its powers. For what else is work but

* *Summa Theol.,* 2, 2, Q. 134.
† Encycl. *Rerum Novarum,* p. 20.

the application of one's forces of soul and body to these gifts of nature
or the development of one's powers by their means?

Labor and Capital. Now the natural law, or rather, God's will manifested by it, demands that right order be observed in the application of
natural resources to human needs; and this order consists in everything
having its proper owner. Hence it follows that unless a man apply his
labor to his own property, an alliance must be formed between his toil
and his neighbor's property, for each is helpless without the other. This
was what Leo XIII had in mind when he wrote: "Capital cannot do without labor, nor labor without capital." * It is therefore entirely false to ascribe the results of their combined efforts to either party alone; and it is
flagrantly unjust that either should deny the efficacy of the other and
seize all the profits.

Excessive Claims of Both. Property or capital, however, was long able
to appropriate to itself excessive advantages; it claimed all the products
and profits and left to the laborer hardly sufficient to repair and refresh
his strength. For by an inexorable economic law, it was held, all accumulation of riches must fall to the share of the wealthy, while the workingman must remain perpetually in indigence or reduced to the barest minimum needed for existence. It is true that the actual state of things was not
always and everywhere as deplorable as the Liberalistic tenets of the so-
called Manchester School might lead us to conclude; but it cannot be
denied that a steady drift of economic and social tendencies was in this
direction. These false opinions and specious axioms were vehemently attacked, as was to be expected, and by others also than merely those whom
such principles deprived of their innate right to better their condition.

The cause of the harassed workingman was espoused by the intellectuals, as they are called, who set up in opposition to this fictitious law an
equally false moral principle: that all products and profits, excepting those
required to repair and replace capital belong by every right to the workingman. This error, more subtle than that of the Socialists who hold that
all means of production should be transferred to the State, or, as they
term it, socialized, is for that reason more dangerous and apt to deceive
the unwary. It is an alluring poison, consumed with avidity by many
not deceived by open Socialism.

Guiding Principles. To prevent erroneous doctrines of this kind from
blocking the path of justice and peace, the advocates of these opinions

* *Ibid.,* p. 11.

should have hearkened to the wise words of Our Predecessor: "The earth even though apportioned amongst private owners, ceases not thereby to minister to the needs of all." * This teaching We Ourselves have reaffirmed above when we wrote that the division of goods which is effected by private ownership is ordained by nature itself and has for its purpose that created things may minister to man's needs in orderly and stable fashion. These principles must be constantly borne in mind if we would not wander from the path of truth.

Now, not every kind of distribution of wealth and property amongst men is such that it can at all, and still less can adequately, attain the end intended by God. Wealth, therefore, which is constantly being augmented by social and economic progress, must be so distributed amongst the various individuals and classes of society that the common good of all, of which Leo XIII spoke, be thereby promoted. In other words, the good of the whole community must be safeguarded. By these principles of social justice one class is forbidden to exclude the other from a share in the profits. This sacred law is violated by an irresponsible wealthy class who, in the excess of their good fortune, deem it a just state of things that they should receive everything and the laborer nothing; it is violated also by a propertyless wage-earning class who demand for themselves all the fruits of production, as being the work of their hands. Such men, vehemently incensed against the violation of justice by capitalists, go too far in wrongly vindicating the one right of which they are conscious; they attack and seek to abolish all forms of ownership and all profits not obtained by labor, whatever be their nature or significance in human society, for the sole reason that they are not acquired by toil. In this connection it must be noted that the appeal made by some to the words of the Apostle: "If any man will not work, neither let him eat," † is as inept as it is unfounded. The Apostle is here passing judgment on those who refuse to work though they could and ought to do so; he admonishes us to use diligently our time and our powers of body and mind, and not to become burdensome to others as long as we are able to provide for ourselves. In no sense does he teach that labor is the sole title which gives a right to a living or to profits.‡

Each class, then, must receive its due share, and the distribution of

---

* Encycl. *Rerum Novarum*, p. 5.
† II Thess. iii, 10.
‡ II Thess. iii, 8–10.

created goods must be brought into conformity with the demands of the common good or social justice, for every sincere observer is conscious that the vast differences between the few who hold excessive wealth and the many who live in destitution constitute a grave evil in modern society.

Bettering Workers' Lot. This is the aim which Our Predecessor urged as the necessary object of our efforts: the uplifting of the proletariat. It calls for more emphatic assertion and more insistent repetition on the present occasion because these salutary injunctions of the Pontiff have not infrequently been forgotten, deliberately ignored, or deemed impracticable, though they were both feasible and imperative. They have lost none of their force or wisdom for our own age, even though the horrible condition of pauperism during the days of Leo XIII is less prevalent to-day. The condition of the workingman has indeed been improved and rendered more equitable in many respects, particularly in the larger and more civilized States, where the laboring class can no longer be said to be universally in misery and want. But after modern machinery and modern industry had penetrated with astonishing speed and taken possession of many newly colonized countries no less than of the ancient civilizations of the Far East, the number of the dispossessed laboring masses, whose groans mount to Heaven from these lands, increased beyond all measure.

Moreover, there is the immense army of hired rural laborers, whose condition is depressed in the extreme, and who have no hope of ever obtaining a share in the land.* These, too, unless suitable and efficacious remedies be applied, will remain perpetually sunk in the proletarian condition.

It is true that there is a formal difference between pauperism and proletarianism. Nevertheless, the immense number of propertyless wage-earners on the one hand, and the superabundant riches of the fortunate few on the other, is an unanswerable argument that the earthly goods so abundantly produced in this our age which is termed "the age of industrialism," are far from rightly distributed and equitably shared among the various classes of men.

Spread of Ownership. Every effort, therefore, must be made that at least in future a just share only of the fruits of production be permitted to accumulate in the hands of the wealthy, and that an ample sufficiency be supplied to the workingmen. The purpose is not that these become slack at their work, for man is born to labor as the bird to fly, but that by thrift

* Encycl. *Rerum Novarum*, p. 27.

they may increase their possessions and by the prudent management of the same may be enabled to bear the family burden with greater ease and security, being freed from that hand-to-mouth uncertainty which is the lot of the proletarian. Thus they will not only be in a position to support life's changing fortunes, but will also have the reassuring confidence that when their lives are ended, some little provision will remain for those whom they leave behind them.

These ideas were not merely suggested, but stated in frank and open terms by Our Predecessor. We emphasize them with renewed insistence in this present Encyclical; for unless serious attempts be made, with all energy and without delay to put them into practice, let nobody persuade himself that public order, the peace and tranquillity of human society, can be effectively defended against the forces of revolution!

The Question of Wages. This program cannot, however, be realized unless the propertyless wage-earner be placed in such circumstances that by skill and thrift he can acquire a certain moderate ownership, as was already declared by Us, following the footsteps of Our Predecessor. But how can he, by living sparingly, ever save money, except from his wages, who has nothing but his labor by which to obtain food and the necessities of life? Let us turn, therefore, to the question of wages, which Leo XIII held to be "of great importance," * stating and explaining where necessary its principles and precepts.

And first of all, those who hold that the wage contract is essentially unjust, and that in its place must be introduced the contract of partnership, are certainly in error. They do a grave injury to Our Predecessor, whose Encyclical not only admits this contract, but devotes much space to its determination according to the principles of justice.

In the present state of human society, however, we deem it advisable that the wage contract should, when possible, be modified somewhat by a contract of partnership, as is already being tried in various ways to the no small gain both of the wage-earners and of the employers. In this way wage-earners are made sharers in some sort in the ownership, or the management, or the profits.

In estimating a just wage, not one consideration alone but many must be taken into account, as Leo XIII wisely said in these words: "Before deciding whether wages are fair, many things have to be considered." †

* Encycl. *Rerum Novarum*, p. 25.
† *Ibid.*, p. 12.

In this way he refuted the irresponsible view of certain writers who declare that this momentous question can easily be solved by the application of a single principle, and that not even a true one.

Entirely false is the principle, widely propagated today, that the worth of labor and therefore the equitable return to be made for it, should equal the worth of its net result. Thus the right to the full product of his toil is claimed for the wage-earner. How erroneous this is appears from what we have written above concerning capital and labor.

Labor's Double Aspect. The obvious truth is that in labor, especially hired labor, as in ownership, there is a social as well as a personal or individual aspect to be considered. For unless human society forms a truly social and organic body; unless labor be protected in the social and juridical order; unless the various forms of human endeavor, dependent one upon the other, are united in mutual harmony and mutual support; unless, above all, brains, capital and labor combine together for common effort, man's toil cannot produce due fruit. Hence, if the social and individual character of labor be overlooked, it can be neither justly appraised nor equitably recompensed.

From this double aspect, growing out of the very notion of human labor, follow important conclusions for the regulation and fixing of wages.

Wages to Meet Family Needs. In the first place, the wage paid to the workingman must be sufficient for the support of himself and of his family.* It is right indeed that the rest of the family contribute according to their power towards the common maintenance, as in the rural home or in the families of many artisans and small shopkeepers. But it is wrong to abuse the tender years of children or the weakness of woman. Mothers will above all devote their work to the home and the things connected with it. Intolerable, and to be opposed with all our strength, is the abuse whereby mothers of families, because of the insufficiency of the father's salary, are forced to engage in gainful occupations outside the domestic walls to the neglect of their own proper cares and duties, particularly the education of their children.

Every effort must therefore be made that fathers of families receive a wage sufficient to meet adequately ordinary domestic needs. If in the present state of society this is not always feasible, social justice demands that reforms be introduced without delay which will guarantee every adult

---

* Encycl. *Casti Connubii,* Dec. 31, 1930; published by the America Press with study-club questions and bibliography.

workingman just such a wage. In this connection We might utter a word of praise for various systems devised and attempted in practice, by which an increased wage is paid in view of increased family burdens, and a special provision is made for special needs.

Must Not Ruin Business. The condition of any particular business and of its owner must also come into question in settling the scale of wages; for it is unjust to demand wages so high that an employer cannot pay them without ruin, and without consequent distress amongst the working people themselves. If the business make smaller profit on account of bad management, want of enterprise or out-of-date methods, this is not a just reason for reducing the workingmen's wages. If, however, the business does not make enough money to pay the workman a just wage, either because it is overwhelmed with unjust burdens, or because it is compelled to sell its products at an unjustly low price, those who thus injure it are guilty of grievous wrong; for it is they who deprive the workingmen of the just wage, and force them to accept lower terms.

Let employers, therefore, and employed join in their plans and efforts to overcome all difficulties and obstacles, and let them be aided in this wholesome endeavor by the wise measures of the public authority. If the business man has been reduced to extremities, counsel must be taken whether the business can continue, or whether some other provision should be made for the workers. The guiding spirit in this crucial decision should be one of mutual understanding and Christian harmony between employers and workers.

Wages and the Common Good. The wage scale finally must be regulated with a view to the economic welfare of the whole people. We have already shown how conducive it is to the common good that wage-earners of all kinds be enabled by economizing that portion of their wages which remains after necessary expenses have been met, to attain to the possession of a certain modest fortune. Another point, however, of no less importance must not be overlooked, in these days especially, namely, that opportunities for work be provided for those who are willing and able to work. This depends in large measure upon the scale of wages, which multiplies opportunities for work as long as it remains within proper limits, and reduces them if allowed to pass these limits. All are aware that a scale of wages too low, no less than a scale excessively high, causes unemployment. Now unemployment, particularly if widespread and of long duration, as We have been forced to experience it during Our

Pontificate, is a dreadful scourge; it causes misery and temptation to the laborer, ruins the prosperity of nations, and endangers public order, peace and tranquillity the world over. To lower or raise wages unduly, with a view to private profit, and with no consideration for the common good, is contrary to social justice which demands that by union of effort and good will such a scale of wages be set up, if possible, as to offer to the greatest number opportunities of employment and of securing for themselves suitable means of livelihood.

Integrating Economic Life. A reasonable relationship between different wages here enters into consideration. Intimately connected with this is a reasonable relationship between the prices obtained for the products of the various economic groups, agrarian, industrial, etc. Where this harmonious proportion is kept, man's various economic activities combine and unite into one single organism and become members of a common body, lending each other mutual help and service. For then only will the economic and social organism be soundly established and attain its end, when it secures for all and each those goods which the wealth and resources of nature, technical achievement, and the social organization of economic affairs can give. These goods should be sufficient to supply all needs and proper conveniences, and to uplift men to that higher level of prosperity and culture which, provided it be used with prudence, is not only no hindrance but is of singular help to virtue.*

Reforming the Social Order. What We have written thus far regarding a right distribution of property and a just scale of wages is concerned directly with the individual, and deals only indirectly with the social order. To this latter, however, Our Predecessor, Leo XIII, devoted special thought and care in his efforts to reconstruct and perfect it according to the principles of sound philosophy and the sublime precepts of the Gospel.

A happy beginning has here been made. But in order that what has been well begun may be rendered stable, that what has not yet been accomplished may now be achieved, and that still richer and brighter blessings may descend upon mankind, two things are particularly necessary: the reform of the social order and the correction of morals.

When we speak of the reform of the social order it is principally the State we have in mind. Not indeed that all salvation is to be hoped for from its intervention, but because on account of the evil of Individualism,

* Cf. St. Thomas, *De Regimine Principum,* I, 15; Encycl. *Rerum Novarum,* p. 20.

as We called it, things have come to such a pass that the highly developed
social life which once flourished in a variety of prosperous institutions
organically linked with each other, has been overthrown and all but
ruined, leaving thus virtually only individuals and the State, no little
harm being done to the State itself. Social life lost entirely its organic form.
The State, which now was encumbered with all the burdens once borne
by associations rendered extinct by it, was in consequence submerged
and overwhelmed by an infinity of affairs and duties.

Gradation in Functions. It is indeed true, as history clearly proves, that
owing to the change in social conditions, much that was formerly done
by small bodies can nowadays be accomplished only by large corporations.
None the less, just as it is wrong to withdraw from the individual and
commit to the community at large what private enterprise and industry
can accomplish, so too it is an injustice, a grave evil and a disturbance of
right order for a larger and higher organization to arrogate to itself functions which can be performed efficiently by smaller and lower bodies. This
is a fundamental principle of social philosophy, unshaken and unchangeable, and it retains its full truth today. Of its very nature the true aim
of all social activity should be to help individual members of the social
body, but never to destroy or absorb them.

The State should leave to these smaller groups the settlement of business
of minor importance and the management of troublesome details. It will
thus carry out with greater freedom, power and success the tasks belonging to it, because it alone can effectively accomplish these, directing,
watching, stimulating and restraining, as circumstances suggest or necessity demands. Let those in power, therefore, be convinced that the more
faithfully this subsidiary rôle be followed, and a graded hierarchical order
exist between the various organizations, the more excellent will be both
the authority and the efficiency of the social organization as a whole and
the happier and more prosperous the condition of the State.

Now this is the primary duty of the State and of all good citizens: to
abolish conflict between classes with divergent interests, and thus foster
and promote harmony between the "vocational groups."

Harmony by New Grouping. The aim of social legislation must therefore be the reëstablishment of vocational groups. Society to-day still remains in a strained and therefore unstable and uncertain state, being
founded on classes with contradictory interests and hence opposed to each
other, and consequently prone to enmity and strife. Labor, indeed, as has

been well said by Our Predecessor in his Encyclical,* is not a mere chattel, since the human dignity of the workingman must be recognized in it, and consequently it cannot be bought and sold like any piece of merchandise. None the less, under the prevailing conditions, the demand and supply of labor divides men on the labor market into two classes, as into two camps, and the bargaining between these parties transforms this labor market into an arena where the two armies are engaged in fierce combat. To this grave disorder which is leading society to ruin a remedy must evidently be applied as speedily as possible. But there cannot be question of any perfect cure, except this opposition be done away with, and well-ordered members of the social body come into being anew, "vocational groups" namely, binding men together not according to the position they occupy in the labor market, but according to the diverse functions which they exercise in society. For as nature induces those who dwell in close proximity to unite into municipalities, so those who practise the same trade or profession, economic or otherwise, combine into vocational groups. These groups, in a true sense autonomous, are considered by man to be, if not essential to civil society, at least its natural and spontaneous development.

Bond of Union in Common Good. Order, as the Angelic Doctor well defines, is unity arising from the apt arrangement of a plurality of objects; hence, true and genuine social order demands various members of society, joined together by a firm bond.† Such a bond of union is provided on the one hand by the common effort of employers and employees of one and the same "group" joining forces to produce goods or give service; on the other hand, by the common good which all "groups" should unite to promote, each in its own sphere, with friendly harmony. Now this union will become powerful and efficacious in proportion to the fidelity with which the individuals and the "groups" strive to discharge their duties and to excel in them.

From this it is easy to conclude that in these associations the common interest of the whole "group" must predominate: and among these interests the most important is the constant directing of the activities of each vocation to the common good of the State. Regarding cases in which interests of employers and employees call for special care and protection whenever they are in opposition, separate deliberation will take place in

* Encycl. *Rerum Novarum*, p. 11.
† St. Thomas, *Contra Gent.* III, 71; cf. *Summa Theol.*, 1, Q. 65 a. 2, i.c.

their respective assemblies and separate votes will be taken as the matter may require.

It is hardly necessary to note that what Leo XIII taught concerning the form of political government can, in due measure, be applied also to vocational groups. Here, too, men may choose whatever form they please, provided that both justice and the common good be taken into account.*

Freedom of Association. Just as the citizens of the same municipality are wont to form associations with diverse aims, which various individuals are free to join or not; similarly, those who are engaged in the same trade or profession will form free associations among themselves, for purposes connected with their occupations. Our Predecessor explained clearly and lucidly the nature of free associations. We are content, therefore, to emphasize this one point: not only is man free to institute these unions which are founded on a private right, but also to adopt such organization and such rules as may best conduce to the attainment of their respective objects.† The same liberty must be claimed for the founding of associations which extend beyond the limits of a single trade. Let those free associations which already flourish and produce salutary fruits make it the goal of their endeavors, in accordance with Christian social doctrine, to prepare the way and to do their part towards the realization of that ideal type of vocational groups which we have mentioned above.

Evil Effects of Individualism. Still another aim must be kept in view. Just as the unity of human society cannot be built upon class warfare, so the proper ordering of economic affairs cannot be left to free competition alone. From this tainted source have proceeded in the past all the errors of the "individualistic" school. This school, ignorant or forgetful of the social and moral aspects of economic matters, teaches the State should refrain entirely in theory and practice from interfering therein, because these possess in free competition and open markets a principle of self-direction better able to control them than any created intellect. Free competition, however, though within certain limits just and productive of good results, cannot be the ruling principle of the economic world. This has been abundantly proved by the consequences that have followed from the free rein given to these dangerous individualistic ideals. It is therefore very necessary that economic affairs be once more subjected to and gov-

---

* Encycl. *Immortale Dei,* Nov. 1, 1885, *Catholic Mind,* Oct. 22, 1937, with study-club supplement.
† Encycl. *Rerum Novarum,* p. 32.

erned by a true and effective guiding principle. Still less can this function be exercised by the economic supremacy which within recent times
has taken the place of free competition: for this is a headstrong and
vehement power, which, if it is to prove beneficial to mankind, needs to
be curbed strongly and ruled with prudence. It cannot, however, be
curbed and governed by itself. More lofty and noble principles must
therefore be sought in order to control this supremacy sternly and un-
compromisingly: to wit, social justice and social charity.

Justice and Charity Needed. To that end all the institutions of public
and social life must be imbued with the spirit of justice, and this justice
must above all be truly operative. It must build up a juridical and social
order able to pervade all economic activity. Social charity should be, as it
were, the soul of this order and the duty of the State will be to protect
and defend it quickly and effectively. This task it will perform the more
readily if it free itself from those burdens which, as We have already
declared, are not properly its own.

Further, it would be well if the various nations in common counsel and
endeavor strove to promote a healthy economic coöperation by prudent
pacts and institutions, since in economic matters they are largely dependent one upon the other, and need one another's help.

If then the members of the social body be thus reformed, and if the true
directive principle of social and economic activity be thus reëstablished,
it will be possible to say, in a sense, of this body what the Apostle said of
the Mystical Body of Christ: "The whole body being compacted and fitly
joined together, by what every joint supplieth, according to the operation
in the measure of every part, maketh increase of the body, unto the edify-
ing of itself in charity." *

Within recent times, as all are aware, a special syndical and corporative
organization has been inaugurated which, in view of the subject of the
present Encyclical, demands of Us some mention and opportune comment.

Syndical Organization. The State here grants legal existence to the
syndicate or union, and thereby confers on it some of the features of a
monopoly, for in virtue of this recognition, it alone, according to the kind
of syndicate, can represent workingmen and employers, and it alone can
conclude labor contracts and labor agreements. Affiliation to the syndicate
is optional for everyone; but in this sense only can the syndical organiza-

* Ephes. iv, 16.

tion be said to be free, since the contribution to the union and other special taxes are obligatory for all who belong to a given trade or profession, whether workingmen or employers, and the labor contracts drawn up by the legal syndicate are likewise obligatory. It is true that it has been authoritatively declared that the legal syndicate does not exclude the existence of trade associations, not recognized by law.

The corporative organizations are composed of representatives of both unions (i. e., of workingmen and employers) of the same trade or profession, and as true and genuine organs and institutions of the State they direct and coördinate the activities of the unions in all matters of common interest.

Strikes are forbidden. If the contending parties cannot come to an agreement, public authority intervenes.

Little reflection is required to perceive the advantages of the institution thus summarily described; peaceful collaboration of the classes, repression of Socialist organization and efforts, the moderating influence of a special Ministry.

Benefits and Drawbacks. But in order to overlook nothing in a matter of such importance, and in the light of the general principles stated above, as well as of that which We are now about to formulate, We feel bound to add that to Our knowledge there are some who fear that the State is substituting itself in the place of private initiative, instead of limiting itself to necessary and sufficient help and assistance. It is feared that the new syndical and corporative institution possesses an excessively bureaucratic and political character, and that, notwithstanding the general advantages referred to above, it risks serving particular political aims rather than contributing to the initiation and fostering of a better social order.

Guidance of the Church. We believe that to attain this last-named lofty purpose for the true and permanent advantage of the commonwealth, there is need before and above all else of the blessing of God, and, in the second place, of the coöperation of all men of good will. We believe, moreover, as a necessary consequence, that the end intended will be the more certainly attained the greater the contribution furnished by men of technical, commercial and social competence, and, more still, by Catholic principles and their application. We look for this contribution, not to Catholic Action, which excludes from its field any strictly syndical or political activities, but to Our sons, whom Catholic Action imbues with these principles and trains for the Apostolate under the guidance and direction of the Church, of the Church We say, which in the above-mentioned sphere, as in all others where moral questions are discussed and regulated, cannot forget or neglect its mandate as custodian and teacher given it by God.

However, all that We have taught about reconstructing and perfecting the social order can in nowise be brought to pass without a reform of manners. Of this, history affords the clearest evidence. At one period there existed a social order which, though by no means perfect in every respect, corresponded nevertheless in a certain measure to right reason according to the needs and conditions of the times. That this order has long since perished is not due to the fact that it was incapable of development and adaptation to changing needs and circumstances, but rather to the wrong-doing of men. Men were hardened in excessive self-love and refused to extend that order, as was their duty, to the increasing numbers of the people; or else, deceived by the attractions of false liberty and other errors, they grew impatient of every restraint and endeavored to bring all author-ity into disrepute.

It remains for Us then to turn our attention to the actual condition of the economic order and to its bitterest adversary and accuser: We mean Socialism. On these We shall pronounce a frank and just sentence; shall examine more closely the root of the present grave evils, and shall indi-cate the first and most necessary remedy, which lies in a reform of morals.

III. THE MODERN SCENE: ITS CAUSES AND CURE

Since the time of Leo XIII important changes have taken place both in economic conditions and in regard to Socialism. In the first place, it is obvious to all that the entire economic scene has greatly changed. You are aware, Venerable Brethren and beloved children, that Our Predecessor, of happy memory, in his Encyclical, had chiefly in mind that economic regime in which were provided by different people the capital and labor jointly needed for production. He described it in a happy phrase: "Capi-tal cannot do without labor, nor labor without capital." *

Leo XIII's whole endeavor was to adjust this economic regime to the standards of true order; whence it follows that the system itself is not to be condemned. And surely it is not vicious of its very nature; but it violates right order whenever capital so employs the working or wage-earning classes as to divert business and economic activity entirely to its

---

* Encycl. *Rerum Novarum,* p. 11.

own arbitrary will and advantage without any regard to the human dignity of the workers, the social character of economic life, social justice, and the common good.

It is true that even to-day these economic conditions do not everywhere exist exclusively, for there is another economic system which still embraces a very large and influential group of men. There are for instance the agricultural classes, who form the larger portion of the human family and who find in their occupation the means of obtaining honestly and justly what is needful for their maintenance and cultural development. This system, too, has its difficulties and problems, of which Our Predecessor spoke repeatedly in his Encyclical, and to which We Ourselves have more than once referred in the present letter.

But the capitalist economic regime, since the world-wide diffusion of industry, has penetrated everywhere, particularly since the publication of Leo XIII's Encyclical, so that it has invaded and pervaded the economic and social sphere even of those who live outside its ambit, influencing them, and, as it were, intimately affecting them by its advantages, inconveniences and vices.

When We turn Our attention, therefore, to the changes which this capitalistic economic order has undergone since the days of Leo XIII, We have regard to the interests, not of those only who live in countries where "capital" and industry prevail, but of the whole human race.

In the first place, then, it is patent that in our days not alone is wealth accumulated, but immense power and despotic economic domination is concentrated in the hands of a few, and that those few are for the most part not the owners, but only the trustees and directors of invested funds, who administer them at their good pleasure.

Domination of Wealth. This power becomes particularly irresistible when exercised by those who, because they hold and control money, are able also to govern credit and determine its allotment, for that reason supplying, so to speak, the life-blood to the entire economic body, and grasping, as it were, in their hands the very soul of production, so that no one dare breathe against their will.

This accumulation of power, the characteristic note of the modern economic order, is a natural result of limitless free competition which permits the survival of those only who are the strongest, which often means those who fight most relentlessly, who pay least heed to the dictates of conscience.

This concentration of power has led to a threefold struggle for domination. First, there is the struggle for dictatorship in the economic sphere itself; then, the fierce battle to acquire control of the State, so that its resources and authority may be abused in the economic struggles; finally, the clash between States themselves.

This latter arises from two causes: because the nations apply their power and political influence, regardless of circumstances, to promote the economic advantages of their citizens; and because, vice versa, economic forces and economic domination are used to decide political controversies between peoples.

You assuredly know, Venerable Brethren and beloved children, and you lament the ultimate consequences of this Individualistic spirit in economic affairs. Free competition is dead; economic dictatorship has taken its place.

Economic Dictatorship. Unbridled ambition for domination has succeeded the desire for gain; the whole economic life has become hard, cruel and relentless in a ghastly measure. Furthermore, the intermingling and scandalous confusing of the duties and offices of civil authority and of economics have produced crying evils and have gone so far as to degrade the majesty of the State. The State, which should be the supreme arbiter, ruling in kingly fashion far above all party contention, intent only upon justice and the common good, has become instead a slave, bound over to the service of human passion and greed. As regards the relations of peoples among themselves, a double stream has issued forth from this one fountainhead: on the one hand, economic nationalism or even economic imperialism; on the other, a not less noxious and detestable internationalism or international imperialism in financial affairs, which holds that where a man's fortune is, there is his country.

Social Justice the Cure. The remedies for these great evils We have exposed in the second part of the present Encyclical, where We explicitly dwelt upon their doctrinal aspect. It will, therefore, be sufficient to recall them briefly here. Since the present economic regime is based mainly upon capital and labor, it follows that the principles of right reason and Christian social philosophy regarding capital, labor and their mutual cooperation must be accepted in theory and reduced to practice. In the first place, due consideration must be had for the double character, individual and social, of capital and labor, in order that the dangers of Individualism and of Collectivism be avoided. The mutual relations between capital and labor must be determined according to the laws of the strictest justice, called commutative justice, supported however by Christian charity. Free competition and still more economic domination must be kept within just and definite limits, and must be brought under the effective control of the public authority, in matters appertaining to this latter's competence. The public institutions of the nations must be such as to make the whole of human society conform to the common good, i. e., to the standard of social justice. If this is done, the economic system, that most important branch of social life, will necessarily be restored to sanity and right order.

Changes in Socialism. Since the days of Leo XIII, Socialism, too, the great enemy with which his battles were waged, has undergone profound changes, no less than economics. At that time Socialism could fairly be termed a single system, which defended certain definite and mutually coherent doctrines. Nowadays it has in the main become divided into two opposing and often bitterly hostile camps, neither of which, however, has abandoned the principle peculiar to Socialism, namely, opposition to the Christian Faith.

Communism. One section of Socialism has undergone approximately the same change through which, as we have described, the capitalistic economic regime has passed; it has degenerated into Communism. Communism teaches and pursues a twofold aim: merciless class warfare and complete abolition of private ownership; and this it does, not in secret and by hidden methods, but openly, frankly, and by every means, even the most violent. To obtain these ends, Communists shrink from nothing and fear nothing; and when they have attained power it is unbelievable, indeed it seems portentous, how cruel and inhuman they show themselves to be. Evidence for this is the ghastly destruction and ruin with which they have laid waste immense tracts of eastern Europe and Asia, while their antagonism and open hostility to Holy Church and to God Himself are, alas! but too well known and proved by their deeds. We do not think it necessary to warn upright and faithful children of the Church against the impious and nefarious character of Communism. But We cannot contemplate without profound sorrow the heedlessness of those who seem to make light of these imminent dangers and with stolid indifference allow the propagation far and wide of those doctrines which seek by violence and bloodshed the destruction of all society. Even more severely must be condemned the foolhardiness of those who neglect to remove or modify such conditions as exasperate the minds of the people, and so prepare the way for the overthrow and ruin of the social order.

Mitigated Socialism. The other section, which has retained the name of Socialism, is much less radical in its views. Not only does it condemn recourse to physical force; it even mitigates and moderates to some extent class warfare and the abolition of private property. It does not reject them entirely. It would seem as if Socialism were afraid of its own principles and of the conclusion drawn therefrom by the Communists, and in consequence were drifting towards the truth which Christian tradition has always held in respect; for it cannot be denied that its programs often strikingly approach the just demands of Christian social reformers.

Class war, provided it abstains from enmities and mutual hatred, is changing gradually to an honest discussion of differences, based upon the desire of justice. If this is by no means the blessed social peace which we all long for, it can be and must be an approach towards the mutual co-operation of vocational groups. The war declared against private ownership has also abated more and more, in such a way that nowadays it is not really the possession of the means of production which is attacked but that type of social rulership, which, in violation of all justice, has been seized and usurped by the owners of wealth. This rulership in fact belongs, not to the individual owners, but to the State.

If these changes continue, it may well come about that gradually the tenets of mitigated Socialism will no longer be different from the program of those who seek to reform human society according to Christian principles.

For it is rightly contended that certain forms of property must be reserved to the State, since they carry with them an opportunity of domination too great to be left to private individuals without injury to the community at large.

Just demands and desires of this kind contain nothing opposed to Christian truth, nor are they in any sense peculiar to Socialism. Those therefore who look for nothing else, have no reason for becoming Socialists.

Is Compromise Possible? It must not be imagined however that all the Socialist sects or factions which are not Communist have in fact or in theory uniformly returned to this reasonable position. For the most part they do not reject class warfare and the abolition of property, but merely are more moderate in regard to them. Now, when false principles are

thus mitigated and in some sense waived, the question arises, or is un-
warrantably proposed in certain quarters, whether the principles of Christian truth also could not be somewhat moderated and attenuated so as to
meet Socialism, as it were, halfway upon common ground. Some are engaged by the empty hope of gaining in this way the Socialists to our
cause. But such hopes are vain. Those who wish to be apostles amongst
the Socialists should preach the Christian truth whole and entire, openly
and sincerely, without any connivance with error. If they wish in truth
to be heralds of the Gospel, let their endeavor be to convince Socialists
that their demands, in so far as they are just, are defended much more co-
gently by the principles of Christian faith, and are promoted much more
efficaciously by the power of Christian charity.

But what if, in questions of class war and private ownership, Socialism
were to become so mitigated and amended, that nothing reprehensible
could any longer be found in it? Would it by that very fact have laid
aside its character of hostility to the Christian religion? This is a question
which holds many minds in suspense; and many are the Catholics who,
realizing clearly that Christian principles can never be either sacrificed or
minimized, seem to be raising their eyes towards the Holy See, and earnestly beseeching Us to decide whether or not this form of Socialism has
retracted so far its false doctrines that it can now be accepted without the
loss of any Christian principle, and be baptized into the Church. In Our
fatherly solicitude We desire to satisfy these petitions, and We pronounce
as follows: whether Socialism be considered as a doctrine, or as a historical fact, or as a movement, if it really remain Socialism, it cannot be
brought into harmony with the dogmas of the Catholic Church, even
after it has yielded to truth and justice in the points We have mentioned;
the reason being that it conceives human society in a way utterly alien to
Christian truth.

Opposition in Basic Ideas. According to Christian doctrine, man, endowed with a social nature, is placed here on earth in order that he may
spend his life in society, and under an authority ordained by God,* that
he may develop and evolve to the full all his faculties to the praise and
glory of his Creator; and that, by fulfilling faithfully the duties of his
trade or other calling, he may attain to temporal and eternal happiness.
Socialism, on the contrary, entirely ignorant of or unconcerned about this
sublime end both of individuals and of society, affirms that living in com-

* Cf. Rom. xiii, 1.

munity was instituted merely for the sake of advantages which it brings
to mankind.

Goods are produced more efficiently by a suitable distribution of labor
than by the scattered efforts of individuals. Hence the Socialists argue that
economic production, of which they see only the material side, must necessarily be carried on collectively, and that because of this necessity men
must surrender and submit themselves wholly to society with a view to
the production of wealth. Indeed, the possession of the greatest possible
amount of temporal goods is esteemed so highly, that man's higher goods,
not excepting liberty, must, they claim, be subordinated and even sacrificed to the exigencies of efficient production. They affirm that the loss of
human dignity, which results from these socialized methods of production, will be easily compensated for by the abundance of goods produced
in common and accruing to the individual who can turn them at his will
to the comforts and culture of life. Society, therefore, as the Socialist conceives it, is, on the one hand, impossible and unthinkable without the use
of compulsion of the most excessive kind: on the other it fosters a false
liberty, since in such a scheme no place is found for true social authority,
which is not based on temporal and material advantages, but descends
from God alone, the Creator and Last End of all things.*

If, like all errors, Socialism contains a certain element of truth (and this
the Sovereign Pontiffs have never denied), it is nevertheless founded upon
a doctrine of human society peculiarly its own, which is opposed to true
Christianity. "Religious Socialism," "Christian Socialism" are expressions
implying a contradiction in terms. No one can be at the same time a
sincere Catholic and a true Socialist.

Cultural Socialism. All that We have thus far laid down and established by Our sovereign authority bears application also to a certain new
Socialist phenomenon, hitherto little known, but nowadays common to
many sections of Socialism. Its main aim is the formation of minds and
manners. Under the appearance of friendship, it attracts little children in
particular and attaches them to itself, though its activity extends to all
the people, to make of them convinced Socialists, upon whom to build
society modeled on Socialistic principles.

In Our Encyclical Letter, *Divini Illius Magistri,*† We have expounded

* Encycl. *Divinum Illud,* June 29, 1881.
† Encycl. *Divini Illius Magistri,* Dec. 31, 1929, published by the America Press with
study-club supplement with questions and bibliography.

at length the true principles on which Christian education rests and the end which it pursues. The contradiction between these and the actions and aims of cultural Socialism is so clear and evident as to require no comment. Nevertheless, the formidable dangers which this form of Socialism brings in its train seem to be ignored or underestimated by those who are little concerned to resist it with strength and zeal, as the gravity of the situation demands.

It is a duty of Our pastoral office to warn these men of the grave danger which threatens. Let us bear in mind that the parent of this cultural Socialism was Liberalism, and that its offspring will be Bolshevism.

This being so, you can understand, Venerable Brethren and beloved children, with what grief We perceive, in certain countries particularly, not a few of Our children, who, while still preserving, as We are convinced, their true faith and good will, have deserted the camp of the Church and passed over to the ranks of Socialism. Some openly boast of its name and profess Socialistic doctrines: others, either through indifference or even almost in spite of themselves, join associations which, in theory or in fact, are Socialist.

In Our paternal solicitude, therefore, We have meditated and sought to understand what can have been the reason of their going so far astray; and We seem to hear what many of them allege in excuse: the Church and those professing attachment to the Church favor the rich and neglect workingmen and have no care for them: they were obliged therefore in their own interest to join the Socialist ranks.

Cloaking Greed under Religion. What a lamentable fact, Venerable Brethren, that there have been, and that there are even now some who, while professing the Catholic Faith, are well-nigh unmindful of that sublime law of justice and charity which binds us not only to give each man his due, but to succor our needy brethren as Christ Our Lord Himself; * worse still, that there are those who out of greed for gain are not ashamed to oppress the workingman! Indeed there are some who abuse religion itself, attempting to cloak their own unjust imposition under its name, that they may protect themselves against the clearly just demands of their employees.

We shall never desist from gravely censuring such conduct. Such men are the cause that the Church, without deserving it, may have the appear-

* Cf. St. James ii.

ance and be accused of taking sides with the wealthy, and of being little moved by the needs and sufferings of those who have been deprived of what is quite their natural inheritance. That these appearances and these accusations are undeserved and unjust, the whole history of the Church clearly shows. The very Encyclical, the anniversary of which we are celebrating, affords the clearest evidences that these calumnies and contumelies have been most unfairly passed upon the Church and upon her teaching.

Invitation to Return. But so far indeed are We from being angered by these injustices or dejected by Our pastoral sorrow, that We have no wish to drive away or repel Our children who have been so unhappily deceived, and who are wandering so far from the paths of truth and salvation. On the contrary, We invite them with all possible solicitude to return to the maternal bosom of the Church. God grant that they listen to Our voice. God grant that whence they set out, thither they may return, to their Father's house: that where their true place is, there they may remain, amongst the ranks of those who, zealously following direction promulgated by Leo XIII and solemnly repeated by Ourselves, unremittingly endeavor to reform society according to the mind of the Church on a firm basis of social justice and social charity. Let it be their firm persuasion that nowhere, even on earth, can they find an ampler happiness than in company with Him, who being rich became poor for our sakes; that through His poverty we might become rich: * who was poor and in labors from His youth: who invites to Himself all who labor and are burdened that He may refresh them bounteously in the love of His heart,† who, in fine, without any respect for persons, will require more of him to whom more has been given,‡ and "will return to each one according to his work." §

Reform Needs Christian Spirit. However, if we examine matters diligently and thoroughly, we shall perceive clearly that this longed-for social reconstruction must be preceded by a profound renewal of the Christian spirit, from which multitudes engaged in industry in every country have unhappily departed. Otherwise, all our endeavors will be futile, and our social edifice will be built, not upon a rock, but upon shifting sand.||

We have passed in review, Venerable Brethren and beloved children,

* II Cor. viii, 9.
† Cf. Matt. xi, 28.
‡ Cf. Luke xii, 48.
§ Matt. xvi, 27.
|| Matt. vii, 24–27.

the state of the modern economic world, and have found it suffering from the greatest evils. We have investigated a new Socialism and Communism, and have found them, even in their mitigated forms, far removed from the precepts of the Gospel.

"And if society is to be healed now"—We use the words of Our Predecessor—"in no way can it be healed save by a return to Christian life and Christian institutions," * for Christianity alone can apply an efficacious remedy for the excessive solicitude for transitory things, which is the origin of all vices. When men are fascinated and completely absorbed in the uncertain things of the world, it alone can draw away their attention and raise it to Heaven. And who will say that this remedy is not urgently needed by society?

For most men are affected almost exclusively by temporal upheavals, disasters, and ruins. Yet if we view things with Christian eyes, and we should, what are they all in comparison with the ruin of souls?

Nevertheless, it may be said with all truth that nowadays the conditions of social and economic life are such that vast multitudes of men can only with great difficulty pay attention to that one thing necessary, namely, their eternal salvation.

Constituted pastor and protector of these innumerable sheep by the Prince of Pastors who redeemed them by His blood, We can scarcely restrain Our tears when We reflect upon the dangers which threaten them. Our pastoral office, moreover, reminds Us to search constantly, with paternal solicitude, for means of coming to their assistance, appealing to the unwearying zeal of others who are bound to this cause by justice or charity. For what will it profit men that a more prudent distribution and use of riches make it possible for them to gain even the whole world, if thereby they suffer the loss of their own souls? † What will it profit to teach them sound principles in economics, if they permit themselves to be so swept away by selfishness, by unbridled and sordid greed, that "hearing the Commandments of the Lord, they do all things contrary"? ‡

Causes of Defection. The fundamental cause of this defection from the Christian law in social and economic matters, and of the apostasy of many workingmen from the Catholic Faith which has resulted from it, is the disorderly affections of the soul, a sad consequence of original sin. By

* Encycl. *Rerum Novarum*, p. 16.
† Cf. Matt. xvi, 26.
‡ Cf. Judges ii, 17.

original sin the marvelous harmony of man's faculties has been so de-
ranged that now he is easily led astray by low desires, and strongly
tempted to prefer the transient goods of this world to the lasting goods
of Heaven.

Hence comes that unquenchable thirst for riches and temporal possessions, which at all times has impelled men to break the law of God and
trample on the rights of their neighbors; but the condition of the economic world to-day lays more snares than ever for human frailty. For the
uncertainty of economic conditions and of the whole economic regime
demands the keenest and most unceasing straining of energy on the part
of those engaged therein; and as a result, some have become so hardened
against the stings of conscience as to hold all means good which enable
them to increase their profits, and to safeguard against sudden changes
of fortune the wealth amassed by unremitting toil. Easy returns, which a
market unhampered by laws offers to anyone, lead many to interest
themselves in trade and exchange, their one aim being to make clear
profits with the least labor. By their unchecked speculation prices are frequently raised and lowered arbitrarily and out of mere greed for gain,
thus making void all the most prudent calculations of manufacturers.

The regulations legally enacted for corporations, with their divided
responsibility and limited liability, have given occasion to abominable
abuses. The greatly weakened accountability makes little impression, as
is evident, upon the conscience. The worst injustices and frauds take
place beneath the obscurity of the common name of a corporative firm.
Boards of directors proceed in their unconscionable methods even to the
violation of their trust in regard to those whose savings they administer.
In the last place must still be mentioned the unscrupulous but well-
calculated speculation of men who, without seeking to answer real needs,
appeal to the lowest human passions. These are aroused in order to turn
their satisfaction into gain.

A stern insistence on the moral law, enforced with vigor by civil authority, could have dispelled or perhaps averted these enormous evils.
This, however, was too often lamentably wanting. For at the time when
the new economic order was beginning, the doctrines of Rationalism had
already taken firm hold of large numbers, and an economic science alien
to the true moral law had soon arisen, whence it followed that free rein
was given to human avarice.

As a result, a much greater number than ever before, solely concerned with adding to their wealth by any means whatsoever, sought their own selfish interests above all things; they had no scruple in committing the gravest injustices against others.

Those who first entered upon this broad way which leads to destruction,* easily found many imitators of their iniquity because of their manifest success, their extravagant display of wealth, their derision of the scruples of more delicate consciences, and the crushing of more cautious competitors.

With the leaders of business abandoning the true path, it is not surprising that in every country multitudes of workingmen too sank in the same morass: all the more so, because very many employers treated their workmen as mere tools, without any concern for the welfare of their souls; indeed, without the slightest thought of higher interests. The mind shudders if we consider the frightful perils to which the morals of workers (of boys and young men particularly), and the virtue of girls and women are exposed in modern factories: if we recall how the present economic regime and above all the disgraceful housing conditions prove obstacles to the family tie and family life; if we remember the insuperable difficulties placed in the way of a proper observance of the holy days.

Matter Exalted, Men Degraded. How universally has the true Christian spirit become impaired, which formerly produced such lofty sentiments even in uncultured and illiterate men! In its stead, man's one solicitude is to obtain his daily bread in any way he can. And so bodily labor, which was decreed by Providence for the good of man's body and soul even after original sin, has everywhere been changed into an instrument of strange perversion: for dead matter leaves the factory ennobled and transformed, where men are corrupted and degraded.

Remedy in the Gospel. For this pitiable ruin of souls, which, if it continue, will frustrate all efforts to reform society, there can be no other remedy than a frank and sincere return to the teaching of the Gospel. Men must observe anew the precepts of Him who alone has the words of eternal life,† words which, even though Heaven and earth be changed, shall not pass away.‡

All those versed in social matters strenuously demand a rationalization of economic life which will introduce sound and true order. But this

* Cf. Matt. vii, 13.
† Cf. John vi, 69.
‡ Cf. Matt. xxiv, 35.

order, which We ourselves earnestly desire and make every effort to promote, will necessarily be quite faulty and imperfect, unless all man's activities harmoniously unite to imitate and, as far as is humanly possible, attain the marvelous unity of the Divine plan. This is the perfect order which the Church preaches with intense earnestness, and which right reason demands: which places God as the first and supreme end of all created activity, and regards all created goods as mere instruments under God, to be used only in so far as they help towards the attainment of our supreme end.

* * *

[For interpretation of this encyclical see John A. Ryan, *A Better Economic Order*, New York, Harper & Brothers, 1935, and R. A. McGowan, *Toward Social Justice*, New York, Paulist Press, printed for the Social Action Department, National Catholic Social Welfare Conference.

There are interesting relations between the doctrine of this encyclical and the corporative organization of Italy (totalitarian), the corporative state of Portugal (rejecting totalitarianism), and the movement toward "integral nationalism" in France. See S. G. West, *The New Corporative State of Portugal*, London, 1937 (King's College Inaugural Lecture), and W. C. Buthman, *The Rise of Integral Nationalism in France*, New York, Columbia University Press, 1939.]

20

F. D. ROOSEVELT ON THE DEMOCRATIC
WELFARE STATE

[Franklin D. Roosevelt was born in 1882 at Hyde Park, N.Y. He was educated at Groton, Harvard, and the Columbia Law School. He served as Assistant Secretary of the Navy, 1913–1920. In 1921 he suffered a severe attack of infantile paralysis, but in subsequent years he recovered the partial use of his legs. He was governor of New York, 1929–1933, and President of the United States from 1933 until his death on April 12, 1945.

His second inaugural address on January 20, 1937, surveyed the achievements of his first term and the problems requiring further action. It is presented as an expression of the New Deal philosophy of democracy.

This address has been reprinted in various volumes, including *The Public Papers and Addresses of Franklin D. Roosevelt, 1937 Volume,* New York, The Macmillan Company, 1941.]

When four years ago we met to inaugurate a President, the Republic, single-minded in anxiety, stood in spirit here. We dedicated ourselves to the fulfillment of a vision—to speed the time when there would be for all the people that security and peace essential to the pursuit of happiness. We of the Republic pledged ourselves to drive from the temple of our ancient faith those who had profaned it; to end by action, tireless and unafraid, the stagnation and despair of that day. We did those first things first.

Our covenant with ourselves did not stop there. Instinctively we recognized a deeper need—the need to find through government the instrument of our united purpose to solve for the individual the ever-rising problems of a complex civilization. Repeated attempts at their solution without the aid of government had left us baffled and bewildered. For, without that aid, we had been unable to create those moral controls over the services of science which are necessary to make science a useful servant instead of a ruthless master of mankind. To do this we knew that we must find practical controls over blind economic forces and blindly selfish men.

We of the Republic sensed the truth that democratic government has innate capacity to protect its people against disasters once considered inevitable, to solve problems once considered unsolvable. We would not admit that we could not find a way to master economic epidemics just as, after centuries of fatalistic suffering, we had found a way to master epidemics of disease. We refused to leave the problems of our common welfare to be solved by the winds of chance and the hurricanes of disaster.

In this we Americans were discovering no wholly new truth; we were writing a new chapter in our book of self-government.

This year marks the one hundred and fiftieth anniversary of the Constitutional Convention which made us a nation. At that Convention our forefathers found the way out of the chaos which followed the Revolutionary War; they created a strong government with powers of united action sufficient then and now to solve problems utterly beyond individual or local solution. A century and a half ago they established the Federal Government in order to promote the general welfare and secure the blessings of liberty to the American people.

Today we invoke those same powers of government to achieve the same objectives.

Four years of new experience have not belied our historic instinct. They hold out the clear hope that government within communities, government within the separate States, and government of the United States can do the things the times require, without yielding its democracy. Our tasks in the last four years did not force democracy to take a holiday.

Nearly all of us recognize that as intricacies of human relationships increase, so power to govern them also must increase—power to stop evil; power to do good. The essential democracy of our Nation and the safety of our people depend not upon the absence of power, but upon lodging it with those whom the people can change or continue at stated intervals through an honest and free system of elections. The Constitution of 1787 did not make our democracy impotent.

In fact, in these last four years, we have made the exercise of all power more democratic; for we have begun to bring private autocratic powers into their proper subordination to the public's government. The legend that they were invincible—above and beyond the processes of a democracy —has been shattered. They have been challenged and beaten.

Our progress out of the depression is obvious. But that is not all that you and I mean by the new order of things. Our pledge was not merely to do a patchwork job with second-hand materials. By using the new materials of social justice we have undertaken to erect on the old foundations a more enduring structure for the better use of future generations.

In that purpose we have been helped by achievements of mind and spirit. Old truths have been relearned; untruths have been unlearned. We have always known that heedless self-interest was bad morals; we know now that it is bad economics. Out of the collapse of a prosperity whose builders boasted their practicality has come the conviction that in the long run economic morality pays. We are beginning to wipe out the line that divides the practical from the ideal; and in so doing we are fashioning an instrument of unimagined power for the establishment of a morally better world.

This new understanding undermines the old admiration of worldly success as such. We are beginning to abandon our tolerance of the abuse of power by those who betray for profit the elementary decencies of life.

In this process evil things formerly accepted will not be so easily condoned. Hard-headedness will not so easily excuse hard-heartedness. We are moving toward an era of good feeling. But we realize that there can be no era of good feeling save among men of good will.

For these reasons I am justified in believing that the greatest change we have witnessed has been the change in the moral climate of America.

Among men of good will, science and democracy together offer an ever-richer life and ever-larger satisfaction to the individual. With this change in our moral climate and our rediscovered ability to improve our economic order, we have set our feet upon the road of enduring progress.

Shall we pause now and turn our back upon the road that lies ahead? Shall we call this the promised land? Or, shall we continue on our way? For "each age is a dream that is dying, or one that is coming to birth."

Many voices are heard as we face a great decision. Comfort says, "Tarry a while." Opportunism says, "This is a good spot." Timidity asks, "How difficult is the road ahead?"

True, we have come far from the days of stagnation and despair. Vitality has been preserved. Courage and confidence have been restored. Mental and moral horizons have been extended.

But our present gains were won under the pressure of more than ordinary circumstance. Advance became imperative under the goad of fear and suffering. The times were on the side of progress.

To hold to progress today, however, is more difficult. Dulled conscience, irresponsibility, and ruthless self-interest already reappear. Such symptoms of prosperity may become portents of disaster! Prosperity already tests the persistence of our progressive purpose.

Let us ask again: Have we reached the goal of our vision of that fourth day of March, 1933? Have we found our happy valley?

I see a great nation, upon a great continent, blessed with a great wealth of natural resources. Its hundred and thirty million people are at peace among themselves; they are making their country a good neighbor among the nations. I see a United States which can demonstrate that, under democratic methods of government, national wealth can be translated into a spreading volume of human comforts hitherto unknown, and the lowest standard of living can be raised far above the level of mere subsistence.

But here is the challenge to our democracy: In this nation I see tens of millions of its citizens—a substantial part of its whole population—who at this very moment are denied the greater part of what the very lowest standards of today call the necessities of life.

I see millions of families trying to live on incomes so meager that the pall of family disaster hangs over them day by day.

I see millions whose daily lives in city and on farm continue under conditions labeled indecent by a so-called polite society half a century ago.

I see millions denied education, recreation, and the opportunity to better their lot and the lot of their children.

I see millions lacking the means to buy the products of farm and factory and by their poverty denying work and productiveness to many other millions.

I see one-third of a nation ill-housed, ill-clad, ill-nourished.

It is not in despair that I paint you that picture. I paint it for you in hope—because the Nation, seeing and understanding the injustice in it, proposes to paint it out. We are determined to make every American citizen the subject of his country's interest and concern; and we will never regard any faithful, law-abiding group within our borders as superfluous. The test of our progress is not whether we add more to the abundance of those who have much; it is whether we provide enough for those who have too little.

If I know aught of the spirit and purpose of our Nation, we will not listen to Comfort, Opportunism, and Timidity. We will carry on.

Overwhelmingly, we of the Republic are men and women of good will; men and women who have more than warm hearts of dedication; men and women who have cool heads and willing hands of practical purpose as well. They will insist that every agency of popular government use effective instruments to carry out their will.

Government is competent when all who compose it work as trustees for the whole people. It can make constant progress when it keeps abreast of all the facts. It can obtain justified support and legitimate criticism when the people receive true information of all that government does.

If I know aught of the will of our people, they will demand that these conditions of effective government shall be created and maintained. They will demand a Nation uncorrupted by cancers of injustice and, therefore, strong among the nations in its example of the will to peace.

Today we reconsecrate our country to long-cherished ideals in a suddenly changed civilization. In every land there are always at work forces that drive men apart and forces that draw men together. In our personal ambitions we are individualists. But in our seeking for economic and political progress as a nation, we all go up, or else we all go down, as one people.

To maintain a democracy of effort requires a vast amount of patience in dealing with differing methods, a vast amount of humility. But out of the confusion of many voices rises an understanding of dominant public need. Then political leadership can voice common ideals, and aid in their realization.

In taking again the oath of office as President of the United States, I assume the solemn obligation of leading the American people forward along the road over which they have chosen to advance.

While this duty rests upon me I shall do my utmost to speak their purpose and to do their will, seeking Divine guidance to help us each and every one to give light to them that sit in darkness and to guide our feet into the way of peace.

[For comparisons between democracy and other ideals, see Joseph A. Leighton, *Social Philosophies in Conflict: Fascism and Nazism, Communism, Liberal Democracy*, New York, Appleton-Century-Crofts, Inc., 1937; C. E. Merriam, *The New Democracy and the New Despotism*, New York, Whittlesey House, 1939; Kurt London, *Backgrounds of Conflict*, New York, The Macmillan Company, 1945.]

21

ALFRED E. SMITH ON CATHOLICISM AND AMERICAN POLITICS

[Alfred E. Smith (1873–1944) was born in New York City. He entered politics in 1895. He rose through various local and state offices to the governorship of the state, which he held for four terms (1919–1920 and 1923–1928). In 1928 he ran for the presidency on the Democratic ticket, but his opponent, Herbert Hoover, won the office by a large majority.

In May, 1927, Governor Smith published a letter in the *Atlantic Monthly*, denying that there was any conflict between a man's religious duties as a Catholic and his civic duties as a public official in the United States. This letter was republished in *Progressive Democracy, Addresses and State Papers of Alfred E. Smith*, edited by Henry Moskowitz, New York, Harcourt, Brace and Company, 1928.

The occasion for this letter is described by Moskowitz as follows:

The April, 1927, issue of the *Atlantic Monthly* contained "An Open Letter to the Honorable Alfred E. Smith," by Charles C. Marshall, "an experienced attorney of New York City who has throughout his active life been closely associated with the Anglican Church and has made himself an authority upon canon law."

The letter expressed, in a spirit of fairness and with much display of erudition, what many non-Catholics were feeling "as to certain conceptions which your fellow citizens attribute to you as a loyal and conscientious Roman Catholic, which in their minds are irreconcilable with that Constitution which as President you must support and defend, and with the principles of civil and religious liberty on which American institutions are based."

The following paragraphs are taken from Governor Smith's letter, published under the heading, "Catholic and Patriot: Governor Smith Replies":]

In your open letter to me in the April *Atlantic Monthly* you "impute" to American Catholics views which, if held by them, would leave open to question the loyalty and devotion to this country and its Constitution of more than twenty million American Catholic citizens. I am grateful to you for defining this issue in the open and for your courteous expression of the satisfaction it will bring to my fellow citizens for me to give "a disclaimer of the convictions" thus imputed. Without mental reservation I can and do make that disclaimer. These convictions are held neither by me nor by any other American Catholic, as far as I know.

*   *   *

But, beyond this, by what right do you ask me to assume responsibility for every statement that may be made in any encyclical letter? As you will find in the *Catholic Encyclopedia* (Vol. V, p. 414), these encyclicals are not articles of our faith. The Syllabus of Pope Pius IX, which you quote on the possible conflict between Church and State, is declared by Cardinal Newman to have "no dogmatic force." You seem to think that Catholics must be all alike in mind and in heart, as though they had been poured into and taken out of the same mold. You have not more right to ask me to defend as part of my faith every statement coming from a prelate than I should have to ask you to accept as an article of your religious faith every statement of an Episcopal bishop, or of your political faith every statement of a President of the United States.

*   *   *

Your first proposition is that Catholics believe that other religions should, in the United States, be tolerated only as a matter of favor and that there should be an established church. You may find some dream of an ideal of a Catholic State described. But, voicing the best Catholic thought on this subject, Dr. John A. Ryan, Professor of Moral Theology at the Catholic University of America, writes in *The State and the Church* of the encyclical of Pope Leo XIII, quoted by you:

In practice, however, the foregoing propositions have full application only to the completely Catholic State. . . . The propositions of Pope Pius IX condemning the toleration of non-Catholic sects do not now, says Father Pohle, "apply even to Spain or the South American republics, to say nothing of countries possessing a greatly mixed population." He lays down the following general rule: "When several religions have firmly established themselves and taken root in the same territory, nothing else remains for the State than to exercise tolerance towards them all, or, as conditions exist today, to make complete religious liberty for individual and religious bodies a principle of government."

That is good Americanism and good Catholicism. And Father Pohle, one of the great writers of the Catholic Church, says further:

If religious freedom has been accepted and sworn to as a fundamental law in a constitution, the obligation to show this tolerance is binding in conscience.

The American prelates of our Church stoutly defend our constitutional declaration of equality of all religions before the law. Cardinal O'Connell has said:

Thus to every American citizen has come the blessed inheritance of civil, political, and religious liberty safeguarded by the American Constitution . . . the right to worship God according to the dictates of his conscience.

Archbishop Ireland has said:

The Constitution of the United States reads: "Congress shall make no laws respecting an establishment of religion or prohibiting the free exercise thereof." It was a great leap forward on the part of the new nation towards personal liberty and the consecration of the rights of conscience.

Archbishop Dowling, referring to any conceivable union of Church and State, says:

So many conditions for its accomplishment are lacking in every government of the world that the thesis may well be relegated to the limbo of defunct controversies.

I think you have taken your thesis from this limbo of defunct controversies.

[Pope Leo XIII's encyclical on the *Catholic Constitution of States*, repeatedly quoted in Marshall's letter, appeared in 1885.]

*   *   *

I come now to the speculation with which theorists have played for generations as to the respective functions of Church and State. You claim that the Roman Catholic Church holds that, if conflict arises, the Church must prevail over the State. You write as though there were some Catholic authority or tribunal to decide with respect to such conflict. Of course there is no such thing. As Dr. Ryan writes:

The Catholic doctrine concedes, nay, maintains, that the State is coördinate with the Church and equally independent and supreme in its own distinct sphere.

What is the Protestant position? The Articles of Religion of your Protestant Episcopal Church (XXXVII) declare:

The Power of the Civil Magistrate extendeth to all men, as well Clergy as Laity, in all things temporal; but hath no authority in things purely spiritual.

Your Church, just as mine, is voicing the injunction of our common Saviour to render unto Caesar the things that are Caesar's, and unto God the things that are God's.

What is this conflict about which you talk? It may exist in some lands which do not guarantee religious freedom. But in the wildest dreams of your imagination you cannot conjure up a possible conflict between religious principle and political duty in the United States, except on the unthinkable hypothesis that some law were to be passed which violated the common morality of all God-fearing men. And if you can conjure up such a conflict, how would a Protestant resolve it? Obviously by the dictates of his conscience. That is exactly what a Catholic would do. There is no ecclesiastical tribunal which would have the slightest claim upon the obedience of Catholic communicants in the resolution of such a conflict. As Cardinal Gibbons said of the supposition that "the Pope were to issue commands in purely civil matters":

He would be offending not only against civil society, but against God, and violating an authority as truly from God as his own. Any Catholic who clearly recognized this would not be bound to obey the Pope; or rather his conscience would bind him absolutely to disobey, because with Catholics conscience is the supreme law which under no circumstances can we ever lawfully disobey.

[Further references on the relation of church and state: John A. Ryan and Francis J. Boland, *Catholic Principles of Politics,* New York, The Macmillan Company, 1940; Jacques Maritain, *True Humanism,* London, Geoffrey Bles: The Centenary Press, 1938; Sidney Hook, *Reason, Social Myths and Democracy,* New York, The John Day Company, 1940 (criticizing Maritain); Jacques Maritain, *The Rights of Man and Natural Law,* New York, Charles Scribner's Sons, 1943, pp. 21–29; George Seldes, *The Catholic Crisis,* New York, J. Messner, Inc., 1939.]

22

THE BRITISH LABOR PARTY: DEMOCRATIC SOCIALISM

[The British Labor Party works toward socialist aims by peaceful, gradual, and democratic means. It combines the strength of the trade unions with the thinking of socialist intellectuals.

From its foundation in 1883 onwards, the Fabian Society was an organization of socialist intellectuals. Among its leaders were Sidney and Beatrice Webb and George Bernard Shaw. In the same period the trade unions were growing in size and influence. In 1900 the Labor Representation Committee was founded as a federation of trade unions with the Fabians and other socialist societies. After 1906 it became known as the Labor Party.

The Labor Party gradually increased its strength in Parliament, until in 1923 it held 192 out of 640 seats, and in 1929 it held 288 seats. It controlled the government in 1924–1925 and in 1929–1931. But in these periods it lacked an absolute majority and could pass only such legislation as was approved by its allies of the Liberal Party. It suffered a severe defeat in 1931, electing only 52 members.

When Hitler invaded Poland in 1939, the Labor Party supported Britain's entry into the war. It helped to oust Chamberlain from his post as Prime Minister in May, 1940, and joined in the coalition government with Churchill. During the war Labor ministers held many of the most important cabinet posts, among them being Attlee, Greenwood, Morrison, Bevin, and Dalton.

In 1945, after the defeat of Germany and before the defeat of Japan, a general election was held in which Labor won 394 out of 640 seats. Having for the first time an absolute majority, the Labor Party took control of the government and began to put its program into effect step by step.

See Harry W. Laidler, *Social-Economic Movements,* New York, Thomas Y. Crowell Company, chapters 18 and 31; *Encyclopedia Britannica,* articles "Fabian Society" and "Labor Party"; *Encyclopedia of the Social Sciences,* articles "Fabianism" and "Labor Parties, Great Britain."

The paragraphs below are taken from a declaration of the National Executive Committee of the Labor Party entitled "Labor's Home Policy." It was unanimously adopted by the annual conference of the Party at Bournemouth on May 14, 1940, after having already been circulated as a pamphlet. It is printed as Appendix III on pp. 191–195 of the *Report of the Thirty-Ninth Annual Conference of the Labor Party,* published by the Labor Party, Transport House, London.]

THE NEW SOCIETY

The Labor Party is a Socialist Party; therefore it conceives of reconstruction in Socialist terms. But its Socialism is built upon a profound faith in the people of Britain, and a determination to press for necessary social changes upon the basis of Democracy and Justice. We reject all demands for Dictatorship, whether from the Left or from the Right. We take our stand upon that faith in reason which looks to the declared will of the people as the only valid source of power. So long as that will is nationally respected, we are confident that the historic forms of Parliamentary Democracy provide a highroad along which the nation can pass peacefully from an acquisitive to a Socialist society. We warn the enemies of Democracy, whether open or secret, that the declared will of the people *must* prevail. The majority of the nation is entitled to be master in its own house.

For the Labor Party a Socialist Britain is not some far-off Utopia but an ideal that can be realized within our time. We seek a society in which there is a just distribution of wealth, and where the essential instruments of production are publicly-owned.

Such a society will establish that national minimum standard of living which is a vital test of civilization. It will abolish the irrational privileges which disfigure our present order. It will secure genuine equality, and a high level of educational opportunity. It will make economic freedom real by its ability to offer security and a rising standard of life to the worker, both urban and rural. It will make justice responsive to the needs of the many, and not only of the few. It will care with a new intensity for the health of the people, and will nourish the opportunity for the creative use of leisure. Because its Socialist principles are built upon a faith in the power of reason, the Labor Party can give to science that place and scope which Capitalism frustrates.

*   *   *

THE NEW ECONOMIC ORDER

. . . The main outlines of the new order are clear.

Those key industries and services, upon which the well-being of the nation depends, must be transferred to public ownership. Financial power is central to the whole economic structure; therefore, the banks must be subject to public control. The direction of investment is a public trust to be determined in the public interest; left to the chance of private decision, it breeds domestic waste, colonial exploitation, and, only too often, war. There must also be public ownership and control of coal and power, of the basic forms of transport, and, on a steadily-increasing scale, of the land. Without these first measures of public ownership, effective planning in the interest of the whole nation is impossible.

The industries and services so brought under national direction will have to be reorganized as a condition of their efficiency, and this task will be pursued with vigor. Those still in private hands will be required to plan their structure and methods; for the nation can no longer tolerate the grotesque waste of man-power and wealth which arises from unregulated private ownership. Individual initiative and ability must not be restricted, but must be directed to the service of the community.

There must be, also, that control of the location of industry which is urgent for the public health, for the preservation of the countryside, and for a new life in the distressed areas. . . .

There must be a fuller recognition of the functions of Trade Unions in the national life. . . . The Trade Union—as the experience of Dictatorships has made manifest—is not only the worker's primary safeguard; it is also the obvious instrument of the democratic control of industry. The Labor Party insists that the principles of constitutional government apply not less fully to the economic than to the political life of a nation. It is through the Trade Union that the immense technical knowledge of its members can be made available to improve industry and agriculture. The Trade Unions, also, must be freed from the mean restrictions of the present law.

The proper organization of the consumers in the Co-operative Movement has its essential place in any scientifically-planned society. That great Movement has already established for the benefit of some five million families a great equalitarian sector in industry, and is destined in the future to play an even greater part within that sphere which it has made so specially its own.

The Labor Party is an alliance of workers by hand and brain. Therefore its program for building a Socialist Britain is not less urgently addressed to the black-coated worker than to his fellow in field, factory, and mine. Only the scientifically-planned use of the national resources offers to the black-coated worker the prospect that his services can be used to full advantage. Alike to the scientist in his laboratory and the administrator in his office, Socialism offers relief from servitude to financial interest and business nepotism. The Labor Party was born of the immediate needs of the working class; but each year of its experience has shown more fully the essential identity of interest between the worker by hand and the worker by brain. Through their joint effort, the resources of Britain will be restored to her people.

*   *   *

A Fair Distribution of Wealth

Any great social change necessarily requires a wise administration of the national income; and no administration is wise that is not founded also in justice. The Labor Party differs from its critics in its tests of fiscal wisdom. These critics believe that the less the income of the rich is reduced, the more prosperous is the community; they are even sceptical whether expenditure on public health and public education is as fruitful as private expenditure on luxuries. This view, Labor emphatically condemns. In common with enlightened economic opinion all over the world, Labor unhesitatingly affirms that urgent national requirements, as judged by democratic opinion, should be the first charge on the national income.

It is both economically right and socially just to raise the sum required for a vigorous social policy from those elements in the nation who contribute relatively little to social efficiency and too often waste their resources unproductively. A socialist policy in public finance is not less vital to the clerk and the teacher, the professional man and the technician, than to the wage-earner.

Two-thirds of the private wealth in this country belongs to less than 500,000 persons, many of whom, under our property system, have done nothing to earn it. The Labor Party, therefore, proposes to revise drastically the system of death-duties, not only as just in itself, but to help in breaking that ugly tradition which binds poverty in one generation to poverty in the next, and perpetuates great fortunes by unearned inheritance. It will further steepen the graduation of income tax and surtax. Other taxes, falling on excess profits and other forms of unearned increment, will be employed. The Labor Party will deal firmly with the shameless practices of tax evasion which have developed in recent years. To grapple with the inert mass of war-debt, an annual capital tax during the war, and a bold capital levy afterwards, are indispensable.

The Labor Party does not seek to treat harshly those who have profited by an outworn and unjust system. But we are convinced that the existing vast differences in wealth poison the relation between classes in a way that is incompatible with the achievement of a common good. They increase every difficulty in meeting the needs of a rapidly changing world. They make privilege ever less conscious of social obligation.

Social Planning

Socialist planning of the nation's economic life will make possible a new direction for the social services. The Labor Party holds the view that, wisely provided and efficiently administered, these services are a definite addition to national well-being.

The provision by the community, for its members, of security against the economic deprivations of unemployment, ill-health, and old age, and of services which develop bodily and mental health and generous living, is in the forefront of Labor's program.

For those in need, assistance must be sufficient. The aged and infirm must be given that security and modest comfort which, hitherto, have been denied them. The unemployed and the sick must be adequately maintained. The blind and the deaf must be given the full chance of a self-respecting life, untainted by private charity. The harsh injustices of the "means test" must go.

The Labor Party will give the unemployed a fair deal; but it does not accept the view—inherent in the capitalist system—that large-scale unemployment is either necessary or beyond the nation's power to prevent.

The Prevention of Unemployment

The great depression revealed the inability of private enterprise to cope with the disasters it produced. There is a tragic sense in which war is a great public works program in relief of Capitalism in crisis. The organization which is essential to the safety of the nation in war, and without which victory is impossible, is, in its underlying principles, equally necessary in times of peace. The Labor Party is not prepared again to watch the grim spectacle of distressed areas and decaying men, when a policy of Socialist development can transform the one into sources of national wealth, and the other into active and valuable citizens. The Labor Party is not prepared to watch resources and workers lie idle—at the cost of the future—until it seems profitable to private enterprise to use them; nor to see them left stagnant and wasting, after the profit has been squeezed out of them.

Unless, however, there is careful planning now, in War-time, for a great program of economic and social development after the War, the end of hostilities may well bring industrial disaster. The Labor Party proposes such a program, to include, among other items:—

The re-equipment of socialized industries, and also of industries not yet socialized but requiring drastic measures of reorganization under public control.

Electrification, including the electrification of the socialized railway system.

The erection of publicly-owned plants in the mining areas for the extraction of oil and other valuable by-products from coal, to be worked in conjunction with the socialized mining industry.

Building, in conformity with careful regional planning, to include houses, schools, hospitals, holiday camps, village halls, and other public buildings and amenities.

Land drainage.

Water supply.

Agricultural development, including a vigorous extension of afforestation and forest holdings, based on the public ownership of the land.

Road and bridge-building, and harbor development.

This program would provide extensive employment in many industries and in many different districts. As part of the development of publicly-owned and publicly-administered resources, it would go to the root of the unemployment problem. It would add to the national wealth, and save expenditure on unemployment benefit and assistance. Above all, it would arrest the decay of men.

HEALTH, HOUSING, AND EDUCATION

Ill-health and ill-feeding compete with unemployment in taking heavy toll of our people. Socialist economic planning will raise the standard of living, and will be supplemented by a wide range of social services. The Labor Party will utilize medical discovery to the full. The extension of maternity and child welfare, of the care of children in the pre-school years, and of open-air nursery schools, is urgent. Many more special schools and classes are needed for children with physical or mental defects. The provision of school milk and meals must be greatly increased. The school medical service must be rapidly developed, to secure the early detection and treatment of all physical defects and illness. Full medical care will be made available, through the Local Authorities, for everyone who needs it, whether in the home, in the hospital, or at the clinic. Lack of means must not be a barrier to the best prevention and relief, including specialist care, that medical science can provide. Ill-health is a loss to the nation, against which the nation owes its citizens the best possible safeguards.

After the War of 1914–1918, at long last, the nation began to deal with housing. The Labor Party proposes that the end of this War shall see a determined effort to deal with the problem decisively. There must be a great program of houses to let at rents which the workers can afford, drastic and rapid slum clearance, and the abolition of overcrowding. There must be ample provision of parks and open spaces, a rigorous planning and control of developing areas, and the constructive preservation of the countryside. General planning, closely associated with the proper location of industry, must be conceived on regional lines; the grim debris of industrial devastation must be cleared away. Socialist Local Authorities, with courage and imagination, have shown what can be done within their present powers. Labor demands that this courage and this imagination shall be given full national opportunity. This post-war period will, like the last, see a great housing shortage and a demand for new standards. The community must not again be left exposed to the jerrybuilder and the rack-renting profiteer; nor must tenants be left without protection against excessive rents.

The Labor Party insists that an immense development must take place without delay in education. We must not economize at the expense of the spiritual capital of our people. A nation, the overwhelming majority of which still leaves school at fourteen years of age, has not yet been given the instruments of intellectual freedom which are a main bulwark of Democracy. The school-leaving age must be raised to sixteen as rapidly as possible, with adequate maintenance grants; there must be a drastic reduction in the size of classes; there must be such a reorganization of secondary and university education as to prevent them from being, and being regarded as, a privilege reserved for an exceptional minority of children. Labor proposes, therefore, so to reshape the educational system as to bring within reach of all children and young persons, irrespective of parental income or occupation, the opportunity for the fullest development of their powers. Because we refuse to perpetuate a vicious class distinction in the training of the national mind, our aim is a unified system of education through which all children shall pass.

* * *

23

COMMUNIST STRATEGY AND TACTICS

[The strategy and tactics of revolution are an essential part of Communist political ideals. Communists do not recognize that non-Communist governments have any rights that they are bound to respect. Such governments are described as instruments for the suppression of the masses by their exploiters (landlords or capitalists). In the transition from capitalism to communism, suppression is still necessary, but the rôles are reversed: the dictatorship of the proletariat must suppress the formerly exploiting classes.

The Communist Party is therefore not a party like other parties, which accept majority rule, work within the framework of a constitution, and share with opposing parties a common loyalty to the nation. It is a disciplined organization working for the overthrow of non-Communist governments. From the Communist viewpoint it is a matter of strategy and tactics what measures to propose, what slogans to use, whether to form united fronts or to go it alone, whether to work legally and aboveboard or illegally and "underground."

The passage quoted below is part of the program drafted at the Fifth Congress of the Communist International in 1924, and adopted in revised form at the Sixth Congress in 1928. The English version was published in 1929 by Modern Books, Ltd., in England, and republished in 1935 by International Publishers, New York, 1935, in a *Handbook of Marxism* edited by Emile Burns, pp. 1032–1042.

The (Third) Communist International was founded by Lenin in 1919. It was dissolved in May, 1943, in an effort to lull the suspicions of Russia's allies in World War II. It is practically certain that Communist leaders throughout the world continued to take orders from Moscow. In October, 1947, the formation of a Communist Information Bureau was announced; it included representatives from the Communist Parties of France, Italy, and the eastern European nations dominated by Russia.]

The Fundamental Tasks of Communist Strategy and Tactics

The successful struggle of the Communist International for the dictatorship of the proletariat pre-supposes the existence in every country of a compact Communist Party, hardened in the struggle, disciplined, centralised, and closely linked up with the masses.

The Party is the vanguard of the working class, and consists of the best, most class-conscious, most active and most courageous members of that class. It incorporates the whole body of experience of the proletarian struggle. Basing itself upon the revolutionary theory of Marxism and representing the general and lasting interests of the whole of the working class, the Party personifies the unity of proletarian principles, of proletarian will and of proletarian revolutionary action. It is a revolutionary organisation, bound by an iron discipline and strict revolutionary rules of democratic centralism—which can be carried out owing to the class-consciousness of the proletarian vanguard—to its loyalty to the revolution, its ability to maintain inseparable ties with the proletarian masses and to its correct political leadership, which is constantly verified and clarified by the experiences of the masses themselves.

In order that it may fulfil its historic mission of achieving the dictatorship of the proletariat, the Communist Party must first of all set itself to accomplish the following fundamental stategic aims:

Extend its influence over the majority of the members of its own class, including working women and the working youth. To achieve this the Communist Party must secure predominant influence in the broad mass proletarian organisations (Soviets, trade unions, factory councils, coöperative societies, sport organisations, cultural organisations, etc.). It is particularly important for this purpose of winning over the majority of the proletariat, to capture the trade unions, which are genuine mass working-class organisations closely bound up with the everyday struggles of the working class. To work in reactionary trade unions and skilfully to capture them, to win the confidence of the broad masses of the industrially organised workers, and to remove from their posts and replace the reformist leaders, are all important tasks in the preparatory period.

The achievement of the dictatorship of the proletariat pre-supposes also that the proletariat acquires leadership of wide sections of the toiling masses. To accomplish this the Communist Party must extend its influence over the masses of the urban and rural poor, over the lower strata of the intelligentsia, and over the so-called "small man," i. e., the petty-bourgeois strata generally. It is particularly important that work be carried on for the purpose of extending the Party's influence over the peasantry. The Communist Party must secure for itself the whole-hearted support of that stratum of the rural population that stands closest to the proletariat, i. e., the agricultural labourers and the rural poor. To this end the agricultural labourers must be organised in separate organisations; all possible support must be given them in their struggles against the rural bourgeoisie, and strenuous work must be carried on among the small allotment farmers and small peasants. In regard to the middle strata of the peasantry in developed capitalist countries, the Communist Parties must conduct a policy to secure their neutrality. The fulfilment of all these tasks by the proletariat—the champion of the interests of the whole people and the leader of the broad masses in their struggle against the oppression of finance capital—is an essential condition precedent for the victorious Communist revolution.

The tasks of the Communist International connected with the revolutionary struggle in colonies, semi-colonies and dependencies are extremely important strategical tasks in the world proletarian struggle. The colonial struggle pre-supposes that the broad masses of the working class and of the peasantry in the colonies must be won over to the banner of the revolution; but this cannot be achieved unless the closest coöperation is maintained between the proletariat in the oppressing countries and the toiling masses in the oppressed countries.

While organising under the banner of the proletarian dictatorship the revolution against imperialism in the so-called civilised States, the Communist International supports every movement against imperialist violence in the colonies, semi-colonies and dependencies themselves (for example, Latin-America); it carries on propaganda against all forms of chauvinism and against the imperialist maltreatment of enslaved peoples and races, big and small (treatment of negroes, "yellow labour," anti-semitism, etc.), and supports their struggles against the bourgeoisie of the oppressing nations. The Communist International especially combats the chauvinism that is preached in the Empire-owning countries by the imperialist bourgeoisie, as well as by its social-democratic agency, the Second International, and constantly holds up in contrast to the practices of the imperialist bourgeoisie the practice of the Soviet Union, which has established relations of fraternity and equality among the nationalities inhabiting it.

The Communist Parties in the imperialist countries must render systematic aid to the colonial revolutionary liberation movement, and to the movement of oppressed nationalities generally. The duty of rendering active support to these movements rests primarily upon the workers in the countries upon which the oppressed nations are economically, financially, or politically dependent. The Communist Parties must openly recognise the right of the colonies to separation and their right to carry on propaganda for this separation, i. e., propaganda in favour of the independence of the colonies from the imperialist State. They must recognise their right of armed defence against imperialism (i. e., the right of rebellion and revolutionary war) and advocate and give active support to this defence by all the means in their power. The Communist Parties must adopt this line of policy in regard to all oppressed nations.

The Communist Parties in the colonial and semi-colonial countries must carry on a bold and consistent struggle against foreign imperialism and unfailingly conduct propaganda in favour of friendship and unity with the proletariat in the imperialist countries. They must openly advance, conduct propaganda for, and carry out the slogan of agrarian revolution, rouse the broad masses of the peasantry for the overthrow of the landlords and combat the reactionary and mediæval influence of the priesthood, of the missionaries and other similar elements.

In these countries, the principal task is to organise the workers and the peasantry independently (to establish class Communist Parties of the proletariat, trade unions, peasant leagues and committees, and—in a revolutionary situation—Soviets, etc.), and to free them from the influence of the national bourgeoisie, with whom temporary agreements may be made only on the condition that they, the bourgeoisie, do not hamper the revolutionary organisation of the workers and peasants, and that they carry on a genuine struggle against imperialism.

In determining its line of tactics, each Communist Party must take into account the concrete internal and external situation, the correlation of class forces, the degree of stability and strength of the bourgeoisie, the degree of preparedness of the proletariat, the position taken up by the various intermediary strata, etc., in its country. The Party determines slogans and methods of struggle in accordance with these circumstances, with the view to organising and mobilising the masses on the broadest possible scale and on the highest possible level of this struggle.

When a revolutionary situation is developing, the Party advances certain transitional slogans and partial demands corresponding to the concrete situation; but these demands and slogans must be bent to the revolutionary aim of capturing power and of overthrowing bourgeois capitalist society. The Party must neither stand aloof from the daily needs and struggles of the working class nor confine its activities exclusively to them. The task of the Party is to utilise these minor everyday needs as a starting point from which to lead the working class to the revolutionary struggle for power.

When the revolutionary tide is rising, when the ruling classes are disorganised, the masses are in a state of revolutionary ferment, the intermediary strata are inclining towards the proletariat and the masses are ready for action and for sacrifice, the Party of the proletariat is confronted with the task of leading the masses to a direct attack upon the bourgeois State. This it does by carrying on propaganda in favour of increasingly radical transitional slogans (for Soviets, workers' control of industry, for peasant committees, for the seizure of the big landed properties, for disarming the bourgeoisie and arming the proletariat, etc.), and by organising mass action, upon which, all branches of Party agitation and propaganda, including parliamentary activity, must be concentrated. This mass action includes: strikes; a combination of strikes and demonstrations; a combination of strikes and armed demonstrations and finally, the general strike conjointly with armed insurrection against the State power of the bourgeoisie. The latter form of struggle, which is the supreme form, must be conducted according to the rules of war; it pre-supposes a plan of campaign, offensive fighting operations and unbounded devotion and heroism on the part of the proletariat. An absolutely essential condition precedent for this form of action is the organisation of the broad masses into militant units, which, by their very form, embrace and set into action the largest possible numbers of toilers (Councils of Workers' Deputies, Soldiers' Councils, etc.), and intensified revolutionary work in the army and the navy.

In passing over to new and more radical slogans, the Parties must be guided by the fundamental rôle of the political tactics of Leninism, which call for ability to lead the masses to revolutionary positions in such a manner that the masses may, by their own experience, convince themselves of the correctness of the Party line. Failure to observe this rule must inevitably lead to isolation from the masses, to putschism, to the ideological degeneration of Communism into "leftist" dogmatism, and to petty-bourgeois "revolutionary" adventurism. Failure to take advantage of the culminating point in the development of the revolutionary situation, when the Party of the proletariat is called upon to conduct a bold and determined attack upon the enemy, is not less dangerous. To allow that opportunity to slip by and to fail to start rebellion at that point, means to allow the initiative to pass to the enemy and to doom the revolution to defeat.

When the revolutionary tide is not rising, the Communist Parties must advance partial slogans and demands that correspond to the everyday needs of the toilers, and combine them with the fundamental tasks of the Communist International. The Communist Parties must not, however, at such a time, advance transitional slogans that are applicable only to revolutionary situations (for example, workers' control of industry, etc.). To advance such slogans when there is no revolutionary situation means to transform them into slogans that favour merging with the capitalist system of organisation. Partial demands and slogans form generally an essential part of correct tactics; but certain transitional slogans go inseparably with a revolutionary situation. Repudiation of partial demands and transitional slogans "on principle," however, is incompatible with the tactical principles of Communism, for in effect, such repudiation condemns the Party to inaction and isolates it from the masses. United front tactics also occupy an important place in the tactics of the Communist Parties throughout the whole pre-revolutionary period as a means towards achieving success in the struggle against capital, towards the class mobilisation of the masses and the exposure and isolation of the reformist leaders.

The correct application of united front tactics and the fulfilment of the general task of winning over the masses pre-supposes in their turn systematic and persistent work in the trade unions and other mass proletarian organisations. It is the bounden duty of every Communist to belong to a trade union, even a most reactionary one, provided it is a mass organisation. Only by constant and persistent work in the trade unions and in the factories for the steadfast and energetic defence of the interests of the workers, together with ruthless struggle against the reformist bureaucracy, will it be possible to win the leadership in the workers' struggle and to win the industrially organised workers over to the side of the Party.

Unlike the reformists, whose policy is to split the trade unions, the Communists defend trade union unity nationally and internationally on the basis of the class struggle, and render every support to, and strengthen, the work of the Red Trade Union International.

In championing universally the current everyday needs of the masses of the workers and of the toilers generally, in utilising the bourgeois parliament as a platform for revolutionary agitation and propaganda, and subordinating all partial tasks to the struggle for the dictatorship of the proletariat, the Parties of the Communist International advance partial demands and slogans in the following main spheres:

In the sphere of Labour, in the narrow meaning of the term, i. e., questions concerned with the industrial struggle: the fight against the trustified capital offensive, wages questions, the working day, compulsory arbitration, unemployment; which grow into questions of the general political struggle, big industrial conflicts, fight for the right to organise, right to strike, etc.; in the sphere of politics proper: taxation, high cost of living, Fascism, persecution of revolutionary parties, white terror and current politics generally; and finally in the sphere of world politics, viz., attitude towards the U.S.S.R. and colonial revolutions, struggle for the unity of the international trade union movement, struggle against imperialism and the war danger, and systematic preparation for the fight against imperialist war.

In the sphere of the peasant problem, the partial demands are those appertaining to taxation, peasant mortgage indebtedness, struggle against usurer's capital, the land hunger of the peasant small-holders, rent, the metayer (crop-sharing) system. Starting out from these partial needs, the Communist Party must sharpen the respective slogans and broaden them out into the slogans: confiscation of large estates, and workers' and peasants' government (the synonym for the proletarian dictatorship in developed capitalist countries and for a democratic dictatorship of the proletariat and peasantry in backward countries and in certain colonies).

Systematic work must also be carried on among the proletarian and peasant youth (mainly through the Young Communist International and its Sections) and also among working women and peasant women. This work must concern itself with the special conditions of life and struggle of the working and peasant women, and their demands must be linked up with the general demands and fighting slogans of the proletariat.

In the struggle against colonial oppression, the Communist Parties in the colonies must advance partial demands that correspond to the special circumstances prevailing in each country, such as complete equality for all nations and races, abolition of all privileges for foreigners, the right of association for workers and peasants, reduction of the working day, prohibition of child labour, prohibition of usury and of all transactions entailing bondage, reduction and abolition of rent, reduction of taxation, refusal to pay taxes, etc. All these partial slogans must be subordinate to the fundamental demands of the Communist Parties, such as complete political national independence and the expulsion of the imperialists, workers' and peasants' government, the land to the whole people, eight-hour day, etc. The Communist Parties in imperialist countries, while supporting the struggle proceeding in the colonies, must carry on a campaign in their own respective countries for the withdrawal of imperialist troops, conduct propaganda in the army and navy in defence of the oppressed countries fighting for their liberation, mobilise the masses to refuse to transport troops and munitions, and in connection with this, to organise strikes and other forms of mass protest, etc.

The Communist International must devote itself especially to systematic preparation for the struggle against the danger of imperialist wars. Ruthless exposure of social chauvinism, of social imperialism and of pacifist phrase-mongering intended to camouflage the imperialist plans of the bourgeoisie; propaganda in favour of the principal slogans of the Communist International; everyday organisational work in connection with this in the course of which constitutional methods must unfailingly be combined with unconstitutional methods; organised work in the army and navy—such must be the activity of the Communist Parties in this connection. The fundamental slogans of the Communist International in this connection must be the following: "Convert imperialist war into civil war"; defeat the "home" imperialist government; defend the U.S.S.R. and the colonies by every possible means in the event of imperialist war against them. It is the bounden duty of all Sections of the Communist International, and of every one of its members, to carry on propaganda for these slogans, to expose the "socialistic" sophisms and the "socialistic" camouflage of the League of Nations, and constantly to keep to the front the experiences of the war of 1914–18.

In order that revolutionary work and revolutionary action may be coordinated and in order that these activities may be guided most successfully, the international proletariat must be bound by international class discipline, for which first of all, it is most important to have the strictest international discipline in the Communist ranks.

This international Communist discipline must find expression in the subordination of the partial and local interests of the movement to its general and lasting interests and in the strict fulfilment, by all members, of the decisions passed by the leading bodies of the Communist International.

Unlike the social-democratic Second International, each Section of which submits to the discipline of "its own," national bourgeoisie and of its own "fatherland," the Sections of the Communist International submit to only one discipline, viz., international proletarian discipline, which guarantees victory in the struggle of the world's workers for world proletarian dictatorship. Unlike the Second International, which splits the trade unions, fights against colonial peoples, and practises unity with the bourgeoisie, the Communist International is an organisation that guards proletarian unity in all countries and the unity of the toilers of all races and all peoples in their struggle against the yoke of imperialism.

Despite the bloody terror of the bourgeoisie, the Communists fight with courage and devotion on all sectors of the international class front, in the firm conviction that the victory of the proletariat is inevitable and cannot be averted.

"The Communists disdain to conceal their views and aims. They openly declare that their aims can be attained only by the forcible overthrow of all the existing social conditions. Let the ruling class tremble at a Communistic revolution. The proletarians have nothing to lose but their chains. They have a world to win.

"Working men of all countries, Unite!"

[For the development of Communism in ideology and methods up to 1944, see Harry W. Laidler, *Social-Economic Movements,* New York, Thomas Y. Crowell Company, 1944, Part Four: "Communism"; for Stalin's utterances on method, see Historicus (pseudonym), "Stalin on Revolution," *Foreign Affairs,* vol. 27, no. 2, January, 1949, pp. 175–214.

Tactics recently employed by the Communists include:

1. (a) Securing increased representation in parliaments by forming a "united front" with other parties; (b) then securing key positions in a cabinet, especially those controlling police, army, press, and radio; (c) then rigging elections or plebiscites in their own favor.

2. Discrediting religious groups by trying their leaders on charges ranging from illegal importation of currency to treason.

3. Occupation by armed forces promoting the formation of communist regimes.]

24

JAPANESE IMPERIALISM: THE TANAKA MEMORIAL

[Two aspects of the Japanese political ideal were expounded in Chapter 18: the exalted position of the Emperor and the code of Bushido. A third aspect, imperialism, is definitely expressed in the *Tanaka Memorial*. In 1927 the Japanese premier, Baron Tanaka, held a conference in Mukden, Manchuria, with civil and military officers, which lasted eleven days. Some report must have been made to the Emperor. Chinese journalists claimed to have obtained a copy of this report, which they published as *The Tanaka Memorial*. Japanese authorities declared it a forgery. But it is closely in line with previous utterances of Japanese leaders, and in the 1930's and 1940's Japanese policy conformed closely to it. The matter is discussed by Carl Crow in the introduction to his book, *Japan's Dream of Empire, The Tanaka Memorial*, New York, Harper & Brothers, 1942, from which the following selection is taken.

We should not imagine that military defeat necessarily destroys the dogma of superiority or quenches the spirit of imperialism. Fichte's stirring *Addresses to the German Nation* were delivered while Berlin was occupied by Napoleon's troops; Germany's defeat in 1918 was followed by Hitler's drive toward world power. Russia's collapse in 1917 has been followed by the expansionist policy of Stalin. Japan's present humiliation may create pressure for future expansion.]

The Tanaka Memorial

MEMORIAL PRESENTED TO THE EMPEROR OF JAPAN ON JULY 25, 1927, BY PREMIER TANAKA, OUTLINING THE POSITIVE POLICY IN MANCHURIA

Since the European War, Japan's political as well as economic interests have been in an unsettled condition. This is due to the fact that we have failed to take advantage of our special privileges in Manchuria and Mongolia and fully to realize our acquired rights. But upon my appointment as premier, I was instructed to guard our interests in this region and watch for opportunities for further expansion. Such injunctions one cannot take lightly. Ever since I advocated a positive policy toward Manchuria and Mongolia as a common citizen, I have longed for its realization. So in order that we may lay plans for the colonization of the Far East and the development of our new continental empire, a special conference was held from June 27th to July 7th lasting in all eleven days. It was attended by all the civil and military officers connected with Manchuria and Mongolia, whose discussions result in the following resolutions. These we respectfully submit to Your Majesty for consideration.

GENERAL CONSIDERATIONS

The term Manchuria and Mongolia includes the provinces Fengtien, Kirin, Heilungkiang and Outer and Inner Mongolia. It extends an area of 74,000 square miles, having a population of 28,000,000 people. The territory is more than three times as large as our own empire, not counting Korea and Formosa, but it is inhabited by only one-third as many people. The attractiveness of the land does not arise from the scarcity of population alone; its wealth of forestry, minerals, and agricultural products is also unrivaled elsewhere in the world. In order to exploit these resources for the perpetuation of our national glory, we created especially the South Manchuria Railway Company.

The total investment involved in our undertakings in railway, shipping, mining, forestry, steel manufacture, agriculture, and cattle raising, as schemes pretending to be mutually beneficial to China and Japan, amounts to no less than Yen 440,000,000. It is veritably the largest single investment and the strongest organization of our country. Although nominally the enterprise is under the joint ownership of the government and the people, in reality the government has complete power and authority. In so far as the South Manchuria Railway is empowered to undertake diplomatic, police, and ordinary administrative functions so that it may carry out our imperialistic policies, the Company forms a peculiar organization which has exactly the same powers as the Governor-General of Korea. This fact alone is sufficient to indicate the immense interests we have in Manchuria and Mongolia. Consequently the policies toward this country of successive administrations since Meiji [Emperor from 1868 to 1912] are all based on his injunctions, elaborating and continuously completing the development of the new continental empire in order to further the advance of our national glory and prosperity for countless generations to come.

Unfortunately, since the European War there have been constant changes in diplomatic as well as domestic affairs. The authorities of the Three Eastern Provinces [i. e., Manchuria] are also awakened and gradually work toward reconstruction and industrial development following our example. Their progress is astonishing. It has affected the spread of our influence in a most serious way, and has put us to so many disadvantages that the dealings with Manchuria and Mongolia of successive governments have resulted in failure. Furthermore, the restrictions of the Nine Power Treaty signed at the Washington Conference have reduced our special rights and privileges in Manchuria and Mongolia to such an extent that there is no freedom left for us. The very existence of our country is endangered.

Unless these obstacles are removed, our national existence will be insecure and our national strength will not develop. Moreover, the resources of wealth are congregated in North Manchuria. If we do not have the right of way here, it is obvious that we shall not be able to tap the riches of this country. Even the resources of South Manchuria which we won by the Russo-Japanese War will also be greatly restricted by the Nine Power Treaty. The result is that while our people cannot migrate into Manchuria as they please, the Chinese are flowing in as a flood. Hordes of them move into the Three Eastern Provinces every year, numbering in the neighborhood of several millions. They have jeopardized our acquired rights in Manchuria and Mongolia to such an extent that our annual surplus population of eight hundred thousand have no place to seek refuge. In view of this we have to admit our failure in trying to effect a balance between our population and food supply. If we do not devise plans to check the influx of Chinese immigrants immediately, in five years' time the number of Chinese will exceed 6,000,000. Then we shall be confronted with greater difficulties in Manchuria and Mongolia.

It will be recalled that when the Nine Power Treaty was signed which restricted our movements in Manchuria and Mongolia, public opinion was greatly aroused. The late Emperor Taisho called a conference of Yamagata and other high officers of the army and navy to find a way to counteract this new engagement. I was sent to Europe and America to ascertain secretly the attitude of the important statesmen toward it. They were all agreed that the Nine Power Treaty was initiated by the United States. The other Powers which signed it were willing to see our influence increase in Manchuria and Mongolia in order that we may protect the interests of international trade and investments. This attitude I found out personally from the political leaders of England, France and Italy. The sincerity of these expressions could be depended upon.

Unfortunately just as we were ready to carry out our policy and declare void the Nine Power Treaty with the approval of those whom I met on my trip, the Seiyukai cabinet suddenly fell, and our policy failed of fruition. It was indeed a great pity. After I had secretly exchanged views with the Powers regarding the development of Manchuria and Mongolia, I returned by way of Shanghai. At the wharf there a Chinese attempted to take my life. An American woman was hurt, but I escaped by the divine protection of my emperors of the past. It seems that it was by divine will that I should assist Your Majesty to open a new era in the Far East and to develop the new continental empire.

The Three Eastern Provinces are politically the imperfect spot in the Far East. For the sake of self-protection as well as the protection of others, Japan cannot remove the difficulties in Eastern Asia unless she adopts a policy of "Blood and Iron." But in carrying out this policy we have to face the United States, which has been turned against us by China's policy of fighting poison with poison. In the future if we want to control China, we must first crush the United States just as in the past we had to fight in the Russo-Japanese War. But in order to conquer China we must first conquer Manchuria and Mongolia. In order to conquer the world, we must first conquer China. If we succeed in conquering China the rest of the Asiatic countries and the South Sea countries will fear us and surrender to us. Then the world will realize that Eastern Asia is ours and will not dare to violate our rights. This is the plan left to us by Emperor Meiji, the success of which is essential to our national existence.

The Nine Power Treaty is entirely an expression of the spirit of commercial rivalry. It was the intention of England and America to crush our influence in China with their power of wealth. The proposed reduction of armaments is nothing but a means to limit our military strength, making it impossible for us to conquer the vast territory of China. On the other hand, China's sources of wealth will be entirely at their disposal. It is merely a scheme by which England and America may defeat our plans. And yet the Minseito [a liberal party] made the Nine Power Treaty the important thing and emphasized our TRADE rather than our RIGHTS in China.

This is a mistaken policy—a policy of national suicide. England can afford to talk about trade relations only because she has India and Australia to supply her with foodstuffs and other materials. So can America, because South America and Canada are there to supply her needs. Their spare energy could be entirely devoted to developing trade in China to enrich themselves. But in Japan her food supply and raw materials decrease in proportion to her population. If we merely hope to develop trade, we shall eventually be defeated by England and America, who possess unsurpassable capitalistic power. In the end, we shall get nothing. A more dangerous factor is the fact that the people of China might some day wake up. Even during these years of internal strife, they can still toil patiently, and try to imitate and displace our goods so as to impair the development of our trade. When we remember that the Chinese are our principal customers, we must beware lest one day when China becomes unified and her industries become prosperous, Americans and Europeans compete with us; our trade in China will be wrecked. Minseito's proposal to uphold the Nine Power Treaty and to adopt the policy of trade toward Manchuria is nothing less than a suicide policy.

*   *   *

After studying the present conditions and possibilities of our country, our best policy lies in the direction of taking positive steps to secure rights and privileges in Manchuria and Mongolia. These will enable us to develop our trade. This will not only forestall China's own industrial development, but also prevent the penetration of European Powers. This is the best policy possible!

The way to gain actual rights in Manchuria and Mongolia is to use this region as a base and, under the pretense of trade and commerce, penetrate the rest of China. Armed by rights already secured, we shall seize resources all over the country. Having China's entire resources at our disposal, we shall proceed to conquer India, the Archipelago, Asia Minor, Central Asia, and even Europe. But to get control of Manchuria and Mongolia is the first step if the Yamato race wishes to distinguish itself on Continental Asia.

Final success belongs to the country having food supply; industrial prosperity belongs to the country having raw materials; the full growth of national strength belongs to the country having extensive territory. If we pursue a positive policy to enlarge our rights in Manchuria and China, all these prerequisites of a powerful nation will constitute no problem. Furthermore, our surplus population of 700,000 each year will also be taken care of.

If we want to inaugurate a new policy and secure the permanent prosperity of our empire, a positive policy toward Manchuria and Mongolia is the only way.

[The preceding quotations constitute about one eighth of the whole memorial; the remainder consists of detailed proposals for carrying out this general plan.]

25

CONFLICTING IDEALS IN CHINA

[The founder of the Chinese Republic was Dr. Sun Yat-Sen. He was born on a Chinese farm in 1866. He came in contact with American and British ideas as a schoolboy in Honolulu and a student in Hong Kong, which was both a Chinese sea-port and a British colony; there he graduated from Queen's College and Hong Kong Medical College. Beginning in 1895, he traveled among Chinese groups abroad, obtaining support for revolutionary uprisings in China. His aim was to overthrow the corrupt Manchu dynasty and build a new China in which there would be equality of opportunity and economic progress. In 1911 this movement caused the fall of the Manchu dynasty.

Since 1911 progress toward Dr. Sun's ideals has been hampered by many causes, including Japanese aggression and the present split between Nationalists and Communists.

Dr. Sun's program was embodied in a series of writings from 1918 to 1925. The most important of these is a series of lectures on *Three Principles of the People* (San Min Chu I). These lectures were begun in 1924 and interrupted by his death in 1925. The three principles are (1) The Chinese must advance from clan loyalty to national loyalty, while preserving their ancient moral ideals. (2) They must advance from political confusion to solid democratic organization. (3) They must advance from mass poverty to a just and productive economic order.

For the work and thought of Dr. Sun, see Gung-Hsing Wang, *The Chinese Mind*, New York, The John Day Company, 1946, pp. 159–185. See also Leonard S. Hsü, *Sun Yat-Sen, His Political and Social Ideals*, Los Angeles, University of Southern California Press, 1933, which includes a translation of the *Three Principles* differing from the one used below.]

San Min Chu I, the Three Principles of the People *

PART I. THE PRINCIPLE OF NATIONALISM

LECTURE 1

The Chinese people have shown the greatest loyalty to family and clan with the result that in China there have been family-ism and clan-ism but no real nationalism. Foreign observers say that the Chinese are like a sheet of loose sand. . . . The family and the clan have been powerful unifying forces; again and again Chinese have sacrificed themselves, their families, their lives in defense of their clan. . . . But for the nation there has never been an instance of the supreme spirit of sacrifice. The unity of the Chinese people has stopped short at the clan and has not extended to the nation (p. 5).

LECTURE 6

China did not reach her former position of greatness by one road only. Usually a nation becomes strong at first by the expansion of its military power, then by the development of various forms of culture; but if the nation and the state are to maintain a permanent standing, moral character is essential. Only by attaining a high standard of morality can the state hope to govern long and exist at peace (p. 124). [He says that the Mongols conquered a vast empire but lost it soon through lack of moral character.]

Because of the high moral standards of our race, we have been able not only to survive in spite of the downfall of the state, but we have had power to assimilate these outside races. So, coming to the root of the matter, if we want to restore our race's standing, besides uniting all into a great national body, we must first recover our ancient morality—then, and only then, can we plan how to attain again to the national position we once held.

As for China's old moral standards, they are not yet lost sight of by the people of China. First come Loyalty and Filial Devotion, then Kindness and Love, then Faithfulness and Justice, then Harmony and Peace. The Chinese still speak of these ancient qualities of character. But since our domination by alien races and since the invasion of foreign culture, which has spread its influence all over China, a group intoxicated with the new

* Translated by Frank W. Price, edited by L. T. Chen, under the auspices of China Committee, Institute of Pacific Relations, The Commercial Press, Limited, Changsha, China, 1938 (first printed in 1927).

culture have begun to reject the old morality, saying that the former makes the latter unnecessary. They do not understand that we ought to preserve what is good in our past and throw away only the bad. China now is in a period of conflict between old and new currents and a large number of our people have nothing to follow after (p. 125).

In a democracy it stands to reason that we should still show loyalty, not to princes but to the nation and to the people. Loyalty to four hundred millions must naturally be on a much higher level than loyalty to one individual; so I say that the fine moral quality of loyalty must still be cherished.

Filial Devotion is even more a characteristic of China, and we have gone far beyond other nations in the practice of it. Filial duty as revealed in the "Canon of Filial Piety" covers almost the whole field of human activity, touching every point; there is no treatise on filial piety in any civilized country today that is so complete. Filial Devotion is still indispensable. If the people of the democracy can carry out Loyalty and Filial Devotion to the limit, our state will naturally flourish. . . .

Since our foreign intercourse began, some people have thought that the Chinese ideal of kindness and love was inferior to the foreigners' because foreigners in China, by establishing schools and carrying on hospitals to teach and relieve the Chinese, have been practicing kindness and love. In the practical expression of the fine qualities of kindness and love, it does seem as though China were far behind other countries, and the reason is that the Chinese have been less active in performance. Yet Kindness and Love are old qualities of Chinese character, and as we study other countries let us learn their practical methods, revive our own kindness and love, the spirit of ancient China, and make them shine with greater glory.

Faithfulness and Justice. Ancient China always spoke of Faithfulness in dealing with neighboring countries and in intercourse with friends. In my estimation, the quality of faithfulness is practiced better by Chinese than by foreigners. This can be seen in business intercourse: Chinese in their business relations do not use written contracts; all that is necessary is a verbal promise which is implicitly trusted. Thus, when a foreigner places an order for goods with a Chinese, no contract is necessary; there is simply an entry on the books and the bargain is closed (p. 128). . . .

Justice. China in her mightiest days never utterly destroyed another state. Look at Korea, which was formerly a tributary of China in name but an independent nation in reality (p. 131). . . .

China was a strong state for thousands of years and Korea lived on;

Japan has been a strong state for not over twenty years and Korea is already destroyed. From this one can see that Japan's sense of "faithfulness and justice" is inferior to China's and that China's standards have advanced beyond those of other nations.

China has one more splendid virtue—the love of Harmony and Peace. Among the states and the peoples of the world today China alone preaches peace; other countries all talk in terms of war and advocate the overthrow of states by imperialism. Only in recent years, since the experience of many great wars and huge, tragic death losses, have they begun to propose the abolition of war. . . . But the representatives of the various nations have met to discuss peace out of fear of war, out of a feeling of necessity rather than out of a natural desire on the part of all citizens for peace. The intense love of peace which the Chinese have had these thousands of years has been a natural disposition. In individual relationships great stress has been laid upon "humility and deference"; in government the old saying was, "He who delights not in killing a man can unify all men." All of this is very different from the ideals of foreigners. China's ancient virtues of Loyalty, Filial Devotion, Kindness, Love, Faithfulness, and such are in their very nature superior to foreign virtues, but in the moral quality of Peace we will further surpass the people of other lands. This special characteristic is the spirit of our nation and we must not only cherish it but cause it to shine with greater luster; then our national standing will be restored (p. 132).

China has a specimen of political philosophy so systematic and so clear that nothing has been discovered or spoken by foreign statesmen to equal it. It is found in the "Great Learning": "Search into the nature of things, extend the boundaries of knowledge, make the purpose sincere, regulate the mind, cultivate personal virtue, rule the family, govern the state, pacify the world." This calls upon a man to develop from within outward, to begin with his inner nature and not cease until the world is at peace (p. 134).

China from the beginning of her history has never put democracy into practice; even in the last thirteen years we have not had democracy. In all these four thousand years, through periods of order and disorder, China has seen nothing but autocracy. If we ask history whether autocracy has really been a good thing for China or not, we find its effects have been about half advantageous and half disadvantageous. But if we base our judgment upon the intelligence and the ability of the Chinese people, we come to the conclusion that the sovereignty of the people would be far more suitable for us. Confucius and Mencius two thousand years ago spoke for people's rights. Confucius said, "When the great doctrine prevails, all under heaven will work for the common good." He was pleading for a free and fraternal world in which the people would rule. . . . Mencius said, "Most precious are the people; next come the spirits of land and grain; and last, the princes." Again: "Heaven sees as the people see. Heaven hears as the people hear." He, in his age, already saw that kings were not absolutely necessary and would not last forever, so he called those who brought happiness to the people holy monarchs, but those who were cruel and unprincipled he called individualists whom all should oppose. . . . Democracy was then what foreigners call a Utopia, an ideal which could not be immediately realized (pp. 169–170).

Now that Europe and America have founded republics and have applied democracy for one hundred and fifty years, we whose ancients dreamed of these things should certainly follow the tide of world events and make use of the people's power if we expect our state to rule long and peacefully and our people to enjoy happiness (p. 171).

PART II. THE PRINCIPLE OF DEMOCRACY

LECTURE 6

[Beginning on p. 350, Dr. Sun describes the powers of suffrage and recall, to control officials, and initiative and referendum, to control laws. He then continues:]

For direct control of the government it is necessary that the people practice these four forms of popular sovereignty. Only then can we speak of government by all the people. This means that our four hundred millions shall be king, exerting their kingly authority . . . by means of the four powers of the people (p. 351).

On the side of the government there must be five powers—executive, legislative, judicial, civil service examination, and censoring. When the four political powers of the people control the five governing powers of the government, then we will have a completely democratic government organ, and the strength of the people and of the government will be well balanced (p. 354).

PART III. THE PRINCIPLE OF LIVELIHOOD

LECTURE 1

[Dr. Sun rejects Marxian ideas and proposes four peaceful methods of economic improvement.]

The first one—socionomic reform—means the use of government power to better the workingman's education and to protect his health, to improve factories and machinery so that working conditions may be perfectly safe and comfortable. . . . The second new practice means putting electric and steam railways, steamship lines, and all the big business of the postal and telegraph service entirely under government management (p. 386).

The third feature of modern economic reform, direct taxation, is also a very recent development in the socionomic method. It is applied by means of a graduated tax scale which levies a heavy income tax and inheritance tax upon capitalists and secures financial resources for the state directly from capitalists. Because of the large income of capitalists, direct taxation by the state "gets much without seeming oppressive" (p. 387).

The fourth new economic activity, socialized distribution, is a most recent development in Western society. . . . England, for example, has introduced consumers' coöperative societies which are social organizations for the distribution of commodities. The most modern municipal governments in Europe and America themselves undertake the distribution of water, electricity, and gas, bread, milk, butter, and other foods for the community. This saves the merchants' profit and reduces the loss which the consumers suffer (p. 388-389).

LECTURE 2

The Kuomintang some time ago in its party platform settled upon two methods by which the Principle of Livelihood is to be carried out. The first method is equalization of landownership and the second is regulation of capital (p. 409).

[In order to "equalize landownership" Dr. Sun proposes the following system:]

The landowner reports the value of his land to the government and the government levies a land tax accordingly. Many people think that if the landowners make their own assessment, they will undervalue the land and the government will lose out. . . . But suppose the government makes two regulations: first, that it will collect taxes according to the declared value of the land; second, that it can also buy back the land at the same price. . . . According to my plan, if the landowner makes a low assessment, he will be afraid lest the government buy back his land at that value and make him lose his property; if he makes too high an assessment, he will be afraid of the government taxes according to this value and his loss through heavy taxes. Comparing these two serious possibilities . . . he will strike a mean and report the true market price to the government. . . . After the land values have been fixed, we should have a regulation by law that, from that year on, all increase in land values, which in other countries means heavier taxation, shall revert to the community (p. 432).

[Regarding "regulation of capital" Dr. Sun says:]

China has never had any great capitalists; if the state can control and develop capital and give the benefits to all the people, it will be easy to avoid the conflicts with capitalists (p. 442). [He proposes to borrow foreign capital to create government-owned railroads, factories, and mines.] In the solution of the social problem, we have the same object in view as that in foreign countries: to make everybody contented and happy, free from the suffering caused by the unequal distribution of wealth and property (p. 443).

LECTURE 3

[Dealing with agricultural problems.] A large majority of the people in China are peasants, at least nine out of every ten; yet the food which they raise with such wearisome labor is mostly taken away by the landowners. . . . If we are to increase the production of food, we must make laws regarding the rights and interests of the farmers . . . and allow them to keep more of the fruit of their land. . . . Later, when the problems of the farmer are all solved, each tiller of the soil will possess his own fields— that is to be the final fruit of our efforts (p. 456).

In dealing with agricultural production, we should study not only this question of liberating the peasants but also the seven methods of increasing production. These methods are: use of machinery, use of fertilizers, rotation of crops, eradication of pests, manufacturing, transportation, and prevention of natural disasters (p. 457).

CHINESE COMMUNISM AND MAO TSE-TUNG

[The Communist Party of China was formed in Shanghai in July, 1921. Among those present was Mao Tse-Tung. Mao was born in 1893 on a farm not far from Changsha.

In 1923–24, Sun Yat-Sen accepted the aid of Russian Communist advisers in reorganizing his party, the Kuomintang. At this period both Chiang Kai-Shek and Mao Tse-Tung served on the combined executive committees of the Kuomintang and Communist parties. After Dr. Sun's death in 1925, Chiang came to dominate the Kuomintang. When Chiang broke with the Communists in 1927, Mao formed the nucleus of a Red Army and maintained Soviet Republics in Kiangsi and neighboring provinces.

In 1934–35, pressure from Chiang's forces led the Communists to make their famous Long March of 6000 miles in 368 days, westward, northward, and finally eastward to Yenan, in Shensi, which thereafter was the center of Communist activity. See John K. Fairbank, *The United States and China,* Cambridge, Massachusetts, Harvard University Press, 1948; Paul M. A. Linebarger, *The China of Chiang Kai-Shek,* Boston, World Peace Foundation, 1941, Chapter VI; Edgar Snow, *Red Star Over China,* New York, Random House, 1938, pp. 111–167, Mao's account of his own life; Freda Utley, *Last Chance in China,* Indianapolis, The Bobbs-Merrill Company, 1947, Chapters VI, VII, VIII. Early in 1949, Mao's forces controlled the north half of China.

In 1940, Mao wrote *China's New Democracy,* which illustrates the application of communist strategy to Chinese conditions. The following paragraphs are reprinted from *Mao Tse-Tung's "Democracy," a digest of the Bible of Chinese Communism, Commentary by Lin Yutang,* New York, Chinese News Service, An Agency of the Chinese Government, 1947, pp. 9–14.]

China's New Democracy

China's revolution is a magnificent part of the world revolution! . . . The first step or stage of this revolution is certainly not to, and certainly cannot, establish a capitalist society dictated by the bourgeoisie, but to establish a New Democracy under the joint dictatorship of several revolutionary classes. After the accomplishment of this first stage, it will be developed into the second stage—to establish the socialist society of China. . . .

The Democratic Republic of China which we are aiming to construct now can only be a joint dictatorship of all anti-imperialist and anti-feudal people. It is a Republic of New Democracy, or a Republic of the genuine, revolutionary San Min Chu I that includes Dr. Sun's three revolutionary policies.

This Republic of New Democracy is different on the one hand from the old Western-style capitalist republics that are under the dictatorship of capitalists and are already out-of-date. On the other hand it is also different from the newest, Soviet-style socialist republic, under the dictatorship of the proletariat. This kind of republic has already arisen and grown strong in the Soviet Union, and furthermore will yet be established in the different capitalist countries, and will undoubtedly become the type of government of all progressive countries through the Union of Nations and of political power. Nevertheless, in a certain historical period, the Soviet-style republic cannot be fittingly practised in colonial and semi-colonial countries, the national policy of which must therefore be of a third type—that of the New Democracy. This is a national policy for a certain historical period, and is therefore transitional in character, but it is a form indispensable and un-alterable.

Hence, according to their social character, the forms of government of all the countries of the world fall fundamentally into three categories: (a) republics under the dictatorship of the capitalist class; (b) republics under the dictatorship of the proletariat, and (c) republics under the joint dicta-torship of several revolutionary classes.

The first category comprises the countries of the old democracy. Today, after the outbreak of the second imperialist war, the breath of democracy has already disappeared from all capitalist countries. All have become, or are about to become, blood-smelling, military dictatorships of the capitalist classes. Certain countries under the joint dictatorship of the landlords and the capitalist classes can be grouped under this heading.

The second form of republic is fermenting in the various capitalist coun-tries, besides its realization in the Soviet Union. It will become the form of world rule in a certain period.

The third form is the transitional form in the revolutionary colonial and semi-colonial countries. . . . .

. . . Capitalist elements are accustomed to conceal the truth about class status, and to resort to the term "nation" to camouflage the actuality of one-class dictatorship. Such concealment gives no benefit to the revolutionary people and therefore should be clearly exposed. The term "nation" can sometimes be used of course, but it does not include the traitors and the counter-revolutionary elements. It (the national structure) means a dictatorship of all the revolutionary people—and revolutionary classes over the traitors and counter-revolutionaries. Such is the kind of country we want today.

* * *

Big banks, big industries and big business shall be owned by the Republic. . . .

It will adopt certain measures to confiscate the land of big landlords and distribute it to the peasants who are without land or have too little of it, to realize Dr. Sun's slogan "Land to those who till it," and to liquidate the feudal relation in rural districts. . . .

. . . We can never let the few capitalists and landlords "manipulate the life of the people," nor can we construct a capitalist society of the European or American style. Whoever dares to act against this direction shall not be able to accomplish his work, and he himself shall find his head broken.

* * *

We cannot be separated from the socialist state or from the aid of the international proletariat, if we wish to seek for independence. That is to say, we cannot separate ourselves from the assistance of the Soviet Union or from the victory of the anti-capitalist struggles of the proletariat of Japan, Great Britain, the United States, France and Germany. Their victories help us. Although we cannot say that victory in China must be preceded by the success of revolutions of the above countries, or at least in one or two of the above countries, it is doubtless true that we can only win our victory with their assistance. This is especially true of the aid of the Soviet Union, an indispensable condition for the final victory of China's war of resistance. To refuse Soviet aid will surely bring about the failure of the revolution. Is not this the clear lesson of China's anti-Soviet movement after 1927? . . .

* * *

Communism is the proletarian system of thought, and is also a new kind of social system. It is different from any other ideological system or social system in that it is the most complete, the most progressive, the most revolutionary, and the most rational system in human history. The feudal ideology and social system have now become fit for the museum of historical relics; a part of the capitalist ideology and social system has already entered historical museums. And the remaining part of it is "like a setting sun, breathing its final breaths," and "not knowing in the morning whether it can still survive in the evening." It is soon to enter historical museums. It is only the Communist ideology and social system that grow and spread in the world, with a mighty thundering force that can level mountains and overturn seas, and maintain their flowering youth. . . . The world now depends on Communism as its star of salvation, and so does China.

26

POLITICAL AIMS AND METHODS IN INDIA

THE CONGRESS PARTY

[The Indian National Congress is an association for the discussion of political and social problems that gradually became a sort of political party. It has never been a body with power to enact laws. It was founded in 1885, and its character has changed under the influence of changing conditions. From 1919 on it was deeply influenced by Gandhi, but it continued to supplement his spiritual methods by more ordinary ones.

Persistent aims of the Congress have been (a) to achieve increasing degrees of unity and self-government for India, and (b) to defend the cultural heritage of India against Western influences that were considered detrimental.

Members of the Congress have often disagreed on questions of method and tempo. As the decades passed, increasingly radical demands were pressed.

Useful accounts of the Congress are to be found in *Indian Crisis, The Background,* by John S. Hoyland, New York, The Macmillan Company, 1943, and in *Political India, 1832–1932,* edited by Sir John Cumming, London, Oxford University Press, 1932, pp. 39–64.

One phase of the growing aspirations of the Congress is to be found in the following Resolution, reprinted from *The Unity of India, Collected Writings, 1937–1940,* by Jawaharlal Nehru, New York, The John Day Company, Inc., 1942, Appendix A, pp. 406–408.]

The Karachi Resolution, 1931

The Karachi Congress resolution on Fundamental Rights and Economic Programme, as varied by the All-India Congress Committee in its meeting held in Bombay on August 6, 7, and 8, 1931, runs as follows:

This Congress is of opinion that to enable the masses to appreciate what "Swaraj," as conceived by the Congress, will mean to them, it is desirable

313

to state the position of the Congress in a manner easily understood by them. In order to end the exploitation of the masses, political freedom must include real economic freedom of the starving millions. The Congress therefore declares that any constitution which may be agreed to on its behalf should provide, or enable the Swaraj Government to provide, the following:

FUNDAMENTAL RIGHTS AND DUTIES

1. (i) Every citizen of India has the right of free expression of opinion, the right of free association and combination, and the right to assemble peacefully and without arms, for a purpose not opposed to law or morality.

(ii) Every citizen shall enjoy freedom of conscience and the right freely to profess and practice his religion, subject to public order and morality.

(iii) The culture, language, and script of the minorities and of the different linguistic areas shall be protected.

(iv) All citizens are equal before the law, irrespective of religion, caste, creed or sex.

(v) No disability attaches to any citizen by reason of his or her religion, caste, creed or sex, in regard to public employment, office of power or honor, and in the exercise of any trade or calling.

(vi) All citizens have equal rights and duties in regard to wells, tanks, roads, schools and places of public resort, maintained out of State or local funds, or dedicated by private persons for the use of the general public.

(vii) Every citizen has the right to keep and bear arms, in accordance with regulations and reservations made in that behalf.

(viii) No person shall be deprived of his liberty, nor shall his dwelling or property be entered, sequestered, or confiscated, save in accordance with law.

(ix) The State shall observe neutrality in regard to all religions.

(x) The franchise shall be on the basis of universal adult suffrage.

(xi) The State shall provide for free and compulsory primary education.

(xii) The State shall confer no titles.

(xiii) There shall be no capital punishment.

(xiv) Every citizen is free to move throughout India and to stay and settle in any part thereof, to acquire property and to follow any trade or calling, and to be treated equally with regard to legal prosecution or protection in all parts of India.

LABOR

2. (a) The organization of economic life must conform to the principle of justice, to the end that it may secure a decent standard of living.

(b) The State shall safeguard the interests of industrial workers and shall secure for them, by suitable legislation and in other ways, a living wage, healthy conditions of work, limited hours of labor, suitable machinery for the settlement of disputes between employers and workmen, and protection against the economic consequences of old age, sickness, and unemployment.

3. Labor to be freed from serfdom and conditions bordering on serfdom.

4. Protection of women workers, and especially, adequate provision for leave during maternity period.

5. Children of school-going age shall not be employed in mines and factories.

6. Peasants and workers shall have the right to form unions to protect their interest.

TAXATION AND EXPENDITURE

7. The system of land tenure and revenue and rent shall be reformed and an equitable adjustment made of the burden on agricultural land, immediately giving relief to the smaller peasantry, by a substantial reduction of agricultural rent and revenue now paid by them, and in case of uneconomic holdings, exempting them from rent, so long as necessary, with such relief as may be just and necessary to holders of small estates affected by such exemption or reduction in rent, and to the same end, imposing a graded tax on net incomes from land above a reasonable minimum.

8. Death duties on a graduated scale shall be levied on property above a fixed minimum.

9. There shall be a drastic reduction of military expenditure so as to bring it down to at least one-half of the present scale.

10. Expenditure and salaries in civil departments shall be largely reduced. No servant of the State, other than specially employed experts and the like, shall be paid above a certain fixed figure, which should not ordinarily exceed Rs. 500 per month.

11. No duty shall be levied on salt manufactured in India.

Economic and Social Program

12. The State shall protect indigenous cloth; and for this purpose pursue the policy of exclusion of foreign cloth and foreign yarn from the country and adopt such other measures as may be found necessary. The State shall also protect other indigenous industries, when necessary, against foreign competition.

13. Intoxicating drinks and drugs shall be totally prohibited, except for medicinal purposes.

14. Currency and exchange shall be regulated in the national interest.

15. The State shall own or control key industries and services, mineral resources, railways, waterways, shipping, and other means of public transport.

16. Relief of agricultural indebtedness and control of usury—direct and indirect.

17. The State shall provide for the military training of citizens so as to organize a means of national defense apart from the regular military forces.

GANDHI

[India is a country in which a man like Gandhi was able to exert enormous political influence. Religion was the basis of all he did. He wrote, "I am surer of God's existence than of the fact that you and I are in this room. I can testify that I may live without air and water, but not without Him" (*Harijan,* May 14, 1938). His character has been described as "marked by simplicity, humility, faith in the unseen forces of the Spirit, and above all, by self-identifying, loving and redemptive compassion for the poor, the needy, and the suffering" (John S. Hoyland, *Indian Crisis, The Background,* New York, The Macmillan Company, 1943, p. 173).

Gandhi's distinctive method of political and social action was first called Ahimsa (harmlessness or non-violence), but later, more positively, Satyagraha (defense of truth, or truth-force). ". . . Satyagraha teaches that, although wrong and man-made pain cannot be ended by violence, they can be ended by the redemptive good will which is willing to seek out ways of taking the suffering upon oneself, and sharing it to the utmost, without resentment or recrimination towards the evil-doer, but patiently and lovingly" (*ibid.,* p. 175). For a full account, see R. R. Diwakar, *Satyagraha: The Power of Truth,* Hinsdale, Illinois, Henry Regnery Company, 1948.

Gandhi was born in 1869. After studying law in London he practised it in Bombay. From 1893 to 1915 he lived in South Africa and developed his method of Satyagraha in the struggles of the Indian colony against government oppression. After 1919 he repeatedly applied Satyagraha, sometimes through widespread movements of "non-violent non-coöperation" and sometimes single-handed by fasting. He said, "It is my frequent prayer to God that I may lay down my life in the service of the poor" (Hoyland, p. 172). This prayer was granted on Jan. 30, 1948. As the assassin's bullet struck him down, he pressed his hands together in sign of forgiveness.

The origin of Gandhi's non-violence is described in the following passage from C. F. Andrews, *Mahatma Gandhi's Ideas,* New York, The Macmillan Company, 1930, pp. 191–194.]

. . . It is obviously of great importance to understand, as far as possible from Mahatma Gandhi's own lips, the main motives that urged him forward in this unique moral direction with such singular spiritual power. These had been published in a small and comparatively unknown volume by the Rev. J. J. Doke, Baptist minister in Johannesburg, who was one of Mr. Gandhi's closest friends. The record is given of a conversation regarding the way in which Passive Resistance, or Soul-Force, became a living inspiration to Mr. Gandhi himself. Mr. Doke writes as follows:—

One day I questioned Mr. Gandhi concerning the source from whence he derived his original idea.

"I remember," he told me, "how one verse of a Gujarati poem, which I learned at school as a child, clung to me. In substance it was this:

'If a man gives you a drink of water and you give him a drink in
    return, that is nothing.
'Real beauty consists in doing good against evil.'

Even as a child this verse had a powerful influence over me and I tried to carry it out in practice. Then came the Sermon on the Mount."

"But," said I, "surely the Bhagavad Gita came first?"

"No," he replied. "Of course I knew the Bhagavad Gita in Sanskrit tolerably well; but I had not made its teaching in that particular a study. It was the New Testament which really awakened me to the rightness and value of Passive Resistance.

"When I read in the Sermon on the Mount such passages as 'Resist not him that is evil; but whosoever smiteth thee on thy right cheek, turn to him the other also,' and 'Love your enemies; pray for them that persecute you, that ye may be sons of your Father which is in heaven,' I was simply overjoyed, and found my own opinion confirmed where I least expected it. The Bhagavad Gita deepened the impression, and Tolstoy's *The Kingdom of God Is Within You* gave it a permanent form.

"I do not like the term 'Passive Resistance.' It fails to convey all I mean. It describes a method, but gives no hint of the system of which it is only a part. Real beauty—and that is my aim—is in doing good against evil.

"Still I adopt the phrase because it is well known and easily understood, and because at the present time the great majority of my people can only grasp that idea. Indeed, to me the ideas that underlie the Gujarati hymn I have quoted and the Sermon on the Mount should in time revolutionize the whole of life.

"Passive Resistance is an all-sided sword: it can be used anyhow: it blesses him who uses it, and also him against whom it is used, without drawing a drop of blood. It produces far-reaching results. It never rusts and cannot be stolen. The sword of Passive Resistance does not require a scabbard, and one cannot be forcibly dispossessed of it.

"Jesus Christ, Daniel, and Socrates represented the purest form of Passive Resistance, or Soul-Force. All these teachers counted their bodies as nothing in comparison with their souls.

"Tolstoy was the best and brightest modern exponent of the doctrine. He not only expounded it but lived according to it. In India the doctrine was understood and commonly practised long before it came into vogue in Europe. It is easy to see that Soul-Force is infinitely superior to body-force. If people, in order to secure redress of wrongs, resort only to Soul-Force, much of the present suffering would be avoided. There is no such thing as failure in the use of this kind of force.

* * *

The Passive Resisters endeavor to meet and conquer hatred by love. They oppose the brute or physical force by Soul-Force. They hold that loyalty to an earthly sovereign or an earthly constitution is subordinate to loyalty to God and His constitution.

"In interpreting God's constitution through their conscience they admit that they may possibly be wrong. If they are wrong they alone suffer and the established order of things continues."

[A "confession of faith" drawn up by Gandhi at the age of forty, toward the close of his residence in South Africa, is presented by Andrews on pp. 186-189 of the same work:]

His *Confession of Faith*, 1909, runs as follows:—

(1) There is no impassable barrier between East and West.

(2) There is no such thing as Western or European Civilization; but there is a modern form of Civilization which is purely material.

(3) The people of Europe, before they were touched with modern civilization, had much in common with the people of the East.

(4) It is not the British people who rule India, but modern civilization rules India through its railways, telegraph, telephone, etc.

(5) Bombay, Calcutta, and other chief cities are the real plague-spots of Modern India.

* * *

(8) It is simply impertinence for any man, or any body of men, to begin, or to contemplate, reform of the whole world. To attempt to do so by means of highly artificial and speedy locomotion, is to attempt the impossible.

(9) Increase of material comforts, it may be generally laid down, does not in any way whatsoever conduce to moral growth.

(10) Medical science is the concentrated essence of black magic. Quackery is infinitely preferable to what passes for high medical skill.

(11) Hospitals are the instruments that the Devil has been using for his own purpose, in order to keep his hold on his kingdom. They perpetuate vice, misery, degradation, and real slavery. I was entirely off the track when I considered that I should receive a medical training. It would be sinful for me in any way whatsoever to take part in the abominations that go on in the hospitals. If there were no hospitals for venereal diseases, or even for consumptives, we should have less consumption and less sexual vice amongst us.

(12) India's salvation consists in unlearning what she has learnt during the past fifty years. The railways, telegraphs, hospitals, lawyers, doctors, and such like have all to go, and the so-called upper classes have to learn to live consciously, religiously, and deliberately the simple peasant life, knowing it to be a life giving true happiness.

(13) India should wear no machine-made clothing, whether it comes out of European mills or Indian mills.

(14) England can help India to do this, and then she will have justified her hold on India. There seem to be many in England today who think otherwise.

(15) There was true wisdom in the sages of old having so regulated society as to limit the material conditions of the people: the rude plough of perhaps five thousand years ago is the plough of the husbandman today. Therein lies salvation. People live long under such conditions, in comparative peace, much greater than Europe has enjoyed after having taken up modern activity; and I feel that every enlightened man, certainly every Englishman, may, if he chooses, learn this truth and act according to it.

It is the true spirit of passive resistance that has brought me to the above almost definite conclusions. As a passive resister I am unconcerned whether such a gigantic reformation (shall I call it?) can be brought about among people who find their satisfaction from the present mad rush. If I realize the truth of it I should rejoice in following it, and therefore I could not wait until the whole body of people had commenced. . . .

[The following utterances of Gandhi during World War II are drawn from T. A. Raman, *What Does Gandhi Want?* Oxford University Press, 1942. The first selection expresses his conviction that non-violence is the best defense, even against Hitler.]

In spite of your disbelief, I must adhere to my faith in the possibility of the most debased human nature to respond to non-violence. It is the essence of non-violence that it conquers all opposition.

That I may not express myself that measure of non-violence and others may express less, is highly probable.* But I will not belittle the power of non-violence or distrust the Fuehrer's capacity to respond to true non-violence.

*   *   *

You will please excuse me for refusing to draw distinction in kind between the forces I have had to cope with hitherto and what I may have to cope with if the Fuehrer attacked India. The prospect of his killing every Satyagrahi causes neither terror nor despair. If India has to go through such a purgatory and if a fair number of Satyagrahis face the Fuehrer's army and die without malice in their breasts, it would be a new experience

* This awkward sentence probably means, "It is highly probable that I myself may not express that degree of non-violence, and that others may express even less of it." Ed.

for him. Whether he responds or not, I am quite clear that these Satyagrahis facing the army will go down in history as heroes and heroines, at least equal to those of whom we learn in fables or cold history. . . . (pp. 41–42).

[The following selection shows Gandhi's attitude toward Great Britain and the United States.]

Both Britain and America lack the moral basis for engaging in this war unless they put their own houses in order by making it their fixed determination to withdraw their influence and power from Africa and Asia and remove the color bar.

They have no right to talk of protecting democracy, civilization and human freedom until the canker of white superiority is destroyed in its entirety.

*   *   *

Let me sum up my attitude.

This unnatural prostration of a great nation [i. e., India] must cease if the victory of the Allies is to be ensured. They lack a moral basis.

I see no difference between the Fascist or Nazi powers and the Allies.

All are exploiters, all resort to ruthlessness to the extent required to compass their end.

The American and British are great nations, but their greatness will count as dust before the bar of dumb humanity, whether African or Asiatic.

They have no right to talk of human liberty until they have washed their hands clean of pollution and so gained the surest insurance of success in the good wishes, unexpressed but certain, of millions of dumb Asiatics and Africans. Then, but not till then, will they be fighting for the New Order (pp. 64–65).

NEHRU

[Jawaharlal Nehru was born in 1893. His father, Motilal Nehru, was a successful lawyer and a leader in the Congress party in the 1920's. The younger Nehru was educated at Harrow and Cambridge and became far more Westernized than Gandhi. Like Gandhi he sought Indian unity and self-government and condemned the profit-motive. But he never completely shared Gandhi's exclusive reliance on purely spiritual methods. He rejected Gandhi's attempt to replace manufactured cloth by hand-spun and hand-woven clothing. Instead he sought to obtain the benefits of industrialism without its drawbacks. He also sought to reorganize agriculture and to get rid of usury. Gandhi looked more to the past; Nehru looks more to the future.

Since Gandhi's death, Nehru has been the outstanding leader in India. See *Political India, 1832–1932*, edited by Sir John Cumming, pp. 192–195; John S. Hoyland, *Indian Crisis, The Background*, New York, The Macmillan Company, 1943, pp. 181–188.

The paragraphs printed below express Nehru's outlook in 1939. They are taken from "A Survey of Congress Politics, 1936–1939" in *The Unity of India*, New York, The John Day Company, 1942, pp. 117–119.]

The Marxian philosophy appeals to me in a broad sense and helps me to understand the processes of history. I am far from being an orthodox Marxist, nor does any other orthodoxy appeal to me. But I am convinced that the old Liberal approach in England or elsewhere is no longer valid. Laissez-faire is dead, and unless far-reaching changes are made, with reasonable speed, disaster awaits us, whether we live in England or India. Today the community has to be organized in order to establish social and economic justice. This organization is possible on the Fascist basis, but this does not bring justice or equality, and is essentially unsound. The only other way is the Socialist way.

Liberty and democracy have no meaning without equality, and equality cannot be established so long as the principal instruments of production are privately owned. Private ownership of these means of production thus comes in the way of real democracy. Many factors go to shape opinion, but the most important and fundamental of them is the property relation, which ultimately governs our institutions and our social fabric. Those who profit by an existing property relation do not, as a class, voluntarily agree to a change which involves a loss of power and privilege. We have reached a stage when there is an essential contradiction between the existing property relation and the forces of production, and democracy cannot effectively function unless this relation is transformed. Class struggles are inherent in the present system, and the attempt to change it and bring it in line with modern requirements meets with the fierce opposition of the ruling or owning classes. That is the logic of the conflicts of today, and it has little to do with the good-will or ill-will of individuals, who might in their individual capacities succeed in rising above their class allegiance. But the class as a whole will hold together and oppose change.

I do not see why under Socialism there should not be a great deal of freedom for the individual; indeed, far greater freedom than the present system gives. He can have freedom of conscience and mind, freedom of enterprise, and even the possession of private property on a restricted scale. Above all, he will have the freedom which comes from economic security, which only a small number possesses today.

I think India and the world will have to march in this direction of Socialism unless catastrophe brings ruin to the world. That march may vary in different countries and the intermediate steps might not be the same. Nothing is so foolish as to imagine that exactly the same processes take place in different countries with varying backgrounds. India, even if she accepted this goal, would have to find her own way to it, for we have to avoid unnecessary sacrifice and the way of chaos, which may retard our progress for a generation.

But India has not accepted this goal, and our immediate objective is political independence. We must remember this and not confuse the issue, for else we will have neither Socialism nor independence. We have seen that even in Europe the middle classes are powerful enough to suppress today any movement aiming at vital social change, and, when danger threatens, have a tendency to go to Fascism. The middle classes in India are relatively at least as strong, and it would be the extremity of folly to estrange them and force them into the opposing ranks. Our national policy must therefore be one which includes a great majority of them on the common basis of political independence and anti-imperialism, and our international policy must be one of anti-Fascism.

Marxism and Socialism are not policies of violence, though, like most other groups, capitalist or Liberal, they envisage the possibility of violence. Can they fit in with the peaceful methods of the Congress, not only as a temporary expedient, but in a straightforward bona-fide manner? It is not necessary for us to discuss the whole philosophy underlying the doctrine of non-violence or to consider how far it is applicable to remote and extreme cases. For us the problem is that of India and of India of today and tomorrow. I am convinced that the way of non-violence is not merely the only feasible course for us, but is, on its merits, the best and most effective method. I think that the field of its application will grow as its effectiveness is recognized. But here in India large numbers of people have recognized it, and it has become the solid foundation of our movement. It has proved effective enough already, but it is quite possible, with further experience, to extend its applications in a variety of ways. It is easy to belittle it and point to its failures, but it is far easier to point out the innumerable failures of the method of violence. We have seen powerfully armed countries collapse and sink into servitude without a struggle. India, with all her lack of armed might, would never have succumbed in this way.

THE CLASH OF POLITICAL IDEALS

27

TOWARD ONE WORLD

[Men have long dreamed about "the parliament of man, the federation of the world." The events of World War II, especially the use of the atomic bomb, have turned this dream into an urgent practical problem. *No one in the world is safe until the world is united under an effective government, but every one sees risks in forming such a government.*

A draft of a world constitution has been prepared by a committee organized for that purpose. Among its members were university administrators and professors of various subjects including law, political science, literature, and anthropology. They were aided by a staff of associates.

The members of the committee did not expect that their draft would ever be adopted in its present form. Their aim was to clarify men's thoughts about world government by framing a specific proposal that could be analyzed and discussed.

The following paragraphs are reprinted from *Preliminary Draft of a World Constitution,* Chicago, University of Chicago Press, 1948.]

Preliminary Draft of a World Constitution

Since November 1945 the Committee to Frame a World Constitution, with headquarters at the University of Chicago, has been at work on the preparation of a preliminary draft for federal union. The publication of this document, dedicated to Gandhi, is a milestone on the road to a democratic federation of the people of the world. The members of the Committee and the signers of the draft are Robert M. Hutchins, G. A. Borgese, Mortimer J. Adler, Stringfellow Barr, Albert Gérard, Harold A. Innis, Erich Kahler, Wilbur G. Katz, Charles H. McIlwain, Robert Redfield, Rexford Guy Tugwell. Comments on the draft and an index to Committee documents are published with the Constitution in the March issue of

325

Common Cause, Vol. I, No. 9; previous issues of the magazine contain articles relevant to the work of the Committee as it has developed.[1]

Preamble

The people of the earth having agreed that the advancement of man in spiritual excellence and physical welfare is the common goal of mankind;

that universal peace is the prerequisite for the pursuit of that goal;

that justice in turn is the prerequisite of peace, and peace and justice stand or fall together;

that iniquity and war inseparably spring from the competitive anarchy of the national states;

that therefore the age of nations must end, and the era of humanity begin;

the governments of the nations have decided to order their separate sovereignties in one government of justice, to which they surrender their arms;

and to establish, as they do establish, this Constitution as the covenant and fundamental law of the Federal Republic of the World.

Declaration of Duties and Rights

A. The universal government of justice as covenanted and pledged in this Constitution, is founded on the Rights of Man.

The principles underlying the Rights of Man are and shall be permanently stated in the Duty

of everyone everywhere, whether a citizen sharing in the responsibilities and privileges of World Government or a ward and pupil of the World Commonwealth:

to serve with word and deed, and with productive labor according to his ability, the spiritual and physical advancement of the living and of those to come, as the common cause of all generations of men;

to do unto others as he would like others to do unto him;

to abstain from violence,

except for the repulse of violence as commanded or granted under law.

B. In the context therefore of social duty and service, and in conformity with the unwritten law which philosophies and religions alike called the Law of Nature and which the Republic of the World shall strive to see universally written and enforced by positive law:

[1] *Common Cause,* 975 E. 60th St., Chicago 37.

It shall be the right of everyone everywhere to claim and maintain for himself and his fellowmen:

release from the bondage of poverty and from the servitude and exploitation of labor, with rewards and security according to merit and needs;

freedom of peaceful assembly and of association, in any creed or party or craft, within the pluralistic unity and purpose of the World Republic;

protection of individuals and groups against subjugation and tyrannical rule, racial or national, doctrinal or cultural, with safeguards for the self-determination of minorities and dissenters;

and any such other freedoms and franchises as are inherent in man's inalienable claims to life, liberty, and the dignity of the human person, and as the legislators and judges of the World Republic shall express and specify.

C. The four elements of life—earth, water, air, energy—are the common property of the human race. The management and use of such portions thereof as are vested in or assigned to particular ownership, private or corporate or national or regional, of definite or indefinite tenure, of individualist or collectivist economy, shall be subordinated in each and all cases to the interest of the common good.

Grant of Powers

1. The jurisdiction of the World Government as embodied in its organs of power shall extend to:

(a) the control of the observance of the Constitution in all the component communities and territories of the Federal World Republic, which shall be indivisible and one;

(b) the furtherance and progressive fulfillment of the Duties and Rights of Man in the spirit of the foregoing Declaration, with their specific enactment in such fields of federal and local relations as are described hereinafter (Art. 27 through 33);

(c) the maintenance of peace; and to that end the enactment and promulgation of laws which shall be binding upon communities and upon individuals as well.

(d) the judgment and settlement of any conflicts among component units, with prohibition of recourse to interstate violence,

(e) the supervision of and final decision on any alterations of boundaries between states or unions thereof,

(f) the supervision of and final decision on the forming of new states or unions thereof,

(g) the administration of such territories as may still be immature for self-government, and the declaration in due time of their eligibility therefor,

(h) the intervention in intrastate violence and violations of law which affect world peace and justice,

(i) the organization and disposal of the federal armed forces,

(j) the limitation and control of weapons and of the domestic militias in the several component units of the World Republic;

(k) the establishment, in addition to the Special Bodies listed hereinafter (Art. 8 and 9), of such other agencies as may be conducive to the development of the earth's resources and to the advancement of physical and intellectual standards, with such advisory or initiating or arbitrating powers as shall be determined by law;

(l) the laying and collecting of federal taxes, and the establishment of a plan and a budget for federal expenditures,

(m) the administration of the World Bank and the establishment of suitable world fiscal agencies for the issue of money and the creation and control of credit,

(n) the regulation of commerce affected with federal interest,

(o) the establishment, regulation, and where necessary or desirable, the operation of means of transportation and communication which are of federal interest;

(p) the supervision and approval of laws concerning emigration and immigration and the movement of peoples,

(q) the granting of federal passports;

(r) the appropriation, under the right of eminent domain, of such private or public property as may be necessary for federal use, reasonable compensation being made therefor;

(s) the legislation over and administration of the territory which shall be chosen as Federal District and of such other territories as may be entrusted directly to the Federal Government.

2. The powers not delegated to the World Government by this Constitution, and not prohibited by it to the several members of the Federal World Republic, shall be reserved to the several states or nations or unions thereof.

THE FEDERAL CONVENTION,
THE PRESIDENT, THE LEGISLATURE

3. The sovereignty of the Federal Republic of the World resides in the people of the world. The primary powers of the World Government shall be vested in:

(a) the Federal Convention,
(b) the President,
(c) the Council and the Special Bodies,
(d) the Grand Tribunal, the Supreme Court, and the Tribune of the People,
(e) the Chamber of Guardians.

4. The Federal Convention shall consist of delegates elected directly by the people of all states and nations, one delegate for each million of population or fraction thereof above one-half million, with the proviso that the people of any extant state, recognized as sovereign in 1945, and ranging between 100,000 and 1,000,000, shall be entitled to elect one delegate, but any such state with a population below 100,000 shall be aggregated for federal electoral purposes to the electoral unit closest to its borders.

The delegates to the Federal Convention shall vote as individuals, not as members of national or otherwise collective representations; (except as specified hereinafter, Art. 46, paragraph 2, and Art. 47).

The Convention shall meet in May of every third year, for a session of thirty days.

[Sections 5 and 6 provide for the election of the President of the World Republic and a World Council of ninety-nine members.]

7. The primary power to initiate and enact legislation for the Federal Republic of the World shall be vested in the Council.

The tenure of the Council shall be three years.

The Council shall elect its Chairman, for its whole tenure of three years.

Councilors shall be re-eligible.

[Sections 8 and 9 provide for the establishment of several advisory bodies.]

10. The executive power, together with initiating power in federal legislation, shall be vested in the President. His tenure shall be six years.

The President shall not have membership in the Council.

The President shall not be re-eligible. He shall not be eligible to the Tribunate of the People until nine years have elapsed since the expiration of his term.

No two successive Presidents shall originate from the same Region.

11. The President shall appoint a Chancellor. The Chancellor, with the approval of the President, shall appoint the Cabinet.

The Chancellor shall act as the President's representative before the Council in the exercise of legislative initiative. The Chancellor and the Cabinet members shall have at any time the privilege of the floor before the Council.

But no Chancellor or Cabinet member shall have a vote or shall hold membership in the Council, nor, if he was a member of the Council at the moment of his executive appointment, shall he be entitled to resume his seat therein when leaving the executive post unless he be re-elected at a subsequent Convention.

No one shall serve as Chancellor for more than six years, nor as Cabinet member for more than twelve, consecutive or not.

No three Cabinet members at any one time and no two successive Chancellors shall originate from the same Region.

The Council shall have power to interrogate the Chancellor and the Cabinet and to adopt resolutions on their policies.

The Chancellor and the Cabinet shall resign when the President so decides or when a vote of no confidence by the absolute majority of fifty or more of the Council is confirmed by a second such vote; but no second vote shall be taken and held valid if less than three months have elapsed from the first.

12. The sessions of the Council, as well as those of the Grand Tribunal and the Supreme Court, shall be continuous, except for one yearly recess of not more than ten weeks or two such recesses of not more than five weeks each, as the body concerned may decide.

[Sections 16 to 25 provide for a judicial system including a Grand Tribunal of sixty Justices (assigned to five benches) and a Supreme Court of seven members.]

THE TRIBUNE OF THE PEOPLE AND THE WORLD LAW

26. The Federal Convention, after electing the Council, shall elect by secret ballot the Tribune of the People as a spokesman for the minorities,

this office to be vested in the candidate obtaining the second largest vote among the eligible candidates; ineligible to the office of Tribune being any candidate having also been nominated by any Electoral College for the office of President in the current Convention, or having been a President or Acting President or Alternate or a member of the Grand Tribunal at any time in the nine years preceding said Convention, or originating from the same Region as the President simultaneously in office.

The Tribune of the People shall not have membership in the Council.

The tenure of the Tribune of the People shall be three years. He shall have power to appoint a Deputy, subject to the same ineligibilities as above, with tenure to expire not later than his own.

He shall not be re-eligible, nor shall he be eligible to the office of President or Alternate or Justice of the Grand Tribunal, until nine years have elapsed from the expiration of his present term.

The Tribune, or his appointed Deputy, shall have the privilege of the floor before the Grand Tribunal and, under such regulations as shall be established by law, before the Supreme Court; but no vote in either; and he shall not be present when a vote is taken.

27. It shall be the office and function of the Tribune of the People to defend the natural and civil rights of individuals and groups against violation or neglect by the World Government or any of its component units; to further and demand, as a World Attorney before the World Republic, the observance of the letter and spirit of this Constitution; and to promote thereby, in the spirit of its Preamble and declaration of Duties and Rights, the attainment of the goals set to the progress of mankind by the efforts of the ages.

28. No law shall be made or held valid in the World Republic or any of its component units:

(1) inflicting or condoning discrimination against race or nation or sex or caste or creed or doctrine; or

(2) barring through preferential agreement or coalitions of vested interests the access on equal terms of any state or nation to the raw materials and the sources of energy of the earth; or

(3) establishing or tolerating slavery, whether overt or covert, or forced labor, except as equitable expiration endured in state or federal controlled institutions and intended for social service and the rehabilitation of the convicted criminal; or

(4) permitting, whether by direction or indirection, arbitrary seizure or

search, or unfair trial, or excessive penalty, or application of ex post facto laws; or

(5) abridging in any manner whatsoever, except as a punishment inflicted by law for criminal transgression, the citizen's exercise of such responsibilities and privileges of citizenship as are conferred on him by law; or

(6) curtailing the freedom of communication and information, of speech, of the press and of expression by whatever means, of peaceful assembly, of travel;

paragraphs 5 and 6 to be subject to suspension according to circumstances, universally or locally, in time of emergency imperiling the maintenance and unity of the World Republic; such a state of emergency, worldwide or local, to be proposed by the Chamber of Guardians and proclaimed concurrently by a two-thirds majority of the Council and a two-thirds majority of the Grand Tribunal for a period not in excess of six months, to be renewable on expiration with the same procedure for successive periods of six months or less but in no case beyond the date when the time of emergency is proclaimed closed, on the proposal of the Chamber of Guardians by simple majority votes of the Council and of the Grand Tribunal concurrently or, if the Guardians' proposal is deemed unduly delayed, by three-quarters majority votes of the Council and of the Grand Tribunal concurrently.

29. Capital punishment shall not be inflicted under federal law.

30. Old age pensions, unemployment relief, insurance against sickness or accident, just terms of leisure, and protection to maternity and infancy shall be provided according to the varying circumstances of times and places as the local law may direct.

Communities and states unable to provide adequate social security and relief shall be assisted by the Federal Treasury, whose grants or privileged loans shall be administered under federal supervision.

31. Every child from the age of six to the age of twelve shall be entitled to instruction and education at public expense, such primary six-year period to be obligatory and further education to be accessible to all without discrimination of age or sex or race or class or creed.

Communities and states unable to fulfill this obligation shall be assisted by the Federal Treasury with the same proviso as in Art. 30.

THE CHAMBER OF GUARDIANS

35. The control and use of the armed forces of the Federal Republic of the World shall be assigned exclusively to a Chamber of Guardians under the chairmanship of the President, in his capacity of Protector of the Peace. The other Guardians shall be six Councilmen elected by the Council and the Grand Tribunal in Congress assembled, for terms of three years. (But the Grand Tribunal shall not participate in the first election.)

One former President shall also sit in the Chamber of Guardians, the sequence to be determined term for term, or, if he resign or die, for the fractional term, according to seniority in the presidential office; he shall have the privilege of the floor in the deliberations of the Chamber, but no vote in its decisions.

Officers holding professional or active rank in the armed forces of the Federal Republic, or in the domestic militia of any component unit thereof, shall not be eligible as Guardians.

41. The Chamber of Guardians, assisted by a General Staff and an Institute of Technology whose members it shall appoint, shall determine the technological and the numerical level that shall be set as limits to the domestic militias of the single communities and states or unions thereof.

Armed forces and the manufacture of armaments beyond the levels thus determined shall be reserved to the World Government.

[Sections 42 to 47 deal with the Federal Capital, the Federal Language and Standards, the Amending Power, Ratification, and Preliminary Period.]

28

EPILOGUE
1949

You who read this will be of various national origins, various religions, various political views, various colors of skin.

This variety is to be welcomed and cherished. The world would be a dull place if all its inhabitants were alike.

Industry and trade, airplanes and radio, have made the world *one* in the sense that events in any nation can affect the fate of people in all nations. What can make the world *one* in the sense that all men may live together in peace and fruitful coöperation?

Military conquest by one power would impose peace, but it would make the world a prison.

Fruitful coöperation requires union by consent. There must be external organization animated by an inner spirit.

It is easier to devise an external organization than to achieve the spirit of coöperation. How is this spirit to be achieved?

Is it possible that one of our spiritual traditions will convert all men to it? Will all men become Catholics or Methodists or Mohammedans or Confucians or disciples of Gandhi?

There is little hope of that.

But there is hope that if men of each tradition will live up to the *best* in their tradition, the spirit of brotherhood implied in each tradition will prevail.

The people of the world have nothing to lose by world union but their hates and fears. They have everything to gain.

Inhabitants of the world, unite!

GENERAL REFERENCES

ASHLEY-MONTAGU, M. F., *Man's Most Dangerous Myth: The Fallacy of Race* (New York, Columbia University Press, 1942).

BURNS, Emile, *Handbook of Marxism* (New York, International Publishers Co., 1935).

BUTLER, R. D'O., *The Roots of National Socialism* (New York, E. P. Dutton & Co., Inc., 1942).

CATLIN, George, *The Story of the Political Philosophers* (New York, McGraw-Hill Book Company, Inc., 1939).

COKER, F. W., *Readings in Political Philosophy,* rev. ed. (New York, The Macmillan Company, 1938).

———, *Recent Political Thought* (New York, Appleton-Century-Crofts, Inc., 1934).

EBENSTEIN, W., *Man and the State* (New York, Rinehart & Company, Inc., 1947).

EDMAN, Irwin, *Fountainheads of Freedom* (New York, Reynal & Hitchcock, 1941).

LAIDLER, H. W., *Social-Economic Movements* (New York, Thomas Y. Crowell Company, 1944).

LEIGHTON, J. A., *Social Philosophies in Conflict: Fascism and Nazism, Communism, Liberal Democracy* (New York, Appleton-Century-Crofts, Inc., 1937).

LONDON, Kurt, *Backgrounds of Conflict* (New York, The Macmillan Company, 1945).

OAKESHOTT, N., *The Social and Political Doctrines of Contemporary Europe* (Cambridge, England, Cambridge University Press, 1939).

RYAN, J. A., and BOLAND, F. J., *Catholic Principles of Politics* (New York, The Macmillan Company, 1940).

SABINE, G. H., *A History of Political Theory* (New York, Henry Holt and Company, Inc., 1937).

(6)